*Welcome to Paris, "The City of Lights"---where the only requirement to visit is being "Undead."*

*Struggling with a past tragedy and growing unrest with my sister, I accepted an invitation to visit my very close friends in Paris.*

*My early morning flight had just arrived in Paris. As I made my way through the busy concourse, timed seemed to stop. All my mind could register were the three friends standing in front of me. Janine and her two brothers, Luc and Jaycee.*

*Meanwhile, back in the States my Sister Elena had taken great joy in antagonizing me. Elena's jealousy would come to be the driving force that would lead to the culmination of a showdown that will resolve a past injustice and ultimately lead to the destruction of our relationship, and a much darker, sinister means to an end.*

*Would the love that Luc and I came to share, along with Janine and Jaycee be enough to overcome the deceit, treachery and betrayal we would encounter? Would the secret my friends have destroy me or renew me?*

*Little did I know, they would literally hold my soul in their hands.*

**A JEFF NIEWINSKI NOVEL**

# To Paris With Blood

### Eternity Has Its Price...

## A Novel By Jeffrey Niewinski

# JEFF NIEWINSKI

## To Paris With Blood

Published by:
Shadoe Publishing
Copyright © September 2015 by Jeff Niewinski

**ISBN-13: 978-0692528778**
**ISBN-10: 0692528776**

Jeff Niewinski is available for comments at http://www.jefferyniewinski.com/
as well as on Facebook
https://www.facebook.com/JeffNiewinskiBooksandFans if you would like to
follow to find out about stories and books releases or check with
www. ShadoePublishing.com or http://ShadoePublishing.wordpress.com/.

www.shadoepublishing.com

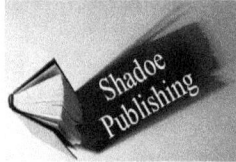

ShadoePublishing@gmail.com

Shadoe Publishing is a United States of America company

Cover Artwork by Candace Niewinski

To Paris With Blood

# ❧ PROLOGUE ❧

Racing through the streets of Paris, the lights and the beauty suddenly turned as grey as the damp night sky. It was very early in the morning. The streets and avenues were quiet as my feet hit the pavement. The sound echoed through the sleeping city. *'Some fucking vacation,'* I thought, as the mist of my breath became visible in the thick night air. *'This isn't exactly the way I had envisioned my trip.'*

"Christ, what have I gotten myself into?" I asked what turned out to be me, myself, and him, not to mention the random Parisians who went screaming in the other direction as soon as they saw the picture unfolding. The scene was set; the cast in place, and the minds of the locals were putting together what was taking place like some sick horror flick, *sans* directors or extras.

Luc's townhouse was about four city blocks ahead. His sister Janine's about eight. Both were located on the breathtaking Rue de Montmorency. Shit! At this point, both might as well be in the next town. The thought of reaching for my cell phone in my pocket and dialing emergency, when I could hear him directly behind me, seemed absurd. *'What was it here? 999? I am so fucked!'* I thought, as I nervously clenched and unclenched my fists.

"Fuck me! Dammit! Why the hell didn't I stay with Luc?" I began to make a run for Luc's apartment. At this point, trying to make it to Janine's was futile. Fuck, who am I kidding? Even trying for Luc's was useless. He could run just as fast as I could. For some reason, he stopped his pursuit. He just bloody stopped in his tracks. With every nerve I had left, I turned toward him. All I could do was take a deep breath and utter, "Oh my God...you?"

"Aller!" he said. It was one word, one simple word.

"Go?" I could hear myself saying it, but if it was audible to him, I couldn't tell. I could only look at him. Actually, more like stare, with I dare say *lust*. I closed my eyes. I had to remind myself to breathe. *'Remember what he did.'* Memories of the limo ride from hell flashed through my head. For a moment, time stood still. He was beautiful, absolutely fucking beautiful. Thick, jet black hair; tanned, smooth skin. His steel blue eyes penetrated me and held me as if they were pulling me to him. *'John, pull yourself together. This bastard is trying to ruin our lives.'* God Almighty, I had everything I could do to turn away. His pure, white fangs framed a perfect smile. Not to mention those fucking feral eyes! But fuck, I really didn't give a shit at the moment. The moment I laid eyes on him, I wanted him. *'God, I hated him. What the hell was he doing to me?'* I thought, as I did everything I could to hold it together. But he had different plans. The moonlight, now piercing the veil of the mist like a soft spotlight, hit his face. It accentuated every line and detail of his incredible, perfect form.

"Go!" he commanded me. "Go before I do to you what I have been craving!"

"So fucking do it already! Just fucking do it!" I had just lost my mind. I was exhausted and just didn't care anymore.

"Don't tempt me, mon amour! You belong to someone else. Turn around now, my love." It was as much a command as it was an endearment.

So I did. As I turned, he smiled. Not at me, but at who was in front of me.

"Bon soir, mon amour. I have been waiting for you for a long time." His white fangs and, oh shit, those eyes...they glistened in the dead of the night.

*'Aahh crap.'*

# CHAPTER ONE

I looked out of my window as the plane made its initial descent into Paris. *The City of Lights.* The landing gear smoothly engaged as the pilot made his obligatory announcement.

"Ladies and gentlemen, we thank you for flying Air France. As we make our final approach to Charles De Gaulle airport, we'd like to take this opportunity to say Bonjour and hope you enjoy your visit to Paris. Currently, it's about nine degrees Celsius and overcast, with a slight mist. We'll approach the gate at our scheduled arrival time, 4 A.M."

Like the weather, my mind was in a fog. *'So this,'* I thought, *'was what jet lag feels like.'* After a restless night of anticipation, I had left Minneapolis International at noon. Nearly nine hours and forty-three hundred miles later, I was here. Tired as hell, I wanted to sleep, but the city awaited me. I had waited too long for this moment and I had friends waiting for me at the terminal. Exhausted but psyched, I was looking forward to what would become, unknown to me, the fight for my life and my immortal soul.

My adventure had started several years back while I was, believe it or not, listening to a song on YouTube. I made a comment regarding my favorite brother and sister song and several days later I received a comment from a gal who, I didn't know at that time, would quite literally hold my very life and soul in her hands. Her name was

Janine. I would come to know her and her family better than my own. Never meeting face to face, my fate was sealed.

The plane pulled into the gate on schedule. *'How the hell do they do that? God, John, that was random!'* I said to myself, half smiling. A little worse for wear, I pulled myself together and rubbed my weary eyes. For some reason, I heard 'Unwell' in my head. Shaking it off, I grabbed my carry-on and made my way off of Airbus A380, the largest jet-liner in the world, built by my beloved France. Magnifique!

"Merci, monsieur," The flight attendant said in a friendly but automated voice.

Friendly yes, but say *that* six hundred and twenty-five times. Oh well, at least this flight wasn't overbooked. Say *that* eight-hundred and fifty-three times! Besides, there were sixteen additional flight attendants on this flight, so it wasn't *that* bad. Anyone who knows me, knows very well that I'm an airplane geek! I love airplanes and I love to fly.

"Thank you very much, ma'am," I replied. "Merci beaucoup!"

*"He thinks he knows French!"* My sister. There she was, in my head again.

This telepathic thing between us was going to be the death of me, or at least drive me nuts! I could just hear my smart-ass sister Elena go off on some tangent about how big a dumbass I was.

A smile crossed my face though. I was in Paris. Take that, Elena! She was back home driving around in a big, red and rusted out Dodge Ram pickup truck. Right smack dab in the middle of the change of a Wisconsin winter to spring. From snow to freezing rain and back again. When I left, we had just gotten fifteen inches of blowing, drifting snow. *'God, Elena, no four-wheel drive? Who's the dumbass now?'* I thought.

Right there in front of the flight attendant, I laughed, hysterically. My sister Elena, God love her, what a freaking red-neck! "Jet lag. Pardon me, madame!" I said, my head down, sheepishly making my way off the airliner… still giggling.

"Americans, God help us!" The flight attendant whispered under her breath.

# ❖ CHAPTER TWO ❖

As I made my way down the ramp, only one thing kept me going, Janine and her family. They came from one of the oldest moneyed families in Paris and graciously made this experience happen for me. For what it's worth, when Janine initially told me, I did resist her generosity. You see how well that went! The trip was on them. Right down to the black charge card they sent to me. In case you're wondering, a black card has *no* credit limit. Aucun...keiner...zaden...geen...zip...nada. *'Would it be wrong of me to run and get a new wardrobe before the trip?'* I shook my head, thinking, *'No, not a way to make a good first impression.'*

I walked into the terminal entrance of de Gaulle and if it could really happen, my jaw would have hit the ground. My carry-on did instead. I took in the sight like some lost puppy looking for its master. I rubbed my eyes, shook my head, and took in several deep breaths of air. I honest to God thought that the airport was empty except for the vision in front of me.

Janine was a vision of complete beauty. Long, flowing, silky black hair. Perfect complexion and, God help me, she was beautiful. No, Janine was simply stunning. 'A long, cool woman in a black dress!' The song references, get used to it. I was a radio personality for some twelve years.

"Bonjour, mon amour! Jacques, over here!" she shouted excitedly, waving her arms in the air.

'*The voice of an angel,*' I thought. "Oh, for Pete's sake. Get a grip, John!" I muttered. Thousands of voices, thousands of people, and this voice, soft and delicate, was beckoning me. She belonged in the Musee du Louvre. Exquisite, Janine! I had never heard her voice, but through our time online, I knew who I was looking for and was now looking at. Janine was the portrait of Parisian beauty. She was wearing Christian Lacroix. Why wasn't she a cover girl? Ah, Vogue, hello?

'*Where the hell is my Visine?*' I thought, as I rubbed my bleary, tired eyes.

Standing on either side of her were her brothers. Luc, who I had met and talked to online, and her elusive and mysterious other brother, Jaycee. I never spoke to Jaycee, I had only seen pictures of him. They both were wearing black, tailor-made suits. Holy shit! They say pictures paint a thousand words? I had a whole fucking art gallery in front of me. Screw the Louvre.

Janine came running to me, embraced me, and gave me a kiss on each cheek. "Bonjour, my precious Jacques, mon cher!" she said breathlessly.

Much to the joy of my weary mind and body, Luc and Jaycee reciprocated in the same fashion. I had died and gone to heaven. Pulling myself together and trying to hide the obvious feelings, well at least to me they were obvious, I turned my attention back to Janine.

"Bonjour, mon amour! Janine, it is so good to be here with you and your brothers! Merci!"

"*Jesus, John. How gay are you anyway? Idiot!*"

"*Oh for God's sake! Elena, get out of my head and take a ride in your big red friggin' truck!*"

Janine took my hands and looked at me. Really looked at me. I felt at once warm and welcomed, then as quickly as that feeling came over me, I swore I saw concern in her eyes. If not concern, I could have sworn I saw fear. A sudden chill ran down my spine. '*Jesus, that's new.*' I quickly shrugged it off.

# CHAPTER THREE

"So let me get this straight," Elena started. "You're going to Paris? After all I've fucking done for you, this is the way you repay me? You simply are the most ungrateful brother I could have possibly hoped to have! You, dear bro, are one daft prick!"

Yep, that's my sister Elena. How do I describe her to you? She's seven years younger than me and, thanks to her typically mid-western, redneck boyfriend, not afraid to speak her mind.

She wasn't like that when she was younger. I swear to God, she was sweet, innocent, and adored her big brother. Hell, she looked up to me. Although she would deny that under penalty of death. Mine!

Then there was an attitude adjustment, thanks to that boyfriend of hers. Not afraid to say what is on her mind, she lets me know exactly what she's feeling. I'm embarrassed to admit it, but thanks to that new attitude I've heard "I told you so" more times than I can count. But it was beginning to wear thin on me, as I no longer had a private life. As a matter of fact, I was still pissed off at her for ruining my latest attempt at happiness.

An eighties throwback, Elena wears boots all summer long. Goth Girl, no, but if her closet is any indication, I'd swear she was. She takes the whole spiritual medium thing to a whole new level. Do I consider Elena a witch? No. Absolutely not. But her premonitions have been uncanny. More than once she saved my ass from disaster.

Oh, did I mention we are telepathic. You're probably thinking cool, right? Well, speaking from experience, try a week. It's annoying as hell!

"Elena, please calm down. I'm doing this! Tell father I've done the best I can. I'm tired of being judged. I'm gay! Deal with it! God made me this way!" Trying to convince her. "I'm not angry. I'm just saying sometimes these things can lead to a second chance." Shit, now I'm trying to convince myself.

"Brother," Elena looked at me and, taking my arms, shook me. Shook me with more strength than her four foot eight inch frame let on.

*'Her boyfriend, Trace must have been giving her lessons,'* I thought to myself. God help anyone who gets on his bad side. Take for instance, me.

"John, I had a vision." Elena looked at me. I knew that look quite well. Part terrified, part serious. Serious as someone could get without pulling a gun. At this point, if she would have pulled a gun on me, I wouldn't have been surprised. Elena was dead serious.

Elena's visions started when she was fourteen. Premonitions, if you will. Some vague. Some deadly accurate. When it came to me, she was always one hundred percent right. Dead on. If it weren't for my Elena, I'd be dead, more times than a cat has lives. I did appreciate that.

"What is it, sis?" I looked at her and saw total fear in her eyes.

"You can't go. Please, just fucking listen to me!"

"Why? Having a 'Final Destination' moment, Elena?" I felt a half-smile forming on my face. WHACK! Her hand struck my face. I immediately regretted saying that. "Damn, Elena, that fucking hurt! What is your fucking problem?" I shouted, rubbing my face.

"God, John, if only it were a jet exploding!" Tears flowed from her eyes.

# ❧ CHAPTER FOUR ❧

"Jacques...Jacques?" That voice.

"Mon cher, is something wrong?" I felt Janine's hand on my forehead, the way someone does when they are checking if you have a temperature.

"No, I'm okay, really," I said softly, trying to reassure her. "Pardonnez-moi, Janine, nothing to worry about. I'm just really tired, jet lag." I had become aware that not only Janine, but Luc and Jaycee had surrounded me, and judging by the expressions on their faces, they were deeply concerned about me as well. The looks in Luc's and Jaycee's eyes were, to say the least, making my heart skip a beat. What the hell was that feeling coming from them? Concern? Friendship? I'm not even going to go further with what I was feeling. Not yet. No. It couldn't be.

"Why don't we head to Luc's apartment, Jacques? You can shower and rest up. After all it's only five in the morning! From what you've told me, you're not exactly a morning person!" She softly laughed. "After that, Paris is yours, mon amour!" Janine smiled.

"That sounds sooo good, Janine!" Despite rubbing my eyes, I managed a small smile.

"John," Luc, choosing to use the American pronunciation as he always did, looked at me. "I have some Visine for those eyes of yours! I need it all the time!"

'OKAY, John,' I thought. 'Visine? How the hell...and he needs it all the time?' I shrugged it off as a coincidence, returning to reality.

Luc was still leaning into me, his eyes gazing into mine. God, that smile. He was going to be the death of me.

"You've got that right, John."

"Shut up, Elena...just shut the fuck up!"

On the way out of the airport, surrounded by my Parisian friends, I couldn't help but notice the activity in the main concourse. It seemed like every eye was focused on us.

As we made our way through the terminal, we stopped at a coffee shop for some much needed caffeine. I had offered to treat Janine, Luc, and Jaycee to a cup. Janine, I made a mental note, ordered a latte. The boys declined, saying that if they had any more they'd be bouncing off the walls.

Janine chuckled. "Jacques, sweetheart...they're right. They were so excited to be here that they must have drunk two pots apiece."

"We didn't want to sleep through the alarm and miss your arrival!" Luc winked at me.

'Oh my God! What a little flirt! No,' I thought, 'this can't be happening. He's, oh for the love of all things holy, half your age, if that!' I felt a little better. The caffeine was kicking in, so we decided to make our way out of the airport. I couldn't wait to be out of there and get my first look at Paris! I couldn't help notice how people were making way for us. The looks in their eyes were part respect, part fear and, as they looked at me, I swear to God, pity. What the fuck?

I looked to Janine and Luc, who were to my left, and Jaycee, extremely close to my right side. I made an observation of their demeanor. Janine was breathtaking. A smile radiated from her face. Her walk, one of poise and elegance. Luc, the handsome little shit, walked with such a confidence and attitude it made me, oh for Pete's sake, hornier than hell. Turning to Jaycee, who by now had snaked his strong, capable fingers through mine as he guided me through the crowd of people, I saw he had a look of, dare I say, 'He's mine.'

'Come on, John!' I thought. 'These are my friends. I'm here! Paris! If they don't like what they see, fuck 'em! Fuck 'em all!' The look on my face seemed to reflect that to the on-lookers. I had this strange feeling Jaycee saw it too. His grip tightened around my hand. Damn I was happy!

# ❧ CHAPTER FIVE ❧

Shit, that was short-lived.

A tingle went through my spine. It was Elena. Our connection was strong. It always has been. Without saying a word to each other, we could finish each other's thoughts. Hell, just before I left we produced a one-million dollar music video for Elena's friend, Jared. My sister went to college for production and directing, along with other degrees. She drove me crazy, a total perfectionist and her own worst critic.

The amazing part about it was that no words had to be spoken. We just looked at each other, and our thoughts and emotions were transmitted to each other.

Before I left we 'hit a wall', so to speak, on Jared's music video. Total mind blank. I decided to step out and have a smoke. Yes, I smoke. Bitch at me all you want. I took a drag, shivered at the fucking cold weather, and it hit me.

"Elena! Elena!" I yelled, as I bolted through the door.

Elena's cat Norm raced down the steps like it was the second coming. I had to stop and giggle. Norm, as usual, looked at me from the bottom of the steps, his eyes burning into mine.

I could swear he meowed, "Bitch!"

"Jerk!" I replied.

"John, leave the cat alone and get in the living room!" she yelled.

"You know, Elena," I started as I came around the kitchen corner into the living room, "you don't have to yell at me! Just think me to death, why don't you!" I glared at her, with a half-smirk on my face.

*"You, dear brother, are an asshole."* Elena rolled her eyes.

*"See, wasn't that far more enjoyable?"* I couldn't help the shit-eating grin I had on my face. I had her this time, or so I thought!

"So, Elena, I got it! Picture this. Sharp-dressed Wall Street dude gets out of a..."

"Hot sports car!" Elena blurted out.

"Damn it, sis...You take the joy out of everything!"

"I live for it," Elena said. The smirk on her face drove that fact home.

I came back to reality absolutely humiliated, finding myself flat on my back about two hundred feet away from the exit. This, by the way, did not help the already on-edge people passing by.

"Jacques? Hey, Jacques!" Jaycee knelt next to me. His hand came down to my face, palm side up, stroking my cheek.

My weary eyes continued to focus and there, on my other side was Luc, his fingers intertwined with mine. As he knelt over me, his deep blue eyes were full of concern. He knelt lower and pressed his forehead to mine as he gently brushed his lips against mine. *'My God.'* I thought. *'So this is heaven. Breathe, John, breathe.'*

"Jacques, what the hell happened? Are you okay?"

"Yeah, Jaycee," I said, my eyes gazing into his. "I felt myself black out and Elena..." *'Ahh, crap.*

*That, I did not want to come out.'*

"Elena? Your sister?" Luc questioned.

Not yet. Not in the middle of an airport. It was a conversation best served up over coffee, or better yet never! They'd think I was completely nuts.

"Where is Janine, Jaycee?"

"She went to get you help, Jacques. You scared her half to death."

"Oh, Jesus. Luc, Jaycee, I am so sorry for putting you through this. Please forgive me. This isn't exactly the way I thought my visit would start. Honestly guys..." My voice became agitated. "S'il vous plait, pardonnez-moi?"

"John, there is nothing to forgive," Luc stated, as he and Jaycee started to help me to my feet. These two beautiful young men handled me like something priceless. Their hands strong, yet gentle on me. Luc to my left, Jaycee to my right. I was still a bit woozy and unsteady on my feet. I didn't mind the attention. Both of their strong, young bodies pressed tightly to my sides. Protecting me. Their faces showing nothing but concern and a warmth that actually gave me chills. Then to my amazement, taking turns, they gently kissed my forehead.

"You, love, are ours," Jaycee stated, with a gentle, but passionate smile.

# ❖ CHAPTER SIX ❖

"Jacques, mon cher. Are you okay?" Janine asked, her fingers gently stroking my face.

Janine had found her way back to where I had recently taken a *trip* and where, much to my amazement and total confusion, there were two abso-fucking-lutely perfect brothers who had inclinations towards me that went beyond your normal, everyday Parisian amities.

*'You, love, are ours. What the fuck?'* I thought. *'Now I'm property. Hell, not that I'm complaining, but again, for lack of a better way to describe my feelings, what the fuck?'*

"Mon amour? Jacques, mon cher?"

"Oh, Janine, sweetheart, I feel like such a fool!" I said, snapping back to reality. If this was reality.

Wait, maybe I'm still unconscious.

Luc and Jaycee still had their hands on my arm, steadying me. I looked at both of them. Their eyes much more intense than I remembered. Their grip just a bit firmer. Their smiles were hypnotic. "You, love, are ours!" Jaycee repeated.

Nope. Conscious!

*"Crap! Elena, if you can hear me, I could really use an explanation here! Elena! Fine time to lose your 'Jedi' mind connection with me, sis! Dumbass!"* I added. Hell, it was the truth.

Janine had brought back a paramedic and insisted on having me checked out. I felt like a complete jackass. The last thing we needed was more attention; we were getting plenty the way it was.

The paramedic did his thing. He gave me the once-over and told me that even though I had banged my head on the ground, I'd be okay. "Monsieur," The paramedic started, leaning into me his lips inches from my ear, "do you know who you are with?" his voice was tinged with fear.

"Sir, these are my good friends. They invited me from the United States to come and visit. Of course I know them! I plan on having the time of my life with them!" I smiled, a little aggravated by his cryptic question.

"The time of your life? More like the time of your impending death!" he whispered, as he packed his equipment and hurriedly left.

*'Time of my death? What the hell did that mean?'* I thought.

"John," Luc squeezed my hand gently, "let's get you out of here and home. You need to rest."

"I'd say, Luc," Jaycee chimed in. "You need rest, handsome. The nighttime awaits!" He leaned in and kissed my cheek. I leaned into him and closed my eyes, letting the feeling of his soft, warm lips touch my face.

"Jaycee! Behave!" Janine said, with a very tempered smile on her face. Luc, not to be outdone, leaned in and brushed his lips against mine.

"Boys!" Janine sighed and rolled her eyes. "What am I going to do with you three?" The tone of seriousness in her voice was overruled by the smile on her face.

# ❖ CHAPTER SEVEN ❖

We departed the airport. Walking out into the fresh air and feeling the warmth of the early morning Parisian sun hitting my face, I couldn't help but notice the absolute beauty of the city that awaited my exploration. Everything from here on out was not up to me, as Janine, Luc, and Jaycee told me that *they* had everything planned out. Just Paris and the four of us.

"John," Luc leaned into me on the left, "you, babe, shall see our city as we see it."

I couldn't help but notice, and didn't care, that Luc still had his fingers intertwined with mine. His thumb gently rubbing my wrist. My God, just that small, intimate action sent a warmth to my very soul.

Jaycee, on my right, looked at Luc with a gentle, but knowing smile on his face. 'You, love, are ours' kept repeating itself like an anthem, a favorite lyric to a favorite song in my head.

Neither Luc nor Jaycee had let me go since my incident in the airport.

Janine, who had been leading the way, turned to us. Approaching me, she wrapped her arms around my waist. For the first time since my arrival, now with the sun shining brilliantly in the sky, I noticed her eyes. My God, they were beautiful. Blue-green with an emerald outline. They looked, I mean *looked* into mine. Almost feral, they mesmerized me. Between them surrounding me and touching me, the world stopped. The beauty that was Paris took a back seat to the three people who had me both emotionally and physically wrapped in their, for lack of a better word, spell.

"Jacques, mon cher," Janine began, "it is early and you have been through so much already. Let us take you home where you can rest. Luc wishes to fix you breakfast, if that's okay? You must be famished! Then you can rest for a while in Luc's bed."

"I couldn't possibly impose..." I never had the chance to finish.

Luc, right there in front of a waiting black limo, turned to me, hand still entwined with mine, and kissed me. Softly his lips met mine, his fingers squeezed tighter, his kiss unleashed a desire I had hidden since I had first seen him when I arrived. Time stood still. His tongue gently pushed my lips open, begging for entrance. I couldn't help but let him in. His tongue explored my mouth, his other hand found its way to my waist and pulled me closer to him. I felt his arousal pressing against my thigh. *'Oh, my God.'* Luc gently pulled away, his arm still wrapped around my waist, tangled with Janine's. Janine's eyes met mine. God, that smile; she approved.

"No imposition, mon ami. You, John, are everything I imagined, and more. You shall share my bed," Luc said breathlessly.

*'Alone? Together?'* I thought. My question would soon be answered. Luc's eyes looked into mine, so fucking deep into mine, I swear he was studying my soul. I was being pulled in. Something powerful was overtaking me. I just couldn't piece it together. I was still weak from the onslaught of what had just occurred. Christ, my knees were shaking.

"Jacques? Hey, Jacques." It was Jaycee. I looked to him, noticing his hand was still holding mine gently, yet possessively.

"My baby brother loves you, as do I," Jaycee spoke. His eyes locked onto mine. "You have much to learn about us," Jaycee continued. "We know you most likely have questions. I promise, mon cher, we will answer them. All in due time, but for now, let us show you a world you never knew could exist. Paris is yours, Jacques. It is yours for the taking, and we will help you take it. Jacques, we love you and you are ours!" Jaycee's lips brushed gently against mine.

# ✤ CHAPTER EIGHT ✤

I was sitting in the living room, back home with Elena. What the hell! Had this just been some dream. Knowing my luck, that's all it was. A dream. A very vivid, erotic, and supernatural dream. The airport. Meeting Janine, Luc, and Jaycee. The so fucking real touching and kisses from Luc and Jaycee. 'You, love, are ours.' Those words! That damn, sweet promise that flowed from Luc and Jaycee's mouths. A promise that would be kept. A promise I would not be able to break away from, nor want to. I was falling… fast.

*"John! Dammit, John. Would you kindly get your head out of your ass and listen to me! Now!"*

*"Elena? What the fuck? What the hell is going on?"*

*"You, brother, are a complete dimwit! Do the names Lestat and Louie ring a bell with you? I thought you told me you read her books? Did you at least see the damn movie?"*

*"Elena, what the fuck are you talking about?"*

*"Good God, John! Do I have to spell everything out for you? How old are you? TWO? Listen to me, dammit. Something is seriously fucking with my connection to you! Just shut up and listen!"*

By this time, Elena, sister or not, was beginning to seriously piss me off. But at the same time, I couldn't help but start giggling.

Looking at her, all I could do was continue to giggle. What Elena was suggesting was so off the wall, even for her, I thought I was losing my fucking mind.

"*Okay, Elena,*" I said, as I tried to get my mirth under control. "*What you're suggesting to me is that...Oh come on, Elena, for God's sake! Luc and Jaycee are vampires? Next thing you're going to tell me is that Janine is a werewolf!*"

Silence. Fucking silence. Chills ran up my spine. "*Sis?*"

Elena just looked at me. That same damn look she gave me every time she knew she was right. Smug, arrogant, but always...always right.

"*John, you do know what this means, don't you?*"

"*No fucking way, sis! Elena, I mean it. You had better get your facts straight before you go making some half-ass 'Underworld' comment like that! I'm serious, Elena! Dead serious!*"

"*You will be.*" Elena glared at me. "*Dead.*"

"*Fuck you, Elena! Fuck you and get the fuck out of my head!*"

"*Fine, bro, but before you let your fucking gay hormones run rampant...*"

"*What the hell does that have to do with anything, Elena?*" I hated this. Fighting with Elena. But damn, I was entitled. I was severely pissed off.

"*Oh come on, John! You know as well as I do! What did Jaycee say? Um...My baby brother loves you, as do I! Yeah, they want you alright, in more ways than one! You don't think I heard that? You want them so fucking bad, you can't see the forest for the trees!*"

"*So what, Elena! Next thing you're going to tell me is that you're going to have a talk with Trace!*" I immediately wished I could take that comment back, but it was too late.

"*If that's what it takes to save you! Save you from your stupidity!*"

"*Let me tell you this once, Elena! If Trace shows up anywhere near Luc or Jaycee, or for that matter, Janine...I'll kill him. Do you understand me, Elena? Do I make myself fucking clear?*"

"*Yeah, you made yourself clear all right! Clear that you are an idiot! Kill Trace...Yeah, that'll happen. You know what he will do!*"

"*Not this time, Elena.*"

Elena looked at me with this grin she had. The one she knew I had grown to hate. One-half superior, one-half just fucking annoying. "*You won't let that go, will you, bro? Trace did not do it!*"
"*You keep telling yourself that, Elena. He will pay! Like I said, Elena, get the fuck out of my head!*"

# ❧ CHAPTER NINE ❧

"Elena! Please just fucking leave me alone!" I found myself shouting.

My body shot upright into a sitting position as my eyes flew open. Disorientated, I felt panic. But at the same time, a set of strong arms wrapped themselves around me and pulled me back, embracing me. I felt a smooth, warm, muscular body press against my back. Panic was being replaced by peace, and yes, arousal. Within an instant, I knew who had me. My baby boy, my precious Luc! My God, I could stay like this forever. A calm swept over me. What I thought I had just gone through with Elena left as quickly as it came.

" Oh my God, Luc," I whispered. "You're here. Really here."

"Shhhhh...be still, my one and only," Luc's voice whispered into my ear. It drifted into my mind, my thoughts, my heart, and, God help me, my soul. "Where else would you have me be, mon cher?" he asked, shutting my doubts down completely.

"John." Luc pulled me closer. "What is going on with your sister Elena? Did something happen before you left for Paris? Do you want to talk about it?" Luc's eyes looked deep into me. The concern and caring he felt for me was so damn obvious all I could do was return his look.

With a slight smile on my face, I answered him. "Luc, babe, I know I owe you and your family an explanation. I promise I will tell you everything. I swear. Can we just put *that* topic on hold for now? Please, baby boy?"

Luc answered me with a kiss. A simple, chaste, sweet kiss.

"God, Luc." I suddenly realized it was once again evening. "How long have I been sleeping?"

"Twelve hours." Luc ran his fingers through my hair. "You were exhausted."

"You've been with me the whole time?"

"Oui, babe. I will *never* leave your side," he whispered.

I nestled my head against the strong, tanned shoulder of the man who now held me with such a steely grip that I felt nothing could touch or harm me. His cock, stiff, hard, and hot, pressed into my lower back. *'Wait! We were naked. When did that happen?'* Luc's hips rocked gently, up and down. *'Who the fuck cared?'* His pre-cum had slicked my back. The friction causing sweet, soft moans, and puffs of air to escape Luc's mouth and caress my ear. I gently pushed my face closer to Luc's, wanting to feel and hear his every breath.

"John, babe. It's okay! I have you, my love. I will never let you go."

"Where are we, Luc?" I asked. For the first time I looked at my surroundings. I found myself in a beautifully decorated room. Pure white down comforters lay softly across our bodies. The room was simply, but elegantly, decorated in the French provincial style that I so loved. A warm fire emanated from the fireplace against the wall. *'God, I could stay here forever and never tire of where I found myself and who I found myself with. This young man I was falling so hard for, falling in love with. Aahh crap!'*

"All you need to know, John, is, as promised, you will share my bed. I hope I haven't overstepped my boundaries," he whispered. "And for that matter, please forgive me if I have taken liberties I shouldn't have." A pause. Silence. Luc's deep blue eyes gazed into mine. "Am I forgiven?" Luc's sincere look on his beautiful, young face melted my heart.

*'A vampire. Elena, you have finally gone off the deep end,'* I thought, as I felt a small smile try to break free.

I turned, staying in Luc's embrace, but needing to see him, face to face. "Luc, my beautiful, precious boy, there is nothing to forgive. God help me, Luc. I know, um, I know this is so soon, but I'm falling for you. Luc..." My breath hitched, "I'm falling in love with you," I said in what was barely a hoarse whisper.

"I already have, John. Please, let me make love to you." A tear rolled down Luc's eye.

"God, Luc, yes. I want you so much! Yes, make love to me! And if I could have my way you could have me forever."

"If that's what you want, then we want the same thing, mon amour." Luc's tears continued to fall down his face.

At that moment, I realized just how inseparable we were becoming. I gently took my thumb and wiped away the tears that had slowly made their way down that incredibly beautiful face.

Still in Luc's arms, he pulled me back with him. Never letting his arms release me, we lay together side by side. Our foreheads touching each other's. Luc's eyes never once left mine. Luc's eyes, a shade of blue I had never seen before, locked onto mine. Without so much as a blink, I felt myself being pulled into his very thoughts, as if we were one. My control was slipping away from me. So were my concerns, fears...the world around me. It was all disappearing, comforting me, enfolding me in peace. All I knew was this beautiful, young man who lay next to me. The expression on his face began to change. A small smile erased the concern I had seen just moments before. His eyes now sparkling with, dare I say, lust emanating from them, continued to watch me with the attentiveness of a guardian, a protector.

"I want you, I need you!" Luc whispered, with a hint of mischievousness in his eyes. The soft, warm glow of the fireplace danced across the walls and the bed we shared.

Covered in the soft down comforter, my eyes shifted just enough to look at the strong, broad shoulders and the arms that were so tightly wrapped around me. The soft light and the white of the comforter magnified his tanned, bronze skin compared to my "much too pale, just arrived from the frozen Tundra of Northern Wisconsin, U.S.A." complexion.

"Luc, babe?" The back of my hand caressed his cheek. "What do you see in me? Why me...I mean, baby...look at me."

I felt his hand travel down my side to my hip. Gripping it tight, and with a definite possessiveness, he pulled me closer than I thought possible.

"John, my love, I see compassion, thoughtfulness, caring, and honesty. Above all, I see *you.* I've waited for you my entire life. I'd wait forever for you. Please, John, no more questions. We have a lifetime to talk. Right now I want you. I need you." His lips brushed mine. "Please, let me show you how much."

Nothing more needed to be said. My arms wrapped themselves around Luc's waist and pulled him tightly to my body. Our mouths joined together in a kiss that went straight to my soul. His mouth was sweet. Our tongues met and we tasted each other. Wet, warm heat began to surge through our mouths.

As we kissed, our hands roamed each other's bodies. Luc's fingers threaded their way through my hair, then gently, his fingers traveled down my spine. As they reached the rise of my ass I felt one of his fingers gently press into the cleft, probing and nearing his destination. Moaning, he added two, then three fingers into me. I wanted him in me, filling me, and making me one with him.

The warmth of the comforter and the fire burning gently in the fireplace, along with our bodies, was too much. Sweat began to coat our bodies. I took my foot and kicked the down comforter off of us, revealing Luc's naked body. *'Fuck!* I had to catch my breath. "My God, Luc...Oh my God, you're perfect." What my hands felt could not compare to what my eyes were seeing. This young man had the body of a Greek God, sculpted pecs and ripped abs. His beautiful ass, firm, round and dimpled, connected to legs with strong, firm thighs and calves. God help me, he was fucking gorgeous.

The light of the fire played across his body. His eyes never left mine. Mine were fucking every part of him that I could see. I needed to feel every part of him. My hands explored his body. Soft, guttural moans escaped Luc as I caressed and touched him. Taught muscles responded to my touch. His cock throbbed, wanting to, needing to be touched. All in due time. Like a piece of fine artwork, this young man needed to be admired and explored.

The exploring only lasted so long, as Luc showed me it was time to "claim" me. With a devious, yet precious, smile on his face, he proceeded to gently push me onto my stomach. I spread my legs ever so slightly. He straddled me, his stiff cock resting in the hot crack of my ass.

I lifted my head and looked over my shoulder at him. *Holy shit! What a sight!* A playful look appeared in his twinkling blue eyes. "Fuck! Have your way with me, Luc! Touch me, dammit!"

Luc's smile was absolutely devious, and for an instant, I could have sworn his eyes flashed completely red at mine.

His hands started with my shoulders, his fingers lightly brushing across them. This was going to be slow torture, and though my boy thought he had the upper hand, I had a few weapons of my own. I canted my hips upwards and the tip of his cock rubbed against my waiting and willing opening. Luc growled.

For once, I was looking forward to a sleepless night.

# CHAPTER TEN

Coming from a deep sleep, I found myself drifting toward an awareness of where I was. The light of the early morning sun filtered through the partially opened silk draperies that hung on the ornate, early baroque style windows of Luc's apartment.

I really don't remember much of how I got from the airport to where I was now. I really didn't care.

My eyes continued to adjust themselves. My eyes found a soft flicker of flames emanating from the fireplace, still giving off a warmth that, last night, had not been needed.

Flashes went through my mind of the passion and feelings that filled our bodies as I gave myself to Luc completely. No boundaries stood between us. I still felt the pull of Luc's beautiful, blue eyes. They drew me to him, like a moth to a flame. A power I could not describe. A power that I let take control of me. *'It was as if,'* I thought, *'Luc knew me. Knew me at every level, in a personal way that no one has ever known me.'*

I was awake now and fully aware of my surroundings. Looking down, I saw his strong arms wrapped tightly and possessively around me. His hard, young body pressed tightly to my back. I could feel his breath, almost non-existent, softly brushing against my shoulder. I turned my body ever so slightly so as not to disturb my sleeping lover. I needed to see him. Once again, the thoughts of last evening came rushing through me as I watched him sleep. From the heated kisses we shared, to feeling Luc enter me, gently at first, slow and deep. Then as our love for each other took over, the thrusts became more powerful. Faster and harder. I came without so much as a touch. Just the constant thrust of his stiff, hard cock driving into me was enough. Hitting my *spot* as he drove himself into me, I came hard. Waves of ecstasy coursed through my body as my cum covered my abs, his chest. At the same time, I felt Luc's body tense. Every muscle in his body contracting and flexing as he drove his hard, pulsing cock into me, filling me with his hot, thick cum. Gently, as our climaxes ebbed, Luc let his body press down upon me. My arms and legs wrapped around him, pulling him as close as I could. His cock, still hard, remained deep in me.

"I will never let you go, Luc...Never," I whispered.

"Please don't, John. My life would mean nothing without you," Luc whispered quietly, his lips brushing mine.

"God, babe...I am so in love with you." My voice trembled with emotion.

Luc's forehead pressed against mine. "I know, John. God, I am so in love with you. I'd be so lost without you." His hands tangled in my hair as he pulled me into a kiss that left us both breathless.

# ❖ CHAPTER ELEVEN ❖

A light, subtle, almost hesitant knock came from Luc's bedroom door. "Do you mind, John, or shall I send them away?"

"Baby boy." I smiled. "This *is* your home!" My lips brushed his.

Smiling, running the back of his hand over my face, Luc turned to the door. "Whoever chooses to announce themselves can come in, providing you have a very good reason!" Luc giggled.

The door to the room opened slowly. With the light of the morning sun and the light from the hallway, I had no problem identifying our visitor. It was Jaycee. *'Oh my God in Heaven*! *For the love of all things holy! It runs in the family!'*

"Bonjour, Jacques...brother!" The smile on his face was almost as bright as the light reflecting through the window.

"I trust you both slept, at least a little?" he said, teasingly.

"Brother, behave. Do not embarrass *our* boy." Luc glanced at me and gave me a quick wink.

*'The little shit!'* I winked back. *'God, I love this man.'* 'You, love, are ours,' came echoing back to me. *'Fuck if I care.'* I thought, as I drank in the view.

"I come bearing something I think both of you could use."

My toes curled. *'If that wasn't a double entendre.'* My thoughts and testosterone were racing. Jaycee was carrying a large, silver serving tray. As he approached the bed, I noticed it had French pastries and other treasures for my appetite, which was suddenly huge, and a decanter of a thick, red liquid.

I was staring now! My God! And no, it wasn't the tray I was staring at.

Dressed in a comfortable pair of grey sweat pants and nothing more, his body I noted, was as incredible as the young man who was lying next to me.

"Like what you see, lover?" Luc said, with a wicked smile on his face. His hand now possessively sliding down my chest to my, shit, once again erect cock.

"Luc, ugh... behave. We *do* have company!" What I said, wasn't what I was fucking thinking.

*'Ménage a trois! Bad, John, BAD! They're brothers for God's sake!'*

Luc continued to stroke my shaft... slowly. It was torture, but with all the power I had, I tried to keep as much proper behavior between us, with his walking, talking, wet dream of a brother in the room. But, God Almighty, my willpower was flying out the window.

By now, Jaycee was standing on my side of the bed. He set the tray down on a table nearby.

"Luc, little brother...are you going to torture me and make me watch, or is there room for one more in your bed?" Jaycee's smile was lethal. His voice should have been a registered weapon. He said it so seductively, with such passion and lust, it had the power to pull-in, reign, and seduce anyone in its path...including me.

"Oh..." Trying to get my mouth to work. "John?" Luc looked at me with equal the power. "Oh fuck." Better than nothing.

With that, Jaycee pulled his sweats off, pulled the comforter back, and slid in by my side. His muscular body and erect, hard cock pressed against me.

"You wanted to say something, babe?" Luc gave me an X-rated stare.

"Fuck...just, FUCK!"

"Well, Luc," Jaycee giggled, "I have to say, he is quite eloquent!"

Luc and Jaycee laughed. The breakfast tray went unnoticed. Luc continued to use his hand on me with a slow and torturous easy slide of his fist, stroking me, oblivious to his brother on the otherside of me.

I was aware of Jaycee's presence, but why question? Who the fuck was I to wonder just where this was going. *'Who the hell cares!'*

"John," Luc pulled himself tightly to my left side, his leg now swung possessively over my waist, "are you okay with this?"

"Jesus!" I responded to another stroke of Luc's fist. "Luc, how can I not be? But..."

"But what?" Jaycee interjected.

"Luc...oh my God. What about Janine? Shouldn't we be meeting her?" '*Where the hell did that come from?*'

"Mon cher," Luc said, lightly kissing my cheek, "it's only nine in the morning. We will be meeting her early this afternoon. Don't worry, John, Janine knows."

I blushed. I fucking blushed.

"She knows?" I looked at Luc, my teeth worrying my lower lip.

"Of course." Jaycee answered. "We have discussed your acceptance into our family. She has, shall we say, come to terms with it."

'*Terms with it?*' I thought, slightly confused.

"She is...how should I put this?" Luc began, "comfortable with our decision, especially the way we feel about you."

"The other way is not an option," Jaycee stated, as he pulled my face to him and gently pressed his lips to mine.

'*Not an option? What option? This needed further explanation... but not now,*' I thought. Jaycee's hand now joined Luc's in stroking my throbbing cock.

∾⤳ ⤲∾

"*John. JOHN!*" It was Elena.

"*What the fuck do you think you are doing, sis? I'm sure you can see what the hell is going on!*"

"*Yeah, you're getting fucked by two FUCKING vampires!*"

"*Fuck you, Elena! Get out of my head!*"

"*That's the problem, John or Jacques, or whatever the fuck your name is these days. Do you know how hard it's been to contact you?*"

"*As if I've cared, Elena. Did you ever think I tuned you out?*"

"*Yeah, right! When have you ever been able to do that! It doesn't work that way! You know that!*"

"*Yeah, I do, but God, Elena...it was nice while it lasted.*"

"*Well, you better fucking listen to me, close and carefully. I'm losing my connection to you...fast! Someone or something is blocking me and I can't get through to you!"*

*"All the better, Elena! In case you haven't seen, I have my hands full at the moment! Or, I mean, other hands...Fuck! Why am I even explaining this to you, Elena?"*

*"Listen, you stubborn idiot, and listen well. I've been researching this family. They are fucking vampires. Generations of them have been ruling Paris for centuries. Oh, and your precious Janine is a werewolf."*

*"Oh, here we go, Elena! Luc and Jaycee are actually centuries old...and wait a minute, wait for it Elena, Janine is...what did you say...a werewolf?"*

*"Yeah, and so is her boyfriend. He turned her."*

*"Elena...please, I can't handle this! Not now, not ever!"*

*"That's just it, John...are you ready to handle being 'one of them' forever?"*

*"Right now, Elena...as pissed as I am...YES!"*

*"John, I've booked a flight. Trace and I..."*

*"No fucking way, Elena! What did I tell you, stay out of my fucking business, and if you bring that boyfriend of yours with you...so help me God, Elena..."*

*"So help me, what? What exactly do you think you can do, John?"*

*"If he comes within eyesight of Luc, Jaycee, or Janine, I WILL kill him! You understand? Elena? Elena! God dammit...answer me!"*

"Elena!" I bolted to a sitting position, my body trembling and sweating. Shit! That was not meant to come out! Before I could even think, in what seemed to be the blink of an eye, both Luc and Jaycee were sitting next to me. Jaycee on my right, Luc on my left. Their foreheads pressed to mine. Their strong arms wrapped tightly and protectively around me.

Luc's voice told me he was scared. "John, what the hell is going on? God, babe, you're shaking. Fuck, baby!" Luc's hand felt my forehead. It was shaking. "You...You're burning up! It was your sister again." It was a statement, not a question.

I felt Jaycee's hand gently stroking my hair. His hand was shaking too. I looked at Jaycee. Tears ran down his face.

"Oh my God. My precious boys...what am I doing to you?"

"You must tell us, John. You are ours. Let us help."

"Luc, I...fuck..." I could hear the frustration in my voice. "I don't know if you'll understand. You'll probably think I'm a total nut job."

"Nut job?" Jaycee interjected, his eyebrows furrowed, somewhat confused.

"You know, a fool, Jaycee." I said, as I felt myself falling apart.

Putting my head down, feeling Luc and Jaycee's protective embrace, I knew I had to let this go if I was to move on. They needed to know. Janine needed to know. *Fuck.* Here goes everything. They'd either understand or Elena had won. *'Again.'*

I took a deep breath, raised my head, and looked at both of them.

First at Jaycee. My lips brushing his lightly. Then to my Luc. My precious Luc. My lips came to his, as his did mine. It was no chaste kiss. I felt passion, concern, and love coming from him. *'That's it.'* My mind was made up. I headed into the fray.

Luc and Jaycee, their hands firm but loving, pulled me down once again, our bodies relaxing into the soft, downy comfort of the bed.

On both sides of me I knew, as I felt their embrace and the look on their faces, I had their full, undivided attention. I would tell them everything. *'Fuck, don't let me regret this.'* I took a deep breath and looked at these two young men, trying to figure out where to start. I just wanted them to keep holding and touching me. I didn't want this to end. My mind was spinning.

"John, mon cher, it's okay." Luc softly said. "Go ahead, my brother. I know something is weighing heavily on your mind. Whatever it is, we are here." As he looked into my eyes, I felt his sincerity and I knew he spoke the truth.

"You, love, are ours." Jaycee stated, as his fingers brushed my lips. Jaycee confirmed it. Their total declaration of love for me. They pulled themselves close to me. Each of them placing one hand on my chest, gently caressing me, showing me they cared and I was loved. I could feel their warmth flowing through me.

*'Here goes. Elena, I swear...'*

"Luc...Jaycee, there's something you need to know about me and Elena. This is going to sound so..." "Nuts!" Jaycee interjected, smiling.

"Yeah, Jaycee. That *is* the word." I couldn't help but grin at Jaycee.

"Go ahead, Jacques." Jaycee whispered as he propped his head up on one hand, the look in his eyes reassuring me.

"Um, Elena and I have this, what the hell can I call it? Think of it as a connection. Since we were young, Elena and I have been able to communicate through our thoughts." *'Yep, John, they think you're nuts!'*

"You're telepathic," Luc stated. Simple, direct. Once again, a statement, not a question. "Luc, how did you know?"

"John..." Luc now looking at me, his head like his brother's, propped up on his free hand. "It was obvious from the moment in the airport." Luc gently rubbed my pecs.

They both had my full, albeit stunned, attention.

"You don't think that Jaycee and I...even Janine, know?"

"I...Luc..." looking and sounding totally dumbfounded, I was finding myself at a total loss for words.

"Listen, John." Luc continued, "This is nothing new to us."

*'Nothing new? What the hell? I am way over thinking this.'*

"Our concern, Jacques," Jaycee took one of his fingers and pulled my face gently towards him, "is that Elena is doing or saying something that is upsetting you. We will *not* allow that to happen. You must tell us what your sister is saying that is upsetting you so much!" His voice now more stern.

Jaycee's eyes locked on to mine, while Luc's hand possessively gripped my waist. "Tell us what Elena is saying, Jacques. Tell us now, mon cher!"

I could feel that pull from Jaycee again. It was by no means threatening. They just wanted to help me. So be it! Dammit, after what I've already put them through, I needed to cowboy up and just fucking tell them already. They deserved that. I took in a deep breath and just looked into his eyes. Eyes that I swore I had just seen flash red.

*'What the fuck! First Luc, now Jaycee?'* Randomly, thoughts of Visine flashed through my head. I really was over thinking this.

Neither Jaycee's nor Luc's eyes had left mine. Their bodies were now pressed so close to mine that the comfort they shared with me warmed me from my head to my toes. My worries, concerns, and fears were falling away. A peace and easiness came over me, but not through my own thoughts or feelings. What I felt was coming from the two men lying on each side of me.

"Elena is driving me completely fucking nuts. She wants me out of Paris and away from the three of you." *'There, I said it. Here goes everything.'* "Elena told me she has information on your family, your, how should I put this... lineage. She says you are...Oh, God...Vampires, and Janine is a werewolf." I waited for the onslaught. What happened next basically confused the living shit out of me.

"Vampires?" Luc giggled. He just shook his head, squeezed my side, and giggled, baring his canines.

His very *human* canines! *'The little shit! Fuck, I loved him.'*

"Vampires, Luc! I'm afraid, my dear brother, he knows too much and we must suck his blood!" Jaycee said, trying his best to imitate Bela Lugosi. He smiled and brushed my cheek with his lips.

Not to be outdone, Luc started to nibble my neck.

"She's right, you know," Luc stated, trying to look deadly serious. I flinched.

"I'm actually three hundred and fifty-seven years old! Jaycee is three hundred and sixty-four!"

"Oh, and, Jacques," Jaycee, trying to control his obvious amusement added, "Janine *is* a werewolf! You see, her boyfriend Alec turned her."

I bolted up. Sitting there, I looked back and down at the two young men laying there. They were still giggling. Their eyes sparkling in the late morning sun. Their smiles, contagious to say the least, took me by complete and utter surprise. What I thought was going to be a complete fucking disaster turned into, for lack of a better word, a joke.

*'How the fuck did they know? John, you are over thinking. John, look at what you've got. Deal with it!'* I started to giggle and found myself being pulled back into Luc and Jaycee's embrace. Fuck it! *"Elena, if you can hear me, remember what I said."*

"You, love, are ours!" Luc and Jaycee said in unison.

They could say that to me one hundred times a day and I wouldn't get sick of it. "Possession is nine-tenths of the law." I said to both of them with a smirk on my face.

"Excusez-moi?" Luc questioned, with a definite feigned look of confusion, one of his eyebrows raised.

Before I could comprehend what the fuck was going on, two of the hottest, beautiful, most perfect men were entwining their bodies around me. Muscular heat to muscular heat. *'Oh fuck!'*

# ❧ CHAPTER TWELVE ❧

Hot, sweaty, muscular bodies wrapped themselves around me. I felt their strong hands feeling every part of me. Lips pressed, kissed, and brushed over me. Softly at first, then with passion ignited, hard cocks pressed against my flesh. I felt warm, slick trails of pre-cum on my skin as their cocks slid across me. Pulsing, throbbing, needing release. Hot, wet mouths took turns sucking my cock.

"Mon cher? Babe?" The voice I had come to know so well was there now. In my head. Calling to me. "John! Wake up, lover!"

*'No!'*

"Jacques?" I felt a strong hand wrap itself around my erection.

*'Oh, and God, you too!'* I could feel myself swimming up from a deep sleep where dreams had taken over my mind.

"John? Wake up my love!"

*'God, Luc had the most beautiful voice I had ever heard. Wake up to that every morning? Ya think?' 'That tickles. What the hell, was it raining?'* My eyes were still closed, not wanting to let go of the dream I had been having, but there it was again. Soft, warm drops of water hit my forehead and my chest. I took my hand and brushed the wetness away and with the other I began to rub the sleep from my eyes. I found myself flat on my back and a real live wet dream right above me.

"Jacques." Jaycee smiled. "We thought you were going to sleep all day!"

"Well, big brother, after what we did to him, can you blame him?" Luc asked, waggling his eyebrows. Both Luc and Jaycee were kneeling on each side of me, wrapped in white, thick, cotton towels cinched tightly around their slim hips, their hair disheveled and still wet, with bangs hanging down over their impossibly blue eyes. Water droplets dripped from their foreheads on to me. Droplets also ran from their hard, defined pecs and down the indent of their six pack abs, down the slight path of black hair directly to their...God help me!

"Did anyone ever tell Jacques it's impolite to stare?" Jaycee smiled down at me, waggling his eyebrows too.

"I'm glad somebody taught him right!" Luc said, with a devious smile on his face, his eyes twinkling.

*'God, I love that little shit.'*

"Oh God...boys! How long have you been watching me?" I could feel myself turning redder by the moment.

"Long enough to know exactly what you were dreaming about, lover," Luc said, as he reached under the covers, joining his hand with Jaycee's.

"Luc, baby brother, behave. Someone is waiting for us!"

"You're right, Jaycee, but first we must take care of our boy!" His face showing fully his intentions.

Luc leaned over, cupped my face with his warm, strong hand, and kissed me. My mouth opened for him as his tongue found mine. God, he tasted good. He kissed me long and slow. All the while their hands worked together to stroke my cock.

"Uunnhh, boys...Oh my God!" I could feel my balls grow tight as my orgasm approached. My back arched and I could feel my toes curl inward as I came. Luc and Jaycee, not wanting to waste a drop, eagerly bent over my shaft and licked up my cum.

Then, before I could catch my breath, they both leaned toward me and took turns kissing me. I tasted myself in their mouths. Our mouths joined together. We kissed deeply, our tongues exploring each other's mouths. No inhibitions. Just the three of us. *'Would every morning be like this? How the fuck could I survive this? But frankly, what a way to go!'*

Taking my hand, Jaycee pulled me up, throwing the remaining covers back. "We left you plenty of hot water, mon cher," Luc said.

"Go now. Get ready, Jacques! Paris and the beautiful werewolf await us!"

"Wait, what...?" I stammered, startled at first. "Oh fuck...!"

Luc and Jaycee both slapped my ass as I headed to the shower. I could hear them giggling behind me.

# ❖ CHAPTER THIRTEEN ❖

We walked out into the warm, welcoming, Parisian sunshine. It was a perfect day. There was hardly a cloud in the sky.

As we went down the steps at midday, I was oblivious to the people around me. Bustling with activity, everyone seemed to have an agenda. But something strange, yet familiar was beginning to happen, just as it had at the airport. People were beginning to turn and look at the three of us with the same look I had noticed at the airport. Fear? Pity? What the hell?

With Luc to my left and Jaycee to my right as we proceeded, I realized they both held my hands, their fingers entwined in mine. I looked first at Luc, then at Jaycee. They both turned to me and smiled, not a care on either of their faces. Heat coursed through my veins and I felt myself blush. Ah, what the hell. If they don't care, why the fuck should I? I returned their smile. They squeezed my hands tighter, possessively.

"You, my love, are ours!" Luc stated, his voice as smooth as silk.

As if I needed to be reminded. There was no further doubt in my mind. *'Eat your heart out, Elena!'* I thought. A giggle slipped out.

"What's that all about, babe?" Luc asked, still smiling.

"Nothing, baby boy, nothing at all!" With no inhibitions, I leaned toward him and gave him a quick kiss on his lips.

"Whatever you're thinking, babe, don't stop!" Luc leaned into me.

Oh, trust me, precious boy, that will be no problem. *'Or would it?'* I thought.

The same limo that had been waiting for us at the airport yesterday morning was there. It was immaculate, a classic. Holy shit! A Rolls-Royce Phantom. It was, well, stunning. I remember reading about this particular model. Only about five hundred or so were made. This one, I believed to be a nineteen fifty-nine. Mostly used by the Royal Family, introduced to Her Royal Majesty, Queen Elizabeth the Second. I couldn't help but notice its black finish sparkled in the sunlight. This motor car, shit...Well, it was priceless and it looked like it came off the showroom floor.

As we approached, a chauffeur dressed in a perfectly tailored black suit with a crisp white shirt and black tie, tipped his head slightly and opened the door. He looked all of eighteen, if he was a day.

Jaycee, still holding my hand, turned to face Luc and me. With an elegant half bow, he stretched his free arm and hand out.

"Your carriage awaits! So does Paris! Get in you two!"

Luc allowed me to enter the spacious vehicle first. As I did, his hand brushed my ass. "Get in, mon amour. Janine awaits our arrival!"

"Luc," Jaycee started, "you, little brother, are incorrigible!" He chuckled.

*'Fuck if I cared!'*

The chauffeur closed the door.

As the limo began to pull into traffic, I couldn't help but notice that despite its facing leather bench seats, both Luc and Jaycee sat with me.

Once again, Luc to my left, Jaycee to my right. Sitting close to me, their hands never let go of mine. Although the driver had the air conditioning on, I could feel the heat from their bodies infusing into mine. The driver pulled the car into the traffic. As noon approached, the vehicles on the street made for a congestive, slow-moving affair. *'Good,'* I thought. *'I have more time to enjoy the scenery, both inside and out!'*

It was then that I noticed Luc looking at me with his amazing blue eyes. In the light of day they seemed even more blue and bright. *Caribbean blue.* They twinkled, with just a hint of that mischievous look I was getting to know all too well.

"John...where are you?" Luc asked, with a slight concern in his tone.

"I'm right here, baby boy. Any closer, I'd be on your lap!" I couldn't help but chuckle.

"Ah, I meant," The corner of his mouth lifting into a half smile, "in here..." As his finger tapped my forehead lightly.

"Oh crap. Sorry, babe, I was just taking in the sights."

"Inside or out, Jacques?" Jaycee questioned, mischief in his eyes.

"Both, Jaycee. Both."

"Like what you see?" Luc squeezed my hand, smiling at me.

"Definitely, babe!" I pulled Luc's hand up to my mouth and kissed it. "Most definitely!"

Luc and Jaycee leaned into me, and at the same time they gently brushed their lips to each corner of my mouth. Their lips, I noticed, touched each other's. *'Somebody hit me, this can't be happening.'*

"Are you hungry, Jacques? For food?" Jaycee asked, a smirk on his face.

"Yeah. Although, thanks to you two and that incredibly beautiful sister of yours, I have no clue where we are going."

"See over there?" Luc extended his arm, pointing past his brother and out the left window.

"The Eiffel Tower?" *'My God!'* I thought, *'Pictures do not do it justice.'* "They have a restaurant in there?"

"Oui, Jacques," Jaycee answered. "Le Jules Verne. You've heard of him, mon cher." It was a statement. "Very chic. Avant-garde. Then there is '58 Tour Eiffel'. They specialize in classical French cuisine. Janine thought you might enjoy the ambiance there."

I had all I could do not to lean over and hug him. Instead, I smiled at him. My own tour guide.

"Is that to your liking, Jacques? We are meeting Janine at the '58 Tour Eiffel', but if..."

I pressed two fingers to his sensuous, warm lips to quiet him.

"Jaycee, precious, there is no problem! Anywhere with you would be perfect." I made a point to look Jaycee directly into his eyes. "Even that fast food joint over there!"

"Oh, mon dieu!" Luc cringed as he put the back of his hand to his forehead, feigning exasperation. Jaycee and I both looked at him, giggling.

The limo made its way to the Eiffel Tower and Janine. *'Werewolf. Bite me, sis.'*

# CHAPTER FOURTEEN

'58 Tour Eiffel' was located on the second story of the famed Eiffel Tower. When Jaycee told me about it on the way, he mentioned it featured classic French cuisine. My mouth watered at the thought of escargot, beef bourguignon, chicken cordon bleu. Not to mention the desserts! Poire avec Orange, Tartelettes de Framboises au Mascarpone!

"Jacques, mon cher, you're drooling!" Janine giggled.

Oh crap! I had been looking at the menu, my appetite suddenly in full swing after the events of early this morning. I thought about that tray, gone unnoticed, sitting in Luc's room. Memories of what happened played through my head. A warmth like no other I've ever felt coursed through me. I couldn't help but glance at Luc and Jaycee and remember the exquisite union of our bodies. Sweaty, muscular heat to sweaty, muscular heat. Finally, my God, swept away in an orgasm that sent waves of pleasure coursing through me.

"Jacques, mon cher, are you okay?" Janine's voice was telling me she was becoming concerned.

If you only knew, Janine. I felt a small smile escape. "Excusez-moi, ma chere," I said, feeling myself turning just a slight shade of red.

"You, Jacques, are looking much better! I'm so glad! I trust Luc and Jaycee allowed you to rest?"

I couldn't help but notice the knowing look on Janine's face as she looked briefly at the both of them. I also noticed Luc tip his head down and Jaycee blush. They both looked like the cat that ate the canary. Janine knew. We were so busted!

"Jacques?"

"Yes, Janine."

"May I ask you a personal question?"

"Of course, ma chere. What is it, love?"

"While you were in the shower this morning, my brothers relayed the news about Elena," she said, matter-of-factly.

Ahh crap! Now the cat was completely out of the bag. I felt myself starting to blush. "Ah, they...um..." I looked at Janine, clueless as to what or how I was supposed to respond. Now she knew too. Did she think I was nuts?

"Janine, I was planning on telling you, I just didn't know how. Luc and Jaycee took it so lightly, but I didn't know how you were going to respond or what you were going to think of me. I'm really sorry. I didn't..." I started to stutter.

"Jacques, mon cher! Silly boy!" she said, as her face lit up beautifully. She once again took my breath away. "Would you relax! Respirer!"

"Uh?"

"Breathe, Jacques! You're turning blue!"

'*Like Luc's eyes.*' I thought.

My eyes wandered around the restaurant for a moment as I tried to collect my thoughts and return to a calmer state of mind. I couldn't help but notice the view. It was breathtaking, even on the second floor. After lunch, my tour guide, Jaycee, said they would give me a view I would never forget. I thought I got that earlier this morning! Again, visions of heated love-making entered my mind. Luc and Jaycee pressing their strong, young bodies against mine, fucking me senseless. On the way to the restaurant, Jaycee had told me about the history of the tower, and even though he had seen it practically every day, his eyes twinkled as he discussed the view I would take in.

"Hey, John." Luc brushed his hand across my face. "Where did you go? Was it Elena again?"

"Uh...? Oh, Luc, sorry, I was just taking in the view. No, babe, it wasn't Elena."

Should I be concerned? I hadn't heard Elena shooting her smart-ass mouth off for some time now.

Then again, the day was early. Wait, why am I even thinking about this? Then again, Elena's connection with me has never been broken like this. Suddenly, silently. A mixed blessing. A Godsend? John, snap out of it!

"No, baby boy...oops, my bad! Sorry, Janine, I, uh..."

"Jacques, no worries...I know you love him. I've known for some time now." My interest was piqued.

"Janine, you've known for some time?"

"Of course, Jacques! I know you're gay. Remember dear, you told me. You weren't exactly subtle online! I find you quite endearing and a perfect match for my little brother!"

"Luc was smitten with you from practically the beginning!" Jaycee chimed in. "I think it had to do with all your country music posts. All of a sudden, little brother has a Stetson in his closet! Before you arrived he was going around singing, badly I might add, something about, what was it? Oh yeah...'Thinkin' About You'. He's even developed a state-side southern accent!" Jaycee concluded. By the expression Jaycee was wearing, I swear he found great joy in humiliating Luc right then and there.

If he could have, I swear Luc would have, at that moment, slid under the table and cowered like a puppy dog. His eyes were locked on mine with a "help me" look, his eyes as big as saucers. When I could have laughed, I took pity on my baby boy. I reached over and took his shaking hand in mine. My thumb rubbing his knuckles.

"Luc, excusez-moi. I didn't mean to embarrass you in front of your family." I was falling for this young man so hard and so fast that, well, if this all went south, I'd hit so damn hard there would be nothing left of me emotionally. My God, I have never felt anything this intense. Jesus, Luc, what you are doing to me?

"N-n-no-o. It's okay," Luc stammered. "John, I've been putting up with this stuff from Janine and Jaycee for hundreds of years!" His look had turned deadly serious. Did his eyes just flash red?

Uh?" Now it was my turn to stammer. "Hundreds of years? What the..." I looked at Luc, Janine, and Jaycee. Janine was the first to lose it. Well, at least three of the people in the group found it amusing.

"Jacques, oh my God, we've startled you!" Janine said with an apologetic tone in her voice.

"Luc, look what you've done! Shame little brother!" Jaycee's admonishment, I could tell, was light-hearted, but by Luc's reaction he took it seriously.

"John, I am so sorry! Forgive me, my love." Luc's eyes looked into mine with genuine regret. "It's just that I couldn't let go of what you said your sister said about us. I apologize for my rudeness. I promise John, it will not happen again!"

"You have our word." Jaycee reached over and took my hand. His eyes flashed red. "You, love, are ours, always."

Well now, '*Always? That's new,*' I thought.

"Hey, it's okay," I squeezed Luc and Jaycee's hands. I looked at Janine and softly smiled at her.

On cue, as if in a scene from a movie, a waiter dressed in a classic ivory tux with tails, fresh linen draped over his arm, arrived carrying a beautiful, ornate, silver tray. With a flair only the Parisians could master, he put our entrées in front of us. I just had to try the beef bourguignon. After all, this was France. This was Paris and the home to yep, Julia Child. It looked mouth-watering.

"Let's eat!" Janine raised her champagne glass in a toast. "To the newest member of our family! To you, mon cher!"

"Bon appetite!" Luc and Jaycee added.

We clinked the fine crystal together as I looked at my new family. Totally amazed and bewildered, but as happy as I could be, I could only smile at all of them. I could feel my cheeks turning red.

"I'm famished!" Janine said, looking at her plate, her eyes almost feral in appearance.

For the most part, Luc and Jaycee picked at their food. So that's the secret to their incredible bodies. But what about Janine? I watched as I ate. She was devouring her food, although in a lady-like manner.

"Jacques!" Janine looked at me. "Isn't this delicious? I seem to have the appetite of a wolf!" I dropped my fork.

# ❖ CHAPTER FIFTEEN ❖

After lunch I found myself staring at Paris from atop the Eiffel Tower. The view was incredible. The Arc de Triumph, the Louvre, Champs-Elyse...all highly visible. The beautiful Seine River running through Paris. Once again standing next to me, it was Luc to my left and Jaycee to my right. I could feel their fingers intertwined with mine, their thumbs gently rubbing my wrists. Janine stood close by enjoying the view as well. Her gentle looks were ones of thoughtfulness, caring, and concern. Yes, the sights were beautiful, but frankly the conversation we had got a little, oh for crap sake, *weird*. I felt guilty even thinking that way.

"John, babe." Luc leaned into me. "Are you enjoying the view? Any questions our tour guide," he nodded towards Jaycee, "can answer for you?" A smile, one of complete innocence and sincerity, framed my boy's face.

"No, baby boy. This is incredible! I still can't believe I'm here with you! All of you! Merci. Merci beaucoup!" A tear just had to roll down my face. *'Pull yourself together, John.'*

Noticing what was happening and the emotions that were overtaking me, Jaycee released his grip from my hand as Luc turned to me and embraced me. His arms wrapped themselves strongly and possessively around me.

"Kiss me, Luc. Kiss me, my sweet baby boy," I whispered into his ear. I really didn't give a crap where we were. I needed to feel Luc's lips on mine, feel his love flow through me.

With incredible tenderness, he looked up at me. I noticed Luc, too, did not care where we were. He pressed his lips to mine. All of a sudden it was just Luc and I. I don't know if it was from exhaustion, the memories of the early morning love-making, or the spark that went through me at the touch of my lover's lips on mine. I allowed Luc's eager tongue to part my lips. It was slow, passionate, and it caused heat to course through my veins in a way I have never felt.

*'This,' I thought, 'could last forever.'*

*"It will, mon cher... It will..."* Luc's voice whispered in my mind.

I pulled away. Not abruptly. What I thought I heard Luc say to me just gave me pause. Besides that, I had to break away for air.

For just a few moments it was this incredible young man and myself. I found Luc's beautiful, blue eyes gazing into mine.

"Did I make you feel better, love?" Luc asked, still pressed against me.

Oh God, did you ever!

"Yes, babe, merci." My love for Luc only seemed to grow with each moment we were together.

Janine had been watching, and as we pulled away, Luc still held my left hand and Jaycee resumed his possessive hold on my right hand. I was coming to the realization that while Luc was mine, Jaycee would always be a part of our lives. Linked together by what? At the moment, I just didn't care. Answers would come soon enough, with or without Elena's psychic rantings. Where was she? It was a fleeting thought as Jaycee brought me back to my reality.

"We thought we would take advantage of such a beautiful day and give you tours of some of our favorite gardens in Paris!" Jaycee said, his blue eyes looking eagerly at me for approval.

I nodded, looking at Jaycee. "Oui, Jaycee. I am yours and Luc's." Finally accepting their promise.

"Magnifique, Jacques! Yes, you, love, are ours...always! Why don't we head to the car? I gave the driver our itinerary for the rest of the day." I could see Jaycee's excitement in his eyes. I felt Luc's hand squeeze mine as his head came to rest on my shoulder. A moment in time etched into my memory. I kissed Luc on his forehead and heard a sweet and gentle whimper. A whimper that went straight to my heart.

"Later tonight, Jacques." Janine came up to me, her fingers gently brushing down my cheek, "We shall enjoy the nightlife our city has to offer! I can't wait to get you on the dance floor!" I laughed as she took my hands and proceeded to lead me in a brief but sexy dance, right there on the street!

"Get in line, sis!" Luc said. It was meant to be a joke, but for some reason I sensed just a slight possessive streak in the young man, not to mention a flash of red in his eyes.

# ⚜ CHAPTER SIXTEEN ⚜

The day was filled, as I was promised, with visions of unbelievable beauty. The look on Jaycee's face as he described in vivid detail the history behind the gardens we toured, was priceless. His already perfect looks were only made more striking by the afternoon sun. The same could be said for Luc and Janine.

Oh, trust me, I took plenty of pictures because frankly, nobody back in the States would believe me. It seemed to me, that my hosts were more breathtaking than the gardens surrounding us.

From the Palais Royal Garden, with its huge fountains, perfectly trimmed hedges and ornate flowers, to the breathtaking Jardin de l'Arsenal, the visions I saw were forever etched into my mind. They were memories that would last me the rest of my life. Jaycee had a vast, detailed knowledge of the history and design plans. Every detail made it sound like he had watched them design and create them. God, I'd give anything for this moment to last.

*'Hell, I wish it could last me a lifetime,'* I thought.

*"It could...for an eternity, mon cher,"* Luc's answer echoed in my mind.

"What do you mean, babe?" I froze. I just stood there. What the hell had just happened? "Oh my God...Luc?" I slowly turned to face him. I knew my eyes were showing him surprise and a hint of disbelief.

It took a few moments before I realized that Luc was caressing my face with his hand. His eyes studied mine. I was in no way upset, but I think he realized he had just shocked the hell out of me.

We were just leaving the Cours-La-Reine. Jaycee and Janine, walking ahead of us, turned and looked at what was happening.

"Luc, baby boy, did you just um, did you just..." I cupped my hands to his face.

"Oh shit, John. What was I thinking? Are you all right?"

"Oui. It was a bit of a shock, but then again I'm kind of used to it. You know, babe, my sister." Our foreheads came together. Luc's hands held me at my waist, pulling me close to him.

"John, forgive me for startling you. It's just that after you told us about Elena...I...I just couldn't stop myself."

"Stop yourself? Luc?" Jaycee asked. Jaycee and Janine had made their way back to us. How did they hear our exchange? Huh?

"From what?" Janine asked. "What did you do?" One of her perfect eyebrows arched.

Luc put his head down, worrying his bottom lip almost as if he were ashamed. A lock of his beautiful, black hair fell into his eyes as he looked down at the path we were on and nervously started kicking the ground with the front of his shoe. I put my hand under his chin and tilted his head so his eyes met mine. His eyes begged me for forgiveness as I gently brushed the lock of hair away. And as I did, I leaned toward him and brushed my lips over his.

"It's okay, my sweet boy. You have nothing to be worried about."

Luc took my hand and leaned into me, putting his head on my chest. I wrapped my arm around his waist, pulling him to me.

"He *talked* to me, Janine." I rested my head on Luc's.

"Like...how?" Jaycee questioned.

"Like Elena and I do. Please do not be angry with him." I felt Luc tremble and pulled him closer. I took my hand and rubbed the small of his back. I kissed Luc on the top of his head, nuzzling my nose into his thick, black, shaggy hair. My God, he smelled good. I wasn't trying to be rude. I knew Janine and Jaycee were standing right by us. I understood their concern, but the protective nature I had developed for Luc told me that I needed to place all my attention on the man that I had fallen for, and at the same time let him know and realize that I was, by no means, angry with him.

"Are you okay with that, mon cher?" Janine asked. "We weren't going to divulge that to you, just yet. Were we, Luc." It was a statement, not a question. It came off kind, yet somewhat stern.

"Janine, my love, it's okay. No explanations are needed now. I realize that I have fallen for your brother and I find myself in love with him. I don't want secrets between us...all of us. Is that okay with you? Janine? Jaycee?" I could feel Luc pulling himself closer to me.

*"Baby boy, I love you. I have you and, God knows, you have me. Talk to me all you want."*

*"I love you too, John...with all my heart,"* his words softly spoke to me. I could feel him relax.

"Of course, John," Janine replied. "It's just that there are things about our family that we want to share with you."

"But we just wanted to wait a bit," Jaycee added.

For the first time, still holding Luc, I looked up at them. "It's okay. No secrets. The three of you mean so much to me that nothing you say will affect me or change the way I feel about you."

"You, love," Janine came up to me and Luc, "are a blessing to us. I promise you, we will tell you about our family." She leaned over and kissed Luc on the top of his head and then, turning to me, she brushed her soft lips across mine.

"I look forward to that, and I will do the same."

"You love our baby brother." Jaycee caressed my cheek. "That is the most important thing to us. Janine and I love you too, mon cher." He leaned over and gently kissed me. "You are so easy to love!" Then to my total surprise, he reached his hand to Luc's face, touching him gently. Jaycee took my free hand, and at the same time leaned into his brother who was now looking at me with tears coming down from his eyes, and gently kissed his brother's cheek. It was one of the most loving and touching things I have ever seen.

"It's okay, Luc. Janine and I couldn't be happier that you can share your gift with John. It's okay." It was a simple affirmation that spoke volumes about the love that was the foundation of this family.

Still in my embrace, Luc slowly lifted his head to look at his brother and sister. A serene smile greeted them. "Merci, Janine. Merci, Jaycee." Luc's voice was barely a whisper.

I softly kissed his forehead, then turned my attention to Janine and Jaycee. "What's not to love?" I gently tousled Luc's hair.

Janine took a few moments to look at both of us. "Let us put this behind us. We have one more surprise for you before we show you Paris the way it should be seen...at night."

I couldn't help notice how big Luc's smile became. He threw both his arms around me and kissed me, his tongue begging for entrance. With no hesitation, I let him in. I gave as good as I got. My hands reaching for, and running through, his thick, black locks of hair. As I did, I heard his now familiar soft whimper and, as always, it made my heart thud and my knees knock.

*"Make love to me tonight, Luc. I need you so damn much! Make me yours, babe."*

*"Oh God, John...I've wanted you from the first moment I saw you. Yes, I will...completely."*

Luc's words, running through my head, made me dizzy. I took a deep breath and looked at the young man I had fallen for so deeply. I realized, there and then, that my life was now with Luc and his family, who, unbeknownst to me, would be changing my life forever.

"Ah, boys." I felt Janine's finger tapping my shoulder. "Save some of that for tonight!" Looking at Janine, the wink she gave us said it all.

Not letting go of Luc's hand, we turned towards Janine and Jaycee.

"Luc, baby bro, you are one of a kind!" Jaycee smiled, tousling Luc's hair as he spoke.

As Janine led the way, once again with Luc to my left and Jaycee to my right, their fingers intertwined with mine, we walked through the exit of the garden to the waiting black limousine. I could only imagine what was next on the agenda.

*"You'll love it, John!"* Luc's voice ran through my head. *"I'm sure I will, especially with you by my side."*

*"What about me?"* Jaycee asked, giving me puppy dog eyes?

# ❧ CHAPTER SEVENTEEN ❧

After touring the Gardens, the black limousine gracefully made its way through the late afternoon traffic of Paris.

Once again, Luc sat to my left and Jaycee to my right. Once again, protectively and lovingly, they sat pressed as close as they could get to me, their hands holding mine. Janine sat opposite us, in the facing, plush leather bench seat. Janine had a fondness for music of the nineteen-eighties and had the driver softly play the music while I sat and watched the sights roll by outside the window.

"What the?" I couldn't help but notice that even with the one-way blackened windows, as we passed cars, the occupants were staring at the vehicle. It apparently had no effect on Janine, Luc, or Jaycee.

Squeezing my hand, Luc leaned into me. "Is everything all right?"

"Yep!"

"You seem preoccupied, mon cher," Jaycee responded.

"No. Really, Jaycee, I'm fine."

"It's the stares, isn't it?" Luc asked.

"Well, I have to admit, I am a little bit taken aback by the attention you seem to receive. I noticed it at the airport and the restaurant...even the gardens. Are you royalty?" I felt a half smile form on my lips.

"You could say that." Janine spoke, as she blushed. "We have, how should I say this, history in this town. People are very familiar with our family heritage."

~ ~

*"John. John? John!"*

Holy shit. It couldn't be. What the fuck! *"Elena?"*

*"Yeah, idiot, but then again, I guess you'd have to wonder which voice was invading your head lately."*

*"You mean..."*

*"Exactly, big brother. Listen, and listen carefully. I don't have much time! I have been struggling to get in touch with you since we last spoke! Don't you fucking tune me out, either!"*

*"First of all, I didn't 'tune you out'."* I was beginning to wish I could...*"How the hell did you know?"*

*"John, I don't have time for this. They are trying to read me as I speak to you!"*

*"They?"* I almost choked.

*"Your little lover boy and Jaycee. They are on to me!"*

*"What the fuck, Elena! Have you totally lost it?"* I was getting pissed again, waiting for the vampire comment to come from her.

*"You, big brother, have your head shoved so far up your ass you just can't see it! Now, for the love of God...listen!"*

*"Go ahead, Elena. Do I really have a choice? But don't you dare start in on this vam-"* I was cut off mid-thought.

*"They are fucking vampires and you're the next course. And yes, God help me, Janine is a werewolf! I was there with you in the restaurant! Her appetite. Her feral eyes. Not to mention the red flashes in Luc's and Jaycee's eyes."*

There it was. Vampires and werewolves. Oh for crap sake. I was waiting for lions, tigers and bears...oh my.

*"Jesus, Elena. Even if what you were telling me is true, and I'm having a hard time grasping this, why haven't I been "turned" or "mauled" by the supernatural trio you think I'm with?"*

*"John! For the love of all things holy, you have got to get out of there! If you don't, or won't listen to me...then just wait until this evening. They plan on telling you EVERYTHING!"* Now it was Elena's

turn to be pissed off. *"Maybe then you'll fucking believe me!"*

*"Okay, Elena...that's it! You probably already know-"*

Elena cut me off in mid-thought. Christ, she was good at that. And the more she did it, the more I was beginning to hate it.

*"You're in love with Luc. I know that. I knew from the minute he sent you those pictures online! He wants you for eternity!"*

*"Would that be so bad, sis? Really?"*

*"Yeah, well...God, John, this is so damn hard..."* Elena faltered. *"Jaycee has designs on you too! And if you love your baby boy as much as you say you do...I'll tell you this once and only once. Jaycee is willing to kill him to have you for himself!"*

*"Oh for crap sake, Elena! You are going too far! I will not tolerate this from you, sister or not! That is enough!"*

*"John, I'm losing you, but hear this! Trace and I will be there in a matter of hours!"*

*"No, absolutely not!"* Dead silence. *"Elena...?"*

"Fuck! Leave me alone!" I shouted. Shit, I said it out loud.

Luc's voice gently entered my thoughts. *"It was Elena. Babe, I heard every word."*

*"Oh my God, Luc, please tell me my sister is just pulling this bullshit on me to try and ruin this. She's always been so fucking jealous of me."*

*"John, I wish I could, but,"* He squeezed my hand, *"I will explain to you tonight. Everything. It is not what you imagine...Elena..."* Luc paused, his teeth worrying his lower lip. *"Babe, your sister is just...how shall I put this...misinformed."*

*"Luc, baby boy, I believe you. I fucking love you!"*

*"I know, John. God, I feel the same way you do. Do you trust me?"*

*"With my life, mon cher."*

*"Tonight, babe. Tonight we will explain. I promise you."* His eyes were moist with tears about to spill down his young, perfect face. *"I need you, John...please?"*

*"Baby boy, I'm so sorry you had to hear that, and yes, I want you too. I want you deep inside me, so deep, Luc, that we become one. Making love to you is more important than anything you need to tell me. I love you so damn much!"*

*"Oh God, John...I...I...love you. I promise, mon amour, there will never be any secrets."* Just then a tear ran down his face. Not one of sorrow, but one of love.

Luc leaned into me, and as I tilted his chin up, he pressed his lips to mine and once again time stood still. I felt the love this young man had for me flow through me, making me go weak. I had fallen. Hard. Whatever the outcome, I would never regret, and I would never let go. I would live for Luc; I would die for Luc.

I felt Jaycee's hand squeeze mine, gently but firmly, and Janine, God bless her, leaned forward and put her hand on my knee. Without so much as another word, the understanding between us deepened to another inexplicable level. It was if they were taking possession of my very soul. So be it.

The rest of the ride was mostly quiet, yet pleasant. I couldn't help but notice that the mood had once again lifted to its former place, before Elena invaded my mind. Just the four of us enjoying each other's company.

I was looking out the window, once again listening to Jaycee, this time explaining the intricacies of the Seine River and the part it played in the infrastructure of this magnificent European city.

I looked like, Luc noted with a giggle, a puppy dog.

"Jaycee." Luc tapped his brother's knee. "Keep the window up. I fear John will be sticking his head out the window for a better view."

"I've got a better idea!" Janine leaned over and pressed the intercom. "Adrian, please open the sunroof!"

I watched the large pane of glass open to let in the warm, golden, late day sun.

'*Yep, Elena. Vampires.*' The sun accented the natural highlights of Janine's long, silky hair. Luc and Jaycee looked up and let the sun warm their tanned, perfect skin. '*Nope, no sudden spontaneous combustion. No piles of ashes. Explain this one, sis!*'

Luc grabbed my arm and before I knew it, the four of us were standing up and looking at the sights with half our bodies exposed to the warm breeze, courtesy of the open sunroof. The car next to us almost veered off the road.

Whatever Luc, and I'm sure Jaycee and Janine, were going to share with me later this evening, it had a totally logical explanation, nothing preternatural or supernatural.

We enjoyed the views and Jaycee once again pointed out and shared his vast knowledge of the city.

"Oh look, baby boy," I pressed my forehead to Luc's, "another burger joint!"

"Oh my Lord!" There it was again, that feigned look of disgust, and once again Luc placed his hand on his forehead. He giggled.

"What? French fries!" I poked Luc with my elbow.

"That was wrong in so many ways!" Jaycee chuckled as he squeezed my hand.

"See that park?" His voice was happy as a four year old getting a pony for his birthday, which he probably did. "That, dear Jacques, is the Champs de Mars! Hungry, love?"

"When am I not?"

"Me too!" Janine chimed in. "Like a wolf!"

Silence. You could have heard the veritable pin drop. Then all four of us started to giggle, then just plain laugh, remembering the events that unfolded earlier with Elena.

As the limousine started to pull into the park, Luc and Jaycee put their hands on my head and gently pushed me back down inside the limo.

"Mon cher," Jaycee rubbed his hand up and down my thigh, "time for a little respite before our big night!"

Frankly, after all that happened since this morning, I didn't know if I had the energy to even continue.

*"You better, lover! We've only just begun."* Luc's hand began to roam, as his voice in my head sent heat scudding through my veins.

*"You know, Luc, you're right! You promised to give me something later!"* I *said* to Luc.

*"Uuhhnnn!"* Luc leaned back, closing his eyes.

Oh yeah, he wanted me!

*"Oh, brother!"* I watched Jaycee roll his eyes. *"Have either of you no shame?"* Luc turned his head to look at me, his eyebrows waggling. The little shit!

*"Boys, what shall I ever do with you?"* Janine added.

Why was I not surprised? The whole family knew my thoughts, and I, theirs.

"But, mon cher, trust us. When it comes to matters of the heart, Janine and I will be, shall we say, minding our own business?" Jaycee squeezed my thigh and winked. Another flash of red permeated his eyes.

Why I wasn't concerned about that, I didn't know. Frankly, I didn't care. There was a very normal explanation for it.

The limousine pulled into a reserved parking area. No other people were present. All the parks I had seen that day were wonderful. This one was breathtaking! Imagine being at the top of the Rockies or gazing at the Grand Canyon. The majestic beauty. Now, just imagine that beauty multiplied tenfold!

Adrian got out and came to the rear of the vehicle to open the door.

"My Lady...My Lords...Sir Jacques, mon cher," Bowing politely as he addressed us, once again, like royalty. God, I could get used to this. Hell, I was!

As I stepped out of the limousine, Luc and Jaycee resumed their possession of my hands. Janine came up to me and lightly kissed me on the cheek.

"Jacques, there is something you should know," Janine's expression had turned slightly serious, but not enough to alarm me.

There before me, amongst the flowers and ornate decorations, was a table set for royalty with fine, white linen, and china that defied explanation adorning it. Two wait staff dressed in tuxes with white wing collar, formal shirts and black vests of tapestry silk stood at attention, waiting to take care of our every need. Good God...No...It couldn't be? Janine didn't need to clue me in. That face, that body. Oh my God. It was Alec, Janine's fiancé.

*'Aahh crap!'*

# ❦ CHAPTER EIGHTEEN ❦

I was beginning to wonder what it would feel like if this were ever taken away from me. It was something that, since I met them, began to nag at me. Worry me. I had fallen so hard for Luc that if it ended, I would be hit so damn hard emotionally and physically, I would shatter, with no one to pick up the pieces. Everything they said to me drew me further into their lives both physically and emotionally. Like their promise or pledge or whatever the hell you want to call it...'You, love, are ours...always.' I was, and God help me, I would fucking die if I lost this.

We approached the table, and Alec, with Luc to my left and Jaycee to my right, each holding one of my hands. *'Don't ever stop doing that, boys!'* I thought to myself. Their fingers gripped mine just a little tighter. Luc, Jaycee, and for that matter Janine, knew exactly what I was thinking and how my emotions were affected by situations that presented themselves. But, and I have to emphasize this, they never seemed to intentionally pry. I would know, I could tell. They had the same *connection* to me that Elena did but, dare I say it, more powerful. Now I realized why Luc and Jaycee were signaling me with their hands. Alec. They felt my apprehension growing and, as if on cue, their hands held mine just a little tighter.

When I first met Janine and Luc online, Janine only spoke of Alec as her 'BF', never going any further than that, not even a picture. Why the fuck would he have a problem with that? The man was a walking wet dream. He had thick black hair like Luc and Jaycee, only his was tipped with blond highlights. Blue eyes. No surprise there! He was about six feet four inches tall, his broad shoulders framed his solid pecs and tapered waist. He had an ass that, well, if I thought any more about it...The look in Luc's eyes told me to...

"*Stop drooling, John! You know, if you're that horny I'll take you back home right now and have my way with you!*"

"*I just might take you up on that offer, baby boy! But Luc, you know there's only one man that will ever have me the way I want to give myself, and that is you, precious boy. You have my word!*"

"*God, I love you, John.*"

"*I love you too, babe!*"

After embracing his beloved Janine, Alec turned to Jaycee and Luc and kissed them both on the cheek. Then he approached me. I began to put my hand out to shake his, but this was not to be.

"Jacques, Janine has told me all about you! Welcome to the family, mon ami!"

His smile was mesmerizing. Kissable lips. Perfect white teeth. Perfect, hell...everything. Before I knew it he embraced me, and with no hesitation, he kissed me. Yep, full soft lips...and, oh crap, his tongue came out to play. Briefly. Then, just as soon as it started, it was over. He kissed me on the cheek, smiled, and fuck, when his eyes met mine, they had the same 'feral' look Janine had. No, I will not accept this. Elena has messed up my mind good.

"Alec..." Luc's eyes, I noted, flashed red. "Careful. John is mine!"

For a brief moment I noticed Luc's voice became possessive, almost...no, it couldn't be...a warning? Alec's eyes once again turned feral. The whites suddenly disappeared from his eyes. They stood there staring at each other. What...? I had a picture of these two marching ten paces and...'*Oh, for crap's sake...fire! What the hell?*' I thought. The tension between the two of them was so thick you could have cut it with the proverbial knife, but I will admit, Luc's possessiveness of me was just...well...hot!

For some reason vampires and werewolves came into my mind. I quickly buried that thought. Good God, could Elena actually be on to something? No. They just don't exist. But vampires and werewolves are mortal enemies! Oh, for the love of all things holy! No, really, haven't you seen 'Underworld'? Oh for crap's sake! I found myself standing there arguing with myself and silently cursing Elena.

"Jacques?" Jaycee brushed his lips across my forehead. "Don't mind, my baby brother..." He gave Luc a nudge..."He is very protective of what is his."

"No worries, Jaycee. Luc has me. I am in love with your brother more than you will ever know, mon cher, but merci just the same!" I gave Jaycee a kiss on his cheek. He blushed.

"Oh, I'm sure Jaycee will have plenty of time to know just how much you love Luc!" Alec interjected. "Won't you, Jaycee?" Alec's voice was thick with sarcasm.

*'Where the hell did that come from?'* I thought to myself. I couldn't help but notice Jaycee's face turning red, not to mention his eyes.

"Have you told him yet, Janine?" Alec took her arm and pulled Janine close to him, his arm wrapped possessively around her.

If I hadn't been watching, I would have missed Janine pull away from Alec. It was subtle, but her eyes gave away a definite dislike for how Alec spoke to her sibling.

"Not yet, my love. Later tonight. You still plan on joining us, mon cher, don't you?"

"Of course!" Alec said with a twinkle in his eye. "How could I miss this? He has absolutely no idea? God, I can't wait to see the look on his face!"

"His name is Jacques!" Jaycee glared at Alec. "Show some fucking respect, Alec!"

My comfort level was slowly going to shit and Luc and Jaycee immediately picked up on it. Leaning into me, Luc brushed his lips against mine. "It's alright, John. I'm right by your side. Janine just thought it would be nice to have the whole family together for our, how do you say it in the States, chat?"

"Chat, baby boy? I'm getting the distinct feeling that the fur is going to fly!" It was meant to be an attempt at humor.

Luc, bless his heart, looked at me, his eyebrows furrowed, with an utterly confused look on his face. "Pardonnez-moi, babe." I lightly caressed his cheek.

I tried to smile. Elena's accusations still nagged at me. No. This was exactly what my sister wanted to do, create reasonable doubt. Elena, you have finally lost it. There is no fucking way they were going to tell me they are vampires and werewolves.

"Relax, Jacques." Jaycee stroked my arm. "Alec is excited to make your acquaintance, despite the fact he's an asshole!" His voice and demeanor, I noticed, were more at ease, as well as the color in his face, but I knew Jaycee was doing this for my benefit.

"I can tell, Jaycee." God, if I didn't know any better, I would swear Alec wanted to fuck me senseless, despite his smart-ass attitude. Bad, John! BAD! But the pull I felt from him, from those feral eyes, was undeniable.

# ❧ CHAPTER NINETEEN ❧

For the most part, our early dinner, or respite, as Jaycee had put it, was without any further tension. Alec seemed to be more cordial. Polite, if that was possible. The conversations were light and Luc took every available chance to let me know what he was after. His hands were letting me know exactly what he wanted!

"Unh...Luc...Is this the most appropriate time and place to have your hand on my..." I half moaned, half whispered.

Reluctantly, he released his grip from my crotch. He softly chuckled and resumed eating.

"Sorry, love," he whispered back. The way he was looking at me, I could tell he wanted ME as the main course!

The sun was beginning to set as we finished what turned out to be more than a snack, if you'll pardon the American vernacular. When Jaycee mentioned respite I got the idea it would be a bunch of chips, salsa, and a soda. My French family's idea...escargot, French baguettes, and several dishes I had no clue about. Luc, by the way, found that particularly endearing and took great joy in educating me. At one point in the meal he reached over, grabbed my hand, and asked if I wanted a hot dog.

*"No. What I want is you, Luc!"*

That comment earned me one of his whimpers, which was quickly becoming something of an endearment, not to mention the cause of the heat that scudded through my veins.

Shit, I'm not complaining, but once again I couldn't help but notice that Janine, and now Alec, looked like they hadn't eaten for days! Although both of them had impeccable manners, they ate their food with such voraciousness, it was like a lion devouring his prey. Shit!

When we had finished with the main course, the wait staff cleared the table. Crystal wine glasses were then placed in front of us. No, there were no red plastic cups at this picnic!

"How was your meal, my love?" Luc leaned into me, kissing me on the cheek.

"Magnifique, mon cher!" But I couldn't help noticing Luc had not eaten much. "Babe, you hardly touched anything! Are you feeling okay?"

"Oui, mon cher! Just thirsty!" As he let his tongue run across his upper lip. "Mostly for you!" With the X-rated stare he gave me, and the smirk on his face, I knew exactly what he meant.

I had never become that aroused, that fast, in all my life. Seriously. "You, my baby boy, are going to be the death of me!" What came next wasn't me, rather it was Luc.

"Oh my God!"

I felt myself take in a sharp, sudden breath. There went Luc's eyes. A flash of red, only this time he locked onto my eyes, smiled and...What. The. Fuck! No, absolutely not. This was just Elena and her mind games again. I will not, nor will I ever...but...no! If that wasn't enough, for a split second I'd seen Luc's canines extend...into fangs. My heart felt like it was going to beat through my chest. John, you either need sleep or you need to let Luc fuck you into next week.

The gentle touch of Luc's hand on my shoulder brought me out of what felt like a trance. I was looking directly at Luc. His beautiful blue eyes. Perfect, pure, white teeth. Damn you, Elena!

"John...Mon cher?"

I brushed my fingertips across his lips. "I'm here, babe."

The wait staff was pouring what looked like a very thick wine into everyone's glass...except mine. A different waiter came with my own personal bottle, which I noticed was white. Everyone else was sharing the other bottle. Red. Oh well, I preferred white. *What don't they know about me?'* I thought. The perfect hosts. *'God, Elena, I could kill you!'*

"Sir Jacques, mon cher? Wine, monsieur?" "Oui! Merci."

Janine and Alec seemed oblivious to us, and hell, I felt the same way when I was with Luc. Though the constant touch of Jaycee reminded me that he had, oh fuck, feelings for me too!

*"He's going to kill Luc to get to you!"*

Elena's voice came blaring through my brain like a tornado siren on a hot Wisconsin day. What the...? "You okay? How is your wine, John?" Luc leaned into me, squeezing my hand.

What was she doing to me?

"Huh? Oh Luc...Yeah, the wine...Um, to tell you the truth, I've never tasted anything so..."

"Wonderful!" Janine finished my comment. "You could say that, ma chere. It's simply..."

"Wonderful!" Alec parroted sarcastically.

It's a shame to say, Alec was beginning to annoy me, but as I looked into his eyes...shit.

"John." Luc squeezed my arm and whispered in my ear. "Do you want Alec?" The smile on his face looked sincere, but his eyes were telling me something else. My God, Luc was genuinely concerned I would turn away from him. He worried his lower lip and stared into my eyes with such vulnerability that I went weak at his devotion to me. All I wanted to do was pull him into my arms.

*"My precious boy."* I relayed to him. *"You, my handsome young man, are the only one that I hunger for. When I'm with you, I can't get close enough. When I'm away, all I want is to be with you. You make my knees weak and all I want is to make love to you. Luc, I am yours...always! Don't ever doubt that, baby boy!"*

"Oui, John. Oui, my love. God, John, I can't imagine my life without you." His eyes were misting over.

I took my hand and gently brushed it across his face, then I pulled him close for a kiss. Jaycee's hand squeezed my thigh.

*"I envy my baby bro, Jacques."* Jaycee's head was tipped down as he swirled his glass of wine in his hand. The thick liquid clung to the sides of the glass.

Was that...? No, it couldn't be! But, holy shit, it looked like...blood?

*"He's mine, Jaycee. The sooner you realize that, the sooner we can get on with our lives. Please, can we stop this, Jaycee...Now!"*

What I overheard wasn't a polite request. Luc had staked his claim and was not giving Jaycee the opportunity to question him, or for that matter, challenge him as to my affections. It was a statement almost, no, not almost...it was what it was...a demand.

"This tension between you two," Janine looked at Luc then Jaycee, "has got to stop! If we are to bring Jacques totally into our family, you two have got to understand that our man is not a possession. He is here because he loves us. Jaycee? Jaycee!" The young man was staring into his glass, and for the first time, I saw a tear fall down his face. "Jaycee, Jacques is in love with Luc. Luc is in love with Jacques. I couldn't imagine it being any other way, even if it were for an eternity." Janine looked at me with a resolve that left no room for questions or discussions.

Eternity? I found myself draining my glass of wine. I had never heard Janine speak like this. Her usually calm demeanor was replaced with an authoritative tone that brought everyone's attention to her, even her shithead of a fiancé. It was totally apparent that Janine meant every word she said and she would not tolerate any further rifts between her siblings.

I lifted my glass and, on cue, it was filled again. "Please, just leave the bottle," I said to the waiter.

He nodded, set the bottle of wine down to my right, and quickly turned and walked away.

"Yes, my dear sister, I understand. Jacques is Luc's. It's very apparent to me. They are beautiful together!" Jaycee did his best to smile, but I knew a little bit of him was dying inside. Despair punctuated every word the young man was saying.

'God, I felt bad for him. I recalled what the three of us shared in bed. Crap, Jaycee did have feelings for me. Damn! For the first time since I met him at the airport and felt his strong hand take mine, Jaycee's confidence was failing him. Was Jaycee in love with me? No... please. I don't want that. Sure, I was flattered. Who the hell wouldn't be? Jaycee is an incredible man. How the fuck could I ever think of hurting his feelings. Yes, I love him. I care about him deeply. I know he will be an integral part of our life, and what about his love for his brother? It was apparent. Very apparent. Jaycee killing Luc? No! God dammit, Elena! For once in your life, be wrong. Just please be wrong!' I looked at Luc. His eyes told me they knew exactly what I had been thinking.

"It's okay, my love. I understand. Elena has really messed with your head. Forgive me, mon cher, but I don't like what she is doing to you. She does not have the facts. I assure you babe...we do...and you *will* have things set straight before the night is over. I promise you, lover!"

"There is no need for forgiveness, Luc. Trust me, I will not tolerate any more of her accusations."

"Do me a favor, John, will you please?" He could have asked me to jump off the Arc de Triomphe and I would have.

"Anything, Luc." I reached for his hand. I was amazed at how perfectly it fit into mine.

"Show him. Show Jaycee how much you care. It warms my heart, the love you have for him. I love my brother and I would not want to be in his position. He is hurting, John. He is in love with you too." Luc's eyes penetrated mine, and with a statement that, I swear, came from his soul, he looked at me, caressed my cheek, and said "You, babe, and my brother, are the most important men in my life! Kiss him, John. Kiss him and make him better."

"If that is your wish, my love." *'Was I hearing right?'*

"It is." *'And yes, your hearing is just fine.'*

"God, Luc. Have I told you lately how much I love you?"

"Oui. You, love, are mine...ours...always and forever."

As I softly shook my head, I looked at my boy. I hadn't heard that for a while and was beginning to worry. But that declaration, our pledge and promise to each other, seemed to put to rest any doubts I may have had about where Luc and I, with Jaycee by our side, were headed with our relationship. Though unique, I wouldn't trade it for anything. I could live this life forever.

*"Keep it up, John...and you will!"*

*"Just shut the fuck up, Elena!"*

Leaning over, I gently kissed Jaycee and, with my hand, caressed his cheek. At first I felt his body tense up, but then after gently nipping his lower lip, his tongue begged for entrance to my mouth. I let him in. God forgive me, but it felt so good. Just like Luc, I could literally feel the love he had for me course through me from my head to my toes. But something was different. He gave as good as he got. Oh God, *yes,* he was in love with me! His kiss was charged with emotion. It was incredible, but as great as it was, there was a difference in his kiss, his touch. Unlike Luc's, which emanated love and passion...an equal partnership, Jaycee's kiss felt more like *possession.*

Needing air, I gently broke away from his kiss. "Jaycee, you, mon cher, are incredible!  The three  of us share something incredibly special, and Jaycee..."

My eyes met his and Jaycee's eyes met mine.  His teeth were worrying his lower lip. Pressing his forehead to mine, I could tell he was waiting for the conclusion to my thought. His whole body was trembling. From the kiss? Possibly, but if I didn't know him better, I might guess fear. Fear of rejection? God, in the short time I knew this man, he never showed this much vulnerability.  I needed to reassure him.

I couldn't help but feel Luc's hand rubbing the nape of my neck. Warmth crept through his fingers, soothing and *telling* me that this was okay. Luc was reassuring me. "Go ahead, John. It's okay. I didn't think I could love you any more than I do." His hand now resting on my thigh, Luc whispered into my ear "Lover, release my brother from his fear."

Mine and Jaycee's eyes continued to gaze into each other's. I let the words speak from my heart. "Jaycee, I love you. You know that. Never ever doubt that, I beg you!" My voice hitched. "Luc and I are in love, but that doesn't mean that I can't be a part of your life too. I promise you, Jaycee, I don't plan on going any place for quite a long time." My hand brushed his cheek as I gently kissed his lips.

The relief in Jaycee's eyes and body were palpable.  Leaning into me, he pressed his forehead against mine.

"You're damn right you're not!" It was Alec. Dickhead. Yeah, pretty boy, you definitely are  getting on my fucking nerves.

# ❧ CHAPTER TWENTY ❧

It was going on six in the evening when we made our way back to the waiting limo. Adrian, appearing out of nowhere, opened the door for us.

"I trust all of you had an enjoyable meal?"

"Oui, Adrian! Yes, we did! That couldn't have been planned better!" Janine answered happily. "Alec and I were starved!"

*'Like wolves, Janine?'* I said to myself. *'Where the hell did that come from?'* What the fuck is wrong with me? How the hell can I even make a comment like that about Janine? Yeah sure, Alec is turning out to be a first-rate prick, but Janine?

*"Pull yourself together, John!"*

*"Elena, so help me, if you can hear me, stay out of this! Everything is fucking falling apart, and it hasn't even started! Elena? Elena! I mean it! Leave us alone!"*

*"Like hell I will!"*

*"Elena? Where the fuck have you been?"*

*"Back off, bro! I'm surprised you know who I am! You've got so many voices going through your head, I'm surprised you can even think straight!"* Elena snickered.

*"What's so damn funny, Elena?"* Not quite catching the "gay" reference.

*"God, bro...You are soooo slow! You can't even think straight!"*

She put the emphasis on straight. *"Ha ha, Elena. Just get on with it already. What the hell do you want?"*

*"Well, brother of mine, I can't help but notice you are questioning things that you are seeing and hearing."*

*"Oh really, Elena...like what?"*

I really wanted to get pissed off at my sister, but I couldn't, and THAT was pissing me off. Elena was once again on to something. Something I knew that I was experiencing too.

*"I'm waiting, Elena!"* I just wanted her to get it over with and get out of my fucking head, which was starting to hurt.

*"Well, Luc's and Jaycee's red eyes. Luc's fangs. Alec's and Janine's feral eyes. Their hunger...and your lover and his brother's lack of appetite. Should I go on? What about the separate bottles of wine?"*

*"The wine? Oh for fuck sake, Elena. You know I drink white wine! Wait...Oh. My. God. You know, you're right! I noticed the label on the bottle! Hmmm, oh yeah, a type B negative, aged to perfection! How could I have overlooked that? Christ, sis, you're good!"* It was meant to be sarcastic.

*"Actually, it was O positive."* My sarcasm meant nothing to her. There was absolutely no humor in her voice. It was a statement meant to prove a point, and right now, thank God, I wasn't with her, or I would have slapped her fucking smart-ass mouth.

*"You'd try!"* she snapped back.

*"Damn it, Elena...Fuck you! I can't accept this. I know there is a logical explanation for this!"*

*"FUCK YOU!"* Elena screamed. My head had hurt, but now I had a migraine. *"Ouch! Elena! Dammit, sis, don't 'think' so loud!"*

*"Somebody is listening in,"* her voice for the first time, quieted.

*"Listening in?"*

Just like that, my sister was gone. All I had to show for it were the shakes and a very bad headache.

"John?" I felt Luc's hand on my forehead. "You're flushed! God, babe, you're burning up! What is your sister doing to you?" His eyes flashed red. "She has no right doing this to you. Damn it! Damn her!" My baby boy was seriously pissed off.

I let my eyes focus and noticed we were seated in the limo. Shit, how long was I out of it? Luc and Jaycee in their usual spots, and facing us, Janine and Alec. Luc had turned toward me, his hand

TO PARIS WITH BLOOD

trailing down my face. His arm came up around my shoulder, pulling me to him. God, my head was pounding. I let Luc pull my head gently to his shoulder. I pressed my face into his neck. He smelled so good. Luc's very essence. I let myself relax into his strong arms and let the warmth from his body comfort me. With no words spoken, Luc's hand began to rub and massage my pounding forehead.

Jaycee's concern was evident as well. He brushed his hand, palm side up on my face and, leaning over, gave me a soft, tender, concerned kiss. Then, excusing himself, he leaned over me and gave Luc that same gentle kiss on his lips. I have never seen anything so incredible. My heart fluttered and my breath 'hitched' as I witnessed the pure love of two brothers.

Jaycee resumed his place next to me and brushed his lips across mine. The love he had for me was evident in the smile he gave me. His handsome face, without a word, was saying, "I love you, Jacques."

"I love you too, Jaycee." No words, no telepathic communication, just a look.

"This hurts me, little brother. I don't want this for Jacques."

I lifted my head from Luc's shoulder for a moment. I noticed Janine looking at us with complete understanding.

The same could not be said for that dumb-ass boyfriend of hers. God, what a douche bag! The look Alec gave me actually sent a jolt of fear up my spine. Leaning over, and placing his mouth against my ear, in a tone only I was meant to hear, he spoke..."So how was your conversation with Elena? She sure is one nosy little bitch!"

Alec, the idiot, completely forgot that there were no thoughts, when it came to my wellbeing that would not be 'heard' by the others. He still didn't get it. I was being protected. Sure, he was Janine's fiancé, but he wasn't winning any popularity contests, especially with Luc and Jaycee.

Luc's head abruptly turned and he glared at Alec. Luc heard the remark Alec made to me.

"Alec..." Luc's eyes were red, his nostrils flaring. "I suggest you get away from John. Now! Do you fucking hear me? You have been taunting John since you met him and frankly, I am sick of the way you are treating him. I am tired of your bullshit! If you value your life, you will shut your fucking mouth! Remember this, Alec, when you insult him, you insult me...And, Alec..." Luc hesitated. It was so quiet it was deafening. "I will not fucking tolerate that from you or anyone. John is mine! Mine! Do. You. Understand?"

Luc DID have fangs!

"That makes two of us, Alec!" Jaycee's voice was full of anger. "Back off and leave Jacques alone. If you remember one thing, Alec, you sure as hell better remember this: you so much as say or do one more thing to Jacques and I will beat you senseless. Because, Alec, I love Jacques too. As my brother said, what you do to Jacques, you do to my brother. And get this through your thick skull, you do it to me as well! I sincerely believe you owe Jacques an apology for what you said about Elena. If you can't do that, then you sure as fuck aren't going to be coming back home with us."

Jaycee turned away from Alec and directed his attention to Janine. "Sis, pardonnez-moi. I fully understand and respect your wishes when it comes to Jacques and Luc, but this has to stop! With all respect, put your wolf on a leash, would you!"

'*Wolf! ...Aahh crap!*' My mind was reeling. I watched Janine's reaction, waiting for all hell to break loose, but damn, it didn't. What I heard next surprised the shit out of me.

Turning to Alec, Janine's eyes turned feral. The whites of her eyes were completely gone, showing only pure brown. What the? My belle was pissed, but not at me or her brothers. Janine looked like she was ready to tear Alec apart, limb by limb.

"Keep it up, Alec...and I'll..."

"You'll what, Janine? Bitch me to death?" Alec grinned and shook his head.

What the hell was he doing? My heart was racing. Alec, you stupid fool. You are not helping the situation or yourself. Do you have anything in that beautiful, empty head of yours?

"On the contrary, Alec..." Janine glared at Alec and said something to him in French. My command of the language was extremely limited so what she said, I had no idea, but what she said had an immediate effect on Alec. His attitude and demeanor did a 180 in a matter of seconds. His cocky grin disappeared just as quickly, and putting his head down, he looked like a puppy that just got his favorite chew toy taken away. That chew toy happened to be me.

I could tell as he turned his sights to me, this was something he did not want to do. "S'il vous plait, pardonnez-moi."

'*You've got to be fucking kidding me. Forgive you?*' His blue eyes looked into mine. Wait...blue? I had all I could do to even look at him, but out of respect to the others I extended my hand, more out of manners than friendship. "Merci, Alec." I grimaced. *'Thanks for nothing, asshole!'* I thought,  glaring into his eyes.

Luc gently cupped my chin and turned my head to face him. I immediately felt a wave of peace wash through me.

"John, my love, please forgive us..." His eyes pleaded with me..."I am so sorry for the distress we caused you. I love you, John. God, what have we done?" His voice was trembling. Luc's head fell down to his chest and a lock of his beautiful black hair fell into his eyes. Almost to hide his...shame? A quiet, yet noticeable, sound of...oh shit...Luc starting to cry. It emanated throughout the limo. Tears began to streak his face.

Oh no, I'll be damned first. This in no way was his fault, nor Jaycee's or Janine's for that matter. It was that fucking arrogant prick sitting across from me. No wonder Janine had such a stressful time with him. What in all that is holy made her come back to him? She was just too good for this arrogant, selfish prick. Pissed? Damn right I am! Until this asshole came along, the four of us were perfect together. He was after something, or should I say someone. Me. I sure as hell was going to find out what was going on in Alec's twisted head and what his problem was.

I couldn't help but think that Elena's warning was not about Jaycee 'offing' Luc. He loved his brother. Unconditionally. A cold chill ran down my spine, as I realized that Alec was capable of doing the unthinkable to destroy me. All it would take would be to...Oh my dear God, the realization hit me like a punch in my gut. Kill Luc, destroy me. A chill ran through me and I almost threw up the lunch I had eaten.

Janine knocked on the tinted window, which divided the rear passenger seats from Adrian, our  driver.

The limo quietly pulled away from the park.

"Luc, babe?" I gently lifted his chin so his eyes made contact with mine. I took a finger and gently brushed the lock of hair away from his forehead, uncovering his blue eyes, although, this time they were red from crying. "Listen to me. Hey...Luc." I almost started crying myself as I wiped the tears away from his face. He was doing his best to stay his sobs, but the quiet whimpering and his shaking  shoulders tore me apart. It broke my heart to see him this way. "Are you with me, precious boy?" I took his  hand. He held mine with a steely grip.

"Oui, mon cher..." he sniffled..."I am so..." Another apology was coming from him.

"No, baby...Stop! Stop right there!" I pressed two of my fingers to his lips. "This is not your, Jaycee's, or Janine's fault. None of it!" I pulled myself together and forged ahead. I knew that what I was about to say could be a 'deal breaker' for any relationship my family and I would have.

I turned my attention to Janine. "Please, ma chere...All I care about are Luc, Jaycee, and you, love." My eyes begged her for understanding.

In silent confirmation, Janine nodded, and I knew I had her total attention. Without even knowing what I was going to say, she would accept whatever my thoughts were.

"Jacques, I know you do. As do we. Please, say what's in your heart." Then, right in front of Alec, she leaned forward and took my hands in hers; her delicate fingers stroked my wrists. "You see, Jacques, we care about you too."

A lump formed in my throat. "Merci." Janine had released her hold of my hands and I reached for Luc, pulling him close to me, his head coming to rest on my shoulder. "I need to say this, Janine. I sure the hell am not going to sugarcoat it, because the asshole sitting next to you needs to know one thing!" I looked directly into Alec's eyes, leaving no doubt in his mind just how serious I was.

"Who the fuck you calling asshole?" Alec interjected.

"Shut up, Alec! Shut up and listen!" I took one of Jaycee's hands into mine, gently squeezing it in silent thanks.

"Alec, I'm trying to believe you love Janine, at least giving you the benefit of the doubt. I know you are her fiancé. Other than that, I know nothing about you. Since I met you, I have done nothing but show you respect, because after all, Alec," I took a breath, "the most gorgeous, kind, and compassionate woman I have ever met has said yes to your proposal of marriage. Frankly, from what you've shown me so far, you don't deserve her! You don't deserve to be a part of this family."

I noticed Alec move forward. His breath was shallow and his face began to flush. I had definitely struck a nerve. Jaycee firmly squeezed my hand and an immediate rush of confidence coursed through me.

Matching Alec's move, I leaned forward. "Furthermore, you see this young man sitting next to me?" I looked at my precious baby boy and smiled. "I adore him. I am forever in love with him! I fucking belong to him!" Luc whimpered.

"Je t'aime, John."

"Je t'aime aussi, Luc." I let my lips brush across his.

Alec just sat there and stared at me. What was with his fucking eyes? Where the hell did the whites go? Fuck, they were no longer blue, they were, oh for crap's sake, gray! Well, John, you've come this far... just finish this.

"You see this young man?" I turned my head to acknowledge Jaycee. "I love him too! Maybe not in the same way I love Luc, but I love him. I am his too!" Jaycee squeezed my hand and I reached up to wipe away the tear that was falling down his face.

It looked like Alec was going to begin to speak. I halted his progress. I took Luc's and Jaycee's hands, entwining our fingers together. Although it was a simple gesture, what it meant to us spoke volumes. The three of us, our lives and our love for each other, linked together in a chain that no one would ever break. I knew they felt the same way. I could feel their bodies press closer to mine as their thumbs gently rubbed the pulse point of my wrists.

"Just wait, Alec. I'm not finished! I'll let you know when. And maybe, just maybe, if you can talk to me and the others in this vehicle like a real man and not an arrogant, self-righteous prick, I'll let you speak. In the meantime, shut up!"

Alec was trying to keep his composure, but it wasn't working. I noticed his hands clench into fists, his eyes burning into mine.

He was pissed off, but I just didn't care.

"You see that amazing woman sitting next to you? If it weren't for her, I would never have even had the privilege of being here with them. Alec, God only knows what Janine sees in you. Yeah, you have it all on the outside, but there is only so far that shallow, fucking perfect, façade is going to take you. You, Alec, are rude, egotistical...fuck, who am I kidding? Alec, do me and my men a favor...and Janine, for that matter...Fuck off! Bastard!"

*"Easy, lover."* Luc 'said' to me calmly. *"God, John...I love you so damn much! No one has ever stood up to Alec like that. No one! But, baby, please...Stop! I'll explain...I swear. You will know everything there is to know about Alec soon! Just ease up, babe."*

Luc's thoughts said something entirely different than what his eyes were 'saying' to me. His eyes, for the first time while he looked at me, had turned red. For some reason, which I knew he would explain, I felt no fear. Curiosity, yes. Fear, no. But if I didn't know any better, what was a sincere concern running through my mind, was actually an order. For my own good, he was protecting me. Luc's eyes returned to their blue and he softly smiled at me. Shit, I didn't care anymore if they turned black. I was too far gone. I'd fallen hard for Luc, and God help me, I was forever, unequivocally, in love with him.

*"Of course. Anything for you, Luc. My mind, my body, my soul... They are yours. Forever."*

Luc leaned over, his lips brushing my ear. I closed my eyes as arousal and need for him swept through me.

"What is it, baby boy?" Our foreheads were now pressed together. "Unhhh...Luc!" His hand was rubbing my cock through my pants, not giving a shit who was seeing his actions...or my reactions.

"Luc horny now!" He put his mouth to my ear. His voice was soft, but thick with desire.

"Oh my God, Luc!" I was out of my mind.

*'Fuck. Me.'* I did everything I could to maintain my composure.

*"That's the idea, John."*

There was a giggle, yes, a giggle, coming from Jaycee. Yep, he was a little shit too! "Merci beaucoup, Jacques." Jaycee rubbed his hand on my thigh.

*"Uunnh...that is not helping the situation."*

*"Oh, you like that, Jacques?"* Jaycee continued rubbing my thigh.

*"Consider it my way of thanking you, Jacques."* Jaycee's 'voice' was absolutely X-rated.

*"For... Uunnhh...Oh God...Jaycee...for what?"*

"That is the first time I have seen Alec speechless." Jaycee chuckled.

"I'm in the car you know," Alec muttered.

"Yeah, how the hell did that happen?" I responded, with a decided note of sarcasm, not even bothering to look at him. I was otherwise occupied.

"I love you boys...both of you are mine, always."

*'Wait, did I just say that? Shit!'*

"And you, love, are ours...always!" The little shit. Now that Luc basically had me a completely frustrated mess, he sat there with this sly, little smile on his face as if nothing had happened. Oh, he would pay for this. But knowing him, he was going to enjoy the payback. Hell, who am I kidding...so would I.

The Jaycee I had first met, shared a bed with, the Jaycee that protected me along with his brother, was returning to his former self. Confident, funny, and completely irresistible.

I leaned over and gave him a quick kiss.

"Je t'aime, mon cher." My hand brushed Jaycee's face.

"Je t'aime...always, Jacques." Jaycee, taking two of his fingers, pressed them to his lips and then, in a gesture that made my heart feel like it skipped a beat, he pressed those fingers against my lips. His eyes never once leaving mine. I knew right then that Jaycee was not obsessed with me...he was in love with me.

"You should take notes, Alec." Janine momentarily looked at the three of us. "That is true love at every level," she said softly, but in a quick turnaround, her demeanor changed. "I'm going to say this to you just one more time, Alec." She turned once again to face her fiancé. "Leave the boys alone! Understood?" Janine's eyebrows furrowed, her eyes looked into Alec's, deadly serious.

"Oui, my love." Unable to look at Janine, humiliated, Alec turned and stared out the window.

# ❧ CHAPTER TWENTY-ONE ❧

Thank God the ride back to the city was relatively quiet. I had taken a big chance by talking to Alec like that. I'd be lying if I said I had no fear in bitching that asshole out. Frankly, it scared the shit out of me. What the fuck did I do to him anyway? If this was going to be the way it was every time we were near each other, how the hell could I continue my self-control? How long before it came to something physical? Christ, he could beat the living shit out of me. Thinking back to my letters from Luc and Janine before I took the trip here, there had been problems between Janine and Alec. At the time, I just brushed it off as 'couple's problems.'

But I had to factor in Luc's apparent fondness for Alec. Back then, before I came here, Alec meant quite a lot to Luc. That fondness was no longer there.

Luc was mine now. And I'd be damned if I let anyone, especially Alec, ruin what we had. I seemed to be the catalyst for whatever was going on with him. But damn, what the hell was setting him off? Was he jealous? It was obvious Alec definitely had a problem with me, but damned if I knew what it was. Maybe tonight's 'chat' would finally clear this crap up and I could get back to enjoying my time here. Specifically, time with my baby boy. The thought of heading back to the States next month was something that ate at the back of my mind. Damn, in just a few, short days, we had fallen in love. Completely. Leaving this young man was not even an option.

Then there was the concern with Jaycee. What the hell was up with that? I hadn't even talked to him prior to arriving in Paris. Yes, Jaycee was a beautiful man. His protective, possessive nature when it came to me, overwhelmed me. I was flattered. Who the hell wouldn't be? He too, had fallen for me. Damn, I could run every moment of my arrival here over and over in my head, but not once did I give him any kind of signal that I was interested in him. It had been Luc from the start. I was in love with Luc even before I arrived.

Confused. Hell, yes, I was confused. Concerned. Hell, yes, I was concerned. In love...ah...hell, yes! Luc was everything to me. What the hell happened? Did I say something to Jaycee? Was I giving him reason to believe I...wait a minute.

*'Aahh crap!'*

**Earlier that morning-**

I watched as Jaycee set the tray down on the table by the window.

Luc was laying on his side, facing me and Jaycee, and had his head propped up on his hand, watching. I noticed the smile that was shared between the brothers. They absolutely adored and loved each other.

Luc possessively swung his right leg up, resting it on my waist. His muscular body pressed greedily against mine. I felt his erect cock as he slowly thrust his hips against my thigh. He softly whimpered. It was the sexiest sound I have ever heard. His hand gently brushed my face, then using several of his fingers, he began to explore and touch my body. They gently felt my lips and then, moving down, Luc stopped at one of my nipples. With a way too fucking sexy smile, he lightly pinched each one of them.

"Unhhhh...Luc..." My head pushed back into the pillow.

I turned my head towards him and looked into his eyes. The smile remained, but there was something about his eyes. Those Caribbean-blue eyes. They looked so deep into mine that, for a moment, I thought I'd have to turn away. The feeling they emanated was intense. Never before had someone so totally and completely given themselves to me. Luc's eyes spoke to me of trust, loyalty, companionship, and above all, love. They say that the eyes are the gateway to a person's soul. I swore I had seen his.

"God, Luc...you are perfection," I said, in what turned out to be a hoarse whisper, "Do you know how much I love you?"

"Jacques, he does."

I turned in time to see Jaycee pull down his sweatpants, revealing a body that rivaled Luc's in perfection. Like his brother, his cock was erect. I looked at Luc and he nodded.

"It's okay, big brother, join us."

Turning back to Jaycee as he slid under the covers next to me, I took my finger and captured the clear, slick fluid making its way out of the slit of Jaycee's engorged cock. I brought my finger to my lips and licked it off. Salty, yet sweet, it coated my mouth. Jaycee tasted incredible. Then, before I could even comprehend what was happening, Luc brought one of his fingers to my mouth with the same offering. As his finger slipped into my mouth, and my tongue tasted Luc's essence, I couldn't help but notice that he tasted just like his brother. "God, boys...you taste incredible." Their pre-cum coated my tongue and lips. "So do you, mon cher." Jaycee had swiped the pre-cum off my cock and was tasting it. As he did, Luc leaned over me and Jaycee put his finger to his brothers mouth. I watched Luc suck Jaycee's finger, savoring the clear liquid, letting it slick his lips.

"What are you up to, baby boy?" My breath was now raspy, as my body and mind were being slowly pulled into the most erotic encounters I could have ever imagined.

"John...I need you...fuck me," Luc's voice was barely a whisper. "I need you in me...fuck me...make me one with you! Please..." Every breath he took was becoming shorter and quicker. Luc's face brushed up against mine. His eyelids were half-closed, heavy with lust. His warm breath silently swept over my neck, as he nuzzled and began to press kisses against my throat. His teeth lightly bit my throat, driving me insane with need.

"You know I will, baby boy. I want you so fucking much...uhnnnhh...I want to be so deep in you that I don't know where I end and you begin."

That garnered a moan from Jaycee. I turned to look at him. "Are you going to be okay?" I reached up and ran a finger across his lips.

"I...fuck...I will be."

Luc let out a deep, long breath as his hand pulled me to him, into an earth-shaking kiss. I could taste him, his brother, and myself. Luc's lips pressed deeply into mine as he took possession of me. My hand grabbed him around the waist, pulling him as tight to my body as I could. I felt his cock press against mine.

"Jacques?" Jaycee's hand was now touching me softly, sending warm waves of heat through me. God, heat scudded through my veins. His muscular, hard body pressed against my back. I was pinned between them, arms and legs wrapped tightly around me. Our bodies writhing against each other.

"Make love to my brother," Jaycee's voice was full of heat. "He needs you desperately." His hands continued their exploration of my body as he pushed and pressed himself against my back. His hard cock nestled in the crack of my ass. His lips pressing kisses on my shoulder. I could feel his teeth lightly bite down, just enough to leave a mark. Oh fuck, yes. Mark me. They both were claiming me as their own.

"You, love, are ours...always...and forever." Jaycee whispered the words with such reverence, I knew it was a vow. It was a pledge and a promise made to me.

Luc was kissing me, his tongue slowly exploring my mouth. His moans of desire made my toes curl. My God, the love I felt from this young man was transfused into my soul. My hands clutched, then tangled, into his thick, shaggy hair, and I pulled his face as close as I could to mine as we continued to kiss. I wanted him to devour me. Luc whimpered. I nearly came. "Fuck...just... FUCK!" Every thought and concern I had was gone. The only thing I knew, the only thing I cared about, were the two young men who were consuming me.

"Oh shit...yes...Luc, my love...Jaycee...I'm yours...Oh God!"

I looked at Luc. His eyes spoke to me...spoke of need, want, and love. "Luc, baby," I reached down and wrapped my fist around his long, erect cock. "I want you now."

With those words, he released his grip from around me, and in one quick move he was on his stomach. He immediately pushed himself up on his hands and knees. Legs spread slightly, he positioned himself for me. His firm ass angled up, waiting for me to take him.

I proceeded to get up on my knees and positioned myself between Luc's athletic, strong legs. I couldn't help noticing how just a light amount of jet black hair covered them and the rest of his body was smooth and tan. I reached down and gently ran my fingertips from his ankles to his thighs, feeling Luc's hard, athletic body. Then my eyes were drawn back to his perfect ass, raised and ready for me. I placed my hands on it, spreading his cheeks, revealing my goal. I could only imagine what my cock would feel like sliding into its tight channel. Leaning down, I let my tongue circle it. That beautiful, sexy, and hot whimper. Shit! His body trembled with need. Then I let my tongue push into him. "Oh fuck... Luc...um!" My tongue circled, then licked, at his tight opening. "You like that?" I pushed my tongue back into him.

"Uunnhhh...John...oh God...Yes!" He pushed his ass back into my face, forcing my tongue deeper into him.

Luc's reaction was more than I could handle. His shoulders arched and his toes curled. Every muscle in his strong, athletic body was flexed. His head thrown back in ecstasy, I continued licking and tasting. All the while my hands fought to feel every part of his young, hard, perfect body. Luc continued to moan. Once again that sweet, soft whimper filled the air. Once again I felt my cock twitch and my balls tighten. I felt like a king, knowing I drew that reaction from him. As I continued rimming Luc, I was vaguely aware of movement behind me. It was Jaycee.

"Relax, Jacques." His hands were caressing my back, slowly moving down towards my ass. "God, Jaycee...You have me too. Fuck, I'm yours."

My baby boy looked back at me, his eyes pleading with me. "John...Please!...Now, John...I need you in me, babe!" Luc's voice hoarse, he gasped for air. His whole body was vibrating.

"Do it, Jacques. Make love to my little brother," Jaycee's voice whispered into my ear.

"Jacques, babe, here." Jaycee took one of my hands and squeezed lube into it. Then reaching around, he swiped the pre-cum from my leaking head, and mixed it with the lube in my hand.

I needed to feel Luc. Be in him. Be one with him. But I dare not hurt him. He had told me earlier in the day that I would be his first and only. I was speechless. To think I was the one he chose, the one he waited for. It was more than I could comprehend. Removing my tongue, I replaced it with two of my now well-lubed fingers. I pushed them in. All the way in.

"Uuunnhh," Luc's soft, guttural moan drifted through the room. "Oh my God...John...it feels so good!"

I pulled back and added a third finger. Stretching and opening him, readying him for my cock. In and out my fingers lubed him. Fucked him. Watching him writhe with passion was the most erotic thing I had ever seen, and that was causing a slight problem. The sight of Luc's body writhing in pleasure was pushing me to the edge. I was so fucking turned on that I swore I felt what Luc was feeling. If I didn't stop, I was going to come without as much as a touch. I pulled my fingers out. Poor boy, he was a mess.

"John...please...I can't take it anymore. I need you!" Luc turned his head to look at me. His eyelids heavy with need.

I leaned forward and whispered in his ear. "Ready for me, baby boy?"

"Always ready, John. I've been waiting for this...for you...nobody else. Please...Now...Please." His sweet whimper echoed through the room.

I wrapped one hand around his waist, and leaning forward, with the other hand, I wrapped my fist around my slick, engorged cock and guided it towards Luc's quivering hole. The tip of my cock breached the opening.

"Uunhh! Fuck me, John. Fuck me...fill me."

I watched my slick, glistening cock disappear into him. I've never seen anything more erotic. My heart ached knowing how much this man loved me. I moaned and threw my head back as I disappeared into his tight, hot channel, inch by inch. I had to watch, I didn't want to miss anything. I watched my boy's body react to every thrust. I noticed Luc's hands fisting the sheets. Then as I pushed forward and my entire shaft entered him, his head once again tilted back and he moaned in pure ecstasy. Pushing back, he impaled himself on me. He was so hot and tight, and every ring of muscle clenched my cock. I could feel him pulsating, grabbing me, and pumping...fucking my cock. I stopped for a moment so I could feel my boy. Deep inside him, we were one.

"I so fucking love you, John," Luc gasped.

With that, I began to thrust in and out of Luc's tight, slick opening. "I so fucking love you, baby boy!" My hands splayed across Luc's sweat-slicked back. I couldn't get enough of the feel of his sinewy, muscular frame. I wanted to touch and feel every part of him. I was brought back to reality by soft, sexy grunts and moans from behind me. Jaycee. I could not help myself. I had to turn my head and look at what he was doing. I dragged in a breath and felt my heart skip a beat. Kneeling behind me, he was stroking his cock to the rhythm of my cock thrusting in and out of Luc. I could see in his eyes that the only thing he was focused on was us. Locks of his long hair stuck to his forehead, sweat trickling down his face. My God, he stole my breath away.

"It doesn't have to be that way, Jaycee. Do...unhh...fuck...do...unhh...Do you want me?" 'Oh my God! Luc was so damn tight,' I thought.

"Yes...but..." Jaycee was so bad off. I knew he loved me. He needed me, oh, who the hell was I kidding, he wanted me, but that was up to Luc.

"Yes, but...unhh...Whaa...What, Jjj...Jaycee?" I was losing it. Even forming a simple word was out of the question.

"I can't, Jacques. You are Luc's." His eyelids were half-closed, his voice filled with a want, a need, so powerful it shook me to my very core.

As I looked into his eyes something else filled them. Trust and love. My God, what the hell did I ever do to deserve this? Luc?

"He. Oh God! He can, John. If you want him to...Uuunnhh!" My cock hit his prostate.

Luc's whole body tensed. Every muscle, from his biceps to his calves, flexed. Even his toes curled. My God, this young man, that means everything to me, has just given me permission to allow his very own brother to take me. His love for his brother and myself overwhelmed me. "Luc...babe...are you sure?" He simply nodded. "God, Luc...you amaze me... You know I am yours."

"I know, John. That's...uunhh...why it's okay. Yes..." Luc assured me, as he pushed back and seated himself against me, driving my cock so far in I thought I would touch his heart. We were one.

"Oh God, baby...you're so fucking tight! I fucking love you so much, Luc."

"God...John! I can't imagine a life without you! Forever isn't...uunngh...Isn't long enough!"

"You'll never have to worry about that, babe. Never! Oh...God..." I began to slowly and gently thrust in and out of my lover.

I turned back to look at Jaycee. Leaning forward, he kissed me. I could feel the swollen head of his cock pressing against my tight opening, his hands firmly grasping my waist, his eyes looking deep into mine.  He was waiting for me...for my permission, even though he had his answer.  "I love you, Jaycee."  Smiling, I reached back and touched his muscular thigh.  I looked into his blue eyes and sent him over the abyss with one simple request.  "Fuck me, Jaycee...fuck me now, before I lose my fucking mind!"  My head was shaking back and forth as Jaycee splayed his hands across my back.

"I love you, Jacques."  It was then he took me.  There was no lead up.  No foreplay.  Jaycee had wanted this, and as he pushed me forward, my chest pressed against Luc's back.  I felt his cock push deep into me.  Slow and gentle.  Just as Luc had done to me, I pushed back and seated myself on him.

"Yes.  Uunnhh!  Oh.  My.  God!  Jaycee...fuck me!  Fuck me deep!"

I clung to Luc, one arm wrapped around his chest, clawing at his hard, defined pecs.  My other hand gripped his rock hard cock.  Pre-cum had gathered at the tip of his cock and I proceeded to use every drop to slick his throbbing member as I began to slowly jack him off.  My cock pulsated in Luc's ass, as I felt Jaycee thrust in, then out...in, then out.  It became a mantra in my head as my hand matched Jaycee's rhythm.  Then, as Jaycee pulled out, I did too.  Within only a few moments, the three of us had set up a rhythm that defied explanation.  We moved as one.  I continued to stroke Luc's cock, and as I pushed deep into him, Jaycee pulled out of me.  This wasn't sex.  This was fucking love.  Alive and real.  A living thing that was controlling us and consuming us.  Our bodies shining with sweat in the morning sun.  "John...uunnnhh...babe...God, I've waited so long."  Luc's head thrown back in pure ecstasy.

"Don't stop.  Please, baby...don't stop."

Jaycee was not having as much luck with his control.  On every thrust in, I relaxed, letting him in.  As he pulled out, I squeezed my muscles.  I wanted to milk the cum out of his beautiful cock.  I wanted to feel it shoot out of him and fill me.  'You, love, are ours...always and forever', was now sealed.  A commitment made, that I knew would be honored.  Luc, Jaycee, and I had become inseparable.

"Jacques.  Oh God...Jacques...I'm going to come."  Jaycee's motor skills flew out the window.  His legs trembled and his hands were shaking as they spread across my back.  I looked back and what I saw only helped push me to my own climax.  Sweat rolled off his brow, running down his perfect face.  Oh shit yeah, this boy was going to come. I could feel his cock stiffen and get harder, if that was even possible.

Luc was feeling the effects of what was going on between Jaycee and I. Both of our cocks were so hard, I thought they were going to burst. As Jaycee pumped his cock into me, I continued to push deep into Luc. Each thrust hit his prostate and my grip on his cock became harder. Luc was out of his mind with need. Then it happened.

"Goeeeffff!" Jaycee pushed his cock into me and exploded. The grip he had around my waist tightened as he pushed deep into me. He gripped me so hard I knew I would have bruises, but I really didn't give a damn! His hot cum filled my ass. I lost all control.

"Luc, baby...God...I'm coming!"

"God, yes, John...please..." Luc turned his head to look back at me. I leant forward and kissed him. "Fill me with your cum, John! Unnh...nn...nn...now!"

With one final thrust I came. My cock, feeling like it would explode, filled Luc with my hot cum. I felt Luc tense up. His ass squeezed every drop of cum from my cock and then he came. I felt his hot cum hit my hand and it pooled on the sheets. Spurting from his cock, every muscle in his taught, young body tensed... flexed. Fuck, he was gorgeous!

"Oh my God, boys...I fucking love you both so much." My body shook from the contractions of my orgasm.

All three of us let out collective moans. Completely sated, we collapsed. Three bodies tangled together, still high on the orgasms we had just experienced...Then Luc and Jaycee, lying on either side of me, their heads resting gently on my chest, took one of my hands and intertwined their fingers with mine. With total love and admiration, Luc looked up at me. His breath softly whispering across my face. "Merci, John. I love you so damn much." A single tear rolled down his cheek. He cuddled closer to me.

"Same here, baby boy, same here." I raised his hand to my lips and kissed each of his fingers. "I don't ever want to leave you...I love you so fucking much. My life is nothing without you, baby boy. I...I...fear I would die without you."

"Jacques?" Jaycee whispered in my ear.

As I did to Luc, I lifted Jaycee's hand, and gently kissed each of his fingers. "Yes, love?"

"Merci, Jacques." He kissed me gently on my chest.

"There is no need to thank me, beautiful boy."
"But, I must.  I...Jacques.  I...I love you."
"I know you do, Jaycee.  I love you too."

# CHAPTER TWENTY-TWO

"Aahh crap! Fuck! What a fucking idiot!" What I was thinking, came out of my mouth before I realized I was saying it. All eyes were on me as I came back to reality as fast as if someone had swatted me across the back of my head.

"John? John, my love...where were you? What's wrong?" I felt Luc's hands caressing my face.

It took me a moment, but I realized it was my boy. My precious Luc. He could barely speak; his breath hitched on every word. His eyes were wet with tears as they streamed down his cheek. He looked scared to death. *Damn it!* Out of pure instinct, and the need to comfort him, I immediately wrapped my arms around Luc and pulled him close. He was shaking so hard that I felt it going through my body.

"Oh God, Luc...It's okay..." I gently kissed his cheek and reached up to stroke his thick, shaggy, black hair. "I am so sorry. I didn't mean for that to happen."

"What have I done, John?" Luc's voice was trembling, the tears still coming from his eyes and rolling down his cheeks.

I pressed my forehead to his. "Babe...No...You did nothing. I, oh God, how do I say this?" I pulled away from Luc and cupped his face in my hands, my thumbs wiping the hot tears that flowed down his cheeks. "Look at me, baby boy. It's just...ah shit...It's me that owes you an apology. You...and..." I turned to look at Jaycee, who wasn't faring much better, "your brother." My hand reached out to touch Jaycee's face. I touched his cheek lightly, then turned my attention back to Luc, but not before I reached for one of Jaycee's hands.

The limousine had been parked in front of Luc's apartment. How long we had been parked there, I had no clue. By the looks on Janine's and that asshole Alec's face, it must have been a while.

"I...God. How do I put this? Jaycee is not to blame for how he feels about me. It's my doing." I looked into Janine's eyes, pleading with her.

"No, Jacques. Don't. Don't blame yourself," Jaycee's voice was shaking. His grip tightened around my hand.

"For what?" Janine leaned forward, her eyebrows raised, a questioning look in her eyes. She showed no anger, just deep, loving concern.

"Janine, don't be too hard on Jaycee. Please? Something happened. Please forgive me, I mean no disrespect, but what happened...God...I wanted it to happen, and it needed to happen."

"John." Luc grabbed my hand. "No, don't blame yourself. You can't...I agreed to it just as much as you did," his voice was pleading with me.

And then it happened.

"You three! Together?" Alec's half smile and crooked eyebrow told me he was enjoying this. So did his fucking sarcastic laugh. "Tell me, Luc...did you let your brother suck your cock? Ah, shit...you fags...no...This is too fucking sweet!" Alec's smile was pure evil. "Jaycee...you fucked your brother up his ass, didn't you...You fucking perverts! I knew Jacques here was a fag, but..." His laugh that followed sent chills through me.

He was the only one. The only one finding any amusement in the situation and his fucking obnoxious ramblings. It was obvious he was taking great pleasure in his fucking wrong assumptions.

It turned deathly silent. Alec had pushed too much. He pushed too far and before I knew it my fist was connecting with his jaw. If they could have, I knew my eyes would be red too. "Shut your fucking mouth, you son-of-a-bitch!" I growled. I wanted to kill him. Only one other time in my life did I feel such hate. "You stupid son-of-a-bitch!" My fist rammed into his gut, causing him to pitch forward. His face etched into a grimace of pain and anger.

"You fucking bastard!" Alec wiped the blood that was flowing from the corner of his mouth. "I'm going to fucking kill you!" He began to lunge forward, toward me.

*'I guess the feeling was mutual.'*

Before I knew it, before I could even visibly comprehend it, Jaycee was on top of Alec with his hands wrapped tightly around Alec's throat. Alec, struggling for air, was grabbing at Jaycee's hands, desperate to get him to release his death grip.

Oh fuck. Alec's eyes were once again a feral grey, the whites gone. Jaycee's eyes were red...Jesus...A low guttural growl came from Jaycee's throat. Jaycee's canines began to...no...this can't be...no...extend into razor sharp fangs. His mouth opened as his head tilted back...Jesus...tilting towards Alec's throat. As fast as it happened, I watched. Part of me wanting to bolt from the limo, but No! These were my boys. Mine. A realization began to creep through me. I would not leave their side.

*"John...get the fuck out of there...now!"*

It was Elena. *"No, sis! Just. NO!"*

"Stop, Jaycee...Stop!" Janine, with a strength I couldn't imagine, reached over and pulled Jaycee off of Alec. Her eyes were pure, deep brown.

As Jaycee landed next to me, Alec went for him, but as quickly as he did, his progress was stopped by Janine's hand, which was now firmly pushing Alec back into his seat.

I grabbed both of my boys' hands in a strong grip that I didn't even know I had. "Hey...easy." My hands gripped them with part fear and part protectiveness. They were mine and I'd be damned if I let this fucker lay his hands on them again.

"Enough, enough Alec! Do you hear me? We are through! Do you hear me Alec?"

Janine regained control of herself, and as the situation climaxed, her eyes remained brown. The whites of her eyes were gone, but then something else started to happen. I watched. Part amazed. Part terrified. Janine's canines began to extend, and as they did Alec's eyes turned feral, but...what the fuck...he was whimpering...whimpering like a...a...wolf.

"Alec, listen and listen well! The most important people in my life happen to be seated across from me. You have gone too far, Alec! I will not let you subject my brothers and Jacques to your obnoxious comments and lewd behavior!" With that, Janine, her eyes locked onto Alec's, took her engagement ring and shoved it into his hand. "Now, Alec, don't say another damn word! We are done! Get the hell out of this car and don't ever bother my family again. If you do, Alec, you might as well consider yourself dead! Get out!" The last two words were punctuated and said with a tone so deadly, so final, that my heart felt like it stopped beating.

Luc and Jaycee were pressed against me. Their hands gripped so firmly with mine that their knuckles were turning white. I didn't know who was protecting whom.

"This isn't over, Janine." Alec's eyes never blinked. His muscles tensed, looking like he wanted to pounce on Janine like...dare I say...prey. "They will pay, and as for you, bitch!"

"Bitch! Why you fucking...!" My anger was at a boiling point.

"Easy, baby." Luc rubbed my chest with his free hand.

"Get out! Get out now, Alec, or so help me God, you will regret it!" Janine's voice was at the breaking point. Anything further would be physical.

That's exactly what occurred. Before I knew what was happening, and could even begin to comprehend it, the limo door closest to Alec flung open.

Jesus, it was Adrian! Without so much as a word, one of Adrian's hands grabbed him by the shirt collar and literally ripped Alec from the limousine, leaving Alec, for all of Paris to see, laying on the sidewalk. In one swift motion, Adrian kicked Alec square in the jaw. Blood spurted from his mouth. Holy Mother of God! Without one word, Adrian closed the door and returned to his place behind the wheel.

"Luc, Jaycee. Precious brothers. Please forgive me for bringing this menace to our family." Janine's eyes focused on Luc and Jaycee. Her eyes returned to their stunning green and her canines retracted to their former self. "Jacques, love, please accept my apologies." Janine's eyes reflected sincerity, but more importantly, the love she had for me. My heart sank though, as I watched a single tear slowly flow down Janine's beautiful face.

When I thought I should be terrified, I was mesmerized. I could only look at Janine and her brothers. When every part of me said run, from somewhere calmness came over me and I sank back in the seat of the limo. My arms immediately went around Luc and Jaycee, pulling them as close to me as I could. I kissed them on their foreheads. They both returned my affection with a kiss placed gently on my face. In one defining moment, I realized one thing that was crystal clear; I meant everything to them. I could only shake my head as a tear rolled down my face, remembering their pledge, 'You, love, are ours, always'. *'Forever.'* I thought.

"There is nothing to forgive, ma chere. Please forgive me, but that sorry son-of-a-bitch didn't deserve you!" As I was speaking to Janine she had taken both of my hands, stroking them softly. I couldn't help but notice how, even though I was calm, my hands were trembling in hers. Janine, fully aware of my emotional state, leaned forward and kissed me on one cheek while she gently caressed my other with her delicate hand.

I knew what I had just seen...witnessed...my God...Elena. Could she be right?

*"Ahh, big brother...do you believe me now?"*

*"Elena...please. I'm going to get the answers tonight."*

*"Get the hell out of there...please, John!"*

*"No, Elena...stop it. NOW! I don't want to talk to you about this any more! They have done*

*nothing but love and protect me since I came here. They are not going to harm me."*

*"Jacques is right."* Jaycee had been *listening.* "OOOhhhhh...kay, this is new," I commented to no one.

*"Elena, meet Jaycee."* I looked at Luc and shrugged. What the hell else could I do?

*"Jaycee...Don't any of you hurt my brother...or so help me..."*

*"Elena, you can stop right there....Jacques is ours now. We love him and plan on making him part of the family."*

*"I bet you will, Jaycee,"* Elena's voice was filled with sarcasm.

*"Elena, please...give them a chance to explain. Listen in if you want, sis...after all, you've proven you're good at that."* I noted my

voice was getting a tone of its own, and it wasn't a nice one, but I had a right and I was seriously pissed off at my sister. Just once, couldn't she cut me some fucking slack! Damn her!

*"You can damn well bet I will, brother..."*

And with that, Elena was gone. Once again her voice shut off. *'What the fuck?'* I thought as I sat there staring into space.

Luc had turned toward me and with his hand he turned my head to face his. "John? Let's go up to my apartment. You will hear the truth...the whole truth."

"So help you God, Luc? Oh shit, I'm sorry babe, I didn't mean for that to come out." I half smiled.

"Oh yes you did, babe," Luc said, a soft smile returning to his face. Though his eyes showed love, there was also a look of concern buried in those blue eyes.

*'Shit. Could I do nothing that would get my baby boy pissed off at me?'* I thought.

*"Believe me, my love...you do not want to do that."* His smile had gone, his face turned deadly serious.

# ❖ CHAPTER TWENTY-THREE ❖

It was going on nine o'clock as we sat in Luc's apartment. From where I was sitting I could see Luc's bedroom, the bed still unmade, the tray sitting where we left it. Untouched. Memories of the morning and the three of us tangled in the sheets making love went coursing through my head.

I realized, yeah, I'm a little slow on the uptake. The words and actions I shared with Jaycee bonded us together, but not like Luc. Ours was a bond made out of love. Jaycee's, the more I thought about it, was not one of possession. Yes, Jaycee loved me too. Luc's was true, from the heart, but (trust me, I was still having a hard time wrapping my mind around this one) so was Jaycee's. I had found love with two men. Confused did not begin to cover what I was feeling. One thing was for sure, I loved Luc and I was his with every single beat of my heart. Fuck, could Elena be right? Was Jaycee planning on...? Oh for crap's sake, John, get a hold of yourself!

Janine was returning from the opposite end of the room where a well-stocked bar was at Luc's disposal. Fine wines, aged to perfection, were the focal point of his collection. Off to the right of the bar I noticed a stainless steel, high tech refrigerator which Janine had just closed. Classical music filled the room. I couldn't help but recall what had happened in the limo and how surreal it was to be where we were. From chaos, no, a horrific nightmare...to, damn it, this. Let it go, John. Let. It. Go.

Luc and Jaycee were seated with me on the sofa. By now I shouldn't have to tell you, but Luc sat to my left and Jaycee to my right. I was so accustomed to it, that if it changed for some reason, I probably would be concerned. Of all things to be thinking about. Seating arrangements?

Good God, I have lost my mind. Feral eyes, fangs...no...Just...no. The heat of the moment had played tricks. Tricks brought on by my sister's very active imagination. There were no such things as vampires and werewolves.

Janine handed Luc and Jaycee a glass of that same thick, red liquid they had enjoyed at the park. God, every part of me wanted to ask. Fuck! It couldn't be! Blood? I wondered what they would do if I asked if I could have a glass? Separately, away from theirs, was my drink.

"Jacques, I remember the comment you made regarding your favorite vodka, with whipped crème flavor, oui? I hope you don't mind, but I took the initiative to make you a drink with it. I hope I did not assume incorrectly, mon cher?"

"Not at all, ma chere!" I took a sip, its warmth spreading through me. Janine had been watching. I sighed and smiled, looking into her mesmerizing, emerald green eyes. "Merci...merci beaucoup!"

"It is my pleasure. It's the least I can do. You, my dear Jacques, were so brave today!" She leaned over and gave me a soft kiss on my cheek. Then Janine placed the tray on the table separating us from the elegantly embroidered, Queen Anne-style, high back chair where she sat down with all the grace of royalty herself.

"We promised you a taste of the nightlife tonight, my love," Luc began. "Are you still up for it? I'll understand if you prefer to stay in. You've been through so much!"

God, this boy was incredible. What the hell did I do to deserve him? This? Luc...hell...everyone went through it, but all concern and attention was turned towards me.

I knew Luc would understand. Part of me wanted to just take my baby boy to bed and feel him next to me. To be cradled in his arms and fall asleep with him pressed against me, safe and secure. I looked at the twinkle in Luc's eyes and saw promises of things to come, along with an assurance that there would be a change from earlier. I wanted that. No, I needed that. I knew Luc, and hell, Jaycee, and

Janine needed it too. I owed it to them after the fucking mess I started with Alec.

"Of course, baby." I squeezed his hand, "provided you do one thing with me."

"I promised you earlier I would, mon cher!" Luc winked at me.

"Well, uh, yeah...that too, baby boy, but...um..."

"I think, dear brother," Jaycee looked at both of us, "Jacques wants you to dance with him."

"Well, that's a given! I have already given the DJ a list of your favorite songs, John!" Luc smiled.

"How the hell? Luc, how do you know?"

"Um, John, I do subscribe to your online play list!"

I felt myself blushing. "Um...Luc...are you, ah, royalty?"

"As I said earlier..," Janine reflected, "we are, in a way. Our family has a...How shall I say this?" Her finger pressed to her lips and her eyes looked off to the side as if gauging her words very carefully. "Our family, Jacques, has a long legacy in Paris. In France, for that matter. As I told you, we come from old money. Our relatives acquired their wealth in the seventeenth century and very carefully made sure that their heirs would be taken care of. We own the club!"

"Holy crap! How cool is that?" I suddenly felt like a little kid given the keys to the candy store.

I heard Jaycee giggle but then, composing himself, he looked at me, his eyes sparkling. "Dear, Jacques," Jaycee paused. "Janine? Luc? May I have the honor of telling him?"

Luc and Janine looked at each other; a soft smile shone on their faces. They nodded yes to Jaycee. "Sure, bro! Tell John. I think a little good news is what is needed right now." Luc squeezed my hand as Jaycee kissed him on his cheek. "Merci, Luc!"

Jaycee looked at me, and taking hold of my hand he stated, "You, Jacques are part owner! We drew the papers up before you arrived. We each hold a quarter percent of the club."

"Also, babe," Luc squeezed my hand, "that means you are on the Board of Directors. My brother took the liberty of contacting our attorneys. You now have personal accounts in Switzerland at two of the highest-rated financial institutions in the Caymans. Jaycee, would you like to take over? You are, after all, the financial genius here!" Luc grinned.

If somebody pinches me and wakes me up, I'll kill myself along with whoever pinched me.

"Right, bro. The most important part! Jacques, I'll get your account books and bank cards together for you later, but we transferred one million euros into each account. As you are now in Europe, you'll be dealing with euros. We'll teach you conversion factors and such, love, but that's about one point five million U.S. dollars in each account. Is three million U.S. dollars enough to start you off?" I looked at him to see if this was for real. It was. As a matter of fact, given Jaycee's expression, it looked like he thought I was disappointed.

I sat there, my face blank. I was absolutely stunned. That could be the reason for Jaycee's concerned look. Realizing I was causing him distress, I quickly snapped out of it and smiled, nodding my approval. I had just become a fucking millionaire.

"Say something, mon cher!" Janine leaned over and caressed my cheek.

"Does our gift meet with your approval?" Luc asked as his forehead pressed softly to mine.

"Th-th-thank y-y-you!" Crap, I was stuttering, but what the hell else could I say.

Luc kissed me. "You're welcome, babe. Remember what we told you? We want to give you the world. This is a start!"

"A ...a...st-st-star...a start?"

"God, John...I just love it when I can get you to do that! Do you know how adorable you are when you stutter like that?"

"Luc? Don't embarrass our boy!" Janine tried on her big sister voice, but with the smile on her face I knew she was enjoying it just as much as Luc and Jaycee.

"The apartment that Luc has, love, has been part of the family for centuries." Jaycee turned to face Luc and me. "Most of the architecture you see is original, though my baby brother has made a few changes. Not many though, Jacques. As you know, he has a great love of the classic architecture."

Jaycee once again smiled, knowing he was on the verge of embarrassing Luc. Something I had finally realized he relished, but as always, there was a deep love for Luc that went beyond what could be considered normal. His taunting and teasing came from pure love. I had no doubt that Jaycee would die for his brother. No, Elena, Jaycee is not plotting to kill Luc.

"Well, I'm trying to broaden his horizons, Jaycee!" I said, smiling at Luc.

Jaycee giggled. "We noticed. Luc, have you shown Jacques your Stetson? You know the one I mentioned earlier?"

*'Oh God, here we go!'*

"Big brother," Luc was turning ten shades of red, "did you have to remind John of that? Really?"

"You're kidding, Jaycee, right?" I desperately tried to feign a serious face, but it wasn't working. A corner of my mouth began to give way to a smile. What I wouldn't give to see him with it on!

"No." Jaycee took a drink from his glass, licking his lips. "Luc is our little country boy!" There was that giggle again. His lips curled into a wicked smile.

Luc, for all intents and purposes, looked like he wanted to disappear into the woodwork. His hand covered his face. Eyes shut tight, he began to slouch down into the sofa.

I squeezed his hand and gave him a kiss on the cheek. "*My* little country boy! Mine...all mine!"

Just when I thought Luc couldn't get any more affectionate, he leaned into me and rubbed his nose against mine. Then brushing his lips lightly over mine, he closed his eyes and whispered, "I love you, John. You are, and always will be, my one and only."

"My thoughts exactly, baby boy. I couldn't imagine my life without you."

"You'll never have to worry about that." It was a promise that, God, I knew Luc would keep.

"Aww." Jaycee leaned back on the sofa. "Love is in the air! What do you think Janine? June wedding?" Jaycee's smile and laugh, little did he know, would be his undoing.

"It's a thought, Jaycee," I looked at Luc, a smile creeping over my face, "but I always wanted to be married in the spring! What do you think, Luc? April? May?"

If his jaw could have dropped, it would have. Luc looked at me. It was absolutely priceless. His eyes were wide open and his mouth agape in total surprise. Then for good measure he let out that sweet, adorable, little whimper.

"Luc, baby." I leaned over and gave him a soft kiss. "Luc, I love you. Will you?" The room was so quiet you could have heard a pin drop. "God, Luc, I'm sorry...if...I mean, hell. What was I thinking?"

"April would be perfect!" Luc pounced on me, and I could only smile as he looked at me and said, in what had to be the sexiest voice I have heard come from Luc, "I accept your proposal, mon cher! I do!" Luc proceeded to seal our engagement with a heated kiss.

"Luc?" I took his hands in mine. "May I ask Jaycee to be our best man?"

Not waiting for permission from Luc, Jaycee jumped up and accepted the offer. "I accept! Wait a minute...you're serious!" Luc and I laughed as we watched Jaycee sit back down, realizing that what had started as a joke, had turned into an honest to God engagement.

"You okay, bro?" Luc leaned over and squeezed Jaycee's hand.

"Yeah...definitely. Now I know how Jacques felt when he found out he was a millionaire! Wow, hey." Jaycee focused his attention on me and winked, flashing me a look that made me blush. "Yeah, I'm more than okay."

"As am I." Janine smiled.

I leaned into Luc and pulled him into my arms. With my hand palm side up, I gently ran it down the side of his face. "Je t'aime, Luc."

"I know. I love you so damn much, John." Our lips met, and as I kissed him I could have sworn that I felt what he was feeling. But how? I was politely brought back to reality when I heard Jaycee clear his throat.

"Sorry, boys." Jaycee blushed.

"Think nothing of it, bro!"

"My brother." Jaycee smiled, and my heart skipped as a single tear fell down his face.

Janine, leaning forward as though to speak, her eyes studying her glass of 'wine', took a pause. I was sure she was collecting her thoughts on how she was going to proceed. Taking a sip of the thick red liquid in her glass, she looked up at Luc and Jaycee. I noticed, without saying a word, the three of them had come to the conclusion that now was going to be the time to disclose information that half of me wanted to hear, while the other half, from a completely emotional standpoint, wanted to bolt out the door. Elena's warnings coursed through my mind. Damn you, sis.

Taking a deep breath, she slowly exhaled. I noticed a resolve in her expression and knew I was about to hear the truth...the whole truth.

"I promise, mon cher. Nothing but the truth." Janine smiled at me.

If there was any relief on my face, I don't think it registered, as both of my boys took one of my hands and squeezed.  Their eyes were trying to reassure me that no matter what I heard, I was safe and no harm would come to me.

"*Get the fuck out of there, John!*"

"*Elena...I love you, but...fuck off!*"

"*Elena.*"  Jaycee entered the conversation.  "*Your protective nature towards your brother is heart- warming to say the least, but I must ask you to back off.  Listen if you want, but I can assure you, Elena, your brother is ours always.  No harm will come to him, the choice...*"

"*Choice, Jaycee?  You expect me to believe you're going to give him a choice?*"

"*Yes, Elena.  We would never hurt Jacques, and yes, the choice will be his and his alone!*"  Jaycee was losing his patience, not to mention the fact he was getting seriously pissed off.

"*Well, before you even utter one more word...*"  Elena snapped back, "*Let it be known that Trace and I are in Paris and we know where you live, Jaycee!  Luc and Janine too!*"

"*Elena...that is...*"  Before I could finish my thought, Jaycee put two fingers on my lips 'mentally' quieting me.

"*If that, Elena, is a threat...*"  Luc's head was cocked to one side, his eyes staring into mine, "*you better know what the hell you are doing and what you are getting yourself into.*"

"*Elena...?*"

"*Yes, Janine...*"

"*Leave us...now!*"

With that Elena, my sister, my overprotective sister, was gone.  But now I knew it was Janine.  My sister's telepathic powers were strong, but my God, Janine could 'tune her out'.  I wouldn't, and didn't, question Janine's actions.  As much as it concerned me, I realized that Elena brought this on herself.

Janine, standing up and moving to a chair closer to the three of us, took my hand.  Her free hand gently brushed my cheek.  "Thank you, Jacques for understanding about Elena.  There are some  details that she is not ready to hear.  Her protective, though impulsive actions, could very easily have  devastating results."

"Of course, ma chere.  Whatever you feel is best.  Thank you though, for understanding Elena's concern."

"All I ask, Jacques, is that you listen.  Please.  Just listen.  What we are about to tell you will probably trouble you. You may find it too incredible to believe, but it's the truth. We will never lie to you or hold anything back. We will never hurt you or force anything on you. But I am thinking, with what you have witnessed, and what Elena has already said to you, you have your own conclusions. Am I right, Jacques, mon cher?"

Jacques, mon cher? My mind began to race. Aahh crap! This was going to be serious. That part of me that wanted to run came crawling into my head again. But looking at Luc, I wouldn't, I couldn't. I loved this boy so fucking much! I didn't care if he turned out to be a...I can't believe I'm thinking this...a vampire! I sat there feeling paralyzed, my hand wrapped so tightly around my drink, I thought I would break the crystal glass. I looked down at it and studied the design, the craftsmanship. Wow...really? Oh shit, John. You have lost it. The possibility of...fuck....vampires and werewolves, and you're admiring the crystal?

"I see you're admiring the wine glass, Jacques." Janine's voice was as pleasant as a warm summer breeze.

"Ah...yeah...pretty dumb, huh?"

"Why would you say that, Jacques?" Janine asked. "You admire fine things! My brothers and I appreciate that. Did you know the glass you're holding in your hands dates back to eighteen ninety-seven? The company itself was founded in eighteen ninety-five. My relatives traveled to Austria to purchase this particular set from the founder himself! They had it custom made. I don't know if you noticed, but our family crest is etched into the pattern." I looked at the design Janine was pointing out.

"Janine, it's breathtaking!" I placed one of my fingers on top of Janine's as she traced it for me. It was subtle and delicate. A quiet understatement meant to be seen only by family, I was guessing.

"Ahh, let's see. Yes, his name was Markus Langes-Swarovski." Then in a move that surprised me, Janine leant forward, and softly kissed me. "It's your crest now too."

Luc whimpered. I heard Jaycee's breathing hitch.

"Janine, um, I, wow!" I immediately, nervously, set the glass on the table. Luc and Jaycee looked at me and smiled.

"Jacques. Relax love. It has survived for centuries!" Jaycee tousled my hair.

"Yes, but my dear, Jaycee, I certainly don't want to make an embarrassing mistake. I can't even afford to touch this!"

"I think," Luc giggled, "My boy has forgotten he's a millionaire!" The three of them smiled, and a soft laugh permeated the room.

"Oh God, big brother. If he's this way over a glass, can you imagine what he's going to do when we give him his other gift later?!"

Visions of fangs piercing my neck flitted through my head. Why the hell was I getting aroused by that? My cock was suddenly very uncomfortable as it strained against my pants.

"G-g-g-if-ift?" *'When did I start to stutter?'*

"There he goes again, Luc!" Jaycee giggled.

Luc squeezed my hand. "Yeah! Damn! He is just so fucking adorable when he does that!"

"But you already told me I'm...I'm partners with you in a club? Not to mention the money." I could feel the sting of tears filling my eyes. "What more do I deserve?" My eyes searched everyone's.

"The world, my love! The world!" Luc's voice was so convincing, I could only do one thing. Believe him.

"God." I could feel warm tears falling down my cheeks. "How do I ever repay you? I'm just me."

"And that's exactly why." Luc pressed his forehead to mine. "Because you, my love, are you. Drop-dead handsome, thoughtful, loving, and sexy you... and you're *mine*! John, baby, I've waited a lifetime for you! We've waited a lifetime for you! You, John, are a priceless gift."

I had never heard anything spoken so truly from the heart, but it was Luc. I was overwhelmed by Luc's declaration.

"Let go, babe, I've got you." Luc pulled me into his arms.

Burying my face in his long, shaggy locks, I let go. As he ran his fingers through my hair, I knew that as long as I was next to him, my life was complete. Pulling back, just enough to see him, I looked into those blue oh-so-loved eyes.

"Better, babe?"

"Much." I felt a tap on my shoulder. As I turned, Jaycee ran a finger down my nose.

"God, bro, you are absolutely adorable! Now can we get going?! You have something waiting for you at our club!"

"Can you give me a hint here?"

"It's waiting for you at the club, babe," Luc said. He had this shit-eating grin on his face as he gazed at my crotch.

*'What the fuck was waiting for me?'*

"Jacques, mon cher, please forgive me, but we need to get back to the main reason we need to talk to you." I knew she did, and I respected her and loved her for her concern. "Luc is right, mon cher. You do deserve the world, and we, love, are going to give it to you!"

"Sis, go ahead. John my love, it'll be okay! I promise you, babe." Luc's promises were never broken. Why the hell would he start now? Looking at him, then Jaycee, and finally Janine, I nodded, ready for the truth. It was at this point I swore that whatever the outcome, I was a part of their lives.

With that, everyone's attention turned back to Janine.

"We are fully aware that you have seen things. Unexplainable things. Your mortal mind is having a hard time comprehending them and that is fully understandable, Jacques."

*'My mortal mind? Oh dear God!'* I thought.

"What we are about to tell you, Jacques, may come as a shock. Then again, your sister Elena has done a fairly good job of clueing you in."

Jaycee had turned and was addressing me. "We want you to know," he continued, "You are in no danger! Do you understand, bro?"

"Yyyyeeaahhh...Ah shit, Jaycee, I'm sorry. I'll be okay. Ah shit, that's not true...I'm sorry...I'm...aahh..."

"Scared? It's okay, lover." Luc had turned toward me as well, his eyes penetrating mine, and at the same time I felt him run his fingers through my hair. Then palm side up, he let his hand slide down my face, caressing me. Warmth spread through me.

"Jacques, do you remember when Luc and Jaycee light-heartedly mentioned their ages?" Janine asked.

"Yes, Janine. How could I forget? Luc is, ah...shit...three hundred and fifty-seven and Jaycee is..." I started to giggle nervously. "Oh God, forgive me, three hundred and, oh come on...three hundred and sixty-four."

"My precious, Jacques, mon cher, I am..." Janine squeezed my hand, "Three hundred and seventy- six." Her eyes never blinked, her face deadly serious.

"I don't. No. This can't..." I began to stand up, but as I did two strong hands, one on each of my shoulders, pushed me back down onto the sofa. There was no threat in the action, I actually felt warmth flow through me. "But how? God, please don't tell me that you are vampires or werewolves or some other preternatural being that exists." Why am I even bothering to ask? Fuck, what more did I need...a neon sign? I looked at Luc, whose eyes gazed into mine. They were once again red. *'Well, there you go John. There's your neon sign!'*

Luc brushed his hand across my face and softly said, "We are. We do, my sweet John." His fingers now entwined through mine.

"Jacques?" I turned to look at Jaycee. His red eyes looked into mine.

"What, Jaycee?" My mind was reeling. Why the fuck didn't I get out of there? Because I loved them."

"It's natural, and it's okay if you are frightened, bro. Just please don't leave until we can put your mind at ease."

"At ease? How the fuck can I be at ease? Oh my dear God, what Elena was trying to tell me was true? How could I be so damn naive? Why the fuck didn't I listen? Jesus!" My head shook sideways in disbelief.

"Babe, yes. Elena was right...to a point. Yes, Jaycee and I *are* vampires. Janine," Luc looked and nodded at his sister, "*is* a werewolf."

"None of us had a choice," Jaycee continued, "Janine was attacked and turned by her fiance, Alec."

"You mean to tell me that son-of-a-bitch is a werewolf too? What...he fucking loved her so much that he decided to turn her into one too? Janine, ma chere, I am so...God...so sorry."

"He wanted me for an eternity, Jacques." Janine squeezed my hand. "It's okay, Jacques. Trust me. I have had centuries to come to terms with this. It's not exactly how I would have chosen to live my life. Alec is out of our lives now. You don't have to worry, mon cher. We will not let him harm you!"

"But, Janine, I'm, aahh crap, I can't believe I'm saying this, I'm..."

"Mortal? Yes, Jacques. My brothers and I are fully aware of that. You were so damn brave standing up to Alec today."

"Shit, Jacques," Jaycee leaned toward me, squeezing my hand, "You showed us how much we mean to you! You put our safety and welfare above your own life. Jacques, you stood up to a werewolf! No mortal, for as long as we have existed this way, has ever shown such bravery, Jacques." He ran his fingers through my hair. "You had no idea what you were up against."

"I just didn't...I didn't care." I felt the sting of tears assault my eyes again. "The bastard was threatening the people that I love!"

"Do you think, my beautiful Jacques," Janine's voice was soft and assuring "we would let Alec hurt you? Never! We adore you, Jacques. We made a pledge that we will protect you, give you your heart's desire, and most of all, you have our eternal love." Janine's voice was now full of emotion. She spoke for all of them.

The love for me was evident. More importantly, as I looked at them, I saw relief.

After all they have done for me, I now knew what I could do to repay them. They wanted nothing from me. There was one thing I could give them. My love. Suddenly, my fears were starting to dissipate. I felt my body slowly relax, my anxiety was slipping away. I looked at Janine. I knew she spoke the truth.

"Merci, ma chere. I...I...believe you. God knows, I love you so much, Janine."

I turned and looked at my boys. Their eyes once again blue, but I knew what they needed to hear. "Luc, Jaycee, hold my hands, I need your touch." They didn't hesitate. I reached out and they took my hands into theirs. "So you're vampires and Janine is a werewolf." I squeezed their hands. "Luc, babe, I adore you and cherish you. I'm crazy for you. I love you, Luc; I belong to you." Luc's lip quivered. "Jaycee, my brother...you're incredible. The love you have for your family warms my heart. Your love for me makes my knees weak. I love you. Only one thing has changed. I didn't think I had any more love to give the three of you. I was wrong. I don't know how it's possible, but my love for you goes beyond any logical explanation. Although I am mortal, my love for you Luc... Jaycee... Janine, is eternal."

"Je t'aime, Jacques. As is ours," Janine answered as I watched tears run down the faces of the three most important people in my life.

There was a moment in time, like that scene in a movie where the main characters just look at each other. Their eyes lock on to each other's, and you know, you just fucking know, that they understand each other and nothing more need be said. I knew it was that way with Janine, but I still needed to ask something of my baby boy.

"Tell me something, Luc...please?" I suddenly had so many questions, but hell, I wasn't going anywhere.

"Anything, love." The relief in his eyes was palpable.

"From what I've witnessed...um..." I looked at Janine, "Janine has, forgive me if I don't know how to describe it, but, Janine has feral eyes. Babe, I'm so sorry...it's just a lot to take in. You know?"

"Babe, after everything you've seen, and what we just told you, you're doing fine! Please don't apologize. Of course you have questions. Ask, babe. Just ask!"

God, it was so good to see the three of them smile.

"Janine, I even saw your canines extend!"

"I'm sorry you had to see that, Jacques. Anger will do that." Jaycee pulled the table out of the way and positioned Janine's chair closer. "It's a natural defense mechanism, like breathing."

"Um...your eyes, Luc, they are..." I reached up to caress his face and he leaned into my touch. "Well,

I noticed they change to bright red, and so do Jaycee's. This is a stupid question, but is that an indicator of, oh shit, I don't mean to be rude, a way to tell whether you are a vampire or a wolf?"

"John, my love, that is not a stupid question. Get that out of your head right now. No question you have for us is stupid." He brushed his sweet lips across mine. "Yes, my love, red eyes and feral eyes, like Janine's, are definitely indicators of who you are with."

"But..."

"How?" Luc interjected.

"Yes, babe. How did you become one?" My hand reached up and I ran my fingers through his hair. I had come to realize that Luc loved when I did that to him. It was nothing he said, it was the way he reacted. The way he leaned into my touch, his eyes closing. This adorable, serene smile appeared, and that whimper.

Luc briefly turned to look at Jaycee, then, once again, his full attention was given to me. "My big brother, Jaycee." He reached to squeeze Jaycee's hand. Jaycee leaned toward Luc and kissed him softly, so damn full of love.

"Jaycee?" I looked at both of them. Stunned.

"You see, mon cher, when Jaycee was turned, he protected me from his Sire."

"His Sire?" Sure, I knew what Luc meant. I had heard that word so many times in movies and TV shows, but to hear it for real was, well, it was just unreal. No. Surreal.

"Yes, Jacques. The same person who claimed me wanted to claim

Luc as well. I had no choice. He threatened to kill my entire family. Luc… Janine...He was a menace. I did not want that life for Luc. I did not want my family dead." A tear fell from Jaycee's face.

"But, Jaycee. You turned my baby boy into one? A vampire?" I told you I was a little bit slow on the uptake.

"Yes, I did. I tried to hold my Sire off, but he was so powerful that...Well, rather than have Luc fall into the control of this barbaric man, I changed my baby brother. Jacques, I love him so much."

"John, my love, Jaycee is right. He did it out of pure love and I have never thought otherwise. I didn't want to be this animal's slave, nor did I want Janine to die. I love my brother dearly; the choice was easy."

"That's why!" Suddenly the closeness and intimacy that Luc and Jaycee had for one another was even clearer to me. The kissing, the touching, even sharing me in bed. My God...Jaycee is Luc's Sire, his protector and guardian. I felt my breath hitch.

"That's right, Jacques." Jaycee had been "listening". "You see, Luc *is* my brother in every sense of the word, but when you become a vampire, the feelings you have for your Sire are complete. Physically and emotionally, brother or not. We love each other completely. We are bound together in every way; bound for eternity."

A sudden wave of guilt washed through me. "Jaycee?" The question begged to be asked. "Then...oh my God...you must hate me. I have no right to come between you and your brother!" Jaycee saw the distress and worry in my eyes.

"Hate you? My God, Jacques. Never, my love. On the contrary, brother, I couldn't be happier for Luc! He loves you… and so do I!"

"But then, that means Luc may want to turn me." I shuddered, but at the same time a thrill ran through me. I knew I couldn't hide anything from them, they could see my apprehension.

I felt Janine gently stroke my arm. "Only if you want that," Janine interjected. "It is you, Jacques, that must make the ultimate decision. Luc will not force you. Nor would he want you to feel obligated to do something you would regret, if only out of his pure and true love for you. He *must* have your permission! Jacques," Janine continued, "Mortal or immortal, we will love you just the same. My dear little brother loves you...adores you...he just can't envision having you for a mere mortal lifetime."

"Babe," Luc leaned over and kissed my cheek, "Janine is right. To think of having you for your mere...um...oh God...mortal lifetime," Luc was choking up. "To see you grow old and to lose you. God, John, I can't...I can't imagine living an eternal life without you by my side. But mon cher, I would gladly have you for your mortal years, if that's what you chose." Luc's emotional pain was visible. So was his love for me.

I ran my hand across his shoulder and brushed the tear falling from his cheek.

"Baby boy...just...just give me some time. Okay? I swear to you, Luc, I won't make you wait long. I swear, precious boy. Just...just give me a little time for this to..." I dragged in a breath, "sink in."

A nervous laugh came out of me at the realization of what I just said.

Luc pressed his forehead to mine. "Of course, my love. Of course. I'll give you all the time you need for it to...sink in." His soft, perfect lips formed a soft smile. "Only God himself knows how much I love you."

I returned the gentle smile that appeared on Luc's face. My God, I never knew I could love someone this much. So completely. Luc had become my world. Life without him? No. That was not an option! As I looked at this exquisite young man, my mind and my heart were coming to the conclusion that would change my life forever.

"But remember, Jacques," Jaycee put his hand on the back of my neck, "The choice is, and always will be, yours!"

"I must admit, I thought for sure this would go a lot worse, given what we told you. I thought I was going to lose your love." Relief began to wash over Luc's face.

"Luc, you will never lose me. I could never and will never love anyone like I love you. You, Luc, are my life." My fingers brushed his hand. "My world. Mortal or immortal, Luc, I am yours."

"You, John, are mine...ours...always. Mortal or immortal." Luc took my hands and pulled me into a kiss. It was soft and sweet and full of need. As he kissed me, he let out that soft, sweet whimper, a sound I could cherish for an eternity.

Pulling back, I looked at him. Luc's smile was contagious. I grinned back and could feel my face flush with the knowledge I had just been given. I had just become a mortal member of a very elite, immortal club. I turned to look at Jaycee. What I saw made my heart skip a beat. To anyone else, it wouldn't have been a big deal, but there he sat, his blue eyes watching us. His smile, and the love reflected on his very expressive face, said it all. He approved.

"Jaycee, God, my head is spinning! May I ask you a question?"

"You need not ask permission, bro, just ask."

"Where is this monster that did this to you and your family, Jaycee?"

"He's dead. A silver knife to the heart, then...well...torched. Nothing more than a pile of ashes." Luc answered for his brother.

"Frankly," Jaycee's voice became quiet, reflective, "The son-of-a-bitch got off easy." Then, realizing the details given to me, Jaycee reached over and squeezed one of my hands, saying apologetically, "Oh God, Jacques, forgive me. I didn't mean to be so graphic. How could I have been so insensitive?"

My hand brushed his cheek. "It's okay, Jaycee. I need to know, um, was it you?" I looked at him, my eyes letting him know I was okay with this. Hell, given the fact I was now loved by vampires and werewolves, these types of conversations were inevitable.

Jaycee's head turned and his eyes met his sister's.

"I killed him, Jacques," Janine answered.

"You mean you...?" Understanding was starting to take hold in my head.

My eyes widened as I turned toward Janine. "Werewolves are the only immortal being that can kill a vampire. You made Alec attack you, didn't you? Oh my God, Janine!" Realization crept through me. "You did it for your brothers. My God, my dear Janine."

"Yes, to get rid of that menace. To make sure he paid for what he forced upon us. It was our only choice."

In a defining moment, I realized this was it. How could I ever walk away from a family that sacrificed themselves for the sake of their love for each other? I was overwhelmed with emotion. *'Hold it together, John.'*

"We, Jacques, are the only three in our family. Elena had that fact wrong, and it's one of the reasons I needed to stop her. There is no lineage. Jaycee's Sire was not part of our family. He was ruthlessly after our family's money. By siring Jaycee, he would force his way into our family and put himself in a perfect position to come after our family's possessions. He didn't care about us at all." Janine's eyes misted over.

I knew this was extremely painful for her. Part of me didn't want or need to hear anymore; what was past was past. But I knew that this was important to them. To once and for all be able to share the terror they went through. The ordeal and sacrifices made to save the three of them. I felt privileged to be entrusted with this family secret, but at the same time, I couldn't help feeling heartbroken, knowing I couldn't help. *'Damn I'm useless!'*

Leave it to Luc to keep watch over me. Once again, he knew what I was thinking. I found myself in his embrace. His face pressed against the side of my head. "Don't you dare...don't you ever say, let alone think, that you are useless. You're here with us and that, my love, means more to us than you could ever imagine." He cupped his hands to my face and pressed his forehead against mine. "Do I make myself clear?"

"Very, babe. Very." Our eyes met. Sometimes Luc is most eloquent in his silence.

Jaycee lightly punched me on the arm. "You had better listen to him, lest I have to have a talk with you." He winked.

I heard Janine softly giggle. "You boys are..."

"We know, sis," Jaycee rolled his eyes, "incorrigible!"

"So, anyway, where were we?" Luc paused. "Right! It was a ruse, John. An evil, almost perfectly planned attempt, to steal our family's fortune. Once he had us where he wanted us, he would have killed us and taken possession of everything."

"But unfortunately, Jacques, we did not see this at the time." Jaycee's eyes began to fill with tears. "Our concern was to ensure the safety of our family. So I... I um..." A tear ran down Jaycee's face as the facts continued to unfold before me. Janine reached over and wiped the tears that were falling down Jaycee's face.

"My God, Jaycee! You..." I was beside myself. "Jaycee, you sacrificed yourself to save your family!" The sacrifice Jaycee made for his family overwhelmed me, not to mention Janine's. I have never known that type of pure, unadulterated love.

Words, at this point, were meaningless. I looked at Luc, and God love him, he nodded his approval. I leaned over, placed my hands on Jaycee's tear-streaked face, and kissed him. Gently, I felt his strong arms wrap around me, pulling me tightly to him. I gently parted my lips from his. I looked into his eyes and tried to show him exactly how much he meant to me. "I love you Jaycee, I really do...and I'm so proud of you." I brushed one of my hands, palm side up across his face.

Jaycee's eyes never left mine. There was no need for him to say anything, his answer was evident in his eyes. He loved me. With a voice that was shaking, he looked at me, and with a sincerity that made my breath hitch, he said, "Jacques, I...I love you too." That was just fine with me.

"As do I," Janine added. "Jacques, there is something else you should know."

"Of course, Janine. Please."

"Jaycee's Sire did not hold to his end of the bargain. After changing Jaycee, he murdered our remaining family: our mother, father..." Janine's voice began to choke with emotion.

"Ma chere...please Janine...don't do this to yourself. My God in heaven, what choice did you have? Janine, God, I love you so much...I understand. Janine, Luc...Jaycee, I am so sorry you all gave so much, sacrificed so much." I was overcome with emotion. Hell, what do you say? My mind was still absorbing everything that I learned, but frankly, all I knew after everything was said, was how I felt. Dragging a deep breath in I looked at them and asked, "Have I told you lately how very much I love you?"

I felt Luc's fingers run through my hair. "You do, love, every minute, of every hour, of every day. There is no need for you to say anything. We know, baby."

I looked at my family. "Well, I need to. I love you all so very much." My voice was breaking apart. I felt my eyes sting with tears. "God, I don't ever want to be apart from you." My declaration was meant for all three of them.

"We know, sweetheart." Janine's eyes, wet with tears, were as perfect as her soft smile. "We love you too, Jacques, mon cher." Janine walked over to me, leaned down, and kissed me gently. "You will never be apart from us. Never."

As the conversation came to an end, I turned to Luc. He brought his hand up to the base of my neck and pulled me into a gentle kiss. Heat scudded through my veins.

"You okay, John?"

"Um...yeah, baby...I'll be okay. It's not every day that you find out you're in love with a vampire." I couldn't help it. I felt a smile, no, a smirk form. "A preternaturally perfect, intelligent, and fucking hot vampire!"

"Fucking hot? Really?" Luc looked at me, his fingers brushing across my lips. "Ah, Jaycee? Did you hear that?" Luc leaned around me, one eyebrow raised up.

"Yeah, I did! Preternaturally perfect, intelligent, *fucking* hot...rub it in, little bro!"

Jaycee was doing better. It was good to see him smile. I only wanted happiness for them. I would do anything to make that a reality. Anything.

I looked at Luc. He was smiling from ear to ear! "May I, baby boy?" He knew what I wanted to do.

"Of course." My beau answered with not one shred of indecision.

I turned back to Jaycee. "Come here!"

"Huh?" Jaycee looked at me, completely puzzled. Damn! He was adorable.

"You heard me!" I took a hand and gently placed it under his chin, pulling his face close to mine. I ran my other hand through that incredible, thick, shaggy black hair, just like Luc's. My eyes met his. Leaning towards him I pressed my lips to his, kissing him, gently, lovingly. Jaycee, God love him, he leaned into me and kissed back. That feeling of possessiveness was no longer there. All I felt was the love of a man who fully accepted what our relationship would be. I don't know if it had something to do with being a vampire, but after what we just shared emotionally, his feelings, true feelings, coursed through me. *Love.* Pulling away, I looked at Jaycee. His eyes were once again wet with tears. Not tears of sorrow, tears of happiness.

"Jaycee? Promise me one thing. Don't ever doubt for one second that you are an important part of my life. Just like Janine and Luc, you are mine, always. I love you, Jaycee. I love you, mon cher." I looked at Jaycee. His eyes fluttered open. "By the way, you, babe, are the bravest, most selfless man I have ever known in my relatively short life and that, my boy, for what it's worth, is just fucking hot!"

"I love you, Jacques." Jaycee's voice was thick with emotion.

"So, um, oh shit. I can't believe I'm going to ask this."

"What, love?" Luc asked.

"The movie...'Underworld'...they had it right?"

Dead fucking silence. John, you idiot. All three of them looked at me like I had lost what was left of my sanity. Then...

"To a point, you goof!" Luc grabbed me and kissed me. His tongue pushing against my lips, his tongue wanting to play. Mine did too, and as my tongue played with his, Luc's fangs extended. I let my tongue run over them. My cock sprang to life.

'Oh fuck!' I thought. This is just too hot! I pulled back. My heart was beating much faster than it should. "One more question?"

"Later, Jacques. Anything you want to know," Janine answered.

"We will answer them," Luc finished Janine's answer, "But now there is something I've wanted to do with you since this morning!"

"Luc, um, your brother and sister are in the room!" I said, feeling my face turn red.

"You goof...that's for later!" He waggled his eyebrows. "Now we want to show you Paris. I want to show you off. Besides, you owe me a dance." He gave me a chaste kiss on the cheek.

"Luc, baby?"

"Yes, love?"

"If I step on your foot, um..." I unconsciously rubbed my neck. "Are you going to bite me?" '*Christ, did I just say that?'*

I heard a giggle from Jaycee.

Luc kissed me on the cheek. "Only if you ask me to!" He smiled, baring his fangs to me. "Smartass!"

I grinned.

Luc leaned into me and let his fangs rub up and down my neck. "You're a smartass?"

"God, yes!" I moaned.

Yeah, Elena. My vampire is abso-fucking-lutely perfect. Score one for me. God that felt good. One up on my smartass sister. Yes, I knew the truth, but I was so deeply in love with him nothing or no one would take me away from him. My baby boy was a vampire. So be it. Fuck, he was the most perfect creature I had seen, or for that matter, would ever see, let alone make part of my life. Damn, I belonged to the young man. I imagined him biting me...feeling those sharp fangs pierce my throat...his warm lips pressed against my neck as he drank my blood, bonding us together for an eternity. 'Oh, shit...Oh, shit...yes...I am yours always, mon cher.' My mind was a blur with the possibilities. I knew what I wanted and that was Luc...for an eternity.

"You know, John." Luc's hand brushed my arm. "I really, really like your canines!" As he looked up at me, his now deep red eyes met mine with a stare that should have been rated X.

"Fuck!"

"I think that's what Luc was aiming for!" I looked at Jaycee.

"Huh?  Oh my God."

# ❧ CHAPTER TWENTY-FOUR ❧

It was nearly midnight as the limo pulled up to a reserved spot directly in front of the nightclub. The ride was quiet, but for some reason I felt relaxed. God only knows why. Here, sitting with me, was a devastatingly beautiful wolf and two incredibly gorgeous, eternally young vampires. Out of the corner of my eye I could see Luc, Jaycee, and Janine looking at me. Shit, staring at me!

"What? What did I do?" I must have looked totally ridiculous. I felt my eyes open wide, looking, for all the world to see, totally confused. You know, deer in the headlight syndrome.

Janine giggled. "You did nothing, mon cher! There is absolutely no need for you to fret."

"God, John, you look fucking incredible!" Luc's eyes were locked on me and his fangs glistened in the dim lights of the limo.

"You're right, baby bro! Our tailor definitely knows his trade. Pardon the pun, but that suits him!" Jaycee had the same look. "What do you think, sis?"

"Good enough to eat!" Janine licked her lips and giggled.

*'Fuck me! Why wasn't I running from this? Why didn't I feel one inkling of fear?'* Why? For one thing, neither Janine, nor her brothers, ever threatened me. They took care of me. Christ, Janine even severed her relationship with Alec. Something deep inside my gut knew they would never harm me. Love me...yes. Hurt

me...absolutely not. I trusted them. Completely.

"Well, um." I felt myself turning red, "If I may say, Luc...Jaycee...for the love of all things holy, he may know his trade extremely well, but those suits don't deserve you, and Janine, that gown!"

"I have my own very well-known dressmaker in Paris."

'*Figures.*'

"Brother, you forget how long we have had to add to our wardrobe! Wait till you see yours!" Janine smiled at me as she gave me a wink.

"Ah yes, Jacques, my sister has gone to great lengths to make sure our incredibly hot mortal looks good...for any occasion!"

"But, Jaycee...the club, the money?"

"Just go with it, babe. You just don't argue with a wolf!" Luc leaned over and gave Janine a brotherly kiss on the cheek.

I knew without a doubt, that when the time came, I would allow...fuck, I'd welcome the chance to become Luc's for an eternity. Yes, I had made up my mind. Shit, I had so many questions, but I knew they would be answered. The way I felt about him, eternity was not enough time.

'*God, John, you have fallen...hard.*'

It didn't matter; I wouldn't change that for anything. '*Sorry, sis. This time you lose. You may have been right about what they are, but Elena, you do not, and will never, know the extent of what they have brought to my life... and what is yet to come.*'

Now, Alec...that was a whole different story. From just meeting him earlier today, I knew he had a hard-on for doing me harm. Not only did I confront him, but I, for all intents and purposes, helped end his relationship, a fucking long relationship, with Janine. If that wasn't enough to come seeking revenge and rip my throat out, I didn't know what was. Worse, what if he harmed Luc? I'd die first.

Oh fuck, then there was my sister and Trace. Did I actually hear Elena right? They're in Paris? No. No fucking way! I remembered the vow I made to Elena. If Trace comes too close or tries to harm Luc, Jaycee, or Janine, I will kill him. That was a fact. They probably knew already, but I had to talk to them about Trace's obsession. As much as they loved and protected me, I would do no less for them.

"Ready, lover?" Luc was pulling on my hand as Adrian held the door open for us.

"Wow! Just...Wow!" I could only stare at the building we were about to enter and my eyes were drawn to the name of the club. In bright red neon it simply read 'Immortalite'. Immortality. Yeah, shit...that sums it up!

I noticed Luc staring at me, his head shaking softly from side to side. "You like, lover?" Luc looked at me expectantly. "After all, you are part owner of this establishment!"

"Oh yeah, my hot, sexy vampire! Merci, mon cher!"

The club itself, from the outside, looked to be seventeenth century French architecture. That was one of the endearing qualities of Paris, France...Europe for that matter. Unlike the States, where if it's old we tear it down, the citizens here appreciated their heritage and their history. Every building had a story. My God, if the walls could talk, imagine the history lessons I could get. But, given my family's true age, I would have no problem in that regard. I had to smile as I realized that Jaycee, explaining the history of the gardens earlier, was probably speaking from experience. My God, he was probably there!

A gathering of well-dressed, extremely good-looking people formed a long line. It did not look like any nightclub I had ever stepped foot in. Elegant, classy beyond words. The thought of what was beyond those doors made me eager to exit the limo. Of course, Luc nearly pulling my arm off gave me a strong indication that he wanted me to move.

So did Jaycee. "Move your hot little ass, Jacques!" Jaycee was directly behind me, one hand firmly holding mine, the other copping a quick feel of my ass.

"Fuck...Jaycee! Hands off the merchandise!" I looked back at him. His red eyes, full of playfulness, pierced the darkness. I couldn't help but giggle!

Luc innocently turned to face us. "What? What did I miss?"

"Your sex-starved brother, Luc!" I smiled.

"Sorry, Jacques. It's just that, well I just can't help it. You look...fuck...incredible!" God, the grin on his face. Those perfect white fangs! Jaycee did his best to apologize with that shit-eating grin of his.

"Luc! Save me!" Feigning, badly I admit, terror, I was laughing as I said it.

"Jaycee! Behave!" Always the proper one, Janine scolded her brother, but I doubt Jaycee was trembling in his shoes with that smile radiating from her face.

We exited the limo and made our way toward a private roped-off entrance just off to the side of the main doors. I turned around to thank Adrian, but by that time he was back in the limo. Curiosity finally got to me.

"Luc, baby?" I leaned in to him, my hand roaming down to brush his tight, little ass.

"Yyyeesss?" Part of me felt bad, but as always, it filled me with heady warmth knowing I was the cause of that reaction.

"I'm sorry, babe."

"For what?" Luc stopped, turned to me, and took one of my hands.

"I should really learn to control myself."

"John...I crave your touch. I need your touch. I am yours...completely. My heart, my soul, my love...my body." Taking my hand he guided it back to his ass. "You had a question, babe?"

"Ah...um...oh God...yeah. This probably isn't my business, but...Adrian?"

"Vampire, babe." Luc smiled.

"Oh...okay! Um, thanks for clarifying that!"

"He'll be two hundred tomorrow!"

"Remind me to get him a card, Luc! No seriously, babe, can't you just see the clerk's face. Yes, dear, I have a friend who is turning two hundred today!"

"John, my love." Luc squeezed my hand. "You are enjoying this too much! Don't stop, lover!"

"Never, baby boy!"

As we approached the roped-off entrance, two extremely good-looking young men came to attention and unhooked the velvet rope for us.

"Bonsoir, my Lords...my Lady...and this must be Sir Jacques, mon cher!"

"Christian...Sam...Bon soir!" Janine let her fingers brush the sides of the young men's faces.

My God, they were perfect! Hello underwear cover boys! The one Janine called Christian was about six foot one with blonde, shaggy hair. *'Just like mine,'* I thought. His shoulders were broad and he was definitely a young pup. Eighteen, if I had to guess. Sam looked a little older. Possibly twenty-eight, give or take a few years. His hair was dark auburn, shaggy, and shoulder length. God, he was tall! If I had to guess, probably about six foot four or five.

Blushing, they half bowed to us as we started to pass, but then we stopped. Janine turned and looked at me, giving me a wicked little wink.

I watched in amazement, and with a little jealousy, as my boys each took turns kissing them. It was then, as I watched this hot scene unfold, that the two young men smiled at Luc and Jaycee and their white fangs glimmered in the lights of the club. Fuck. I was going into the 'House of Dracula'! Cool! Wait... Cool? No. This was fucking awesome!

"John, love? Would you come here a moment, s'il vous plait? Christian and Sam want to meet you!" Luc gestured to me.

Sheepishly, I walked toward them, my head down, my toe kicking at a small stone. Good God Almighty! Was every vampire hot?

"You're right!" Christian looked at Luc. "You are so lucky, Luc!"

*'God, I just don't understand. What is so special about me? My boy, Jaycee, and Janine...and now Christian and Sam. Absolute perfection. Shit...I'm nothing. Yeah, big self-esteem issues.'*

"*Stop that NOW, babe.*" Luc turned and took my hands. "*You are so fucking gorgeous. I don't want you to ever think otherwise. You, John, are perfection.*"

And with that, Luc took me in a kiss. My God, what a kiss. I felt his fangs gently brush against my lips, his tongue playing with mine.

"*You are mine, John.*"

"*My God, I love you for my life.*"

Eventually, realizing we had an audience, I reluctantly let my lips part from Luc's.

"Please excuse us everyone." Luc reached for my hand. I smiled as I realized he was blushing.

"Luc...Jacques...you need never apologize," Sam said. I couldn't help but notice he was looking at me like I was dessert.

"Ahhh, Luc?" I tapped him on his shoulder.

"Yes, love?" He turned to look at me. His eyes twinkled in the light of the entrance and I knew something was about to happen. I quickly found out what.

"I was wondering whmmmff..." My question was swallowed as Christian reached behind my neck and pulled me into a kiss that was as erotically charged as it was loving. A sense of protection coursed through my veins as I felt his strong arms wrap firmly and protectively around me. Once again I could feel the fangs of a vampire. Though deadly, Christian had complete control, only lightly brushing over my lips. I felt secure and safe in his embrace.

No sooner did I get used to Christian's tongue in my mouth, than Sam's strong hand pulled me to him. "Christian...may I?"

"Oui!" Christian winked at me and nodded yes to Sam.

"Bonjour, Sir Jacques, mon cher. Welcome!" I looked up into his dark eyes. He wrapped a big, strong hand around the back of my neck and pulled me to him. Just as Christian had, I felt his strong arms wrap themselves around me. Sam's mouth melted to mine. I felt Sam's lips meld with mine and his razor sharp fangs "made love" To my mouth. I couldn't help myself, I let my tongue rub against one. All willpower left me as I was pulled into his embrace. I was mesmerized and felt no fear, just peace and safety. My hand uncontrollably reached up and grabbed a handful of his thick, auburn hair. As with Christian, I leaned into his embrace. Even though their kisses were intense, there was no threat, and I knew that both Christian and Sam knew who I belonged to.

"Meet your bodyguards, babe. They tend to be...how shall I say this...affectionate? But pity the person who tries to fuck with you." Luc's eyes had gone red. My baby boy was deadly serious.

"Merci, Sir Jacques, mon cher!" Sam released his grip as Luc took my hand. I stood there grinning like an idiot, my knees shaking.

"My Lord, Luc." Sam put a hand on his shoulder, "I must agree with Christian." Sam's eyes met mine. "You are extremely lucky!" The back of Sam's other hand brushed across my face.

"I'm the lucky one, Sam, Christian." Regaining my composure, my eyes turned to Luc's, looking at him as if he were the only man who existed. I knew in my heart Luc *was* the only man who would have my heart. "I'm the lucky one." Luc squeezed my hand, his thumb gently rubbing my wrist.

"Boys?" Luc's eyes were red. "John is mine and I want you to make sure that no one, I mean no one that means him harm, gets near him. You do understand, don't you?"

"Including the two we discussed earlier?" Christian asked Luc.

Shit, that had to mean Elena and Trace! I wasn't upset. Concerned, yes, but I was Luc's. In his heart, he was protecting me as well as letting everyone know just exactly who I belonged to. I knew we would discuss this later; now was not the time. Frankly, I was grateful to Luc. What I had with Luc was priceless. No one, I mean no one, God help me, will take me from my precious boy, my lover, my partner, and for that matter Jaycee and Janine. My God, I thought I knew how much Luc loved me...I had no fucking idea. Just when I thought I knew the extent of Luc's love for me, he surprised me. Our foundation was solid. Our love was, fuck, our love was like no other. Luc is my heart's desire and soon, very soon, Luc will be my soulmate. Did vampires have a soul? John, my boy...way too many vampire books and movies. I was in love, forever in love, with a real vampire. I'd have the answers. I looked forward to it. I could only watch my lover with admiration and pride. Young in appearance, but wise as his years, he had the respect of everyone he knew. I leaned closer to Luc. His hand squeezed mine just a little tighter as he too pressed his body closer to mine.

I continued to observe and listen to Luc. This, I thought to myself as I watched his interaction with Christian and Sam, was the reason he had so much respect from the people he counted on. I couldn't help but feel pride in him. As a mortal, I should be thinking, Okay he's a vampire; powerful and arrogant; controlling. Remind me to ditch my collection of books. What I wouldn't give to put them in their place. God how I wish I could share the mortal world with Luc. He treated the people he depended on with respect. More than respect, with love, but after observing Luc, hell, even Jaycee and Janine, I knew why the respect was there. Quite simply, he respected them and he got the same respect returned to him tenfold.

What the mortal realm could learn from these exceptional people. I had fallen, fallen hard, and God bless him, my boy picked me up and swept me into a world I wouldn't give up.

"Pardonnez-moi, Luc." I was overwhelmed with emotion. I felt bad interrupting him, but God, I needed my boy.

"Je t'aime, mon amour!" Luc said breathlessly. My knees went weak.

I felt a gentle squeeze on my arm. I knew this was business, but oh my God, how I wanted to kiss him.

As he continued his conversation with Christian and Sam, there was no demand or order in Luc's voice. Rather, he asked as if speaking to two old friends. Fuck, they probably were as old as Luc.

"Them especially!" Luc turned his attention back to Sam and

Christian. "I'm concerned, guys. I know they want to rescue John, but I have no idea what they are planning. For John's sake, if they try something, detain them. As for that bastard Alec, he is to be dealt with." I noticed Luc's voice became more agitated.

Luc turned back to me before further addressing his orders to Christian and Sam. "John, love, I need you to know something." He gently cupped his face in my hands. "I know this is by no means pleasant to you, babe, but I have placed a kill order on Alec."

I knew this wasn't easy on my lover. Luc's eyes were a giveaway. I knew this was not a decision Luc was treating lightly. Even though I could tell that, it didn't stop my heart from skipping a beat, but the immediate touch of Luc's hand, once again lightly rubbing my wrist, calmed me down.

"Luc, my love, I understand. I trust you completely. Just...just promise me you won't allow harm to come to my sister. If your boys..."

"*Your* boys, babe," Luc corrected me, "Christian and Sam are *your* bodyguards. John, Elena will not be harmed."

"Trace?"

"That's up to him, John. I need you to tell me what his intentions are. Okay?"

"Of course, Luc. I will not allow him to harm you, Janine, or Jaycee in any way. I promise you, babe, you will know all there is to know about what makes Trace tick."

"The decision will be yours, my love. You understand why I need to do what I did with regards to Alec don't you?"

"Of course, Luc. I wanted to kill him myself. I'd never...oh God, Luc...I'm sorry...that's just not me, but no one will harm you. You're my life, baby." I took his face into my hands. "I am yours...always. Deal with Alec as you see fit, babe." Pulling Luc close to me, I pressed his head to my chest. "Luc, hon, I can't lose you, I'd die. Life without you would be meaningless."

"Nothing will happen to me, John. That bastard, mon cher, has done enough to our family. He has crossed the line and made his intentions evident when it comes to you. Remember, love, he is a werewolf." He wrapped his hands around my arms, firmly. "If there is one thing that you must remember, he can pull you into his spell and do whatever the fuck he wants with you, even if you are a vampire." My blood suddenly ran as cold as ice. I began to tremble, and with no hesitation Luc pulled me into his embrace. "God, John, I don't want to frighten you, but you need to know. Werewolves can play with your emotions, babe. They can make you feel things you don't want. They can control you and make you do things at their whim. Alec is exceptionally capable and will kill!"

I shuddered, but everything that Luc, Jaycee, and Janine had shared and taught me was etched into my memory.

"That is why," Christian approached me, running his hand through my hair, "Sam and I will not let that bastard anywhere near you. You have our vow, Sir Jacques."

*'What's up with the hair? Good God, John! That was random!'*

Sam had joined Christian next to Luc and me. "I couldn't have said that better myself. Sir Jacques...fear not."

"Hear that babe?" Luc's lips brushed across mine. "You, my love, are in good hands."

I turned to Christian and Sam. "Merci beaucoup."

"It is a privilege, Sir Jacques." Christian half nodded, his soft smile imbued nothing but honesty and respect.

Sam's hand reached for my shoulder. "With all due respect, Sir Jacques, you are Lord Luc's and a member of the family. I pray I am not out of line when I say this, but for the first time in centuries it is an honor to have a mortal join our vampire family." With that, both Christian and Sam took turns lightly kissing me on the cheek.

There was a moment of silence between the four of us and then Luc turned to Christian and Sam. With his arm still wrapped around me, Luc took his free hand and turning to Christian, he placed a hand on his face and pulled the young man to him giving him a chaste kiss. Then, the same loving kiss was shared with Sam. "Merci, my loyal friends. Merci. I love you both."

"As do we, Lord Luc."

"John, babe...I promise you, nothing that severe has been ordered for Elena and Trace. They will only be detained. No harm will come to them. You have my word." Luc leaned into me, kissing me gently, sealing his vow.

"You understand your orders, gentlemen?" Luc turned his attention back to Christian and Sam, his fingers once again entwined in mine and once again, though a simple gesture, his thumb gently rubbed my wrist, warming my body and my heart to their very core. My anxiety was almost gone instantly. A walking, talking, immortal

Ativan!

"You have our word, Lord Luc," Christian responded.

"Very good, gentlemen. Merci beaucoup. Oh, and one more thing."

"Yes, Lord?" Christian asked.

"From this point on, and please pass this on to our circle, John is to be referred to as Lord." Luc turned to me and smiled.

*"Lord John?"*

Christian and Sam smiled. "It will be an honor." Christian answered.

"Lord Luc?"

"Yes, Sam?"

"We too, love you, sir..." Sam blushed. "Forgive me if I am out of line. Christian and I love Lord Jacques and nothing will happen to him."

"Merci, gentlemen. He is easy to love, isn't he?" Luc's eyes met mine. "No, Sam, you are not out of line. I want the both of you to treat him as if he were yours."

I felt myself go weak.

"Lord Jacques, mon cher?" Christian half bowed to me. "You need not fear, Sammy and I shall protect you. You have our word."

"If you need anything, anything at all, let us know," Sam added.

"But, how, um, how do I even contact you?" It suddenly occurred to me that not once had I seen or heard a cell phone ring.

*"That is not your worry, Lord Jacques, mon cher,"* Sam's voice rang clear in my mind.

*"No contracts...no dead zones,"* Christian added, smiling.

I looked at my bodyguards, shaking my head and smiling. "Christian. Sam. May I ask a favor?"

"You need not ask, my Lord," Sam responded for both of them.

"I, uh, I appreciate that, but you both have pledged your life to me. You deserve that respect." I moved closer to them and put a hand on each of their shoulders. "I want you to do me one, not quite as life threatening, favor."

"Anything, Lord Jacques, mon cher." Christian half bowed.

"When we are together, please call me John or Jacques, whichever you prefer. Please?"

Sam and Christian looked at Luc, their eyes questioning what I'm sure was a very hard request. "Christian. Sam." Luc put his hands on each of their shoulders. "What did I tell you about John? Please follow his request."

"All I know is, mortal or immortal, he was worth the wait. You have our word, Lord Luc." Sam's compliment went straight to my head.

Sam turned to me and acknowledged my request, and then Sam touched my cheek with his hand. "We will protect you like the treasure that you are."

Once again he embraced me. "Jacques. No one, I repeat, *no one,* will cause you harm. Do not fear."

He pulled back, his eyes deep red and deadly serious. "They will die before they touch you! I promise you this with my life." Still in his embrace he sealed his and Christian's vow with a kiss.

I could feel myself blush. What the hell did I do to deserve this?

Christian approached me and placed his strong hands on my shoulder. "You shall never come to harm, Jacques."

"The four of you," Sam added, "Are all that matter to Christian and I. We would die to save you. Fear not, Jacques."

Then as Sam just did, I felt Christian's strong arms pull me into him, and his lips met mine. His fangs brushed gently over my lips, showing me just how fucking important I was to them. He pulled back, brushed my face with the back of his hand, and smiled. Then, with a half bow, he stepped back and took his place next to Sam.

Well, I'll be damned. If I hadn't looked, I would have missed it. For a split second Sam and Christian held hands. Oh, my precious boy, you have some explaining to do with regards to my bodyguards!

"Enjoy the evening, Lords Luc and Jaycee, Lady Janine, and of course our new friend, Jacques, mon cher!" Christian spoke for himself and Sam. Their deep red eyes telling me just how much I meant to them.

My Lord Luc. I was really starting to love hearing that. Lord Jacques didn't sound too fucking bad either! God, for a moment I looked at Sam. Where the hell had I seen him before? Tall. Extremely tall. Broad shoulders and long, fucking, sexy, shaggy hair...um...no, it couldn't be. I glanced at Sam again, then shook it off. As we started to approach the entrance I heard Christian say, "Come on, Sammy, we got work to do."

*'John, you have far too vivid of a fucking imagination.'*

"Luc, love...was it that?"

"Was it what, my love?"

"Never mind, Luc. I guess now nothing seems impossible... like Sam and Christian!" I nudged Luc in the shoulder.

"Oh, if you only knew, baby. Come on!" Luc took my hand, leading me to the others. "So you noticed! They make one hot couple, don't they?"

"That is an understatement, babe." I took Luc's offered arm.

"Baby," Luc briefly stopped and faced me, "They've been together about one hundred years now." "Holy!"

"Love, babe...eternal love...just imagine, John!"

"Trust me, baby boy...I am."

With that, Luc, myself, Jaycee, and Janine approached the entrance. My eyes had to adjust to the lights as we made our way in. Immediately, it seemed that every eye in the club turned to look at us. Red eyes everywhere! Feral eyes too!

"Are you sure this isn't 'Underworld'? I giggled and nudged Luc.

"You are such a goof!" Luc chuckled and wrapped his arm around my waist.

For a moment I had to stop and think back. They were not the looks that the people in the airport concourse gave us. Nor the people that saw us as we made our way out of the apartment. They were looks of respect and admiration. I knew I wasn't one of them, not yet, but I felt welcomed. Safe. Secure. Then of course, as if on cue, my mind went completely off the set of tracks I was on. For some stupid reason I remembered my concern, and Luc's need, for Visine. Knowing what I knew now, Luc did not need Visine. Even when I met them, Luc was already giving a small, subtle hint as to what I was going to learn. I smiled to myself.

I noticed Janine, Luc, and Jaycee did not seem to pay much attention to the looks they were getting. I, on the other hand, ate it up. I could only look at them with a love that was unexplainable. Well, at least to anyone else.

The music ground to a halt and applause broke out as we made our way in. Yep, fucking royalty. Fucking vampire and werewolf royalty! God! This was too much. I had to smile...and for a brief second, as my tongue felt my canines, I wondered how I would look with fangs!

*"Hot!"* Luc answered. *"Fucking hot!"*

*"Oh crap, baby boy, sorry!"*

*"For what, John? Trust me, my love. I've wondered the same thing!"*

*"You won't have to wonder much longer, baby boy!"*

*"You mean...?"*

Right there, right in front of everyone, I grabbed Luc and pulled him to me and kissed him like I wanted to take his breath away.

*"Yes, baby...make me yours...make me yours forever...I want to start our very own one hundred years."*

I pulled back and looked into his blue, immortal eyes. A tear of red ran down his cheek. His soft, sensuous lips were trembling. Then the one part of Luc that he would give no other, the one thing my man did that signified his love to me and only me, he whimpered that loving, soft whimper. Heat scudded through my veins and before I could even grasp what was happening, Luc, his strong arms enfolding me into him, kissed me. His fangs rubbing against my lips. Our tongues tasting each other.

*"Fuck, baby boy... love you!"*

"Love," Luc's breath hitched, "You...too!"

The applause of an appreciative crowd brought us back to reality. I stepped back, and taking his hands in mine, I knew without a doubt, with no fucking hesitation, that I was on the verge of beginning a new life. A new life with someone that had been waiting for me for...well...a hell of a long time.

The club itself was something else. How the hell do you describe something so incredibly perfect? Sure, I had been in dance clubs but, shit, this place was incredible. As the music started up again and the club-goers began to dance, I watched, mesmerized. Syncronized lights, floods and a sound system that could only be the best money could buy, made the music come alive. Large, high definition screens surrounded the dance floor and brought to life the songs and the accompanying video. Each booming bass note vibrated through my body and intoxicated me with its rhythm. No attention to detail had been spared, including the music. As promised, every song was hand-picked by my boy.

I watched Luc's body start to move. Enrique's 'Tonight I'm Loving you', the *explicit* version, which was so fucking perfect, filled the club with its intoxicating beat and of course his sexy voice. Shit! His sexy everything! I had to make a mental note to check with Luc and see what the odds were of getting Enrique to consider 'Immortal Fame'! If this is the way it was going to be all night, damn, just try to get me off the floor! I glanced over to look at my lover, his eyes locked on to me. I watched his perfect body move effortlessly to the beat of the music. Every part of him matched the rhythm and the beat of the music. Yeah, just try to get me and my baby boy off the floor! Luc had me so turned on that all I wanted was to take my vampire... *'shit, did I just say that...'* and fuck him right there for everyone to see.

"Like what you see, lover?" Luc rubbed his thigh against mine.

"Ah oui, mon cher. I want you so much!"

Luc flashed me such a look that I almost came in my pants. Breathe, John, just breathe.

All of a sudden, out of the corner of my eye, I noticed a revolving circular floor. On it, I saw what could only be described as the hottest thing on four wheels.

"My God, Luc?" I could only imagine I looked like the redneck I thought I left behind in Wisconsin. "Luc...love?" My breath was coming out in short, raspy gasps.

"Yeah, babe, is everything okay?" Giggling, Luc's eyes sparkled and had a hint of playfulness in them.

"Is that what I fucking think it is?"

"You did tell me that you had a weakness for that German luxury motor car, did you not?" He had come up to me, wrapping an arm around my waist.

"Yeah! What are you doing, giving it away? A contest?" I looked at him with what I knew was a puzzled look on my face.

"Well, love," Luc took my hand, "You're part right. We are giving it away...to you! You know that surprise we had waiting here for you?"

"But...Luc... Oh m-my G-God!" I was stuttering. "It...it's...m-m-mine?"

"God, I love it when you do that!" Luc gave me a quick, chaste kiss. "You are so damn cute! It's yours lover, but only if you promise me one thing?" Luc's eyes once again locked onto mine. They had turned to their deep red, which I was beginning to find very hot.

"Anything, Luc!" I turned to look at him. "Anything, baby boy!" I grabbed a handful of his sweet ass and pulled him to me. I could feel our hard cocks pressed against each other.

"Make love to me in the back seat!" he growled. His eyes were filled with lust.

"Fuck, yes! Back seat, front seat...pick a seat!" God, I was smiling so much my face hurt! Luc brushed his hand across my face. "I so love you, babe!"

"Luc. I don't know what to say. I love you too, Luc. I love you so damn much!"

Jaycee and Janine had come to stand next to us as my man presented me with yet another gift. They were watching and listening to our exchange.

"*I have never seen Luc so happy, sis. How do I make this up to you?*"

"*Jaycee, my sweet, beautiful brother, that debt was paid centuries ago!*"

"*Look at them, Janine. God, I have never seen such a perfect love.*"

"*You think Jacques will allow Luc to turn him, sis? I look at how happy they are. How happy Jacques has made Luc. Sis, like Luc, I don't think I could handle ever losing him. I love him, sis. He has brought our family so much happiness and love.*"

"*My precious brother, not a word. Understand?*" Janine placed her hands on her brother's face.

"*Yes. Yes I do. Just look at them.*" Their attention shifted back to us.

I looked at them, and with a sudden realization on their face, both Jaycee and Janine blushed.

"*Hey, you two...merci...I love you both. Jaycee,*" I looked down, lightly kicking the floor with the toe of my shoe, "*your sister is right. Jaycee with your permission, as Luc's Sire, yes... yes I want Luc to turn me.*"

I felt Luc tap me on the shoulder. "Pardonnez-moi, Janine and Jaycee. I believe Luc is wanting my attention."

"Of course, love." Janine touched my arm in approval, giving me a subtle wink.

"Love you, Jacques! Merci beaucoup!" Jaycee smiled. "Come on, sis, let's give our boys some space."

As I turned to face Luc, his one eyebrow was raised as if slightly worried. "Is everything okay, mon cher?"

"I...Luc...I just..." I felt a tear start to run down my face.

"You need say nothing, John, your eyes, your emotions, they say it all." Luc reached up and wiped the tear from my face.

Luc took a quick glance at the two seat convertible. Then even quicker, his eyes were looking back into mine. "I hope you like the color, John." Luc's eyes shifted back to blue.

"Luc, babe...It's...God! It's the color of your eyes. Babe, I don't even think they offer that color." "They don't, John. Custom paint job. One of a kind." He reached for my hand and squeezed it gently. "Like you."

"Luc, I don't know what to say." I brushed my lips across his.

"Take another look."

"I am."

"At the motor car, you goof!" Luc's smile...I knew he wanted me to look, but shit, the boy's smile, his perfect fangs gleaming pearl white. I definitely had a fang fetish! *'Aahh crap!'*

"Holy Mother of...Luc! Am I seeing right?"

The car was making another rotation on the platform. The personalized plate spelled out (I could feel myself choke up) Luc's boy. It was apparent Luc had known all along what my heart, soul, and mind would come to accept. I pulled my lover into my arms and, letting my hands tangle themselves in his thick locks, I kissed him. Tenderly. With love. Luc gave as good as he got. His were sweet and gentle. I looked at him, running a finger down his nose. "I love it, Luc."

"Are you sure, babe?"

"Yes, baby boy." I looked into his eyes. "Yes, I am. We need to talk, Luc."

"I know. We will. I've been thinking about it...us...our life together." His eyes studied me, looking for the answer to the question I knew was on his mind. The only one that mattered.

I gave it to him. "You mean, sweet boy," I kissed his cheek, "Our immortal life together." Luc had no time to answer.

"Come here, Luc! Get your sweet little ass over here." My hand gesturing for him to come to me. "Now!" I pulled him close to me, wrapping my arm around his waist and pulling his body tight to mine. As he looked up, I cupped his chin with one of my hands. The other grabbed a handful of his thick, black hair and I pulled his mouth to mine and proceeded to kiss the fucking shit out of him.

# ❧ CHAPTER TWENTY-FIVE ❧

Most of the evening was spent on the dance floor. The brothers and Janine had made introductions to the friends of the "family" they wanted me to meet. Young and perfect, they were caught in time. All in their late teens to mid-twenties. Werewolves and vampires. All centuries old. All about my family's ages. I was the only mortal there, but that would be changing.

Yes, I know. Elena had warned me. Sad as it was, that whole part of my life was a place I was not going back to, and Elena herself was changing. Her attitude, her motives. I felt an uneasiness. Something in my gut was warning me that things were going to change... for the worse. From where I was standing, Elena had not had, and did not have, anything to worry about. It was apparent that these *friends* had the utmost respect for Luc, Janine, and Jaycee. They must have, after all, vampires and werewolves together? How does that work? Unless...God, it had to be the work and effort of Luc, Janine, and Jaycee.

*'John, don't believe everything you see in the movies!'* I thought to myself with a smile.

I had become a part of their family. I was assured that no harm would come to me. Every one of them assured me that they too would watch over and protect me. Did it really matter? Yes, it did. I was to become a permanent part of the family. Soon. Even if I chose to remain mortal I knew nothing would change, though my mind was already made up. An immortal life with Luc. Bite me! Luc that is.

"*Elena? Sis? If you heard any of this, just know this one thing. You can't stop me. Luc is mine. I am his and will be forever his. Please...please, Elena...go home.*"

"*No, John.*"

"*Elena?*" My heart started to pound. I did not think I would actually get through to her.

"*Yeah, John. Fuck! You can't do this! Just please...Trace is...*"

Just his name brought back feelings I was trying to bury. "*Trace is what, Elena?*"

"*I can't tell you. He's doing this because he loves you, too.*"

"*Bullshit! He loves me? Since when? What more does he want from me? For Christ's sake! We have done nothing to you or Trace!*"

"*We? Listen to yourself. You're not one of them yet!*"

"*Them? They are people, Elena! More importantly, they are more than that...they are family!*"

"*You have completely lost your fucking mind, John! We will be coming to get you!*"

"*For your own good, Elena, leave and take Trace with you. I have chosen my path...my life.*"

"*Soon, John!*"

"*Fuck off, Elena. I mean it. Just once in your life...fuck off!*"

"*I'll be seeing you, big brother.*"

"*Drop dead, bitch!*"

Our connection dissolved.

"Fuck!" I slammed my fists together in frustration.

Luc had been listening. "Babe, take a moment here. It's okay, John. We are handling it."

"Merci, my love." I stayed a sob, but tears streamed down my face. Without a word, Luc wiped them off my face and pressed a gentle kiss to my lips.

"I love you so damn much, John." It was barely more than a hoarse whisper.

"I...I...God, I love you too, Luc." My voice was shaking.

I felt Luc's hand running up and down my back. His touch sent warmth through me. The anger and anxiety I felt was disappearing. A calmness was starting to prevail within me.

"That's it, love. Take it easy." Luc's voice was so gentle and soothing. It was almost hypnotic.

With Luc's help, I shook it off and returned to the present. Luc continued to introduce me. Every introduction was warm and intimate. It was as if these people, who I never met before, had known me all my life. Though, I had to admit, being addressed as Lord Jacques was a little daunting. I gave up trying to convince them to just call me Jacques.

Luc was having the time of his life watching me. What the hell did he say to them?

'*God, I'm just a plain, normal guy from Wisconsin!*'

"*Not anymore, love!*" Luc interjected. "You know that mind thing, baby?"

"Yeah? What about it?"

Luc smirked. "It does have its advantages!"

"Why, you little shit!" I laughed, thinking of the implications.

I was captivated by the eternally young and perfect men and women that surrounded me. I was used to the red eyes, the feral eyes. Hell, even the fangs that shone in the dance club's lights didn't bother me anymore. What kept surprising me, pleasantly I might add, was the way both women and men alike took me in their arms and kissed me. It wasn't just a peck either. It was intimate, personal, and, God help me, kind of hot! Mind you, this was not a *free for all*! Luc and Jaycee kept a continuous presence by my side. Luc to my... Oh for Pete's sake! If you don't have it by now, then forget it. Everyone that I was introduced to knew, without having to ask, who I belonged to. All you had to do was look into their eyes.

"Jacques?" Jaycee leaned into me.

"Yes, mon cher?"

"Can I get you a drink, bro?"

"That would be great, Jaycee, but you don't have to wait on me! I can get one!"

"Oh...alright. I just wanted to..." Jaycee put his head down.

"Jaycee...oh my God! Babe, I'm sorry! It's just that you've done so much for me already. Come here, bro." Jaycee stepped up to me and I cupped my hand around the back of his neck pulling him close to me. I kissed him on the forehead then rested his head on my shoulder. "Hey, it's okay, love. I really appreciate it. I'm just not used to being treated like this."

Jaycee had his arms wrapped tightly around me. "It's just that I fear you may no longer need me." "Jaycee, my God," I buried my face in his hair, "I will always need you. I fucking love you."

Jaycee pulled away just enough to look at me. "Really?"

"Really! Hey, does that offer to get me a drink still stand? Come to think of it, I am really thirsty" I tousled his hair and brushed my lips across his.

"Of course! Janine mentioned you like Mojitos. I'll get you one!" He started to walk away. I took one of Jaycee's arms and pulled him back to me and kissed him. My God, his lips, the feel of that tight waist. I loved him so damn much. We continued to press our lips together, soft, wet and hot. My tongue begged for entrance, wanting Jaycee to open up and play. I felt his fangs lengthen. *'That's my brother!'* I gently parted my lips from his, my eyes looking into his red ones, as he took several breaths. Fuck, I don't know what came over me, but God, I've definitely got a thing for vampires! I felt a smile emerge from my lips. "I'll always need you, Jaycee."

"M-me… t-t-t-too!"

God, he was so adorable when he stuttered. He seemed to pick up my habit. Who would have thought I would be in the company of the most loving vampires, and with just a kiss? So, I kissed him again. Bad John, BAD! But oh, who the fuck was I kidding? I was enjoying every minute of it!

I could hear Luc giggle. "You *are* brothers!"

Poor Jaycee. His knees buckled and I quickly caught him. I felt bad, and outwardly I comforted him, but my Lord, if just a kiss from me does that to him.

"Whoa! I gotcha. I'm so sorry, Jaycee. Forgive me. I don't know what came over me! Yes. A Mojito would be perfect. Merci!" I embraced him and felt him gain control of himself.

"I so fucking love you, Jacques!" He whispered in my ear. "As I do you, precious Jaycee."

"I'll go get our drinks. Janine and Luc thought you would like to sit down and talk to us for a while. I'm sure you have questions."

"That would be great, Jaycee, but I was looking at Luc. Sooner or later I'm going to have to get my baby boy on the floor!"

Luc was oblivious to us. I watched him. The more I watched, the more my cock took notice. He was sex in motion. A fucking, dancing, *wet dream*! Every part of him, from his tight little ass, to his broad, powerful shoulders, moved with the music. Not once did he move more than three feet from me; his eyes never left me. The show he was putting on was meant for me and me alone.

*"Baby boy, I want to fuck you so damn bad! Have mercy on me!"*

*"Uuhnnh..."* Luc rubbed his crotch. *"I want you, baby!"*

Jaycee turned his attention, for a moment, to Luc as well.

"He sure is hot!" Jaycee whispered in my ear. His head shook from side to side and his smile beamed at his little brother.

"Hey!" I exclaimed to Jaycee. Pulling him by the upper arm, I placed a hand on his face and pulled him to me. "You're not so fucking bad yourself!" With that said, I leaned in to him again and kissed him. My tongue feeling his fangs once again extract and grow. *Oh, yeah!* "God, you are fucking hot, Jaycee! You better go get us those drinks!" I kissed him gently on the lips then ran my finger over them.

"I'll be back, Jacques. God, Luc is so lucky."

I ran my fingers through Jaycee's hair. "Yes, he is. He has three people, Jaycee, that would, and will, die for him."

A radiant smile came across Jaycee's face. He turned to go get our drinks. Shit, I just couldn't resist. I patted him on his perfect, hot ass.

Jaycee looked back. A smile spread across his face, framed by two exquisite pure white fangs.

Noticing Jaycee's departure, Luc immediately came to my side. Protectively, he wrapped one of his arms around my waist and pulled me close to him.

"Hi!"

"Hi yourself, Luc!"

"I love the way you move! God, Luc...has anyone told you how hot you are?"

"Yes, but in all my three hundred plus years, it never meant as much as it does when it comes from you."

"Luc, baby, Jaycee went to get us some drinks! You look thirsty, love." For the first time, I noticed his normally perfectly tanned skin looked pale. Preternatural.

"Yeah, I am."

"John?" Luc wrapped his arms around my waist, "Merci, mon cher."

"For what, love?"

"For loving my brother and Sire." His eyes gazed lovingly into mine.

"Oh God...Luc...You saw, didn't you? You know you have my

heart and soul. I...I...um. I didn't go too far, did I?"

"No, baby. I have never seen my brother so happy. I would never deprive him of that. I know you are mine."

"And I, Luc, am yours. Always."

Before I knew it, Luc's mouth was on mine. Our lips locked together in a mind-blowing kiss. Once again, his fangs extended, gently scraping my lips, but not enough to hurt. I noticed how careful he was. Heat, once again, scudded through my veins. It seemed to me that time stopped and everyone disappeared. It was just me and my lover. Luc embraced me, his hands gliding up and down my back. Oh shit, there it was, that sweet little whimper that sent chills through me.

*"I love you, baby boy."*

*"As I do you.*

Not wanting to, but needing air, I gently parted our lips. My hand gently touched his face and Luc leaned into my touch. Closing his eyes, he put his head to my chest.

"Luc?"

"Yes, John."

"Is there a place we could talk. I mean no disrespect. The music you picked for me is intoxicating and yes, I want to be out there feeling your body against mine, but I need to talk with you, our bro, and sis. I need to ask you something. Is that okay?"

"John, of course it's okay! I've got the perfect place and Jaycee and Janine just wanted you to get used to your surroundings. It's not like you walk into The House of Dracula every night!" He smiled, God love him.

"Oh shit, Luc...baby. I'm so sorry. It's just that..."

"Hey, lover." Luc's hand caressed my cheek. God, I loved it when he touched me. "This is a lot to absorb, to comprehend. We threw a lot at you the past two days. Besides, mon cher, you have your sister's concern weighing on you...literally!"

"Luc, I am so sorry about that!"

"Why, John?"

"Well, it's just that she is so over-protective of me sometimes, and I just wish that she would back off."

"John, love...hold on." Luc reached for my hand, his fingers wrapping around mine. "What if Janine hadn't been, what you call over-protective. Think about it, mon cher...you would not be here with us!"

I looked into Luc's eyes, his blue eyes. "God, Luc, you are so right. I know she is only thinking of my safety. She only has my best in mind, but she knows nothing...nothing at all. All she has are her damn assumptions."

"Give her time, John." Luc gave my hand a squeeze.

"With any luck, we'll have the chance to talk with her and her fiancé, Trace, is it?" I sensed he was as concerned as I was. God, I did not want to face Trace again.

"God, if only it would be that easy." My head fell to my chest.

"Baby. Come here!"

With that, I pressed myself into Luc's body. I felt his arms wrap themselves around me and his head came to rest on my chest. "It's going to be okay." His voice was a gentle whisper. "I promise."

There was no doubt that what Luc promised me was true. It *was* going to be okay. With my immortal lover at my side, I knew the decision I was going to make and what I was to become, was what I wanted. Life without Luc? I'd rather be dead!

"Hey, my gorgeous boys. Everything okay?"

I pulled back from Luc just enough to look at Janine. Concern showed on her expressive face. Leaning over, one arm wrapping around her waist, I pulled her close to Luc and myself. "It's more than okay, ma chere...it's perfect."

Janine placed a warm, soft kiss on our cheeks. "Follow me, boys. Jaycee is waiting for us in our suite."

"Suite?"

"You'll see, John...come! I have a feeling that there is something you want, no, *need* to tell us." With that, Luc took my hand, and with Janine leading the way, we followed. My eyes never left Luc.

# CHAPTER TWENTY-SIX

To describe the room as a suite was an understatement.  More like, I don't know, like a penthouse.

We had walked about halfway through the club to where a private elevator took us up three flights.  There we came upon a semi-circle shaped private room.  It took up the entire floor and overlooked the club and dance floor.  From the outside, the windows appeared to be pitch black.  As Janine approached, two large panes of glass parted into a sumptuous, elegantly appointed...shit...penthouse.  As we went in, the panels closed.  I turned and looked back as they slid closed, expecting to not see anything, but I was totally wrong.  One-way glass.  Every part of the club was visible from inside the suite.  The music echoed through the room much more quietly.  Large HD screens monitored the club.  Every angle of the building was being broadcast to the screens in real-time.

"John?"

"Yeah, Luc..."

"You like?"

"Yeah, a lot!" I felt his arm wrap around my waist, pulling me into him.

"You've got entry access now too!  Ownership has its privileges!"

"Jacques love, baby bro, come here.  Make yourselves comfortable." Jaycee took my hand and Luc's, and led us to an original seventeenth century, French provincial sofa. What I saw made me shake my head. Leave it to Jaycee.

"A love seat, Jaycee? Subtle!" I looked at him and smiled, shaking my head.

I could hear Janine giggle. "Jaycee, you are such a romantic. Good Lord, you vampires."

"What's that supposed to mean, Miss Wolf?" Jaycee chuckled.

Luc, I noticed, was starting to laugh. His mirth was so enjoyable that all I could do was watch him. His cheeks were red, and that giggle was driving me fucking mad. Laughter is contagious, and if Luc didn't stop, I was going to catch it...bad.

"Jacques, my love. One thing you'll find with vampires is they are suckers...oops...my bad...I mean..."

I felt so damn bad, but watching Janine start to blush was a rarity and a complete joy. I should feel bad for her, but I just smiled. To hear Janine, proper, reserved Janine, say Oops...my bad...? If they didn't watch it, Luc wouldn't be the only one who was now holding his side. Yep, he had lost it! Luc was beside himself. He was giggling so hard that he was having a hard time catching his breath. *'Good Lord, how my mighty vampire has fallen!'*

Laughing myself, I literally had to hold one of Luc's arms to keep him from falling on the floor. He was doubled over and was laughing so hard he was turning red.

"Breathe, baby boy! Breathe!" I tried to stay serious.

"Janine, my beautiful sister, please can we not get into this. The last thing Jacques needs is to hear about your views on how romantic you think we vampires are! Besides that, look at your baby brother for Pete's sake!" Jaycee's hand motioned toward Luc.

I looked at Janine and Jaycee while rubbing Luc's back. My God, he was so damn precious. I was trying to hold it together, but between Luc's laugh attack, and Jaycee's and Janine's psychoanalysis of vampire love, I just didn't know which I was enjoying more.

"Janine...Jay...hay...hay...cee...Oh God, please continue!" I couldn't help it. I was looking at them trying to hold Luc together and trying my hardest to hold *myself* together!

"Jacques...Janine has this belief that vampires are sentimental fools and love is the ultimate gift." "Janine, pardonnez-moi, but...um, I know this is extremely personal and I don't even want to mention his fucking name..." I needed to ask.

"No offense taken, my love. You're right, but I don't know if you know this? Wolves mate for life. Alec was not my mate."

"God, Janine. I'm sorry. Fuck, you were forced into it. How could I have forgotten? Shit...stupid, stupid, stupid!" I began to slap my forehead. I felt absolutely humiliated. "How could I be so insensitive?"

"Hey!" Luc quickly recovered from his laugh attack. "Stop that!" He pulled my hand away and kissed my forehead.

Janine had walked over to me and, kneeling down, she kissed me lightly on the lips. "Jacques, mon cher. Don't beat yourself up. You had so much thrown at you these past few days. I can't believe you didn't run straight back to the airport!"

I leaned toward Janine and embraced her. "Never! Je t'aime, Janine," I softly whispered in her ear.

"Je t'aime, precious Jacques, mon cher."

"Janine, I'm not going anywhere, my beautiful wolf!" I smiled and ran my hand through her thick, black hair. I could only imagine her in wolf form. That same soft, sensuous, black hair. I felt a warmth flow through me. I guess knowing that vampires and werewolves were real, and I had the privilege of loving three of them, had an effect on me. How could it not?

She softly smiled at me, and taking my hand, she lightly kissed it.

Standing, Janine pulled a chair closer to Luc and me. Jaycee was returning from the other side of the room with a silver tray and our drinks. "Jacques, I believe this is yours!" He handed me my Mojito, the fresh mint swirling through the sweet intoxicating beverage.

"Merci, Jaycee!" I took a sip. "Now, that has to be the best Mojito I have ever tasted."

Luc leaned into me. "Remember what I said lover? Only the best for you!"

In the meantime, Jaycee handed Luc and Janine the same thick red wine they enjoyed so much. With a glass in hand, Jaycee pulled up another chair next to Janine and sat down. We were now in a small, intimate circle. Jaycee had turned off the monitors and music; we were in complete silence.

"Jacques," Jaycee looked into my eyes, "We know you have many questions you want to ask. Is it okay if I ask you just one before we start?"

"Jaycee, of course. Please, ask." I hadn't a clue what Jaycee had on his mind, but at this point no question would go unanswered.

"It's three a.m., Jacques. Would you prefer to get some rest?" I looked into Jaycee's eyes and noticed the genuine concern coming from him. "We don't really require sleep, but, mon cher, you must be exhausted." Jaycee continued. I was deeply touched by his concern for my well-being.

"Jaycee, love. Thank you for your concern, but with everything that is going through my mind, I fear all I would do is stare at the ceiling."

Luc giggled. I turned to him and kissed his forehead. "You, Luc, are a naughty, naughty boy!"

"Would that be so bad? Besides, wouldn't you still be staring…?" I actually heard Jaycee gasp.

"Luc! Really?" Jaycee stammered and Janine, well let's just say the expression on her face was a conflict of emotions. I didn't know if she was going to scold Luc or laugh. She just shook her head.

"Luc…if I've said it once, I've…"

"Yes, Jaycee. I'm incorrigible. I'm sorry, I just can't help myself. I'm in love."

"Don't we know!" Janine grinned.

"Seriously, babe. Do you need to get some rest?" Luc brushed my cheek with his hand.

"Oh, my sweet boy, I'm in love too! I'm fine! I want this. I need this." I took another sip from my drink.

"Jacques, my beloved brother. Just let us know when you want to rest!"

"I promise, Janine. Merci!" I held up my glass and my new family did the same. "Before we go on, I just wanted to say thank you! I love you all so very much!" Turning to Luc, I continued. "My life before this really had no meaning. I'm just plain, ordinary me. The three of you have brought me so much joy, love, and happiness. I don't know how to repay you. Luc, I adore you, cherish you, and above all, I love you with my body and soul. You have my heart…and…" My breath hitched. "I belong to you." On cue, there it was, his whimper. That's all I needed to hear. I brushed my fingers across his lips and, with my thumb, wiped the tear falling down his face.

I turned and looked at Jaycee and continued on. "Jaycee, you know how much you mean to me, how much I admire you for what you did to protect Janine and Luc. I love you in so many ways. For what you've given me… my Luc, I will cherish you all the days of my life."

Finally, looking into Janine's emerald green eyes, I took in a deep breath. "Janine, my love, you are a vision. My belle, my lady, my beautiful wolf. You take my breath away. God only knows how much I love you. For without you… I felt a knot form in my throat...I would not be here."

Our crystal clinked together. We each took a drink of our beverage. Then, as our eyes met each other's, I realized just how blessed I was.

After a brief pause, Luc got up and walked over to his Sire.

With one hand on Jaycee's face, he leaned in and kissed him. I will never get over the sight of Luc and Jaycee kissing. Now, having the facts, it made my heart thud and my knees knock together. The love they showed each other held me in a spell that I could not, and did not want to, break away from. Then, turning to his sister, Luc got down on his knees and gently put his head on her chest. Janine put a hand to his back and stroked his thick, shaggy hair. Luc looked up at her as if asking her a question. She smiled and nodded.

Something was going on. What, I didn't know, but whatever it was, it was something that was going to impact this family more than anything has in decades. Hell, centuries. I could only watch. Luc got up and turned to me. His pearl white fangs had descended, his eyes were red, and once again a tear fell down his cheek. This time that tear was blood red.

I put my drink down and stood up. Suddenly the only thing I wanted to do was wrap my arms around Luc and comfort him, but I realized by the soft, loving smile on his face, it was not a tear of sorrow, it was a tear of absolute joy.

I slowly approached Luc as he walked towards me. We met, and with no hesitation I wrapped my arms around his waist, pulling him close to me. "Hey, Luc." Looking into his eyes, I took one of my fingers and wiped away his tear. Not caring, I put my finger to my mouth and tasted his blood.

"Oh God, Jacques...you shouldn't." Jaycee's voice was trembling.

"It's okay, Jaycee. I can't let this moment go by. There is only one question that I wish to ask of you and Janine. May I?"

"Of course, Jacques." Janine and Jaycee, I noticed, were at the edge of their seats looking at Luc and me.

I once again looked directly into Luc's eyes. "You both know how much I love Luc. He is all I want. A mortal lifetime with him is...is...oh God, Luc...it's not enough!" Luc pressed himself against me. I took my hand and gently pulled his head to my chest.

"John, I love you so fucking much. Go on...s'il vous plait?" I felt Luc's body trembling against mine.

"Luc, babe." My fingers ran through his hair. "You, Luc, are the reason I live, the reason I want to live. Without you, Luc, life has no reason...no meaning. Since I met you, I just want to be with you. I can't seem to get close enough to you. I am poisoned by mortality and it seems, Luc, you are the cure for what is ailing me. The only cure. Please, Luc. Kiss me and make me better."

"John." Luc took in a deep breath. "What have I done to deserve you? Without you, my life would have no meaning. I wouldn't want to go on. For centuries I have waited for you, dreamed of you. I love you so much, John."

I turned to Jaycee and Janine. I knew by the serene smiles on their faces they approved.

"I love you both so much. Luc is my life. Jaycee. Janine. I want Luc to turn me. I want him to make me one with him." There was no question that I was nervous, but there was no question that I would change my mind.

"Jacques, mon cher. Precious Jacques, are you sure?" Jaycee stood up.

"I know we told you it is your decision." She paused and looked at Luc. He nodded. "Earlier Luc had a concern he shared with me. He is frightened that you may grow tired of him. After all, Jacques, eternity is a long time."

I wrapped my arms tighter around Luc. "Janine...never. The only thing I'm frightened of...I kissed Luc's forehead...is a world without him. A world where I would have to say goodbye to him. I just can't accept that. I won't accept that!"

Janine too, had stood up.

I turned back to Luc who was still in my embrace. Tilting his chin up, I gazed into his misty, blue eyes. "Luc, you are my only. We can't and won't say goodbye. I know what I've got to be...immortal. I want to make my journey through eternity with you, only you. I have found a dream that has come true. I am yours, and we need not say goodbye. With all my love for you, we will never say goodbye." Luc's breath hitched. I knew I had completely thrown him.

Fuck, I didn't blame him. I actually knew what was going through his head. Yes, I could pick up on his feelings. *'That's new.'* A warmth rushed through me as he looked at me.

Jaycee and Janine were in tears. I knew all they wanted to do was come to us and hold us, but with the respect due this moment in time, they sat back down. Their hands interlocked with each other.

"John, my love. In my lifetime I have never heard such a sincere and beautiful declaration of love. I'm still trying to figure out what I did to deserve you?" I felt his love for me to the very depths of my soul.

"You don't have to, Luc. Please, babe. Don't worry yourself with those thoughts... ever!" Luc had been worrying his lower lip with one of his fangs. I gently reached a finger to his lower lip and, leaning into the touch, he relaxed. "That's my boy!"

"Janine?" I could hear Jaycee whisper to his sister. *'Interesting'.* "Should we give our boys some privacy?"

"No." I answered without releasing my gaze from Luc's. "Unless my baby boy would rather be alone. Would you, Luc?" I asked.

"I...I...no...John. Whatever you want." I felt Luc's body trembling next to mine.

I turned my head to look at Jaycee and Janine. "Please stay, at least for a while. Please?"

"Of course, Jacques." Janine whispered and nodded.

"Jacques, we are honored that you would allow us to share such an intimate moment with your beloved." Jaycee's sincerity was overwhelming; he was simply beautiful.

The emotions in the room were palpable.

"Jacques," Janine added, "You, mon cher, have our full support and most importantly, our love. This is something we have wished for Luc for such a long time. We are forever grateful it is you that guards our brother's heart."

"Janine, I will guard your brother's heart for eternity. This I swear to you." Then, looking at Jaycee, "I swear to you as well."

"John?" I felt Luc's hand squeeze my arm.

"Yes, love?" The back of my hand caressed his face.

"Um... You... you tasted my blood. Babe, do you know what that means?"

"Yes, baby boy, I do. Like I asked you...kiss me and make me better!"

"But, John..." I felt his concern for me. "You must have so many questions?"

"Luc, my boy, I have the best teacher. My mind is made up. Nothing you could say or do could or would have stopped me from what I did. Nothing could stop me from wanting to spend an eternity with you. Understand?"

"Oui..."

"Merci, my precious boy." I whispered.

Then, leaning forward, I pressed my lips to his and kissed him gently. The warmth I felt coming from his lips ran through my body and warmed me to my very soul.

"Here, Luc, let's sit down." I led him back to the sofa. I noticed Janine and Jaycee were looking somewhat awkward. "Jaycee...Janine... Join Luc and I, please!"

They looked at me hesitantly. "Hey! It's us! I can see it in your eyes! I don't need words from either of you. Yes, I have questions...God knows I have questions, but do you think for one moment the answers would change my mind. Absolutely not!"

The concern in the room was dissipating. Here I was, a mere mortal, calming two vampires and a werewolf. *'Stay on track John...stay on track.'*

"Janine, may I?" My hand reached for the wine glass she was holding.

"Of course." She handed it to me. "What is it, love?"

I took a moment to study the contents. "I am ninety-nine and nine-tenths percent sure...I swirled the thick, red liquid and looked at it, as if testing a fine wine...This is blood, right?"

"But, John..." Luc looked at me..."Um, you know?"

"Luc, my love, vampires? You don't think I see you pick at your food? But you savor this drink like you would a bottle of eighteen sixty-five Chateau Laffite! Pardonnez-moi, with no disrespect, if that's what it was, I'm sure you would be sharing it? No? Damn! I'm really sorry, but my sister knew. She shared her opinion about it when we were having lunch in the park. But for what it's worth, I just thought you and Jaycee were picky eaters."

"You've got yourself one smart man, little brother. You had better make sure you hang on to him!" A smile started to form on Jaycee's face. Oh, thank God!

"Believe me, bro, I plan on it!" Luc's answer was meant for his brother. His look was meant for me.

"Janine, my stunning wolf, I watched you devour your food! Ma chere, forgive me, but only the best cuts of beef and rabbit. Sweetheart, you are *not* a vegetarian! You, my love, happen to be the most beautiful carnivore I have ever seen, let alone loved!"

Jaycee was getting that look on his face. The one that appears right before he usually embarrasses his little brother under the table. Not this time if I could help it.

"Ah, Jaycee?" I half turned towards him.

"Yes, detective. Do I need to come down to the precinct with you?" He smirked.

"Smartass." I chuckled. "Can I get you something? A nice roast beef sandwich? A pork chop? How about a pizza?" I laughed, but not to embarrass. "Jaycee, you and Luc have the same identical eating habits. You *don't*, you goof!"

I looked back at Luc. He was just sitting there with this shit-eating grin on his face. "This is so sweet...finally...John got you, bro!" Luc giggled. Jaycee blushed.

"There. This is exactly what I want. I am so lucky and all I want to do is make you happy. I mean no disrespect, I just wanted you to know that I fucking love you! Being who you are has no effect on how I feel about you. You all made my decision so easy."

I turned my attention to my boy. "Luc?"

"Yes, love?" He reached for my hand and squeezed it.

"I have so many questions, but like I told you earlier, I have made my mind up. I knew it even before I tasted your blood, babe. It's either life with you for an eternity or life is not worth living." I kissed Luc. No doubts about what I wanted. What I wanted was my baby boy. From the feelings I was getting from Luc, they were mutual. What the hell! Oh my God! Suddenly, with no warning, a sharp pain radiated through my stomach. I grabbed at it. *'Aahh crap!'*

"Fuck...Luc...baby. Uuhhh! God in heaven...Luc?" The pain was so intense I grabbed him and doubled over in his lap.

"Damn! Luc!" Jaycee jumped up and moved to my other side.

"Luc, honey. It's happening!" Janine ran to us and knelt down.

"Luc? What's happening to me? Fuck, it hurts!" I felt my hands dig into his thighs, doubling up in pain that I had never felt in my life.

I felt Luc rubbing my forehead.

I could feel Jaycee rub my arms and legs. "Hang on, Jacques. It's going to be OKAY!" My sight was getting blurry, but I could see Jaycee looking at me, trying his best to reassure me.

In the midst of the worst pain of my life, I could hear Janine. *"Yes...Christian! Sam! S'il vous plait! Oh God, hurry...we need your help! It's Jacques!"*

Another spasm of pain hit me. Luc and Jaycee held onto me and I hung onto them. I felt their concern, but for some reason I also knew that they knew what was happening and I was going to be okay. "I...I...uunnhh...I love you."

"Baby...hang on!" Luc's voice tried to remain calm. His hand continued to caress my forehead.

"Bro, Luc has the cure. Hang on, mon cher!" Jaycee's voice sounded like it was miles away. "Tell them to hurry, sis!"

*"Yes, tell Adrian to bring the limo around to the private exit! Do not leave Adrian or the limo out of your sight! Oui. Yes...It's time...Merci."* Janine finished. I looked up at her.

"Janine...God... I...can't...breathe!" I gasped for air.

"Yes you can, Jacques, mon cher. Yes you can." I felt Janine's fingers run through my hair. "Sam is on his way and Christian will meet us with Adrian! We are taking you to Luc's place."

Despite the excruciating pain I was in, my heart skipped a beat when I heard Luc say "Our place, sis." "Hear that, baby...Luc turned my face so I could see him...It's for you and me now, John. *Our home."*

Another jolt of pain hit me. Like a thousand needles being stuck into my skin and a knife slowly being thrust into my gut. I held tight to Luc, needing to feel him against me. *"Ours* babe?"

"Yes. Ours." I felt a tear fall on my face. It was Luc's.

"Luc, honey, don't cry. Jacques needs you. Be strong and brave, little brother. I know how much you love Jacques. Just think, soon you'll share an eternal love. You need your strength. Sam should be here momentarily." Janine started toward the elevator doors.

As if on cue, I heard the private elevator doors opening.

Everything was going black. I reached for, and found, one of Luc's hands. "I...love...you...Luc." I felt him squeeze my hand. I heard him say he loved me too. I saw Sam. Then...nothing.

# ❧ CHAPTER TWENTY-SEVEN ❧

Pain. Unbearable pain. My insides felt like they were being ripped apart. I was burning up; my skin felt like it was on fire. Fuck! It was so hard to breathe and to move. The voice I knew and loved was calling to me, but I couldn't make out what my lover was saying. It felt like I was dying. Oh my God! I *was* dying, and Luc, my precious Luc, I would never have the chance to be with him. My hopes, my dreams, gone...just fucking gone. Well, Elena...are you happy now? Looks like you fucking won...again! Then I felt another sharp, stabbing pain in my stomach, ripping me from unconsciousness to realize what I thought and hoped for was not a nightmare, but something very real.

"Oh my God!" I grabbed my stomach at the same time sitting up. "No, I don't want to fucking die! Luc? God, baby...save me!" I cried out. "Luc, baby boy, where are you?" Strong arms came from behind me and wrapped themselves tightly around my chest. Gently, but firmly, I felt myself being pulled back and coming to rest on the chest of someone I knew so very well.

"Easy, baby! I have you. I am right here for you." It was Luc. I grabbed the strong arms that were holding me as another wave of pain went through my body. "John, sweetheart, listen to me! I know it fucking hurts, but you have to listen to me!" His voice was soft and God, so sweet. He sounded so confident and sure. I clung to his words with a steely grip, not wanting to slip away.

"Yeah, baby. Just please...uunnhh...please make the pain go away!"

"I will, my love, I will!"

"What's...oh God, Luc...what's happening?"

"Babe...remember when you wiped my tear from my face and tasted it?"

Amidst the hellish torture I was going through, I remembered. "Yyy...eess...of course."

"You, God, baby...you started the process. You ingested my blood, vampire blood."

"You mean..."

"Yes, baby...your mortal body is dying."

"No, Luc. God no! I can't leave you...not now! We've only just begun."

Luc brought a hand up and wiped the sweat soaked bangs from my forehead. Running his fingers through my hair, he pulled my head back and nestled my face into the crook of his shoulder.

"Oh shit, Luc..." I grabbed my stomach. "It hurts so damn bad!"

"I know baby, I know." I felt him kiss my forehead. "John, my love, do you trust me?"

"Of course, baby...with my fucking life!"

"Then God, John, please listen to me. I need you to let me take care of you. Is that okay? Do you want to join me...to become immortal?"

Another shot of pain ripped through me. "Oh fuck that hurt! Wait...what? Immortal? Like you, babe?"

"Yes, my love, like me." His voice hitched. "If that is what you truly want? Is it babe? To be like me...a vampire?" His voice was soft and so sweet.

"You...uuhnnn...you know I do, baby! Oh Jesus, Luc...uuhnh. It hurts so damn bad!" Through the pain, I remembered Jaycee and Janine explaining that I had to give Luc permission.

"Luc...oh fuck...yes, mon cher...make me yours! God, Luc, I love you so much...I want to be with you forever. Please...I am yours! Uunnh! Baby, yes...yes...do...uuhnnh...do it!"

And there it was, his soft, sweet whimper.

"God, John...of course, my love! I know it hurts like a son-of-a-bitch, but I need you to do something for me!"

"Anything, Luc!"

"I know this is going to be difficult, but can you lay down on your back for me?"

"Fuck, Luc...uuhhh. Anything for you, baby boy!"

Luc helped me move over on the bed. For the first time since I started my descent into hell, I noticed Luc and I were completely void of clothes. Our naked bodies touching and pressing against each other. God, even in this horrific pain it felt so good to be this close to my lover. We pressed against each other. Fuck, through all the pain, I could only look and realize that this beautiful creature would be mine, as I would be his, for fucking ever. As gently as Luc could, he helped me into a fully supine position. My head nestled on a down pillow. As weak as I was, I needed to touch him, feel him. Reaching up, I let my hands wander across his young, muscular, timeless body. His skin was smooth and warm; his muscles defined and hard. For just a moment I watched him react to my touch. *'Yes, for fucking ever.'* For I have found a dream that has come true.

Another wave of pain went through me. I fisted the sheets. Luc had been straddling my hips, but seeing the agony I was in, he gently laid down, his arms wrapping around me.

"Baby, I know it hurts. Wrap your arms around me and do what you must to help yourself through. Grab me, scratch me. Just let me tend to you. Share your pain with me, lover, share it! Understand?" Luc's eyes were red. He looked deeply into mine. I felt his fingers caressing my face. I felt his love for me warm me from my head to my toes. My eyes never left his.

"I don't want to hurt you, baby boy." I pleaded.

"Baby...let me take the pain...fucking do it for me! I want this! It's the least I can do for the hell you're going through for me!" His eyes glistened with tears, yet his voice was steady and sure.

"Uuunnhhhh. Okay, Luc. I...love...you." With all the strength I could find, I ran my fingers through his hair and pulled his lips to mine, that same warmth flowing through me as our lips brushed over each other's.

"I love you too, John. More than you will ever know. It will be over with soon, babe."

I didn't think the pain could get worse, but it did. What felt like a dagger pierced my heart and sent me over the edge of reason. My fingers dug into Luc's back and tore down it. Fuck, there it was, that precious whimper. He did not turn his attention away from me. He didn't even flinch.

"That's it, John. Let me feel your pain. Let me take it from you!" Never once did Luc lose his composure. He looked at me with enough strength and confidence for the both of us. *'I love him so much!'*

For a moment the pain seemed to subside. Luc's eyes, now deep red, looked into mine. All I saw was his pure love for me. His fangs were now fully extended. Kissing me lightly on my lips, he took his hand and lovingly tilted my head, exposing my neck.

"It's time, babe," he whispered in my ear while softly caressing my neck.

I felt no fear, just the desire to feel his fangs penetrate me. All the times I thought of this moment... it was all coming back to me. God Almighty, I wanted this. Another wave of pain shot through my body. I sank my nails into Luc's biceps. "Unnnhh...Luc...unnhh...do it baby...make me yours!"

"My beloved, John." Red tears streamed down Luc's face.

"Kiss me, Luc. You are my only cure!" My hand wrapped around the base of Luc's neck and pulled him toward me. I felt his warm breath against my neck.

"God, John, I love you, mon cher. You...you, John are mine!" With that, I felt Luc's fangs penetrate my neck.

"God yes, Luc... yes!" My fingers dug into his shoulders. I suddenly found myself somewhere between agony and ecstasy. Luc's warm, naked body pressed tightly against mine, muscled flesh to muscled flesh. I felt his warm lips against my neck, his sharp fangs found their mark, just as I had imagined. Luc began to suck on my throat, drinking in my blood. He was so gentle, so loving. God, it felt so good. My arms wrapped around his back and my legs around his waist. My baby boy, my lover, my partner, my Sire. Fuck, despite the agony and the pain, I wouldn't have traded it for the fucking world.

"Luc?" I felt myself getting weaker. "What's? What's happening?" I looked into my lover's eyes.

Red tears continued to flow from his eyes.

"I've drained you to the point of death, mon cher." He gently licked at the wound on my neck.

"Damn, my book had it right." I whispered.

"John, my love. Only you...only you could joke at a time like this." Luc managed a small laugh, though his concern and his love for me were evident. He had one goal, to save me. No, to make me immortal, a vampire.

"Baby...I...I..."

"Shhhh, don't talk." Luc pressed his forehead to mine, his strong arms now wrapped tightly around me. I could barely move.

"John, my love...You are mine...forever!" His mouth, lips, red from my blood, brushed over mine.

Soft and sweet. His eyes, once again blue, and his fangs had retracted. *'My baby boy. My vampire.'*

I looked at him with bleary eyes, my body barely responding. I could feel my heart beating so slow I thought it had stopped. Through sheer determination I kept my arms and legs wrapped tightly around him, not wanting to let go.

"Hey!" He brushed the sweat-soaked bangs from my forehead. "There is one more thing you need to do for me."

"I know, Luc." I dragged in a breath.

Luc knelt up, his legs straddling me at the waist. Taking his arm to his mouth, he tore open a wound and blood began to course from it. "Here, love. Drink! Drink from me, my love. We will be joined." Luc's breath hitched. "We will be joined together for an eternity."

As weak as I was, I took my hands and pulled his arm to mine with no hesitation. I could taste his sweet blood flow into my mouth. I started gently at first, but then as his life blood began to course through me, it was if I was becoming one with Luc. Just like he said, every one of Luc's thoughts, every memory, like fleeting pictures, went through my mind. My love for him grew into a living thing. I could feel a renewed strength start to course through my body. The pain and agony I was going through was vanishing as quickly as its initial onslaught. As my strength came back, I realized Luc was struggling, growing weaker. Yes, he was giving, and, God in heaven, I was taking. I had to stop. Luc had given enough. My mouth gently parted and at that moment I looked at him. What I saw took my breath away. Fuck, he was more beautiful than before. Was that possible? His head was thrown back, his eyes half closed. Luc was halfway between agony and ecstasy, just like I had been feeling. Sweat cascaded down his forehead to his face. His body was glistening with the effort it took to save me. My God! What I saw took my breath away. Sweat glistened across his defined pecs and his six pack abs.

Sweat trailed down the fine line of black hair towards his cock. Even giving himself to me, he was abso-fucking-lutely perfect. Immediately, with a new strength I had never felt before, I pulled him to me. Pressing my hand against the back of his head, I felt him relax into me, his head falling to my chest. I kissed him on the head, smelling the soft, masculine scent of his thick, shaggy, black hair. God Almighty, he smelled so good! My Luc.

"Luc, my love...are you okay?" My lips brushed against his cheek. Silence.

"Mon cher? Luc?" I nuzzled his neck.

"Ummm." I felt him cuddle closer to me, his muscular body pressing into mine. His face tucked into my neck, where he had just fed.

"My Sire." *'Did I just say that?'* "Are you okay?"

Lifting his head, he smiled. "Never better, John." His voice was still a little shaky.

I whimpered... "I...I didn't hurt you, did I? Do you need blood, baby?" I held one of my arms up. My eyes, full of worry, looked into his.

"Oh, lover, you do have some things to learn!" Luc giggled as he softly smiled at me. "The question, John, is not about me! I'm fine! How are you feeling?"

"Much um, much...Fuck, Luc...I feel great! Luc, baby, I knew it!" For the first time since the ordeal started, I felt myself smiling.

"Knew what, my love?" Luc returned my smile. *'Could it be any bigger?'*

"You kissed me and made me better!" I giggled. I couldn't help it. Wrapping my arms and legs around him, I proceeded to press light kisses on his forehead, his face, neck, shoulders...anywhere I could! There it was, a sound I will cherish for our eternity together, that sweet whimper. Every time I hear that coming from Luc my heart sings!

For a moment, time stopped as I watched him look at me. He rubbed his nose against mine and then gently kissed me. This time I tasted the sweetness of *our* blood moistening my lips.

"Your kiss, baby...your kiss. Please kiss me again! God, Luc, my Sire, my baby boy...kiss me, mon cher!"

Gently my lover pressed his mouth to mine, his tongue begging entrance. I let him in; I gave as good as I got. He kissed me with pure, passionate love. Parting his mouth from mine, Luc looked at me and asked "Are you sure you're okay?" His hand gently caressed my face.

"Of course, baby boy! I feel so good! So alive!" I had been so attentive to Luc that I hadn't noticed the sun coursing through the window.

"Um, Luc?"

"Yes, love?"

"Ah, I've seen you and Jaycee in it before, but...?"

"But what, John?" Luc's eyebrow arched, making him look a little confused. "The sun?"

"You know, lover, we are going to have to keep you away from those books you read!"

"Your heart, Luc. It's...It's still, well... It's still beating!"

"Of course! So is yours! Hey." He put two of his fingers on my lips. "No more questions, my love, but may I show you something?"

I had noticed that Luc had not taken his eyes off of me since I fed on him. A soft, precious smile framed his face.

"Of course, Luc!" I couldn't believe how incredible I felt. Neither could my cock.

As Luc leaned over me, his body rubbed over mine. He was reaching for something on the nightstand.

I felt his stiff erection brush against mine. "Fuck, Luc, being immortal has its advantages!"

"Ah, yes it does, John." He waggled his eyebrows. "Look!" He had picked up a mirror that sat on the nightstand.

I took it from his hand and hesitantly lifted it towards my face. The story of Dorian Gray flashed through my head. *'God, John, that was random!'* "I can't, Luc...I just can't! I'm sure I'm still me."

"Want to bet? You, John, are taking my breath away. And God, babe, you are, and were, fucking hot!" Luc shot me a sexy, wicked grin.

"Were?" I said, with just a bit of confusion in my voice.

"Just look at yourself, John!" His fingers were running through...oh crap...was that my imagination, or did my hair seem...hesitantly I lifted the mirror to my face. I was shocked, stunned, and overwhelmed! There, to my surprise, was a face that I had not seen for quite a few years.

"John, love, you reverted back to the time you reached full physical maturity. It's a little different for each of us, but always late teens to mid-twenties."

"You mean...No...It can't be! I'm twenty-one again?"

"Oh yeah, eternally twenty-one! Fuck, babe, just FUCK!"

"But?" I looked in the mirror again. Reaching up, I touched my face, my young face.

"Baby, you've been through so much! I have an eternity to teach you. I promise love. I will tell you everything."

"God, Luc!" My head jolted up off the pillow. I looked over his shoulder, at his back. "I hurt you!" "Did you?" He gently nuzzled my neck.

My hands gently touched his shoulders, where just minutes before I felt like I was ripping his skin off. "But no...Where are the marks? I remember...God, Luc, I was clawing at your back...I was hurting you!"

"John, I'm surprised!" A smile curled up on his face as he propped his chin up on one hand. "Vampire 101. We heal, babe!"

"God, Luc. I feel like such an idiot. Here I'm questioning scratches on your back and I just became twenty-one again!"

"Silly boy!" He pulled me into a mind-numbing kiss, then rolled off me onto his side. His body remained tightly pressed against mine. "Seriously, my love. Are you sure you're okay?" Luc's hand ran up and down my chest.

Swinging my leg over his waist, propping my head up, I looked at Luc. I really looked at him. Such clarity. God, could it be? He truly was even more beautiful! I just couldn't get over it. Pure, preternatural perfection.

"I'm...I'm...Luc, love...I don't know how to explain it. I don't hurt. I feel like I could run a marathon. All my senses have been heightened and, Luc?"

"Yes, love?" His one eyebrow raised.

"I feel you in me."

Luc looked down at his waist. "Well, babe, um, no...Not yet anyway!" Once again he waggled his eyebrows and giggled.

Smiling and letting one of my hands ghost over his sweet ass, I too had to giggle. "No, not that way lover. I meant, I mean...Oh Christ, Luc, what I mean is..."

Luc possessively tightened his grip on me. "John, I know exactly what you mean. You're feeling me. My feelings, my emotions. Right?"

"Yeah, babe! That's it!" I ran my hand down Luc's face.

"John, you know the closeness that Jaycee and I have, right?"

"Of course, Luc. He's your Sire!"

"Now I am yours! When you drank from me, you became a part of me. Babe, you're going to notice things, well, like you are now!"

"Like?" My curiosity piqued.

"Like, babe...my physical pain...my thoughts. Things like my..." Luc reached down and wrapped my hand around his rock hard cock "...desire for you! Welcome to immortality, love!"

"Uunhh...baby boy...God, I want you so bad!"

"I can tell!" Luc smiled as he looked down at my hand wrapped firmly around his erect cock.

I felt Luc's hand travel down my side to my thigh. His hand found what he wanted, and as he wrapped his hand around mine, I leaned in and kissed him. "What the...?" I felt something pierce my lip and it wasn't Luc. "What the...?" I repeated.

Luc giggled. "What did I tell you, mon cher! They *are* so damn hot!"

My tongue ran across my teeth, across my two newly-acquired fangs. "Oh. My. God!" I giggled at the new discovery. "I'm a...I'm..."

"Go ahead, baby...say it!" My baby boy's face was beaming.

"A vampire! I'm a vampire!" I smiled so big it felt like my face was going to break!

"Jesus, John! You are abso-fucking-lutely perfect! You're MINE! Fuck...just FUCK!" Luc's eyes, deep red, burned into mine with an X-rated stare that sent heat scorching through my veins. His arms wrapped possessively around me and pulled me close. Muscular heat to muscular heat.

I couldn't take my eyes off of my boy. He was so damn happy, and no one, not Elena, Trace, Alec, no one would fucking touch him. I made a vow and I will do anything to protect Luc. I mean anything.

"Fuck! Yeah, baby, I'm all yours! It's you, Luc. Only you!" I wrapped myself tightly around my lover and strongly, passionately, kissed him, nipping at his lips like an aggressive pup.

"Make love to me, Luc! I want you so bad! I need you so bad!"

"We will, lover, but, and this is important, what you are feeling, it's all new. You, love, need to rest. I promise you," He gave me a chaste kiss. "That is the first thing on my agenda...after..."

"We sleep?" I questioned with a definite frown on my face.

"Yes, my love, we sleep. I promise, lover," Luc looked into my eyes. "I'll make it worth your wait." Smiling, he brushed his fingers over my mouth.

As an afterthought, and before I could even think about what was coming out of my mouth, I asked "Where are they?" I looked around the bedroom.

"Where is what, mon cher?"

"The caskets?" I squeaked. I actually fucking squeaked.

"Oh, John! What, in the name of all that is holy, am I going to do with you?" Luc tousled my hair. "I can arrange that, but wouldn't you be more comfortable here in bed with me?"

"God, yes! Je t'aime, Luc! I brushed my lips against his, while wrapping my arms and legs around him, pulling his body tightly against mine.

"Je t'aime aussi, my vampire John!" The smile on his face, framed by those two perfect fangs, took my breath away.

For an eternity, the young man that I had come to know and love, cherish and adore, would be mine...ALL MINE!

"Luc, I love you, baby boy! I really do!" My hand brushed his face.

"I love you too," Luc's lips parted into a huge smile, "My baby boy!" He giggled.

"Huh?" My eyes widened in surprise.

"Well, think about it love. I was turned at twenty-one and..."

"Oh crap...Luc!" Sudden awareness hit me! "I'm..."

"Twenty-one!" Luc answered. "Like I said, *my* baby boy!"

Possessively, I wrapped my arms around this man. This man who quite literally pulled me from the darkness of impending death to the promise of eternal life.

"Luc? Mon cher?"

"Yes, John?"

"I...I don't know how to..."

Then it happened. Nothing supernatural, nothing preternatural. I yawned!

I could feel myself turning ten shades of red, but Luc, God bless him, said nothing. He just smiled and shook his head. His eyes twinkled in the early morning sun and I felt his fingers intertwine with mine.

"Luc." I was so embarrassed, I couldn't even look at him. Here I was, a newly-born vampire, and I yawned. "Pardonnez-moi."

"John, what is there to forgive?" Then at that moment, a moment in time that I would cherish for an eternity, another first, Luc yawned too! "Come closer, John." Luc's hand gripped my waist and pulled me tighter to him. A soft smile formed on his face and, without words, he was letting me know everything was going to be okay. More than okay. Perfect!

I put my head on his shoulder and the soft rise and fall of his chest was like a lullaby. Before I knew it, I, for the first time, slept the sleep of an immortal.

# ❧ CHAPTER TWENTY-EIGHT ❧

I woke in the same position that I was in when I fell asleep; pressed tightly against my still sleeping Sire, on my side, my face resting on Luc's chest. We hadn't moved. For a moment I held my breath. Finally, there it was, almost non-existent, the slow and deep intake of air. The slight feeling of panic that welled up inside of me subsided as I confirmed that Luc was still with me. Is this how I had slept? I watched and waited for Luc to repeat this simple action. *'There. OKAY, John. You can relax.'* Honestly, if someone who didn't know any better were watching us, well, we looked like we were...Dead.

For all intents and purposes, I had lost track of reality. Damn, it was a mystery just knowing what time it was. I didn't even know what day it was. *'What the hell! Who cares?'* I rubbed my eyes and put a finger to my lips. I felt a stinging sensation. *'What the fuck?'* I thought. I put a finger in my mouth and...Fangs! I smiled to myself, remembering my discovery from before we went to sleep. Yeah, I felt like an idiot, but this was no dream. I AM a vampire! I was fascinated. My finger continued to feel the smoothness, and yes, the razor sharp tips.

"Enjoying yourself?" A sleepy voice greeted me. Luc reached and softly ran his hand across my face, causing immediate arousal.

"Huh?" I could feel my teeth retract back to their normal length. I could also feel myself blush. I lifted my head off Luc's shoulder and timidly looked into his eyes. His hair was rumpled and he had the most adorable smile on his face. His fingers gently brushed across my shoulders and, once again, that warmth ran through me as they trailed up and down my spine. God, I loved how he loved to touch me.

"Oh crap! Bonjour, baby boy. I'm...I...I was..."

"Hey," Luc's fingers ran up the base of my neck and he started to play with my hair. "I don't blame you. Besides, I'm going to have to be just a touch concerned." He looked so damned serious.

"Why, Luc?" I said with a worried tone, my eyebrows drawing together in a questioning look.

"Because...You are just too fucking hot of a vampire! I mean, God, I love the feel of this floppy mop of hair you have!" He gently tugged at it, momentarily distracted. Luc's hand and fingers played with my hair. Stroking and feeling my blonde locks, his eyes were transfixed on what he held. I watched him, and a giddiness that I had not felt for a long time, swept through me. I watched my Sire find absolute joy in what he was doing.

"Don't stop, Luc." I let out a soft moan. "Please, lover. Don't ever stop!"

"I can't, baby boy. You are so damn beautiful. What have I done to deserve this?"

I felt myself blush. I was still trying to get used to the radical change and transformation that my body underwent when I became a...Breathe, John...A vampire!

"You, lover, are beyond words!" Luc said, his eyes still showing concern. "Luc, now let me get this straight. You are concerned?"

"Well...Um... Yes." He said sheepishly.

"Why in heaven would you ever even think? Luc, look at me!" I realized my tone was a little harsh, but I was worried. Worried that Luc had nothing to worry about, yet he was worried. Fuck, now I was more than worried; I was concerned.

Luc had put his head down and was looking away from me.

"Luc! You are much older than me in vampire years, but you, my love, will look at me and listen!" Did I just scold my Sire? *'Aahh crap.'* My hand went to Luc's chin and I directed him back to my eyes. "Now here's the thing, Luc! Are you listening?"

Luc was blushing. Were those "puppy dog" eyes I was seeing?

"You, Luc, are my Sire. This I know as a vampire 'fact'." I

gestured a quote around the words with my fingers in the air. "Luc, sweet, dear boy, just days ago I came to this country human and...Hey! Are you listening to me?" I tapped him on his shoulder.

"Yes, mon cher. I'm sorry...I am listening."

"When I came to Paris I was already in love with you. Being with you, making love to you, finding out just who you are, well, Luc... What was it you repeated to me time after time?"

Luc looked at me, feigning ignorance. He was teasing me. I should be mad at him, but God, I loved him too damn much.

"Well, what did you say?" My finger brushed his nose.

"You, love, are ours...always and forever!" A sweet, sexy smile began to emerge on his timeless face.

"That's my boy!" I caressed his face. "I am yours for an eternity. No one, I repeat, no one will ever, ever take your place. You, Luc, are mine...all mine! So you better get used to it! After all, you have me for an eternity! With my eternal life," I was still getting used to that thought. "I promise to you that I am yours! My precious boy, I don't even know if that will be enough time for me to show you how much I love you."

"John...I-"

"SSShhhh!" I put two fingers to his lips, effectively stopping his thought in mid-sentence. "Just wait, okay?"

"Okay, mon cher." He cuddled closer to me. His eternally young, muscular body pressed itself against me.

"We have so much to learn about each other." My fingers now finding their way through his soft, thick, shaggy locks of hair. "I for one, can't wait to learn about you, Luc! Every day of our lives is going to be an adventure. I want you to tell me what happened all those years ago! I want to share my life with you, although, I must admit, it's a little shorter than yours! I want to go to sleep with you, wake up with you, and," I pressed my forehead against his, "I want to make love to you every day," I brushed my lips against his, "in every way! You have me for an eternity, Luc. I, for one, don't want to waste one minute of it!"

"God, John...I love you so damn much! I'm sorry I even thought of the possibility. It's just that, well, like I told Janine, I was afraid you would grow tired of me. Eternity can get a bit daunting, John." He nuzzled his nose against mine.

"Eternity with you, Luc? Daunting?" I couldn't help but smile at him. "How about, like I said, an adventure, a life together, a love together that will last for an eternity! All thanks to...I ran my hand across his cheek...you! Besides, babe, I made a promise to your sister."

"A promise? You made a promise to sis?" I watched his eyes grow wide. "Yes, my love...and Jaycee too!"

"Jaycee?" Luc's hand brushed across my shoulder. "I seem to remember you saying something, but, um, could you refresh my memory here, babe?"

"Of course, Luc. I promised to guard your heart for an eternity. A promise to Janine, our *magnifique loup*, not to mention your brother and Sire. You see where this is going!" I smiled at him, and with a light touch, my fingers tickled his side. I had my reasons. I hadn't heard it for a while, but I knew Luc wouldn't disappoint me. There it was, that adorable little whimper, and for good measure, that giggle of his!

"I guess I have nothing to fear then, do I, mon cher?"

"Nothing whatsoever...except one thing." I tried to feign a serious look, but ended up waggling my eyebrows and smiling at him. Clutching Luc's side, I pulled him to me for a blood-searing kiss. God! That fucking hot, muscular body of his. His cock, engorged and impossibly hard, pressed against my abs. I felt a trail of pre-cum, warm and slick, cover my stomach.

"I think I have an idea what you have in mind." Luc's eyes became intense, but the smile that I adore remained.

"So what do you think that idea is, Luc?" I asked, gripping his side just a bit tighter.

"I fear you shall fuck me to death!" He thrust his hips and I felt his cock slide up my abs.

"Uunhh, Luc..." I gasped. Then, as if that wasn't enough, his strong hand gripped my cock and began to jack me off, matching his thrusts. My pre-cum slicked his hand and my shaft. "Uuunnhhh...fuck...Luc!" I gasped for air.

God, Luc was a sight. His eyes squeezed closed, his nose scrunched. The tips of his fangs showed through his tightly drawn mouth and every muscle in his body tensed. Even his toes curled. Fuck, he was a living, breathing wet dream.

"Ohhhh God...unh...Luc!" I grabbed a handful of his thick hair. "I don't remember that being on the must avoid list for vampires, lover." My lips brushed softly against his.

"It would be fun to try it though. Jesus, John! Oh. My. God!"

I couldn't help but let out a soft laugh. "How about we start now?" I reached down for his cock, my hand achieving its goal. Engorged with blood, Luc's cock throbbed in my hand. Remembering how it felt in me as a mortal, I could only imagine what it would feel like now that I would not only feel my own feelings, but I would feel his, too.

"Unhhh...John, mon cher!"

I wrapped my hand around his cock and gently squeezed. More pre-cum had already gathered at the tip. With a brush of a finger, I brought the hot, slick clear fluid to my mouth and tasted it. *'Oh fuck!'* "Luc, baby...you taste incredible." I pressed my lips to his. As his tongue came into my mouth to play, he licked my tongue, wanting a taste of himself.

"Yum!" he exclaimed with a playful look on his face.

If this is the way it was going to be with Luc, sexually that is, giving myself to him...Well, hell! I thought that what I felt with Luc and Jaycee the other morning was the best thing I could ever feel, but that was no comparison to this. Don't get me wrong, it was unbelievable, but when Luc turned me, all my senses heightened. Every feeling I had, every feeling I ever felt, had been magnified ten fold. It centered on me and this man. This man that I fell for, died for, and now...live for! *'For fucking ever!'*

When Luc gave himself to me, and I merged my blood with his, my soul to his soul, I actually did become part of him. My feelings are his. I could, as strange as this may sound, feel what Luc was giving me. I feel what he is feeling, and he feels what I am feeling, and it is amazing.

Our first time making love, vampire to vampire, was slow and sweet. Luc rolled on top of me. I spread my legs to make room for him and wrapped my legs around his waist, digging my heels into his tight, dimpled ass. We took our time, Luc especially wanted to explore my "young" body. God, it felt so good just having his strong hands touch and feel every part of me. It was like he was mapping me, wanting to know the spots where he touched me that drove me through the roof. That seemed to be everywhere. I felt his fingertips on me, sending soft vibrations through my body.

I couldn't help myself, I had to do the same thing to him. My eyes drank in every part of his muscular, preternatural body. From his broad shoulders, defined pecs, slim waist, tight, defined abs, down to his strong athletic legs. My hands and eyes wanted to explore and feel every part of my lover. As I got to his feet, I licked the bottom of one of them. My tongue traced and tasted his heel, ran up his arch, then gently, I sucked one of his toes. God, his toes curled inward, his hands fisting the sheets. His back arched off the bed. It filled my head with a giddy, euphoric rush.

"Oh fuck! John, baby. Don't stop...please!"

"Oh, babe, I won't! I can't! You are so damn perfect, Luc!"

"Ditto, babe!"

It was just me and Luc. If the rest of the world disappeared I wouldn't care. The only thing that mattered was being with him. Everything else was insignificant, with two exceptions... Janine and Jaycee.

Luc pulled me back so we were once again facing each other. His whole body vibrated. Oh yeah, my boy was definitely turned on! What I was feeling now was...Hell! I couldn't begin to describe what I was feeling. Every part of me, both physical and mental, was linked to Luc. In every sense of the word we were, literally, one!

What started out slow and tender, turned into such searing desire that it seemed Luc had been holding his love for those three hundred plus years, just for me. His body and soul were mine. My Luc, for an eternity.

I was once again on my back. Luc, his body pressed tightly on top of mine, felt so damn good. Flesh to flesh. Muscular heat to muscular heat. His strong arms wrapped tightly around my shoulders, he couldn't get close enough to me. I grabbed his broad shoulders, my legs wrapped around his waist, pulling his body as close to mine as I could. "Luc, uhnnn...you feel so good! I love the way you feel. I can't...Oh fuck, babe...I can't get enough of feeling your warm, hard body pressed to mine. Baby...uhnnnn...Luc, do you feel it?"

"Mon cher, yes...Please, John, I need to feel every part of your body against mine!" One sound, that sweet little whimper from him, sent me into sheer ecstasy. "Please, lover, kiss me!" His red eyes pierced mine, begging, pleading. "John...Oh God, John...I feel your love for me."

I felt the now familiar tingling in my mouth as my canines lengthened. Luc's fangs framed his perfect smile; my lips locked onto his. Our fangs nipping at each other's. "Luc, I feel your love for me too. You are everything to me." I put both my hands to his face. Our eyes locked on to each other's, conveying those three words that sent waves of emotion through me every time I heard them from him. "Please, Luc...Oh God in Heaven, Luc...I need you in me. I need to feel you buried in me. Please, Luc...Now...Lose yourself in me. Uunnhh!" He did. "Jesus, babe!" Luc thrust his rock hard cock into me. Driven by the feeling of my Sire's cock driving into my tight channel, with a burning desire I couldn't control, I buried my fangs into his shoulder.

"Christ, John...uunnhhh! ...Yes! Fuck, yes!" His eyes squeezed shut as his head shook from side to side, his feet digging into the mattress to give him more leverage as he continued to thrust his cock into me.

I was losing my mind. Everything Luc felt, I felt. We were one. I released my bite on his neck, his wound healing instantly.

"Baby boy...Unnh...Luc! Oh God, Luc...Your cock, it's so hard! You feel so good inside me! Please, Luc..." I dug my heels into his ass, helping him to drive his cock deeper inside me. I gripped his biceps, I didn't know where he ended and I began. We were joined as one. God, it felt so fucking good.

So fucking right. Out of my mind with desire for Luc, I let my fingers slide down his spine. My goal, his tight, hot ass. My fingers were nearing their goal. As I traced my way down his lower spine, I felt them approach the rise of his hips, guiding me to my goal. My fingers slid into the crack of his tight cheeks. *'That's it, just a little bit lower.'* I said to myself, smiling.

Luc, anticipating what I was going to do, canted his hips upwards.

Two of my fingers circled his tight hole. Moist with sweat, I felt him relax enough to let my fingers circle around his tight opening. God, I could only imagine what it would feel like to have my cock buried deep inside him. Right now, all I fucking cared about was getting Luc off.

"Baby, just...just...John...fuck my ass with your fingers! Do it...just fucking do it!" Luc's voice was labored. Every word hitched as he tried to catch his breath. "Shove your fingers up my ass baby...fuck my ass!"

He was wet from the anticipation, and with one swift motion I pushed two of my fingers into his tight channel. I buried them up to my knuckles and began to finger fuck him. His ring of tight muscles gripped them. Shit, I wanted my cock up his ass...bad!

"Fuck me, John! Yes. Oh my God...yes, John...YES!" Luc cried out. "There, baby boy, right there! Jesus, babe!"

His forehead was pressed against mine. His thick locks of hair covered my face. They were soft and silky. Christ, he smelled so good. Musky, sweaty, my sweet boy. His scent is, and would be, a part of me, as mine would be his, for now and all eternity. We would be able to find each other among thousands. I was so fucking happy. I never regretted my decision from the moment I wiped, and tasted, his tear of blood. Oh yeah, I could feel that throbbing muscle inside of him. I found it... his prostate. With every thrust of my finger I made sure I hit it, massaged it. My ass slick with his pre-cum, as each touch of his prostate caused more to leak from his throbbing cock. I looked down. I watched as his stiff cock, slick and wet, slid in and out of me. I have never seen anything more sensual and erotic.

"Luc ...unnghh...Luc...forever isn't enough. Love you, Luc! "

Luc's eyes were rolling back into his head. "Love...you...John...Uunnhh!" His hand came up and grabbed me at the base of my neck. Pulling me to him, he kissed me. As his tongue explored every inch of my mouth, my fingers fucked his ass. His cock was getting harder and I felt every part of it.

Suddenly, without warning, Luc grabbed my legs and spread them wide. "Oh fuck, Luc!" He thrust into me in again. "Oh my fucking God, Luc!" My legs tightened around Luc's waist like a vise.

"Like that, baby?" Luc gave me a completely X-rated stare.

"Oh, I think you know the answer to that question, lover!" My voice deeper than normal. The sweet torture continued. Luc continued to let his cock hit my prostate causing ripples of electricity to course through my body. Though sweat covered our bodies, there was no feeling of tiredness. What would have brought me to an orgasm as a mortal, now only continued to drive me to the brink of ecstasy. I wanted so badly to come, yet I wanted the connection between us to continue. We had an eternity! As I looked into Luc's eyes, I saw nothing but pure love and want and need and, good God, lust. This young man was insatiable! No complaints from this vampire! With his red eyes gazing into mine, I knew I was his. I allowed it, I wanted it. He claimed me for his own. No one, nothing, would ever come between us. Till death do us part had no meaning, no dominion over us. "Baby boy...yes...uunhhh...God yes...Luc, please, don't stop!"

"J-j-john-n...I've waited for you for an eternity." His eyes were misting over, his lips quivering. "You are the only one."

"Luc...God...you mean?" I watched my boy as tears started to fall. "You're my first and, babe, my only."

"My God, babe! You truly are a gift. I cherish you, adore you. I am yours completely. Luc...the wait is over. I'm here, babe. I'm yours for fucking ever. Luc...I, unnnh, I cherish you! You are my everything. God in heaven, you are my everything, forever!"

"As are you. God, John, your eyes."

"Just like yours, baby! Uunnhhh!" Then it happened. Luc canted his hips and thrust deep inside me. "Oh fuck, Luc...just FUCK!" My hands reached down and grabbed his ass, pushing him deeper into me.

"Mon cher, I can't, I need to..." I could feel his need to come.

"I know, love. Uuunnhh...it's OKAY. Come for me! Fill me up with your cum!" I dug my heels into Luc's ass, helping him, wanting him to drive his cock into me as deep as he could. With every thrust, his muscles contracted. My hands splayed over his back. Every muscle in his body rippled. I lost it! I just fucking lost it and let my fangs sink into his neck again.

"Uunnhhh! John! Oh, baby...Yeah...Bite me...fff...fff...FUCK!"

I released my fangs from his neck, tasting and savoring the taste of his blood before his wound healed. "God in heaven, Luc...You are incredible."

I watched Luc's fangs extend and as his did, I nipped gently at his neck and his shoulders. I needed to mark him. I knew they wouldn't physically last, but my memory, now linked to his, would remember.

Raw desire took over my lover. This time it was his turn. Before I knew it, before I could react, Luc sank his fangs deep into my neck. I screamed. I fucking screamed.

"Luc...Oh my fucking God...Uunnhh!"

Luc eased his fangs from my neck. "You like that, baby boy?" His eyelids were heavy with lust. He kissed me, sharing my blood with him.

"Oh. My. God! Luc...Yes...Uunhhh...You know I do!" I smiled at him.

I took my hand and cupped Luc's face. Gazing directly into his eyes, I reached down, grabbed his ass, and drove him deep into me, once again penetrating his tight hole with my fingers. "Come on, baby...Come for me! That's it, baby! Fill me with your hot cum! Yeah, baby boy... Come! Fuck me, fill me!"

"But...uunnh...John...I...I… want to please you, make you feel good." He looked at me with such conviction my heart and pulse began to race even faster.

"Then fill me...fill me with your cum. I want to feel you explode inside me."

I had pushed Luc over the edge. I felt his cock become impossibly hard, and with one final thrust I felt his hot cum spill into me. I watched in awe as the muscles in his body contracted and tightened. As his hot, thick cum filled me his head arched back, neck muscles straining. Just watching Luc come to an orgasm hit me with a wave so powerful, that without a touch on my cock, I came. I felt it pumping from me, coating Luc's abs. God, did I come. Waves and waves of cum spurted from my cock. My orgasm was so intense, I felt like my cock was going to burst and I was going to black out... but I didn't. I just went with it. Both of us experienced not only our own, but each other's orgasms. Luc was a mess, a gorgeous mess. I felt his body go weak and, wrapping my arms around him, I pulled him to me.

I couldn't take my gaze off Luc. He was absolutely perfect. I realized then and there how much he deserved this. I was still trying to wrap my head around the fact I was his first, the fact I would be his only. This man who gave me everything, this man that I fell so hard for, he would never have to worry about that again. He had someone to love him unconditionally. My God! What he went through, what he had to endure. I would do anything for this man. This was my solemn vow to him. A vow that I would honor for an eternity... For fucking ever.

"*Merci, mon cher.*" His voice but a whisper echoing through my mind. "*I'd do it all over again, baby boy.*" His head was resting on my chest, his fingertips brushing across my chest. "*Can I hear those words, s'il vous plait?*"

I reached up and buried my hand in his hair. "*You, Luc, are mine. Always and forever.*"

We laid there together, our bodies still entwined. The beating of our hearts, in one single, identical rhythm, further solidified the fact that I was his. Luc was mine. I don't know why, but I remembered our conversation about how wolves mated for life. I guess the same was true for vampires. Luc had waited for me, for...my God...over three hundred years. He was my Sire and now I belonged to him. Hmmm, interesting. We had something in common with wolves.

*'That was random.'*

"Luc?" I whispered into his ear, my fingers still playing with his hair.

"Yes, love?" His head still rested on my chest.

"I...love...you...my vampire."

"I...love...you...my beautiful vampire."

"Always, Luc?"

"Forever, John."

I wrapped my arms tightly around his back, my legs still wrapped around his waist. I did not want to separate myself from this young man who so quickly had become my world, my life. We lay there, the two of us sated after what had turned out to be hours of love-making. Once again we drifted into the sleep of the immortals.

# ❊ CHAPTER TWENTY-NINE ❊

I awoke to a light knocking sound. There it was again. For just a second I had to stop and think where I was. That all changed in a heartbeat when, feeling Luc's head on my chest, I looked down to see my boy sound asleep. All I could do was look at him and smile. My boy, and he was mine. His disheveled, shaggy hair felt so damn good against my chest. His lips slightly upturned into what could only be the cutest damn smile I had ever seen. Fuck, who was I kidding? Any time Luc smiled it was the cutest. God, John, you've got it bad! I watched in fascination as his one hand, the one laying on my stomach, involuntarily opened and closed, gently caressing my skin. His eyelids fluttered, still in a state of sleep that looked human, but I knew full well Luc was still in the deep sleep that claimed our immortal bodies. After last night, he deserved it. I would let him sleep as long as required and no one, or nothing, would make me move. This is where I needed to be, with my boy.

I remember a conversation we had started to have about vampires not requiring that much sleep. The other night, after Luc made me his, I had to ask him why it was so important to sleep when all I wanted to do was let him have my body and make love to me. He was right though, he made it worth the wait.

It seems that, yes, vampires can go without periods of sleep, but the longer we delay, the longer it takes for our bodies to rejuvenate.

That, and the need for food, so to speak. I found it no surprise that our food was blood. I had to smile to myself again, remembering Luc's insistence on not believing everything I read in the books that I loved so much. But I had him this time. Well, I thought I did!

"Luc, baby...this time I gotcha! We cannot ingest food, can we, mon cher?"

"No, my love. You got me, baby boy." He smiled.

Luc calling ME baby boy. I was still getting used to that. I would be, once again and for eternity, twenty-one.

"Luc, my love," I ran my finger across his lips as we lay there, me a newly born vampire. "Fear not, my Sire, it is you who will teach me everything I need to know."

"It would be an honor, John." He brushed his lips over mine, a promise made.

"You must, my love, for I have a promise to keep. I must, and will, with no hesitation, guard your heart for all eternity. It's the least I can do...and even then, Luc..." My voice began to falter.

"Baby, what's wrong? Even then?" Luc looked deeply into my eyes.

I ran my fingers through his hair. It had become an addiction for me. Luc loved that it was. "Even then, Luc, I don't know if that's enough to repay you for what you've done for me." I pulled my lover into my embrace and held him, never wanting to let go.

I was pulled away from my thoughts as, once again, I heard the light rapping on the door. I smiled. I knew exactly who it was.

"Jaycee, my brother." My voice a mere whisper as I knew he could hear me.

This was so incredible. Every sense: sight, smell and hearing, became magnified. "Please, bro. Come in." I whispered. I watched the door knob turn gently and in the light of the hallway, there he stood. Once again dressed in nothing more than his comfortable sweatpants, a vision of perfection. My brother, Jaycee. His lean, muscled body defined by the soft light coming through the door. He carried a tray. This time though, there were no pastries or sandwiches, just glasses, and a bottle of the thick, red liquid. Good God, did my stomach just growl?

"Jaycee?"

"Yes, Jacques?"

"What are you waiting for? Come in, love."

I felt Luc's body softly twitch and his hand once again clutch at the soft hairs on my stomach.

"I'm not disturbing you or Luc, am I?" There was concern in his question, but at the same time, sadness.

Luc still hadn't moved. The look on his face was priceless. He looked like a little boy, innocent and not a care in the world. Damn I adored him.

"Jaycee, my love. Please, come in!" I patted my free hand on the mattress. "What's with you, love?" After a little more coaxing I persuaded him to come into the room. He closed the door behind him.

"Jaycee, put the tray down on the table and come here, okay?"

Jaycee gently set the tray down on the nightstand and approached the bed.

"Come, sit with your brother and I." Jaycee sat down next to Luc. I watched him inch closer to us. "What is it, Jaycee? Why are you so troubled, love?" I could see so many questions dancing through his eyes and, of course, it was Jaycee, so add concern, care, and his absolute love for both Luc and I.

"I...I... um..." A tear ran down his eye. His voice was shaking, "How are you, Jacques?"

I couldn't help but notice the change of subject. "Jaycee," I reached over and touched his face. "I'm fine."

"I...I...was...I was so worried about you, Jacques." He let out a long sigh.

"Sweet Jaycee, I know. God knows how much I appreciate what you did for me. I'm sorry to have put you through that, but please know I love you. Jaycee, I love you... very much."

"I *do* love you, Jacques... so much." He was shaking now and tears flowed down his face.

"Jaycee. It's me, bro. It's okay." I propped myself up on one elbow, careful not to disturb Luc. "What is going on in that beautiful head of yours? What burden are you carrying with you?"

"Jacques...it's just that...um..." He put his head down, a long piece of hair fell from his forehead, hiding his eyes.

"Jaycee!" I reached over and took his hand. "Come here and lay with us." I gently tugged his hand. He entwined his fingers with mine, desperate for my touch. Gently he slipped into bed, pulling himself next to Luc and me, careful not to disturb his sleeping brother. I watched him as he looked at Luc. I have not, and never will, see such dedication, devotion, and love between two brothers. Now, knowing what I do, it was something so rare and intense that I probably was witness to a part of something I will never see again. Jaycee's hand went up to Luc's face, the back of his hand brushed Luc's cheek, and then something we've all become fond of, he gently ran his fingers through Luc's hair. I could feel my pulse quicken as he gently leaned down and softly kissed his brother. After a few moments Jaycee looked up at me, his eyes swimming in tears. "I love him so fucking much, Jacques." It was barely a whisper.

One single blood red tear ran down his face and I had all I could do to catch my breath and hold my emotions in check. Something was troubling Jaycee, and I knew I had to hold my composure together for him, otherwise, hell, I'd fall apart. Then I'd be no good for anyone. It was obvious Jaycee needed me. God, this confident, strong vampire needed me!

"I know you do, Jaycee...I know." I reached up, placing my hand on his cheek. He leaned into my touch. Then I watched as Jaycee spent several more minutes letting his fingers trace and touch his sleeping brother's body. I would never be jealous of that. What Jaycee and Luc had, spanned time...centuries. What they shared was pure love and devotion, and I would do every damn thing to protect that, even if I had to fucking die. No one would separate these two beautiful men who had become my everything. My heart held only the purest form of love for Luc and Jaycee. Knowing what Jaycee did for his brother was the catalyst of my love for him. Yes, my love for Jaycee was different, but I was his as well. Jaycee, mon cher, my brave, loyal, and perfect brother, I will love you forever.

Jaycee looked up at me. In the short time I have been with him, I have never seen the expression that now appeared on his face. He had heard my thoughts. Though tears continued to flow, and his lips began to quiver, his eyes softly showed nothing but love. God, that sweet, serene smile on his face started a flood of emotion in me so strong that, fuck, if I didn't keep it together, the flood gates would open. *'Pull it together, John. Jaycee needs you.'*

"God, Jacques. That means so much to me!" Red tears streamed from his eyes, flowing down his face.

His lips trembled as he tried to maintain his composure.

"Jaycee, you're scaring me, love. What has you so upset?" My hand went for his face, gently touching him and wiping the tears away.

"Be still, bro. Tell me, please?"

Jaycee brought his arm up and I felt his fingers tangle and run through my hair. I leaned towards him, losing myself in his touch. Several minutes passed, then Jaycee's hand gently moved down my head to lightly caress my face. His thumb stroked my cheek. I opened my eyes to find him, his head slightly tilted, looking at me and softly smiling. His white fangs framed that smile. My God. For a moment I was lost, speechless. Despite his smile, his eyes looked deep into mine and gave away his true feelings. No, I would not allow my brother to hurt like this.

"Jaycee?" My hand touched his shoulder. "What, bro?"

"God, Jacques, I am so lucky." He leaned toward me, his lips brushing across mine. "I love you so fucking much, Jacques."

"Mon cher, merci. You know I feel the same way about you. My brother, you take my breath away. I cherish you. I will tell you this for eternity, I fucking love you." I pressed my forehead against his, my fingers softly touching his perfect face. "You have me for an eternity, Jaycee, my amazing brother." I softly smiled at him. "I will be here for you. I will be here for your brother and Janine. Always, babe...forever."

Taking my hand, he leaned toward me. "Jacques, please. Just one kiss?" His eyes pleaded with me. "No, Jaycee...No." I whispered. I knew I was hurting Jaycee's feelings deeply. I saw the hurt in his expressive eyes, but I had a reason, and a point I wanted to make that would hopefully make this man realize just how much I loved him. I know it was cruel, but I was reaching. I needed to get through to him.

"Oh God, Jacques. How could I have asked? Pardonnez-moi?" Jaycee's voice was trembling, he began to turn his face away from me.

Before he could finish, I quickly pulled his face to mine and kissed him... deeply. I opened my mouth and immediately felt Jaycee's tongue begin to explore. I let him, leaning in and letting him take me. As I parted my lips from his, I brushed my hand against his face, and once again softly smiled at him.

"Better, my precious brother?"

"Jacques? I don't...I don't understand?"

The poor boy was utterly confused. I had shaken him and caught him off guard. I immediately felt guilty. Well, somewhat guilty. "One kiss, Jaycee? We have an eternity. How could I give you just one?" I took one of his hands in mine and kissed it finger by finger. "I love you, bro!"

"Jacques, merci." A soft smile started to return to his face, his fangs were still present. His fangs. I remembered a conversation Luc and I had after my transformation...

*"Luc, baby. Are you mad at me?"*

*"Why would you ask that, mon cher?"*

*"Um...Your...Your fangs are showing."*

*"You goof! I'm sorry, babe. Between you, Jaycee, and myself, that will always be a sign of everlasting love, or in our case..."* Luc *giggled and waggled his eyebrows.*

Something primal came over me. I reached over, and with one of my fingers, I softly touched each of Jaycee's fangs. "Thank me for what, bro?" I caressed his face.

"For loving me and my brother."

"It is I that should be thanking you, dear Jaycee. Now, tell me what's going on in that head of yours." I lightly tapped him on his forehead.

Jaycee pulled himself closer to his brother, his one arm reaching over Luc, his hand coming to rest on my side. The need to be close to Luc and I was as evident in his body language as it was in his eyes. Jaycee was hurting so bad. No, this was not acceptable. No way in hell would my boys go through this with me by their side.

"Jaycee, you and Luc, and for that matter, Janine, are the most important people in my life. Mon cher, what in God's name is wrong?" My voice became a little bit demanding, but by no means did I mean to hurt him. I needed to push, but gently. I felt he was finally going to open up to me and I didn't want him to shut down again. "Mon cher, let it go. Tell me so I can make it better. I will babe, I promise."

Luc stirred ever so slightly. Both of us looked down at Luc. Then at the same time, our eyes came back to each other's.

"I thought I lost you both, Jacques." Jaycee's voice choked on every word, his eyes glassed over with tears.

"Jaycee, what the hell brought this on? Brother, why would you even think that?" My hand gently caressed his face.

"I um...Oh God, Jacques, please forgive me. I have never seen Luc so happy. Your declaration of love to him was so sincere, so heartfelt. In all my centuries, I never heard something so beautiful told to Luc."

"But, Jaycee, you knew that to be true."

"But, Jacques, this," his hand waved between Luc and I, "changes everything."

"How, love? Please, Jaycee...How?"

"Jacques, please do not be angry with me."

"Jaycee, anything you have to say to me, you know you can. I adore you, bro! You know that I could never be angry with you!"

"See, Jacques, I am so happy for you and Luc. To know that my little brother has someone now, for an eternity, fills my heart with such happiness and peace of mind, knowing you will always be by his side. It's what I've always wanted for him." Jaycee took one of his fingers and traced his little brother's lips.

"Merci, bro. I owe you everything. You gave me Luc. I owe you everything. And Jaycee, you owe me nothing." Jaycee was trembling. I felt so damn bad.

"Just say what's on your mind." I looked into Jaycee's eyes and leant forward, letting my lips brush his. "Tell me, Jaycee. It's okay." Taking one of his hands in mine, I squeezed it gently, hopefully giving Jaycee a sign that the security and comfort he desperately needed at this moment in time, was there. I could sense that this was one of the hardest things Jaycee had ever gone through. I could feel it in his grip on my hand. It was as if I were to let go, I would be letting him go...literally. "Jaycee, love, tell me. Babe, it's okay!"

"Um...Luc doesn't need me anymore." His breath hitched. "Neither do you, Jacques." The dam broke and Jaycee wept. He was falling apart before my very eyes.

For just a split second, all I could do was lay there and look at my brother, stunned. I could feel the young man's hurt and pain as if it were my very own. "Oh, my beloved Jaycee, my sweet brother!" My hand immediately reached up and cupped his face, stroking his cheek with my thumb. "Whatever could have brought this on?" I was not angry; fuck, how could I be? "I will always need you!" I loved him, and like Luc, there was no way I would allow him to endure any pain or hurt. The now familiar stinging in my mouth gave way to my fangs descending.

I heard Jaycee's breath hitch. He was witnessing my transformation for the first time.

"One will never do!" My hand wrapped around the base of his

neck. "Come here, Jaycee. Now!" I said quietly, but firmly. Gently, I pulled him to me, careful not to disturb Luc. Our foreheads touched. Jaycee's face was wet with tears and my hand came up to wipe them away.

"Jacques...I...I..." He was shaking so hard and my emotional connection allowed me to feel everything. His heart was beating so fast. I felt his angst and his emotional distress. No, this was not acceptable.

Before he could get another word out, or even try to, I placed two of my fingers gently on his lips. "Shhhhhh, my precious boy. Not a word." Once again I pulled him to me and kissed him. With all my heart and feeling I could share, I opened my mind up to him, letting him know how much I loved him, and just how much I needed him. I gave myself up to him. He clung to me, and as he kissed me, he wept. Briefly I parted my lips from his and with all the love I had to give, I looked into his eyes. "Jaycee, my precious brother, let it go. Release yourself from this doubt. You need not fear, Jaycee. Luc and I will need you for an eternity." Once again I joined my lips together with his and proceeded to show him just how true that statement was. I too, wept. The love I felt for him was only second to one person. That person was my baby boy, my Luc.

Parting my lips from Jaycee's, I placed my hands on his face and time stood still. I looked at Jaycee, this powerful vampire. My love for him would be as timeless as it was for his baby brother.

"Jacques, my brother?" Jaycee held my face in his hands.

"Yes, babe?"

"I know I've told you this many times, but I love you," he whispered.

Looking deeply into his blue eyes, I knew it was a declaration that would last for eternity. "As I do you, bro." I pressed my forehead to his. "Jaycee, I asked Luc this question, and I'm going to ask it of you right now, okay?"

"Anything, Jacques...anything, mon cher."

Putting my hand under his chin so his eyes met mine, I looked deep into those blue, soulful eyes and just took a moment to drink in the man who was baring his soul to me. After a few moments I brushed my lips across his. Jaycee shuddered. "Jaycee? Since...my God (I suddenly realized the short time it took to come to this moment), since I've arrived what have you and Luc constantly been saying to me?"

Jaycee looked at me, his eyes, still wet from the remnants of his tears, sparkled like diamonds. Taking a breath, he looked deep into mine and said, "You, love, are ours, always and forever."

"Yeah, babe. I am Luc's, but... and this is the last time I'll say this, okay, because let's face it, saying this for an eternity could get a little, ah..." I couldn't help it. I felt a smile form on my face.

Jaycee shook his head in understanding as he smiled back.

"Jaycee, I'm yours, too. You are mine." I looked down at my beloved, then back at Jaycee, and brushed his nose with my finger. "It's Luc, you, and I for an eternity! Fuck, Jaycee, I love you...I adore you...and, mon cher, Luc and I, if I may speak for my Sire, will always need you!"

"And I will love and need you *both* forever." Luc's sleep-filled voice caught us both by surprise. Jaycee and I looked at each other, eyes as big as saucers. I could immediately see Jaycee's body relax, along with a smile that would light up a room!

"Why, you little shit!" I had to laugh. "How long were you listening? Luc...answer me!" My hand went down and tickled one of the spots I had discovered on him.

"John...please...Luc was giggling uncontrollably. Please, babe...Stop. I give up. You're killing me!"

"Oh, I doubt that!" I chuckled, as did Jaycee. Part of me wanted to continue a little payback, but I knew what torture it was on him.

"Long enough." Luc caught his breath as he explained. "Long enough to know just how lucky I am."

"Jaycee, come here!" I could feel Jaycee's hand on mine, which was resting on Luc's shoulder. Jaycee looked at me, asking for approval. I nodded, smiling from ear to ear. *'God, I'm a lucky man.'*

I had been enjoying Luc's hand on my stomach, but what was happening took my breath away. Luc reached his hand up to his brother, wrapping it lightly around the back of Jaycee's neck and pulled him down, both of their heads resting gently on my chest. Luc, without a word, brought his lips to Jaycee's. My gums tingled and I knew that my fangs were descending.

"I love you, Jaycee...my brother...my Sire. I love you with every part of my being. I will never let you go, nor will I never *not* want you." By now, both Luc's and Jaycee's eyes were red and their fangs had descended.

"Luc...I...Fuck, Luc...I just thought..."

"What did my baby boy just say to you, Jaycee?"

"That..."

"You are ours, always and forever!" Luc finished the question. "As John said, do not question that again...ever! The three of us have something special, brother, and I for one would not give that up for anything."

Once again tears flowed from Jaycee's face. Fuck, I was crying too.

Then, with all the love Luc had in his heart, he pulled Jaycee into a kiss. Their fangs nipped at each other's lips, their hands were running through each other's hair.

I watched and realized that I was part of something very, very special and that nothing, and no one, would take this away. I would literally kill, or be killed, to protect what I had. I felt two very strong hands on my shoulders. Here I was, surrounded by the two most beautiful men I would ever love. Looking into their eyes, I repeated what both had pledged to me and each other. "I am yours...God, I am yours, always...and forever." With a revelation so powerful, I knew, I realized, the brothers had kept their promise, and I was eternally grateful. I was suddenly, willingly, swept away into their embrace.

# ❖ CHAPTER THIRTY ❖

*Growl.*

"What the...?"

I heard Luc giggle as my stomach rumbled.

"So uh, baby boy, I take it you're enjoying this?" I looked down at my boy whose head was resting on my stomach.

"John, you must be starving!" Luc stated as his finger made a circle around my navel.

Jaycee gave me a light kiss on my cheek and, as I turned to look at him, he smiled. Luc, on the other hand was, I swear, intent on listening for the telltale sound again. He was giggling so hard that, even though I was a touch embarrassed, I just didn't care. My boys were happy.

Flashes of what had just occurred replayed through my head. Feeling Luc and Jaycee explore my body with their hands and mouths. Then my back arched off the bed as Luc and Jaycee wrapped their hands around the base of my cock. They were laying on each side of me and I looked down to watch as they took turns wrapping their lips around my swollen, hard cock. Sucking it. They only paused so they could kiss each other and, I imagine, share the taste of me with each other.

"Uungh...Luc...Jaycee..." Each of my hands wrapped and tangled in their shaggy, thick hair. "God...Please...Do something for me. Please!"

I begged.

They both looked up at me. Their eyes, pupils blown wide with desire, showed me I need only ask. "What, Jacques? Tell us. Anything for you!" Jaycee's voice was hoarse with desire.

"Suck each other's cocks. I want to watch."

There was no hesitation. Luc and Jaycee looked at each other, and after sharing a chaste kiss, they rolled their bodies into a sixty-nine position and began to suck each other's cocks.

I watched, mesmerized, as these two boys took each other to the base of their swollen cocks and began to suck each other. Their moans filled the room and I just about blew my load watching them.

I could no longer just watch. Luc was on top, his perfect ass within reach. I needed him and I knew he desired what I was after. Getting up on my knees, I bent over and, taking both of my hands, I spread Luc's ass apart, with one goal in sight. There it was, his tight, pink opening. I buried my face in his ass and began to rim him.

Luc, canting his hips and pressing back into my face, turned back to look at me. "Oh fuck, John...Yes...Please...Don't stop!"

How the fuck could I say no to that? My tongue continued to lick. Damn, he tasted so good. Musky, sweet...my baby boy. My cock felt like it was going to explode.

"Jacques...aargh...fuck...Fuck my..." Jaycee was beyond reason, unable to even form sentences, his muscles taught, his toes curled. "Fuck my baby brother, bro!"

Luc was oblivious to anything except his Sire's cock in his mouth. "Luc, baby boy? I need to be in you."

"Mmphhhh!" Luc's mouth was still wrapped tightly around Jaycee's cock.

"I'll take that as a yes." I moaned.

Kneeling up, I slicked my cock with the pre-cum that was dripping from the tip. I watched as Jaycee lifted and wrapped his strong, athletic legs around Luc's shoulders. Luc spread his legs slightly to give me access. I watched Jaycee bring his hands up to Luc's ass and spread his tight, dimpled cheeks apart to give me access. Wrapping my hand around the base of my cock, I guided it to Luc's opening. Gently I pressed the head of my cock into him. For a split second Luc tensed up, but just as quickly he relaxed. I watched, mesmerized as my cock disappeared into Luc's tight, warm, and wet ass.

Releasing Jaycee's cock from his mouth, Luc looked back at me, his eyes reflecting his love for me. "Go ahead, baby boy...Make love to me. Fill me with your cock. Christ, John, you feel so good! Show me how much you love me, mon cher."

With those words, I gently pushed forward. Luc canted his hips and my cock slid deep into him. Then, thinking I couldn't get any deeper, Luc pushed back and seated himself on my cock. My balls touched his ass. My cock engulfed in his tight, warm, and slick ass. I felt the ring of muscles in him squeeze my cock. Jesus, there was that sweet, adorable whimper.

"Uungh...John...You feel so good! We were meant to be together. God, babe...Fuck me!"

"Luc, baby...I love you." With those words, I began to thrust in and out of my lover's body. Each stroke was like a small orgasm. Once again, I felt what Luc was feeling along with my own. I was going to go nuts! As I made love to Luc, I watched him and Jaycee sucking on each other's cocks. The three of us moved as one. I really had no perception of time. I really didn't fucking care. I didn't want this to end.

*"Neither do I, Jacques!"* Jaycee's voice was a soft whisper in my mind.

This time the boys had a request of me. Fuck if I would say no to that! "Oh fuck, boys...Yes...Yes, of course! I am yours...Take me!"

Oh my God! They did!

I felt Luc and Jaycee making love to me. The three of us joined together in a sexual union that would not, could not, ever be experienced by any mortal. Time again stopped as Luc and Jaycee took turns entering me, joining themselves with me. In the most intimate moments they not only shared their bodies with me, they shared their thoughts, memories...my God, they shared and gave their very essence, their very existence to me.

Afterward, sated, we layed there in silence. There was no need for words. I found myself once again laying between Luc and Jaycee. Luc, his head resting gently on my chest, Jaycee nuzzling my neck. Our arms and legs tangled around each other's bodies. Ripples of our recent orgasms still coursed through us.

It was once again evening. Minutes had slipped to hours and, apparently, into another day. I had lost track of what day it was.

"Boys?"

"Yes, my love?" Luc murmured.

"I think I've died and gone to heaven!" My hands reached down to Luc's and Jaycee's waists and pulled them close to me. At the same time, they each brought one of their legs up and over my waist. Our bodies wrapped tightly around each other, our hands softly caressing each other. We were tangled up in each other, both physically and mentally.

*Growl.*
*'Aahh crap!'*
"Sorry." I felt myself blush.
"Well, Jacques." Jaycee brushed a finger over my face. "You will die if we don't get you something to eat!" I noticed Jaycee's gentle smile was tempered with concern.
"What's happening to me?"
"John, when you initially fed on me you received a very potent supply of blood!" Luc explained.
"It would have lasted a little longer, Jacques, but..." Jaycee put a hand on my chest. "Well, all that physical activity kind of wore you out!"
Luc had quietly slipped out of bed while I was listening to Jaycee. I turned to see him standing next to my side of the bed holding three glasses of the thick, red liquid. Blood.
"Jesus, Luc." I gasped.
"What, baby?" He was handing Jaycee and I a glass and sliding back into bed.
"You are so fucking adorable! What did I do to deserve you, baby?"
"You gave your heart and soul to him. Jacques, you gave your life." Jaycee answered, his voice thick with emotion.
The three of us sat up and Luc and Jaycee sipped on their meal.
I looked down at the glass. I knew it was blood, and I knew this was my new key to life, but I shivered. Who had to die so that I could live?
"Luc...um...who had to..." I started to vocalize my concerns.
Luc and Jaycee, given the look on their faces, had heard my thoughts. "No one, John..." Luc kissed my cheek. "Absolutely no one."
"But..."

"Jacques, love...you can let go of that vampire myth right now!" Jaycee leaned over and brushed his lips across mine. The taste of the blood left on his lips tasted, well it tasted...Hell, who am I kidding, it tasted good!

"Then, if we don't," Luc took my hand, squeezed it, and answered my question before I could ask it. "The blood bank."

"Oh." I could feel my eyebrows furrow together.

"They didn't mention that in their literature!" Luc nudged my arm. "You goof!"

*Growl.*

"Cheers!" Feeling relieved, I put the glass to my mouth and drank it down in one long swallow. What would have repulsed me as a mortal, was now necessary for my existence. It tasted, I don't believe this, delicious. I held the glass towards Luc. "More? Please."

"Who the hell could resist those puppy dog eyes?" Jaycee grinned. "Our boy is hungry!" Luc tousled my shaggy head of hair.

Immediately I could feel a warmth and a renewed strength flow through me. Jaycee had reached for the bottle and was filling our glasses again.

"Baby boy?" I looked at Luc.

"What lover?" I watched as he licked his lips.

"How often do we need to um, drink...feed?" It was Jaycee that giggled this time.

"John, love. Fear not... okay? Usually once a day is enough, but sometimes, under certain circumstances," he glanced down at my once again erect cock, "we need a little extra boost!"

"Let the man enjoy his supper, baby brother!" Jaycee's hand came down and took advantage of my situation.

"Uunnhh...bro...God..." I almost dropped my glass.

"Hey, big brother. If you're going to give advice, shouldn't you follow it?" Luc giggled.

I had plenty of questions and Luc and Jaycee, I quickly found out, had the patience of saints. We basically spent the next several hours discussing, as Luc referred to it, "Vampire 101." Jaycee and I couldn't help but giggle when Luc had the chance to debunk what he referred to as my 'Vampire Do's and Don'ts Rules'. There was plenty to learn, but knowing stakes weren't lethal and garlic did nothing more than repel other people, was a comfort. It did my heart good to know that crucifixes and Holy Bibles would not cause me to burst into flames. Neither could daylight. Now I have to admit that one surprised the hell out of me! The two things that Luc and Jaycee stressed, and would stay with me the rest of my immortal life, were fire and beheading. That, they told me, would very much put an end to our existence.

"There is one more caution, babe, you must take very seriously." Luc stated, squeezing my hand.

"Werewolves, love. They can destroy us." Jaycee stated.

Werewolves indeed were a threat to our existence. Did I just say that...*our* existence? I had brought up the club and questioned the respect they had received. I was extremely proud of them when they told me of the alliance they worked out with the wolves. For the most part, it was all good, but like any society, Luc pointed out there would always be the bad with the good.

I was assured that Sam and Christian would be near me, whether I saw them or not. I knew that, because of their involvement in Paris and France, sometimes my boys would need to attend to business. But Luc, his insistence was adorable, told Jaycee under no circumstance would he be attending to any business without me by his side. Besides, from the way it sounded, I had become an integral part of their corporations and charities. As if being an equal partner in the most successful club in Paris and a multi-millionaire wasn't enough!

"Luc, really, love? What you and your family have done for me is enough. Besides, with all due respect, your love, babe, is priceless. I don't need anything else. I have you!"

"What did I say, John?"

"I know...the world. I'm not going to win this argument am I, Luc?"

"No. Besides, this will give you a chance to show off your new wheels!" Luc squeezed my hand. "Jaycee, where I go, John goes."

"He *is* yours, baby brother...of course!" Jaycee brushed his lips against Luc's. "I feel the same way about you."

"Looks like the three of us are going to be inseparable, hey, bro?" Luc winked at Jaycee.

"That is just fine with me, boys! Pardon my French, fucking fine with me!" I looked at Jaycee, my eyes telling him how much I appreciated what he had just told Luc. "Jaycee, Luc is a lucky man! I love you, brother!" I let my fingers run across Jaycee's chest.

"Holy shit, Luc!" Luc and Jaycee jumped. "Forgive me, but..." I was laying on the bed, my head on Luc's chest, his hand permanently embedded into my shaggy head of blonde hair I had reacquired.

"What's wrong, mon cher?" Luc asked, obviously concerned.

"How is Janine? Is she okay? I mean, after her witnessing everything that happened?"

"She's fine, love!" Luc looked down at me and smiled. "We have kept her informed, John!" Luc tousled my hair. Yep, my Sire had suddenly developed an obsession with my hair!

Jaycee had been lying with his back resting against the headboard. He moved so he was sitting next to his brother and immediately he had to get his hand in on the action. His fingers lightly ran through my hair. Fuck! That feels good! Speaking of obsessions, looks like it runs in the family. Wait a minute, I do it to them! I had developed a kink. Fuck, who am I kidding? Kinks.

"Jacques, please forgive me if this sounds vain, but she knew you were in the very best of care." His hand coming to rest on my shoulder.

"She speaks the truth, Jaycee. I literally gave up my life. I died. I would have never given it to anyone but Luc and you. And I'd do it again, if required." No words were necessary. Jaycee gently squeezed my shoulder and Luc's hand caressed my face.

"Janine asked, if you are up to it, that we meet her in the morning. She would like to show you more of Paris with your vampire eyes!"

"Jaycee?" Luc nudged Jaycee with his shoulder.

"What? What did I say...? Oh shit...!" Jaycee's eyes rolled. I smiled up at Jaycee.

"A quote from his favorite movie." Jaycee sighed.

I couldn't help it. The expression on Jaycee's face, and Luc's little *gotcha* smile, were priceless. I giggled, but then, regaining control of myself, I reached for both of them and pulled them into a kiss that basically left us all shaking.

"Hey, boys, you know what would really feel good right about now?"

"You, dear Jacques, are insatiable!" Jaycee's eyes twinkled.

"Well...yeah...that...but...can a vampire get wet?" I thought I was asking a serious question.

"John, baby boy, you are such a goof!" Luc pulled me to him.

"I suggest," I pulled Luc down into a mind numbing kiss, "we take a shower! Then maybe enjoy a little late night snack?"

"I like the way your lover thinks, little brother!"

Note to self: vampires do not implode in water.

TO PARIS WITH BLOOD

# ❧ CHAPTER THIRTY-ONE ❧

"John, love, what's wrong?" Luc, holding my hand, leaned into me, a note of concern in his voice.

We were leaving the apartment to meet Janine. Jaycee had noted that some fresh air would be good for us, though he had said that the last several days were most definitely worth staying in for. It had been two days since I became a vampire, days that I wouldn't change for anything.

As the doorman opened the doors leading out of the building, I froze... just fucking froze. Luc and Jaycee had assured me that sunlight did not, and would not, make me go "poof" As Jaycee so eloquently and with a giggle, stated. *'The little shit!'*

I couldn't help it. I stared out at the brilliant sunshine of what turned out to be another glorious day in Paris, its rays just footsteps away. I was scared shitless!

"Baby?" I felt my whole body shaking and Luc, feeling my anxiety, squeezed my hand.

"Luc, I can't do this. I, I...the sun, Luc. Fuck! I'm so sorry!" As hard as I tried, my feet wouldn't move; I was frozen in place. "No. I can't do this!" Turning to Luc, I buried my face in his chest.

"John, baby boy." Luc's voice was a calming balm to my nerves, which at this point felt like they were going to overload, and I was going to literally short out.

"I want you to take a deep breath and think about what we told you. Okay? Just think about how Jaycee explained it to you. Remember?"

"Yeah, baby boy, I do." My head now resting on his shoulder.

"Then tell me what your brother said, okay?" He hugged me, rubbing his hands up and down my back.

"Um..." I raised my head so I could look at my boy. "When you became my Sire, I received your attributes."

"That's right." Jaycee interjected. "Think of it like getting, well, hell, Jacques, you did! You got Luc's DNA, Jacques. Do Luc and I go poof in the sun?" He smiled. I looked at Jaycee, rolling my eyes at the mention of poof. I couldn't help but chuckle.

"Luc, baby brother, I think our boy is getting it!" He smiled and gently kissed me on the cheek.

"Fear not. Here's what we are going to do, John. You, Jaycee, and I are going to walk out together. We are going to enjoy this day, and when we get back home, the only thing that's going poof is your collection of misinformed books!"

"Awww..." I pouted. "What about my favorite author?"

Luc giggled. "Oh for Pete's sake, John! Okay! She can stay! I really need to have an interview with her anyway!"

Knowing Luc, he would. My fears, thanks to Luc and Jaycee, dissipated in a heartbeat.

"Besides," Jaycee added, "We have a wolf that has been chomping at the bit to see you! She misses you, mon cher!"

I looked at these two young men who had become my world, took their hands, and with no further hesitation we exited the building into the beautiful city that was Paris.

"That's my boy!" Luc squeezed my hand.

"See, we didn't go poof!" Jaycee pulled me to him.

"Smart ass!" I replied.

"Only if I'm *your* smart ass!" Jaycee squeezed me.

"Like I said, brothers."

# ❧ CHAPTER THIRTY-TWO ❧

We really didn't have to walk that far, and besides the scenery was lovely. Luc stated that Janine's residence was only about four city blocks ahead. The townhouses located on the Rue de Montmorency were gorgeous. I really wasn't that good at European architecture, but if I had to take an educated guess, some, most for that matter, dated back to the seventeenth century. Immaculately maintained, they had been passed down from generation to generation. That is one of the many things I love about Paris. Well, Europe in general. Yes, they built new structures, but they took great care in preserving their past history and the buildings. It showed. Jaycee's apartment was a little further. By limo, my boys did not use taxis, he lived about two miles away. It gave me a sense of peace, and yes happiness, when he told me that, because of recent events, he would be staying in Luc's guestroom. I was one happy camper! *'Wait, where the hell did that come from?'*

Luc and Jaycee were relatively quiet, certainly not out of rudeness though. I was caught up in the magnificence of what I saw, and they were letting me enjoy it. I loved looking through the windows of the shops along the way. My senses were overwhelmed by the smell of roses, lavender, wisteria and peonies. Luc told me that France had perfected, and was well known around the world for, their art of formal gardening. Residents of these homes were obviously proud of that fact, given the landscaping along the way.

Luc squeezed my hand. "Enjoying yourself, John?"

"Luc," I turned to look at him, "it's breathtaking!"

Leaning into me, he wrapped his arm through mine. "If you'd like, babe, why not take the first floor balcony and transform it into our very own garden?"

"Then when you two are done playing house, you can come over and do mine!" Jaycee nudged me with his shoulder and winked.

As we were walking, I noticed once again that people passing on the streets basically *made way* for us, taking extra care to part and allow us a full measure of passage as we walked hand in hand down the sidewalk. I honestly don't think it was the fact that three attractive men were holding hands that bothered them, but how could they sense anything? Looking at us, if I had been one of them, it looked exactly like what it looked like. Three very attractive men...shit, sorry, but I was pretty damn good looking when I was twenty-one...who happened to be gay. Sure, the perfectly tailored designer suits exuded wealth, but other than that? You know what… Fuck them! Neither Jaycee, Luc, Janine, I, or anyone in the family of vampires or wolves, would ever think to lay harm to anyone in this city. Luc had told me the safety record for the citizens of Paris was impeccable. Luc described the various charities and foundations that the vampire and wolf communities were involved in. That should make these people grateful.

"John!" Luc leaned into me. "You're thinking way too much! Relax, love!"

"We have had to contend with this, Jacques, for centuries. Even in your town, love, I'm sure you have dealt with injustices that cannot be explained." Jaycee squeezed my hand.

I looked at him and nodded. "It's still not right, Jaycee."

"Just be thankful you weren't around for the torch-bearing mobs!" Jaycee tried to come off as his usual cute self, but despite his smile, I knew better.

"John, love, remember, this is your first time out of a very safe and secure environment. We still need to be attentive." Luc squeezed my hand.

Luc pulled us all to a stop. I looked at Luc, one eyebrow crooked, intrigued by my Sire's intentions.

Turning, I noticed Jaycee looked at me just as puzzled and shrugged his shoulders.

"John, lover, just wait. You too, brother!" He released my hand and proceeded to walk toward a planter on the steps of a five story townhouse. Jaycee and I watched him as he bent over and picked two perfect red roses. Walking back to me, he first proceeded to kiss me, his tongue brushing my lips. Then, as his blue eyes gazed into mine, he placed one of the perfect roses in my hand. "For you, John! Je t'aime, mon cher."

My breath hitched. I felt a tear fall from my eye.

Then he went to his brother and, disregarding the looks we were receiving, he cupped his brother's face with one hand and kissed him so softly, and with such emotion, I thought for one moment I would have to catch Jaycee before he lost all sense of balance. Luc literally knocked his brother off his feet. Then, as he did to me, he presented a rose to Jaycee.

"Thank you, big brother! Thank you for allowing me to love and be loved. Thank you for letting that someone be John. Thank you, brother, for saving me and for loving me." Luc smiled and gently brushed his brother's face with his hand.

I couldn't help it. I felt the happiness and pride I had for my Sire swell, and my lips started to tremble as tears began to flow from my eyes. I started to cry. My God, this young man took my heart. This young man who loves me, this young man who gave me an eternity with him, this young man was mine. But what really made my heart pound was knowing I was his!

Luc was looking into Jaycee's eyes, wiping the tears from his face, as I gently intertwined my fingers with his.

"Luc, babe? Pardonnez-moi."

"Yes, my lover?" He turned and looked at me. "John, God, you're crying. I'm..." Before he could say anything more I put two fingers to his lips to stop him. I knew Luc was going to apologize. No fucking way! He had nothing to apologize for. The tears I wept were tears of joy.

"I love you. You amaze me, Luc! Luc..." My lips began to tremble again. "Luc, how can I...What can I ever do..." my hand brushed his face, "to repay you?"

We stepped aside to let people pass, as we realized we had more or less been garnering way too many stares.

"My precious baby boy. You... You have given me everything. Your love, your life, your promise to guard my heart forever. My sweet boy," Luc leaned closer to me, "John, I owe you everything...and you, John, you..." his hand brushed my cheek, "owe me nothing."

Frankly, I didn't give a fuck who was watching or what they thought. I pulled Luc as close as I could to me, reached up and tangled my hands in his hair, and gently pulled his face to mine and kissed him. As our lips locked together, I felt the sting as my canines lengthened. Secretly, as our tongues played in each other's mouth, so did our fangs.

"Boys?" Jaycee gently rubbed our backs. "Excusez-moi. We're here," he whispered to us. "Why don't we gain some privacy and go up to Janine's apartment?"

We had been standing in front of Janine's apartment. The roses Luc picked were hers. I glanced up at the building, something *pulled* me to a window. There, on the third floor, a woman stood looking down at us, smiling, from an arched window. The woman looking down on us from the third floor window was, my God, my sister! Our sister. Our stunning, breathtaking wolf!

# ❖ CHAPTER THIRTY-THREE ❖

Apparently vampires were not the only ones with magnified senses. Without so much as a knock on Janine's door, it swung open. There before me was the vision, the woman who, since the day I met her, has taken my breath away. Radiant, beautiful, a vision for all ages. There she stood, her emerald green eyes looking me up and down.

She was dressed in a full length, fitted, ivory robe with pearl and lace trim. God, my sister was breathtaking! Narrow at the waist, the satin robe flared down to the floor, with what looked to be a five foot train flowing behind her. The high, laced collar accentuated the long, black, satin hair that flowed past her shoulders, framing her perfect face. Her smile, always radiant, was made even more so by her perfect, pearl white teeth. I stood there, mesmerized. My wolf. My belle. My Janine. *Ma petite soeur...*my sister!

Before I could compose myself Janine was in my arms. She embraced me with a delicate strength. If people only knew. I felt an overwhelming sense of peace as I let my head rest against her shoulder, my face buried in her soft, silky hair. God in heaven, I could lose myself in her. Her touch, her love for me. With one arm around her delicate shoulders, the other wrapped around her petite waist, I returned the embrace. Not a word was exchanged. I heard Janine's thoughts the same way as I heard my Sire and Jaycee. Stepping back, her emerald green eyes studied my face. Her smile was radiant as the Paris sun.

"Janine!" Luc looked at her, then me. "Is he not the most perfect vampire you have ever seen?"

Taking my hand, Janine led me in first. The boys followed closely behind. Jaycee closed and bolted the door, keying in the alarm code.

"Let me look at you, Jacques!" Holding my hands, she leaned back and looked at me. *'Aahh crap!'* I could feel my face heat up. I was blushing. What a way to make an impression.

Janine had relinquished her hold on my hands. I grinned as I knew, well had a feeling at least, where her hands were headed. Sure enough! Janine's one hand delicately took hold of my waist and pulled me close to her again. My God! She smelled so good! Lilacs? Her other hand brushed my cheek and then, yep, she ran it through my thick, blonde locks of hair.

"Luc...Jaycee?" She continued to stroke my hair.

"Yes, sis?" Luc answered for both of them.

"You are right! Jacques, mon cher, is an absolute vision! But then, mon cher," her eyes looked into mine, "you always were and will forever be! Je t'aime, Jacques." Her hands cupped my face and her soft lips brushed over mine.

Why, at this moment, I couldn't say, but my thoughts turned back to a conversation that I had with Luc and Jaycee before my transformation. Janine, Luc had told me, knew of my feelings since my arrival in Paris. Jaycee had mentioned that they discussed the acceptance of me into their family. I remember the boys saying, "She has, shall we say, come to terms with it." Luc had told me that she was comfortable with our decision and Jaycee said that the other way was not an option. The ultimate, deciding factor was Luc. He had been in love with me since our first conversations online. *'Other way?'* I thought. I couldn't help but picture myself... Blonde fur, four paws, and a tail.

Luc, the little shit, had been *listening*. I looked at Luc, as he and Jaycee had now taken their appropriate places standing next to me.

*"John."* Luc nudged me with a smile. *"You goof!"* He paused for a moment, his finger on his chin. I knew he was painting a picture in his far too imaginative mind. *"Then again, woof! You'd still be hot!"*

*"Just think, babe, a collar around my neck."* I shot back.

Wait for it. There it was! That whimper that drove me out of my mind. *'God, John, be nice.'* I thought. I gave him a quick glance, softly growling and baring my normal canines at him. I so loved to tease him. Quickly though, I returned my attention to Janine and what she had just said. I was still getting used to the open, sincere, and loving compliments that my family bestowed on me. As I felt myself blush, I put my head down, overwhelmed by the outpouring of love.

"Luc, my love? My God, how can you say that?" Even now...Damn those stupid self-esteem issues. They just had to rear their ugly head!

"It's the truth, baby boy," Luc said softly.

I turned to look at my Sire, my partner. Vampires cannot lie, we can only speak the truth. Yet another fact Luc had taught me. Only the truth came from him. I meant no disrespect, but I guess not *ever* hearing these admirations was too much. "No...Just no! Janine, my love. Look what I have standing next to me." I glanced at Jaycee then Luc. "Honestly, how can I compare to them?" My eyes came into contact with Janine's. "They are preternatural perfection."

Her hand hesitantly relinquished my hair as she placed a soft palm on either side of my face. "Jacques, you must understand something. May I explain?"

"Janine, you need not ask!"

"Come. Luc, Jaycee...You too!" Janine led us to a centuries old, burgundy sofa, an elegant piece of seventeenth century craftsmanship. I couldn't help but notice the velvet was like new. Showroom new. "Sit, my brothers! For the love of all things holy, look at you three. My heart sings just looking at you." Her smile seemed to light the whole room with a radiant glow.

As we did, Janine went to the small bar, gracefully. With her gown flowing regally, she brought over a silver tray. Janine looked at me and gave me a wink, knowing I had noticed, once again, the priceless furniture, crystal, and framed works of art that surrounded me. The original painting of *Girl with an Umbrella*? Earlier, she had told me that it was just one of the many endearing little things she adored about me. This time, my eyes went to the crystal she was using. Again, only the finest. Four matching glasses, encircling a beautiful, hand-crafted carafe, completed the service.

"Merci, sis. John seems to have quite the appetite!" Luc lightly nudged his shoulder into mine and brushed my nose with his finger.

Janine had given two glasses to Luc, and he, in turn, handed one to me.

A small gesture, Luc had earlier explained to me, showing his respect and love for me. It was, Luc explained, a custom to show me that, as my Sire, it would be his responsibility to always look after me. I had tried to explain to Luc that it should be the opposite, but then I paused and reflected on how Jaycee took care of Luc. You just don't debate the etiquette of a centuries old tradition. With a vampire, to say the least!

Needless to say, much to Luc's amusement, I put my hands in the air showing a sign of surrender. "I give up, baby boy!"

With a giggle, Luc tousled my hair, looked at me, and shook his head. "You goof!" A term now totally endearing to me.

"Merci beaucoup!" Apparently I was hungry… My stomach growled. "Um, excusez-moi." Luc patted me on the stomach and giggled.

"You, dear brother, shall never apologize to us again. Understand?" Jaycee leaned over and squeezed my hand.

We toasted in silent unity and took a drink. I still couldn't believe I would think that blood tastes as good as a glass of fine wine.

"Better, Jacques?" Janine asked, always the gracious host. "Much!"

"Now, where was I? Ah yes, Jacques, mon cher…You, my dear, are lacking. How shall I say this without hurting my precious brothers' feelings? I say this with complete love for you. You, Jacques, mon cher, need to work on your self-esteem."

Yep! Damn self-esteem, and *fuck,* throw in lack of confidence.

"Sis, he has had a problem with this since I turned him! I even told him that I was concerned over how, pardon my English, *emphasis on English,*" Luc giggled, "I was concerned at how fucking hot he is and was!"

"Touché, baby boy!" I nudged Luc then proceeded to put my head down, a lock of my hair hiding the absolute self-confidence meltdown I was currently having.

"Jacques, mon cher?" Jaycee had brought his hand over and tilted my head back up. "Listen to my baby brother and my sister. You are incredible in every way!"

"Delicious!" Janine added, teasing me by licking her lips. "Jacques, if I may, you have to understand something about us. We do not let just anyone into our lives, let alone our family. My God, Jacques, I'm even just a bit jealous of Luc. And I suspect," she turned her gaze to Jaycee and winked, "so is my other precious brother!"

I noticed Jaycee blush. *'That's new!'* Despite myself, I felt a small smile trying to break through. Then, something that I would never suspect, think, let alone hear, came out of Janine's mouth.

"Why are all the good men either my brothers, gay, or complete fuck-ups like Alec?" Her finger pressed into her chin and her eyes were staring out the window.

"Um...Janine? I, um..."

Then, with a way too sexy smile on her face, she turned to me and, after a moment of silence, she took my hands. "Oh, Jacques. I am just playing with you, love! Please forgive me!"

"There is nothing to forgive, Janine."

"You, Jacques, are a blessing! I felt that the moment we first met at the airport."

"But, Janine..." Her fingers delicately pressed against my lips to suppress my thought. "Listen to me, mon cher."

Luc and Jaycee had moved closer to me and each of them took one of my hands. "Let me try to explain, if I may."

"Of course, sis. Oh God, Janine! I hope that was not too forward of me?"

"No, brother! I *am* your sister!"

Jaycee leaned into me and squeezed my hand. God, could his smile be any bigger? "Jacques, remember what I told you earlier, about gaining Luc's attributes?"

Once again, slow on the uptake, I put it together. I pressed my forehead to Jaycee's, trying to hide my embarrassment. "God, Jaycee. How could I have forgotten? I'm sss..."

Jaycee put his finger to my lips. "Don't you dare! Sorry is not in our vocabulary! You, Jacques, are in every physical sense our brother, and Janine is your sister!" As he spoke to me, the joy on his face reminded me of a young child on Christmas morning. "God, Jacques...You are a gift! Now, thanks to my little bro, I have two brothers! I am so happy he chose you!"

I heard Luc's sweet whimper, and after brushing my lips against Jaycee's, I turned and kissed Luc. Then I turned my attention back to Janine.

"Je t'aime, my brother." She leant forward and gave me a soft kiss.

I felt myself relaxing. Taking another drink, I leaned back between my boys. My eyes were fastened on Janine, showing her, without words, how much I wanted to hear more.

"Jacques, remember the day we met online?"

"How could I forget, Janine!"

"What song did you comment on?"

"I will never forget, sis. 'I Need to be in Love'." My breath hitched, I felt Luc's hand squeeze mine, and I heard Luc's breath hitch too.

"Jacques, I'm sure by now, that when I tell you I could feel what you were thinking as you posted the comment, that you will believe me."

"With all my heart." My eyes started misting over.

"As you made that comment love, I felt the hurt you were going through. All those nights falling asleep alone, then waking up with no one next to you. My heart ached for you." Janine briefly looked away from me, then turning back, she paused just a moment and looked at me. Her face was very expressive and I could feel the compassion and love she held for me. "Jacques, I knew then, without a doubt, just exactly what you needed. I knew then and there I had found that special someone we have been looking for, for centuries. I knew then and there we could give you what your heart desired." Her head slowly turned to look at Jaycee.

Jaycee looked at me and nodded. A tear ran down his expressive face.

I turned my eyes to Luc, who looked at me with nothing but total devotion and love. As I turned back to Janine, I realized I was shaking, and Luc, immediately sensing my stress, pulled me closer to him. "But, Janine, my love...I'm just...I'm just me!"

"That, dear Jacques, is why you are here with us! Yes, Jacques, my love, you are simply beautiful to look at, but the beauty you have goes deeper than that! Your love for Luc, Jaycee, and myself! The way you never doubted us, protected us. Even, mon cher, the way you defended us against Elena's threats and accusations. How you stood up to Alec...as a mortal, no less! But most importantly, your love for Luc! So much so, that you gave your mortal life to become one with Luc!"

Once again, overcome with emotion, I lowered my head, trying to hide the tears now coursing down my face. But like everything else in my short time with them, I knew, I just fucking knew, I could not hide anything from my immortal family.

I could feel Jaycee's hand reach over and lift my chin up and turn my head to face him. He looked into my eyes. "Jacques, my brother," his hand caressed my face, "you *are* the most thoughtful, loving, and kind man I have ever known. Look at what you did for me!"

"Jaycee, my God! What I did for you? You're definitely going to have to clue me in on that one, love, because...I...Jaycee..." I was totally at a loss. "What I did for you?" I could tell my face showed a look of total confusion.

"Jacques, listen, just listen to me and trust me on this. I have seen many, many things in my lifetime! Suitors for my baby brother have come and gone. The one thing they all had in common was their lust, if you will, not for Luc, but for what he could give them. Money and power...Babe, you know how that turned out! Then Janine told us of you! Yes, love...You!"

Luc was rubbing my back and Janine, leaning forward, clasped one of my hands around hers.

"Since the first moment I saw you walk onto the concourse at the airport," Jaycee continued, "I knew. I had no fucking doubt that what Janine felt, and spoke of you, was so damn true! I felt your emotions and your absolute love for us. As you approached us, it was so damn obvious! Now you know," he softly smiled and gave me a wink, "we felt every emotion you were feeling. God, Jacques! I am Luc's Sire! Even before you became a vampire, somehow you knew that."

"You can thank my 'Rules' for that, Jaycee!" Luc nudged Jaycee and giggled.

"Anyway," nudging Luc back, "you respected that. Do you think for one minute, knowing our relationship, it would have gone down any other way? That I would have allowed you to become a part of my precious brother's life?"

"No, Jaycee. God, no! How or why would I want to come between the most perfect love I have ever seen? What you and Luc have is priceless! It's the most incredible expression of love that I have ever witnessed."

"Until now, Jacques." I felt Janine brush my arm.

"Jay...cee," my breath hitched, "what you have given me..." I looked at Luc, softly touching his face. "Jaycee, I'll say this again. You have entrusted Luc's heart to me, and I swear to you, my precious boy, I will protect and guard Luc's heart with my body, mind, soul, and *life*...if required! I am so deeply in love with your brother!" I turned my attention back to Jaycee. "For that, and so many other things, I love you so fucking much, Jaycee."

I could feel the tears sting. Jaycee reached up and brushed them away, but they continued to fall. I just couldn't help it. After everything that had happened to me in this short time, there was one absolute truth. I loved these people, my family. "I would die for any or all of you!"

"That, Jacques, mon cher, our Jacques, mon cher, is why Luc, Jaycee and I would die for you too!"

Janine's promise coursed through me, a pledge that I knew would be kept for eternity. Then it happened. I tried to control it, but everything was conspiring against me. Shit! I wanted to be strong to show Luc, Jaycee, and Janine strength, not weakness. God help me! Why me? Why was I the one to receive such a gift? I know. God, I know. Janine and Jaycee just explained it to me, but I couldn't wrap my head around it. I had to wonder if it was the remnants of mortal feelings still lingering in me.

I looked at Janine, then Jaycee, and by the time I turned to Luc, it was all I could take. I broke down. I wept. The dam burst and the tears poured from my eyes. A total fucking meltdown. All that had happened to me, won out. And knowing who I was with, I let the dam break. Strong arms, the arms of my Sire, wrapped themselves around me. Pulling me into his embrace, Luc gently leaned back, holding and comforting me.

"Let it out, babe. Let it go." I felt him put his hands on my face and his red eyes looked deep into me. "I swear to you, my precious John, I will protect your heart as well. I cherish the day you walked into my life. You are my only. We shall never have to say goodbye. Fate, John, has given me you. I keep you with me in here, in my heart." Luc patted his chest over his heart. "We don't and won't say goodbye. I have found a dream that has come true and that dream, babe, is you. My sweet baby boy, just let it go, because you are mine...Forever."

All I could do was look at this man as his words washed over me. My God! I loved Luc so much, but the floodgates were open and they weren't about to close anytime soon. These were not tears of regret or tears of doubt. These were tears of love, happiness, and utter joy.

Then, without another word spoken, another set of strong arms came up from behind me and embraced me. "Oh God! Jaycee!" I could barely talk. "I… I love…I love you…I love you so much!"

"Jacques, I love you too. Eternity is not enough. I love you so fucking much! Jacques, I too, vow that I will protect you, your heart, and love. I will protect your life, my brother. Normally I don't speak for my sister, but I'm sure she agrees with us. You, Jacques, are ours, and knowing we will be together forever brings us great joy!" Jaycee kissed the tears from my face. "We shall take our journey through eternity together."

"Jacques, mon cher, sweetheart, look at me." Janine had moved to stand before us, by the sofa. As she knelt before me, she lifted my head and brushed my bangs away from my eyes. Placing a hand on my face, she leaned in and kissed me. "You, Jacques," her voice a delicate whisper, "are ours. Always and forever, my beautiful brother and vampire! My beautiful Jacques! Je t'aime, mon cher."

As the words flowed from Luc, Jaycee, and Janine, it seemed like they were soothing me to my soul. Our connection was so strong. So fucking powerful!

"Baby boy?" Luc, still holding me, whispered in my ear. "What can we do? What can we do to help you?"

"Luc, my beloved Sire," my voice was shaking. I reached up and caressed his preternatural face. I wanted, no, I needed to feel Luc's lips on mine. Leaning into Luc, I let my lips brush over his. Not caring, but knowing Janine and Jaycee would not mind, I brought one of my hands to the back of Luc's neck and pulled him into a deep kiss. My tongue begged entry into his sweet mouth. When he let me in, I gave as good as I got. My canines descended and he let me nip at his mouth. Maybe I was just a little too rough, but Luc didn't seem to mind. I needed this, and Luc knew I did. Returning the favor, Luc nipped back. Our blood mixed together. I tasted it, as did Luc. Pulling away for the sake of Janine and Jaycee, I looked at Luc.

"John, baby. Your eyes, your fucking perfect vampire eyes!"

I felt Janine's hand on my thigh. "May I, Jacques?" Janine asked me softly.

My gaze didn't leave Luc's. I felt safe and secure. It was Luc's thoughts and feelings coursing through me. Not a word had to be said. The way he looked at me, his love, God Almighty, his soul said it all to me. He loved me so much and I knew it would be for an eternity.

"Jacques?" Jaycee placed a hand on my shoulder and gently leaned into me, whispering into my ear. "My beloved brother, let Janine look at you."

Slowly, I turned toward Janine. What I saw made my heart skip. Janine just knelt there and looked. A smile began to frame her face. "You are both so right!" Cradling my face in her hands, she looked into my red eyes. Her hand came up and she ran one of her fingers over my fangs. "He is absolutely beautiful! God, Jacques, you are gorgeous!"

# ❦ CHAPTER THIRTY-FOUR ❦

We spent most of the day with Janine, catching up on things that transpired since the other evening when fate intervened, if you believe in that, and I became a full-fledged vampire.

Janine, ever the lady, didn't pry, but, being my sister, I wanted her to know exactly what occurred. Of course, out of pure respect for her, some of the more explicit details were left out, though I'm sure she knew. Janine reiterated her thoughts on what I meant to the family, which she made abundantly clear I was now a part of. So much so, that the family attornies had all my legal documents changed, right down to my driver's license. I had a new last name! But I knew they were still concerned about my self- esteem, and with their combined years of wisdom, well, I didn't stand a fighting chance.

Janine also knew it was extremely important for me to know what happened to her in her monthly transition from human to wolf. It was just as I imagined, no horrible flesh-ripping monster. Luc found great joy in being able to debunk more of my 'things that go bump in the night' theories. Janine had not wanted to get into too many details, but shared about the full moon, which I had great joy holding over Luc's head.

*"Here, Luc...Catch!"* I tossed my DVD of 'Van Helsing' at him.

*"What's this?"* I watched as he looked at the cover.

*"You, goof!"* He fired it back at me.

*"Your goof?"*

I did learn that as the full moon waxed, she would turn. Janine being Janine, embraced me and told me not to fear. I assured her that she didn't need to worry. To be honest, I was curious and excited. I, like Luc and Jaycee, would be able to communicate with her just as we do now. Jaycee described our sister to me in wolf form, and it was no surprise that Janine, being as petite as she was, was just as petite as a wolf. Yes, she was jet black. I wondered if her fur were as soft as her hair in human form. The only other major difference, besides having four paws, was her wolf eyes, which I had already seen.

Luc said what mesmerized him was how exquisite her canine face was. "Yes, babe," Luc softly let his hand touch his sister's face, "she is as breathtaking as a wolf as she is as a human."

Mainly what Janine and her wolf pack would do is satisfy their craving with a hunt. Not a hunt for humans, but rather, just like other wolves (which sounded identical to the ones that roamed our Wisconsin Northwoods), they hunted in packs for their meals. I found out Janine's favorite was rabbit. To be completely honest, I was still trying to wrap my head around this whole transformation Janine would be going through later tonight. The physical part, that is. Was it fast? Did it hurt? My worries, thanks to Luc, were quickly put at ease as he pointed out it wasn't really any different than what occurred to us in our transition. Like I said, forever young, but wise beyond his years.

Something, which I hadn't brought up since the night I tasted Luc's tear and became a new vampire, suddenly sucker-punched me! Even though I didn't want to bring it up, I knew I had to give them the information and an answer to a question that suddenly reared its ugly head. I just did not want to do this. Fuck, just FUCK!

It was going on four o'clock in the afternoon, and this day, even though we did not leave Janine's apartment, was another sweet memory I would cherish.

# ❧ CHAPTER THIRTY-FIVE ❧

As the afternoon slipped by, making way for another evening in the City of Lights, we spent our time talking and sharing special moments from our pasts. Of course comparing my life to those of my new family short story to on of the History Channel's miniseries'. Just being with my family gave me a profound peace that I was very grateful for, but I knew now there was no more need for thanks or gratitude. I was theirs. For an eternity.

We were sitting around a warm, cozy fire that Jaycee had built in the fireplace. For obvious reasons, it was more for mood than actual comfort. The drink I was enjoying was taking care of that warmth. Luc had made my transformation easier from the start, especially the hunger I had for blood. That would probably be the easiest concern I would face. After all, there is no way in hell that I would ever take a human life to satisfy my need to feed, so my family's plentiful supply had simplified things. Of course, Jaycee and Janine had also played a big role in my transformation thus far. How the hell could I ever repay them? Oh, I knew. Dealing with Elena and Trace, and putting an end to their bullshit once and for all. I couldn't let them threaten my family.

The thought of Elena being in the city was enough in itself, but knowing Trace was here was too fucking much to bear. Why couldn't they just leave us alone? *Damn you, Elena! Damn you! You fucking well better be ready to explain yourself.* I was tired of this; it needed to be dealt with. I could not rest, nor would I be comfortable, knowing they were out there.

For the first time since my transformation, I felt rage. Luc had talked to me about it. How to control it but, damn, it wasn't easy. Right now those two made my blood boil! They had no business or right interfering in my life. As hard as I had tried to put them out of my mind, Luc's insistence on us going out tonight, added to Janine's impending transition and hunt reminded me that they were a real threat to my family. God! I didn't want to let Luc, or my brother and sister, see this fear fueled raging side of me, but as a newly-born vampire, I still had a long way to go in terms of control. As hard as I tried, the feelings coursing through me right now were so intense I was losing it. Fuck! I knew my eyes were red, and instantly my fangs descended.

The growl that came out of my mouth scared the shit out of me and Luc! I found myself jumping off the sofa where we had been sitting. Well, I *was* sitting. Luc had been cuddling with me when I felt the gentle touch of his hand on my face. Just his gentle touch shot through me like electricity.

Luc's connection to me, as my Sire, was so strong he immediately stood up and wrapped an arm around me. "John, I'm...I'm so sorry. I didn't mean to startle you. It's just, um, you were so quiet." His eyes met mine, his brow creased, expressing his concern.

"You didn't, Luc. It's not your fault, babe." I kissed him reassuringly. He leaned into me with a sigh of relief.

Jaycee had stood up and walked over from where he was sitting next to Janine. "Jacques? That look on your face. What is it, mon cher? You look so angry." He looked at me, obviously concerned. I could do nothing. I felt frozen to the place I stood. Without a word, Jaycee gently put his hand at the base of my neck. I leaned my head back as I felt his fingers run through my hair. I did not want to do this. Look what I was doing to my family.

By this time Janine had walked over and taken one of my hands. "Jacques, something is deeply troubling you, but none of us can read you. What is it you don't want us to know?" One eyebrow raised as she gently squeezed my hand.

"Sis, please forgive me." I placed a kiss on her forehead. "You are right, I am troubled. God, sis! I did not want to burden any of you with this!"

"What has you troubled, Jacques?" Jaycee asked. Jaycee's touch and Luc's hand on my arm started a chain reaction of warmth that began to flow through me. Once again, their love moved me to my very soul. How in God's name could I ever think of living without them?

"It's, ah, damn! I'm scared." I couldn't hold onto the rage in their embrace, and it was quickly overridden by the fear. I began to feel myself shake.

"Of what, my love?" Luc was still by my side, his fingers now stroking my cheek.

"It's okay, Jacques. We're here. You don't have to be scared." I felt Jaycee place one of his hands on my shoulder. Both my Sire and brother were so close to me I could feel the warmth and concern emanating from their bodies. We were linked together, our minds as one.

"It's...uh...ah shit! I'm just wondering what Elena and Trace are up to. Quite frankly, I don't want to leave here tonight. I don't want anything to happen." A tear leaked from my eye. "Can we please stay in? Please?" I looked at Luc, Jaycee, and Janine expectantly.

"If only it were that easy, mon cher. You realize, I must hunt. I have no control over my transformation, love. Besides, my precious Jacques, mon cher, you forget about Sam and Christian!"

"Janine, I know they are here...well, someplace. I do trust them to look after us, but you don't know what Trace is capable of."

"You, dear Jacques, have no idea... yet," Janine's eyes looked directly into mine, "what they will do to protect us."

"Luc? Be a love and sit down with Jacques and Jaycee, okay?" Janine motioned us to the sofa.

"Sure, sis. Come on, babe, bro." Luc took my hand and led me back to the sofa. With Luc to my left and Jaycee to my right, each holding one of my hands, we turned our attention to Janine. God! The love these two men had for me was indescribable. Their thumbs gently rubbed my wrists, calming me. Like I said, if I had to live my life without them, give me death.

Janine proceeded to walk across the room and stand before us.

"Jacques, mon cher, it's going to be okay." Janine said confidently. Luc and Jaycee squeezed my hands.

"Do you know something, sis?" Luc asked.

"Yes, yes I do." As Janine spoke, I watched Jaycee pull up a chair for Janine and quickly resume his place next to me. My heart skipped a beat as he immediately reclaimed took my hand.

"Could you please tell us, sis? I'm worried sick about all of you. I need to know. I won't, I can't..." I began to shake, my voice began to falter. "I couldn't bear to lose any of you. I just found you!" I was becoming agitated again and Jaycee's and Luc's hands gripped mine just a bit tighter. "I'd die first. I'll die before anything happens to any of you!"

Janine leaned forward, placing her hands on my legs and gently rubbing them. "You, dear Jacques, mon cher, are not dying for us...tonight or ever. We have Elena and Trace. Sam and Christian are with them as we speak."

"What, sis? Really?" With that revelation from Janine, I squeezed Luc's and Jaycee's hands so hard my knuckles turned white. "You have them, Janine?" Relief swept through me like a tidal wave.

"Yes, Jacques, we do. Do not worry, mon cher, they are being taken very good care of, though I hear Trace is not too happy about the situation."

"Sis, that's the understatement of the century!" Though I tried hard not to, I felt a small smile form on my lips. "Sis, how?" I asked.

"They weren't exactly discreet about who they were looking for. You forget, brother, the circle of friends you met at the club were told exactly what was happening and who they should be looking for. They were asked to report any information to Sam and Christian. Jacques, you have been accepted completely into the family, vampires and wolves alike. Yours, Luc's and your brother's safety are of the utmost importance."

"Janine," my voice was shaking, "I hope to God that means your safety as well! Please, Janine, tell me that is true!" My red eyes looked deeply into hers.

"Jacques, of course. You, love, need to calm down." Her voice was soft and reassuring as one of her hands caressed my thigh. Her eyes penetrated mine and a warmth started to flow through me. I could feel my canines return to normal.

Luc had been watching my emotional state. "Breathe, baby boy, breathe. Remember what we talked about." He brushed the back of his hand across my face. "There, love, that's better." I could feel every part of my body relax and an inner peace sweep through me. I turned and pressed my forehead against his. "Merci, babe...pardonnez-moi, mon amour."

"No need, John. I understand." With a gentle smile on his face, Luc leaned forward, tilted his head, and gently kissed me. I felt Jaycee's hand rub my back and Janine's hand lovingly caress my thigh. For several moments we sat there. All attention was turned toward me, but there was no pressure for me to talk. I found myself sitting back, once again seated between my lover and brother. As Luc and Jaycee once again took my hands, Luc looked at me and with a quiet voice began to speak. "John, my love, how are you feeling?"

"Um," I looked into Luc's eyes, "better babe. God, I am so sorry. I only hope you can all forgive me."

"Jacques, my brother, you have such a kind soul." Janine, sitting on the chair facing us, leaned in and continued to speak to me. "I can see," A smile began to form on her face, "that appologizing will be a hard habit to break you of. Brothers," she looked at Luc and Jaycee, "we will not force the issue on him. Jacques' need to vocalize his feelings is, in part, what makes him so very, very special. If our brother needs to apologize or ask for forgiveness, then we shall honor that request, though he shall never have anything to apologize or be forgiven for." I felt Janine squeeze my thigh.

I could feel myself blush. "Merci, sis. I guess that's one mortal habit it's going to take me a while to shake."

As Luc and Jaycee squeezed my hands, Janine, with a soft laugh, looked at me and said "Take all the time you need, mon cher! After all, we have, what? an eternity to break you of it?"

"Sis, with all due respect," Luc looked at Janine, then turned to me, "this is one mortal habit I don't think I want to break him of."

I looked at my Sire and my brother. Both were shaking their heads. Jaycee tousled my hair.

"Babe, can you give us some information here? I know it's hard, but reach down inside you and remember what I taught you. Why don't you tell us what you know, okay?"

"Jacques, there is absolutely no pressure. Take your time, bro." Jaycee's hand brushed across my face as he leaned forward, allowing him to address himself to Luc. "Luc, brother, may I?"

"Of course, Jaycee. You need not ask, though it would be polite to ask John. Would you not agree, brother?"

"Of course, Luc. Merci." Jaycee nodded at Luc.

Here again, I was a little slow on the uptake. I looked at Janine.

The smile on her face, well, like I said, she belongs in the Louvre. Her beautiful demeanor told me everything I needed to know. Janine turned to look at Jaycee for a moment, a serene smile framing her face. Then, just as gently, she turned her head, her eyes capturing mine. "Jaycee needs your attention, Jacques."

I felt a small smile start to form on my face, and with a slight tilt of my head, I nodded and acknowledged Janine's request. I turned to Jaycee, his face now only inches from me.

"Hey, beautiful!"

"Jacques, brother, the courage and strength you are showing us is incredible. You may not think so, but Jacques, I have seen so much in the time since I was turned, and, well..." I could see sadness in Jaycee's eyes. God, so many centuries. What he must have seen, endured! "Others just handle it, but you," Jaycee's voice hitched, "have shown us such grace. For all you've had to adjust to, for what you gave us, we will always be with you. Caring for you, protecting you, teaching you, and most importantly, loving you. There will never be anyone else. Eternity will go by and we will never let you go."

My eyes couldn't leave Jaycee's even if I wanted them to, and then one tear fell down his cheek. I leant forward and kissed it away. At that moment, I knew exactly what Jaycee needed and wanted to do, and damn, I needed it too. "Yes...Yes you can," Before Jaycee could even ask, "and God Almighty, I need you too. Kiss me, brother." With that, Jaycee cupped his hand on my chin and drew me to him. As our lips met, for the first time, a whimper came forth from him, from me as well. Good God! Help me... The kiss was tender, intimate, and our feelings were connected. We felt each other's thoughts. It was incredible. The possessiveness I once thought would be a problem didn't even register. I was truly this man's brother. All I felt was a man who cared so damn much about me. Possessiveness, God, no! Devotion, God, yes!

*"Forever your brother, Jaycee..."*

*"Forever your brother, Jacques..."*

Our lips parted, and as I touched Jaycee's face, his one eyebrow lifted into a questioning expression. "What, brother?" My eyebrows scrunched together. I could feel a puzzled look overcome my face.

"Do you have a twin?" Jaycee's eyes twinkled.

I kissed Jaycee on the forehead, shaking my head back and forth. I gently laughed. I could only imagine.

"If only, brother!"

Janine, ever the lady, had prepared our drinks for us and returned in time to hear our last comments. "Jaycee, my precious brother, have no fear. I have a feeling that once we get through this, Jacques just may have someone worthy of you."

"Sis, you are too kind!" I turned to Jaycee. "Janine is right. Remind me when this nightmare is over and, with your permission, there is someone I would like you to meet!"

"If he's half the man you are, Jacques..."

"Half? Hon, you deserve perfection, and I promise you, he is."

"More reason to end this!" Smiling, Luc tousled his brother's hair.

"That being said, Luc," Janine turned her attention to me, "can we talk a little bit about Elena and Trace and why they are so adamant about ending our relationship with you? When I spoke with Christian, I don't think Elena and Trace are even aware you are a vampire. Just take your time, Jacques, and if I may, I would ask you to share with us some details. I know, love, that you are just as baffled as we are, but they are so driven."

I took a long swallow of my drink and within moments I could feel strength returning to me. A renewed strength to deal with this so we could move on with our lives. Janine softly laughed as I placed the crystal glass gently on the table. I noticed her shaking her head from side to side, and in a soft, almost a whisper, I heard her say "I love you, my sweet vampire."

Smiling at Janine, I took a deep breath and began. "Janine, Elena may talk smart, but it's Trace that I worry about. He has become obsessed with me, and I know for a fact that Elena knows nothing of the reason for this quest he's on... destroying me and the man," I turned my head to look at Luc, "I love." I placed my hand on his chest, then turning my attention back to Janine, I took a deep breath and continued. I owed them this, and before I lost the momentum, I continued. "God! The man has become psychotic. Elena's complete love and devotion for him has completely destroyed her ability to question his reasoning; she is blindly following him. At least those are the vibes I'm getting from her. Honestly, if Elena knew the reason for Trace's behavior, she would want to kill me as well."

Luc brushed his hand across my face. "John, this is why you need to tell us about Trace. What is this vendetta he has for us? He doesn't even know us. Babe, you *must* tell us everything! I love you, John, and I don't plan on losing you. None of us do. I promise you, whatever it is, we will get through this as a family!" Luc pulled me to him as he hugged me.

Fuck! I knew this was going to rear its ugly head, but I could not bury it. I would never try to do that again. I was quickly learning that what you bury always has a way of coming back. You can't bury the fucking truth! Shit! And, I swear...It comes back ten times worse! It went too long as it was. Damn! Like I just told my family, Elena didn't even know about this. Did she? Fuck, now I even had my doubts about that, and how the hell was I supposed to break this to my boy, let alone Jaycee and Janine. I looked at Janine, Jaycee, and then my Sire, Luc. They needed to know the truth, but my God, what would Luc think of me. Fuck! Just FUCK!

While we still embraced, Luc pulled away just enough to look at me. "John? Whatever you need to tell me... us... you know you can. I swear to you, on my eternal life, we will stand by you."

"Babe, it's not that I don't want to tell you. God! I do."

"John, I know it's weighing heavy on you. I know you were someplace else just now. Please, he tapped me on the forehead, let me in!"

"God, Luc, I don't know if I can. I'm so afraid of losing you." My eyes stared into his, pleading for understanding. Even though I knew Luc was speaking the truth, the results could be devastating.

"Jacques?" Jaycee gently turned my head and I looked into his eyes. He leaned toward me, our faces so close that our noses almost touched. "Our brother is right. Whatever you need to tell Luc, it is in the past. As of several days ago, you became family and will be spending a new life with us for eternity. Yes, memories remain, but those are mortal memories. A different life. Do you not realize, my precious brother, that there is no, and never will be any, ill will for things that happened before you became my brother?" He paused long enough to let his lips brush over mine. "Jacques, you must understand one thing... you are ours, always, and forever; and as God is my witness that, Jacques, will not change. Our lives together have only just begun and what you tell us is but fleeting memories of a life that once was. A life that is, for the most part, a memory. What you have with my brother comes along so rarely. It has been sanctified by Luc turning you and accepting you as his lover, his partner. You gave the ultimate gift to Luc and, mon cher, what may have happened in your prior mortal life is but a memory. Cherish it, the good and, yes, my love, the bad, but let it go. Hon… Let. It. Go."

"Jesus, Jaycee." I was so overwhelmed with his words that all I could do for the moment was look at him. Tears coursed down my face and my chest was tight trying to hold back the storm of emotion that was brewing in me. "Merci, brother. I love you." Jaycee's words coursed through me, cleansed me. I knew in my heart that what I was about to say to my Sire, my lover, would not be held against me, but would become a part of a distant memory. A former life. Like a book, it was time to turn the page and start the next chapter, leaving behind memories of pain and betrayal. One I would not go back to. My heart and soul belonged to Luc now. For an eternity I would love only one man, my Luc, my sweet baby boy. I cupped my hand on Jaycee's face and pulled him to me, kissing him gently. As our lips parted, I gently ran the backside of my hand across his face. Framed by his fangs, his smile, so gentle and loving, warmed me. My heart was beating stronger than usual, and I could feel my blood warm me from my head to my toes.

Luc, placing his hand on my chin, turned my head back so I was once again facing him. Taking both of my hands, he smiled. "It's time to set yourself free, John. Share with me. Tell me everything."

"Oui, babe."

# ❧ CHAPTER THIRTY-SIX ❧

After the strength and confidence Jaycee and Janine gave me, I found myself with Luc. Just the two of us, back at *our* townhouse in *our* bedroom. I was reflecting on Luc's words to me *to set myself free*. They radiated through me, and with our connection I came to the realization that Luc would free me from my past. It truly was in the past, but as I paced the room, Luc knew I was scared. Scared shitless! After all, yes, I was a vampire, but for just a handful of days. My former mortal side was showing. *'Aahh crap!'*

"Love?" Luc, sitting at the edge of the bed, brought me out of my pondering. "John, sweetheart, if you keep it up, you'll wear a path in our carpet. Do you want an excuse to remodel? Calm down, babe!"

Our carpet. My God! I stopped in my tracks and looked up and around. I couldn't help but let a small smile out. It still hadn't sunk in. My family promised to give me the world. I was more than happy with what they had already given me! Who would believe, in only a few short days I had become a club owner, received keys to the wheels of my dreams, Provincial townhouses, wealth, and immortality! A vampire, no less. Yes, it was almost too much to comprehend but material things, like the years, fade and disappear. What did not, and would not, sat before me, looking into my eyes. My prayers were answered in the form of this man I called mine. Luc. If all this disappeared tomorrow and all I had was Luc, I would still be the wealthiest man on this planet. My head slowly turned toward him. I could feel that small smile I had was getting bigger. I had to remind myself to breathe because every time I looked at him, he took my breath away. My God! I will never get over just how fucking much I love him.

"What, John? Mon cher, whatever it is, let it go babe. I'm not going anywhere! Remember what Jaycee said...The past is but a distant memory, it has no meaning. You, my love, are, and always will be, mine. Nothing, absolutely nothing, will separate you and me."

"Then, babe, you and I feel the same way." My breath hitched and I put my head down, pausing to collect my thoughts. Taking a deep breath, I lifted my head and slowly turned to face him again, this man I fell so deeply in love with. "It's...ah...God, Luc! I'm afraid the dream is going to end." I nervously ran my fingers through my hair. "Life without you means no life. For you, I would walk through the fires of hell, suffer the unimaginable. I cannot, and will not, accept a life without you. It's not even an option. If I lost you, I would beg for death. It's the only way I can even imagine getting over you." I found myself choking back a sob. "You, my baby boy, have me for all eternity. I just hope you can forgive me." My eyes begged him to understand.

As I walked towards him, he patted his hand on the bed, wanting me to sit next to him. Sitting down as close as I could, I took one of his hands in mine. I squeezed it lightly then, my eyes never leaving his, I brought his hand to my lips and gently kissed it. As I did, Luc's sweet whimper sent a warmth deep within me. I knew how much he needed me. I swear, sometimes he is most eloquent in his silence. His eyes promised he would never leave me; I'd never fall because he would never let me go. Our connection was so deep and powerful, no words were needed, none at all

"It's not a dream, my love. This," his hand gestured around the room, "what you see, what I have, what we, our family, have now, belongs to you as well, babe!" Luc's fingers came up to my face, softly caressing it. "Remember what I said to you, John. The world is yours and I, as well as your brother and sister, have every intention of giving it to you!"

"Luc," I brushed the back of my hand across his cheek, "what you, Jaycee, and Janine have done and given to me, means so much." I shared with Luc what I had been thinking before. "If everything were to be lost tomorrow, and all I had was you, Luc, I'd still be the richest man on earth." As I looked at him, I saw his lips tremble and his eyes start to tear up. He took a deep breath and I took a moment to stroke his hair, letting my hand land at the nape of his neck. There it was, that tingling sensation... My fangs. For a long, quiet moment in time, both of us sat there. We were looking at each other, feeling each other's emotions, forever linked. Luc's eyes were now deep red.

"See, lover, you *are* mine!" A soft smile formed on Luc's lips, the tips of his fangs showing. Luc was right. They are hot! As I let one of my fingers touch them, the memory of them piercing my neck, bringing me eternal life, was still crystal clear, etched forever in my mind. I cupped Luc's chin and pulled him to me. My lips pressed softly against his. I let Luc in, and as our tongues began to play, our fangs lightly nipped at each other. Nicking each other's mouths was of no concern. I relished the taste of my lover's blood mixing with mine. As I pulled back, Luc was looking at me. "Fuck, baby boy, I love you so much. No, Luc! It is a dream!"

Luc looked confused. "Mon cher, no, it's..."

"Yes, love." I placed my fingers on his lips, stopping him in mid-thought. "Baby," I brushed the back of my hand over the side of his face, "it is a dream, an indescribably perfect dream. A dream that is completely, unequivocally, real! Luc," I leaned forward and kissed his forehead, "you are that dream." I pressed my forehead against his, letting every thought and feeling I had flow through my lover, reinforcing what I just said.

'*If I could have only one thing, I would choose you. I need nothing but your love. You, Luc, are mine, as I am yours. Every time I see you, my heart goes thud, my knees knock, and my chest grows tight. Every time you look at me...touch me...I want you...I need you. Loving you, making love to you, and making a life with you, is all that matters. My dream has come true and you, mon cher, are that dream. A dream I never want to wake from.*' Holding his face in my hands, I pulled him to me and kissed him. Slow but urgent. Soft yet desperate. A paradox... A dichotomy... that only Luc and I understood.

After several minutes, Luc pulled back just enough to look into my eyes. He was trembling. "God, John. I know. I feel you, every part of you, and I know. I feel the same way and I know it's the fucking truth."

"Well, babe, as you taught me, vampires can't lie!" I tousled his hair.

"Funny thing of it is, even if we could lie, you just wouldn't, John." He lightly shook his head, and softly smiled at me.

"That means so much to me, Luc."

"It is not necessary to thank me, John, but I promise you, I will honor Janine's request."

"Merci beaucoup. I appreciate that."

"Of course, hon."

I knew I had to do this. I had to tell Luc. He deserved to know. I had asked Jaycee and Janine if they wanted to be with us when I gave Luc the background on why Trace went psycho. God bless them! They both reasoned that they would know. Although it probably would freak someone else out, it didn't bother me. My family needed to know. I appreciated the privacy of being alone with my Sire and I let them know how truly grateful I was for that.

Janine had told me earlier that the reason they could not hear some of my previous thoughts was that when I became a vampire, my already strong telepathic powers were imbued with more strength, stronger than any of them. Without knowing it, I was instinctively protecting them from anything that might hurt them. Talk about feeling like a schmuck! They would not have to worry about that ever again. There would never be any secrets between us.

I thought back to what Jaycee shared with me before we left Janine's apartment.

"When you're ready, Jacques, you will tell us." Jaycee said, as he embraced me. Then he gently tangled his hands into my hair and pulled my lips to his. "Someone I love with all my heart once told me 'one is never enough'." Tilting his head, he pressed his mouth to mine and kissed me. I felt that familiar heat. "I love you, brother. Nothing, absolutely nothing, will change that. Understood?" Our vampire eyes stared into each other's. For a moment, Jaycee wrapped his arms tightly around me and held me close to him. My knees startled to buckle. "Easy, brother. I've got you and I'll never let you go." God Almighty, I loved him!

Now here I was with Luc, the young man I was prepared to die for. The only person, other than myself, that knew Trace was the part of this fucking nightmare that needed to end. I felt my anger once again start to well up inside me. Fuck you, Trace! You will not do this to me again!

As before, it was time. Time to jump into the fray. Damn! The anger that had started was churning inside me and my gut felt like it was on fire. I felt my gums tingle and I knew my eyes were changing color. I reached deep inside me, and with the power I was beginning to tap into, thanks to Luc's help, I took a deep breath and stopped it. I did not want to let my Sire see this side of me. I was saving that for someone else. It would come out soon; very soon, mark my words! Trace had a surprise in store for him if he so much as stepped a foot near my boy, Jaycee, or Janine. May God help him! I had begged Elena, warned her, all to no avail. So help me, if Trace comes anywhere near my family, he better pray I make his death quick and painless. I *will* kill him. I would have no problem ripping his throat open and draining the life from him. For the sake of my sister, I had buried the memory of what Trace had done years ago, but the anger triggered by his continued pursuit was rapidly exhuming ancient history.

A chill ran through me. I found I needed to be close to Luc, much closer than we were now. Sitting next to each other, I wrapped one hand around the back of his neck, the other around his waist, and drew him down on the bed. "Come here, baby boy." My eyes were pleading with Luc's, but there was no need. There was no resistance on Luc's part. I knew he wanted it as much as I needed it. I wanted to be as close as I could humanly get. Humanly? Good one, John! I pulled Luc close to me. Our foreheads touching, our eyes looking into each other's. *"No...This...Now...Luc. Eternity was not enough."* I gently rubbed my nose against Luc's. Oh God, that soft whimper. *"Like a bolt of lightning coursing through my body. If this came crashing down on me, I'd end it! Something as simple as that sweet soft sound, let alone not having him in my life? Fuck that! Where's the guillotine?"*

"Babe! No!" Luc ran his fingers through my hair. "That won't be necessary," Luc said in what was barely a hoarse whisper.

Our connection was back. Never again would I block anything from this young man or my family. I had opened myself up to Luc, and with a mere thought on my part, to Jaycee and Janine as well. *'My family needed to know. Janine, oh God, Janine was going out on her first hunt since I joined the family. It terrified me.'* I felt a tear burn my eye and run down my face. Luc gently kissed it away.

*"Fear not, Jacques. I shall be fine. Remember, mon cher, before*

*you confront Elena and Trace, you must confront your past! Be brave, my beautiful, immortal brother."*

*"I promise, on my immortal life, I will do my best."*

*"I have no doubt, Jacques, mon cher."*

*"We are here, my brother. Listen to what Janine has told you, and know that I love you so damn much. I shall protect, comfort, and cherish you for eternity. Je t'aime, Jacques. Now let it go, brother."*

*"Je t'aime, Jaycee. Janine."*

Luc broke the conversation. "Are you okay with this babe?"

I looked at my Sire. I drank in the sight of him like a fine wine, my baby boy, my lover. "Yeah, Luc. I will never hold any secrets from any of you. You are my family now. There is no turning back. My life, my eternal life, is with you, Jaycee, and Janine."

Luc cuddled closer and brushed his hand against my cheek. "Tell me, lover. Tell me, John. I want to know. I pledge to you that you have nothing to fear. Nothing you could say would change the way I feel about you."

I gently pressed my lips to his, and with the strength of knowing my family was behind me, I took a deep breath and began.

"It was some time ago, Luc. Long before I connected with you. Elena had been dating Trace for years. He was a truck driver at the time. Interstate."

"Ah, let me get a picture." Luc stated, as he put a hand on my hip and drew me closer to him. "Now first of all, John, knowing your taste in men, he must have been younger, um, long, shaggy hair and good looking at the least!"

I found my hand reaching for Luc's hip and pulling him tight to me. God, I just couldn't get close enough to him. His warm, muscular body felt so damn good against mine. Yes, vampires are warm. Blood still courses through our veins, our hearts beat. "You, my love, know me too well!" Smiling, I let my hand ghost across his broad shoulders, down his spine to the cleft where my hand gently caressed one of his firm cheeks. "I wouldn't have it any other way." I smiled softly at him.

"Uuhhnn, I feel the same way about you, babe." I felt his body react immediately. God, I loved to touch him. He didn't need to tell me that he loved me. All I had to do was see his eyes, his smile, and hear that sweet whimper.

"I know, and for that, baby boy, I am eternally grateful!" I let my fangs nibble lightly on his neck.

Luc growled. I watched as his back arched off the bed, his head pressed into the pillow. "Oh, my lover, what you do to me." It took a moment, which I relished, but Luc recovered and went on. "Hey, baby. Continue, s'il vous plait? Dark, handsome, and knew how to handle an eighteen-wheeler. For what it's worth, that is kind of hot!" His eyes twinkled and he had this mischievous look on his face.

"Hey! Who's telling this story anyway?" I lightly squeezed Luc's side, causing him to giggle and press his body against mine. "Yeah, Luc, you are right on the money so far. Since the first day I met him, I felt something from him, but as it happened, I was his boss before he took up trucking and Elena got a job at the same place. It was love at first sight between the two of them. God, Luc!" I paused a moment and let out a slight, albeit nervous, laugh.

"What, John?" Luc asked. His left eyebrow raised in question, waiting for me to continue. "Come on, babe."

I took a moment, smiled, and shook my head.

Luc's eyes pleaded with me to tell him more. "You're killing me here! Tell me, please?" Were those puppy dog eyes I was seeing?

Leave it to Luc, despite the seriousness of the situation, to keep me centered and calm. I actually had to chuckle. "Okay, babe. I remember one day, he was underneath this car doing an oil change and a bolt broke. It soaked him with motor oil. When he came up from under the car, the air was blue. He had ripped his shirt off, but he still had slick oil running down his shoulders and pecs. He was so fucking pissed! All I could do was stand there and watch. I remember looking at Elena. Luc, if her jaw could have, it would have hit the service station floor. I knew, I just fucking knew, that was it. A fire had been lit, so I let it go. They had dated for several years when Trace decided to train to become a truck driver."

"Um..." Luc swung his leg up over my waist. I reached down and began massaging his foot. "I bet Elena's jaw wasn't the only one hitting the proverbial floor!"

I looked at Luc and smirked. His eyes were more interested in another location besides my eyes, but I could tell he was putting this story together faster than I could tell it. The shit-eating grin on his face wasn't helping.

"He asked you to go on a run with him, didn't he?" His eyes traveled up to meet mine, and waggling his eyebrows, he gave me such a hot look I momentarily lost track of where the hell I was.

The more we talked, the more I relaxed. Unaware, I had released my hand from his foot and let my fingertips trace every part of his body. Luc's face was so expressive. I knew I was distracting him, but damn, he had such control. He was concentrating on what we agreed on, putting this to rest, although a little part of him wanted to fuck me senseless. To be quite honest, if he would have brushed the tip of my erect cock, I would have cum. Luc was putting a picture together in his head, and honestly... No, he couldn't! No, just no! Luc pressed his body closer to mine. How could he? Really? My man was enjoying this! I felt like I was telling Luc a bedtime story. A kinky, hot bedtime story. Unfortunately, this bedtime story did not have a happy ending.

I let out a soft grunt. "Yeah, love. That's right. All the way to Miami."

"John, love. Can I ask you something?"

"Of course." My fingers caressed his face. "Anything, Luc. You know that!"

"You were attracted to him, weren't you, mon cher." It was a statement, not a question, but I answered him anyway.

"I had been since I first saw him," I quietly admitted, feeling ashamed.

"I know the feeling." Luc's hand brushed my face, and leaning in, I felt his lips ghost across mine.

Catching my breath, I went on. "Like I said, I buried those feelings when Elena and Trace started dating."

"So, there you were, going cross-country in a big rig with an obviously hot guy behind the wheel!" Luc's eyes twinkled with mischief.

"Yeah, but baby, hands off, you know? This was Elena's man, and, um, let's just say I didn't feel like getting the crap kicked out of me. For all intents and purposes, I had to believe and resign myself to the fact he was straight. So, life went on, at least I thought it would." I paused and took a deep breath, steeling my nerves to go on. "God, Luc," I ran the back of my hand across his face, "I, uh, I started seeing someone else at the shop. It turned out to be Trace's best friend."

Luc looked into my eyes, concern starting to show on his face. Christ, Luc knew. "You called him K.C., didn't you?"

"Babe! My God! How did you know?"

"You actually answered that question yourself. John, you are still a very young vampire. Strong, emotional events, friends, lovers, even the loss of someone, well, they leave an imprint on your mind. Your mortal mind. You still have remnants of K.C. in your memory. I can read those babe."

"Luc, you know I don't doubt anything you tell me, but how can I let go when I will have to live for an eternity with these memories?"

"Babe, you won't. Your mortal memories will disappear, very quickly. John," Luc wrapped his hand in mine, "can I ask you a question? A personal question? I'm not doing this to upset you. I just want to put you at ease. Okay?"

"Luc, love," I gave him a chaste kiss, "of course."

"How did you get to Paris?"

I thought for a moment. "Luc, babe...What do you mean? I've always been here."

Luc pulled me to him, his hand pressing my head to his chest. "It's already happening, love. You flew in from the United States less than a week ago."

"Oh. Shit."

"John, it'll be okay."

"So Elena, Trace...K.C.?"

"Once you've resolved these conflicts, they too, will be forgotten."

I lifted my head and brushed my lips across Luc's. "I don't want to sound cold, but actually, Luc, that's just fine with me. I personally like the memories we've started to create."

"You are one hell of a man, John."

"Thanks to you, babe." I pulled myself up and put my head on Luc's pillow. I needed to be as close as I could to my Sire.

"So, John. Your boy's name was K.C. and he was Trace's best friend?"

"Yeah, babe. What were the odds?" I closed my eyes. K.C.'s face flashed through my mind like a faded photograph. "He, um, Luc...He, well, he reminded me of you." I felt the corner of my mouth quiver.

"How so, John?" Luc pulled me tighter. His one eyebrow raised in question. "It's okay... I want to know."

"God, Luc. He was soft spoken, absolutely adorable, and smart. He had this smile, like yours. He was so damn good looking. He had this sense of humor. Luc, he could make you laugh even when you felt like shit. Huh, he even had your laugh. He was so damn giving. He always put others' needs in front of his own."

"Life, to him, was one big adventure." I took a deep breath, then another, as my hand gently ran up and down Luc's arm. I felt a lump form in my throat. "Babe, his license plate read 'Johns boy'." I turned my head slightly, unable to look at him. I felt like I was betraying Luc.

"John?" Luc put a hand on my chin, pulling my eyes back to his. "It's okay. God, baby boy, I'm sorry...So sorry. You loved him, and it is so obvious he loved you. I can feel that and that's all right. John, you deserved, and you deserve, to be loved."

I felt my heart start to race. I didn't even have to tell Luc the rest of this God-awful story. Luc pressed his forehead against mine. Silence fell between us. Luc's hand reached up and I felt his fingers run through my hair. Then, pulling only far enough away to see me, Luc looked at me. His eyes were deep red. "The bastard killed him. Trace killed K.C. in cold blood, didn't he?" Luc bared his fangs and let out a low, guttural growl. Christ! Luc knew.

"Yeah, babe, he did. As if losing the man I was in love with wasn't enough, they couldn't prove it. Couldn't prove that Trace killed K.C., and it still tears me apart. I knew and, Luc, I think Elena knows too." A tear ran down my face. "I...I just felt so helpless. Luc, I feel so fucking guilty."

Luc pulled me closer, kissing the tear off my cheek. "John, no. Don't do this to yourself. What happened, what Trace did, was not your fault. Let that burden go, babe. Hey, look at me." I did. Luc's deep red eyes pulled me into him. God, the feeling that came over me. It was like Luc was actually taking the sadness I felt away from me, releasing me from the guilt that I felt since K.C. died.

"Trace was involved with Elena. God, Luc, you should have seen him. He had K.C. and I so fooled. He acted like he was fucking happy for us. Elena, well, until recently I thought she was," a lump formed in my throat, "truly happy for us."

"What about the authorities, John?"

"They, um, they..." A sick feeling swept through me. "Babe, they ruled it a suicide. A fucking suicide. God! What a farce! I just couldn't wrap my head around that, Luc. No way in hell he killed himself. K.C. and I were planning a weekend get-away. He was so excited, babe. He even had his truck packed with the gear we were going to use." I felt my eyes sting. Luc, pressing into me, stroked my face with his hand. Tears began to streak down my cheek.

"Baby, take a moment here, okay?" Luc started running his fingers through my hair. "God, John, I am so sorry." I laid there feeling his warmth and love, our eyes looking deeply into each other's. After a few moments, Luc looked at me and, as gently as he could, knowing the emotional precipice I was standing on, asked "Was there a note? Anything?" He already knew the answer.

"Nothing, Luc. We were happy. We were in love. Luc, the day before I lost K.C., he even announced it to everyone at work, and that night he took me home to meet his folks. Nothing, not a damn clue or a shred of evidence was ever found pointing the authorities to the possibility of suicide. Our fucking police force. Shit! Just go with the easiest conclusion. Incompetent assholes!" I closed my eyes and sighed. When I opened them, I found Luc, his face inches from mine, just looking at me. Compassion showed in his deep red eyes.

"John, if it's any consolation, K.C. got the chance to be loved by you."

"Luc, I did love him. My God, he was such a beautiful, young man. Cut down in the prime of his young, sweet life. Trace, that son-of-a-bitch, doesn't deserve to be breathing. Luc, he died be...be...because he loved me. He didn't deserve that."

"John, no he didn't. Please, babe, I can't tell you what to do, but you have to move on...Let this terrible tragedy go. John, remember, for now, the good times you had with him. Remember K.C. and the happiness you shared. When we resolve this situation, you *will* let go. It will no longer linger and torment you."

"I will, babe, but Trace literally got away with murder!" I gripped Luc's arms. "K.C. will have justice. I owe him that. He died because he loved me. Now I fear it's happening again." I tried to control them, but the tears came. I began to cry. "Luc, love... What if...?" I broke down.

"John," Luc pulled me close, "you cannot blame yourself for this." Luc gripped one of my arms. "Trace will pay for what he did!" Luc growled again. My Sire was serious, deadly serious. "You didn't know, babe. How could you?" Luc gently wiped the tears from my face. "John, what I can't wrap my head around is, well, babe, there were no indications...Or were there? Was Trace jealous?" Luc asked, sincerely wanting to know, his hand now pressed against my chest.

I couldn't help but notice Luc's fingers start to work on the buttons of my shirt.

"Well, yes...Now that I think about it." Luc's eyes never left mine, but my shirt was now in a heap on the floor. *'How the hell did he do that?'*

"John, love, I'm deeply sorry about K.C. He sounded like an incredible young man, and John, from what you just shared with me, you gave him happiness, your love, and most importantly, yourself." Luc paused and I watched as his eyes looked at me from head to toe. "Baby boy, you're mine now. You're all I want, you're all I need. You are everything to me. As for Trace, fuck him. What he did is unforgivable." Luc was serious, but I had to hold back a smile. Luc's possessive side was showing and damn, despite it all, it was (although I'm sure Luc wouldn't agree) like watching a little boy throw a temper tantrum when someone tries to take his favorite toy away from him. "You have me now and I swear to you, John, nothing and no one will take you from me. I am so lucky, John."

I don't know how Luc does it, but quite frankly I don't care. Yes, reliving these painful memories helped. God! I tried with my mortal friends, but I would have had better luck talking to a tree. I had loved K.C. deeply. Unlike most of my friends, who couldn't or wouldn't get past the idea of K.C. and I together as a couple, Luc listened. His eyes were full of compassion and understanding, his words were comforting, but it is that incredible preternatural connection that we share. The pain I felt, Luc was feeling too. It was like, how the hell do I explain this, my Sire takes the hurt, the pain and the sorrow I'm feeling, and gives it to himself so I don't have to suffer alone.

"You, Luc? You the lucky one?" I pulled Luc into a mind-numbing kiss. "Baby boy, I was broken before you. I was barely holding on. I really didn't think I could go on after I lost K.C.; now," my breath hitched, "I'm holding on to you. I'm no longer just barely breathing, no longer have a broken heart. Luc, in your name, I found healing, and I'm holding on, holding on to you, for an eternity." Once again I pressed my lips to his and once again time stopped. Our souls connected. The kiss we shared was gentle and sweet. Our fingers tangled up in each other's hair as our bodies pressed tightly together.

I didn't want to stop, but the need for air forced me to. I just laid there and pressed my forehead against Luc's. Our red eyes met each other's and all I could do was gaze at this man. Something about this boy conspired against me, causing me to lose control. Just one touch, one kiss, and I was swept away. Everything and everyone else vanished. Nothing mattered but my connection to my Sire, my Luc.

Huh? No. How the hell? Much to my amazement and absolute delight, Luc and I were now completely naked. Hot muscular flesh to hot muscular flesh.

"What the...?" I couldn't even finish.

"John? Babe, are you okay?" Luc's hands cupped my face, his face showing concern.

"More than okay, mon cher. You just, um, you just drive me wild baby! Takes me a bit to recuperate!" My eyes were now transfixed on the beautiful, young man who lay next to me. "Um, baby boy? How did we...ah...not that I'm complaining, but... fuck...we're...holy shit...our clothes!" I was blabbering like an idiot.

Luc giggled, giving me one of his completely X-rated stares. "We didn't get to that part, did we?" "P-p-pa-ar-rt-?" I stuttered.

Luc giggled again and smiled. "I didn't get to the part about our preternatural ability to move quicker than the actual eye can see! We, babe, put the stealth in stealth. We have the ability to move faster than what the mortal eye can perceive." His hands moved across my body, his eyes tracing every move his hands made. "You have that power, but, as you know, being a newly-born vampire, well..." Luc's hand was rubbing my chest. "What you don't know yet, what's left of your mortal mind is still intact. Right now the abilities you haven't learned, you can't process." For a moment Luc became silent and just looked at me, studying me. "God, baby. Have I told you lately how fucking perfect you are?"

My breath hitched and for a moment I thought my heart stopped. "Yeah, but that's okay. Some things are worth hearing more than once. God help me, Luc, you are too! Preternatural," I kissed his shoulder, "perfection! Show me babe."

"Oh don't worry, love. It'll become a natural ability for you too, but," Luc's eyes locked on to mine, "for now, I prefer it this way!"

Little shit. I was going to complain, but why?

"Unh...You'll get no...Oh God, Luc!" His hands were all over me, touching and groping, "argument from me! Unnhh...Where were we, Luc?" My hand caressed his ass. God, how good he felt. My mind flashed to the last time I thrust into him. Warm, wet, and tight, his muscles clenching my erect cock. Fuck!

"Indications?" Luc moaned, his eyelids half closed, his fangs pressing into his lower lip. *'Mon Luc, mon vampire.'*

"Huh?" The touch of Luc's muscular, warm body pressed against mine caused my thought process to completely derail. Not to mention our hard cocks pressed together. Like I said, fuck!

"Babe, indications about Trace? About his, um," Luc looked away shyly, his face turning red, "his sexual feelings about you?"

I paused briefly. My angel with fangs! "God, Luc, you're blushing. Babe, you have every right to know." I took my hand and gently tilted his head so he was once again looking at me. His face was still flushed. "Oh yeah, well, I don't know if you could call these indications, but, I don't know, after I lost K.C., Trace's affection for me seemed to intensify. He was there for me day and night, consoling me with things like hugs, kisses on the cheek, and intense looks. There was the soft touch of his hand on my shoulder and telling me that he loved me. After K.C. died, Luc, we postponed the run, but then, well," I paused, "our road trip. God, Luc, our road trip. Trace thought it would be good to get me out. Luc, honestly, I took it more as a sign of brotherly affection than actually being physically attracted to me. After all, he had proposed to sis, so I'm thinking brother-in-law, you know?" Luc had propped himself up with his hand. I knew I had his full attention. "Now that I know... Christ! It was all an act." I could feel anger building in me. My chest grew tight and my voice tense. Luc immediately picked up on it and pressed a kiss to my forehead.

"John, it's okay, love. Remember, you had no way of knowing. For all intents and purposes, he used you, used your emotions. You were in a very fragile state of mind and he used that to his advantage." Luc paused and I knew it was to collect his thoughts and help me close this chapter of my mortal life. "Something happened on the way to Miami, didn't it, mon cher?"

"Yeah, something did. I swear, babe, it was something totally unexpected. Hell, Luc. It wasn't even a blip on the Doppler!"

"What was it? What happened? Hot front?" Luc grinned and pressed closer to me, half on top of me.

His now very erect cock pressed firmly against my abs.

"Yeah, babe, but he said... Damn him, Luc! He said he wanted to comfort me, help me through the pain. Luc, he even said I would be helping him, as he loved K.C. too. Bastard!"

"Easy, lover." Luc pulled me to him. "He's evil. He knew exactly what he was doing. Like I said, babe, he will pay. I know it's small consolation, but we will avenge K.C.'s death."

I was trying to wrap my head around what was going on. Here I was, lying next to the man I would be spending eternity with, spilling my guts out and confessing my love for another man. My stomach knotted up at the thought that a cold-blooded killer used me. Yet Luc showed no signs of anger or jealousy toward me. *No, John. He was just completely naked wanting to make love to you!* Why the hell was this bothering me? Why was I waiting for the other shoe to drop? For the first time, my face turned from Luc. God, this was either going to be the nail in the coffin, or Luc was going to be Luc and keep his promise. Given the response I was getting from my boy, Luc was going to be Luc.

Why the fuck am I even doubting or questioning my Sire? What more did he have to do to prove his love for me? Oh shit! Luc's pre-cum slicked my stomach and I felt his hard cock thrust up and down. His hands splayed across my back, grabbing on to me. Luc was tapped into me. Luc knew every one of my thoughts, my memories. He knew the story before I began. Once I opened myself to Luc, he already knew. God, he did this to help me heal. He did this so I could move on. Just when I thought I couldn't love Luc more. Don't get me wrong, what K.C. and I had was, as mortals, right and beautiful. It was real and good, but mortal love compared to immortal love? There was nothing to compare it to. I fucking cherished this man, and in the emotional state I was in, I needed him, wanted him. I wanted Luc to consume me, devour me. The next thing I knew, Luc gently, but firmly, grabbed a handful of my hair and I was suddenly face to face with the man I loved.

"Let it go, baby boy." His eyes, deep red, penetrated mine causing heat to surge through my body.

My cock was so hard it felt like it was going to burst.

Luc canted his hips and thrust his cock against my abs.

"Unh..." I felt the muscles in my body contract, right down to my toes. I looked at him, desperately trying to hold it together, but that was a useless cause. "Trying out my theory, baby boy?" My hands grabbed his ass, pulling him tight to my body.

"Uunnhh...you mean fucking you to death?" Luc was a mess. He was so turned on and God, it felt so good to know I was the one responsible.

"Yeah, Luc. Don't stop. Kill me, baby!" That fucking whimper didn't help!

Then Luc surprised me. He stilled himself and, stroking my hair, he whispered in my ear. "Tell me more, John. Not about Trace, John. Fuck him!" He looked at me with caution in his eyes. "If this is too much...God, John! I shouldn't even be asking you this."

"Luc, baby boy, I told you, you can ask me anything. What do you want to know?"

"Tell me about this young man you were in love with, mon cher." Luc's breath hitched. "Tell me about K.C. Tell me about the first time you made love. I want to get to know this young man."

I was so taken aback by Luc's request that I couldn't even form a sentence. It wasn't that I was angry. It was my baby boy and the undeniable love he had for me. Immediately I could feel Luc tense up, his eyes telling me he wished he could take his request back. "Oh God, John. I'm sorry, babe. I have no right to..."

I placed two of my fingers on his lips. "Shhhhh, baby boy. No, it's okay. I want to tell you. Jesus, Luc, you are the first one who ever even truly wanted to know. Are you sure, babe?"

"Yes, John. Merci, s'il vous plait?" Luc placed his right leg over my hip and, with a hand on my shoulder, pulled me close to him. Looking into my eyes he softly, tenderly said "Tell me, babe, tell me about this young man." Luc's lips brushed mine and then, gently, I wrapped one of my arms around him, pulling his head to my shoulder. With that, I began to tell my Sire about K.C., my one and only mortal love, and the love we shared and made.

Luc, God bless him, listened to every word. He listened to me as I told him about the secret moments we shared at work, our trips, and our dreams. The day we took his boat out on the lake and the last time we made love, the night before K.C. was killed. He laughed with me, cried with me, held me, and comforted me. I don't know how much time had passed, but it was of no concern. Luc brought K.C. back for me. To remember, to mourn, to love, and yes, to help me say goodbye. For that and so many other reasons, I would, as I promised Jaycee and Janine, protect my baby boy's heart and his life.

We lay there. Luc's eyes, which had changed to his deep red, looked into mine. His fangs extended, and with a sweet whimper, he pressed his forehead against mine.

Out of respect to K.C.'s memory, not a word was said. A serene silence filled our bedroom. Then I heard Luc take a deep breath. "John, no wonder you fell in love with him. He sounded...Hell, he was an incredible man. I... I um," Luc abruptly stopped.

"What, love? I... What Luc?" I put a hand on his arm.

"If I would have been there, known you and K.C., I could have..." A tear ran down Luc's face.

"Jesus, Luc. No, don't do that to yourself." I pulled him to me. "I love you so much." My hand caressed his face, my thumb wiped away the tear that was running down his cheek. "Luc, this..." I placed my hand over Luc's heart, then put Luc's hand on mine. "You and I. It was meant to be. What I have in here," I pressed Luc's hand firmly against my chest and my beating heart, "belongs to you now."

"For that, John, I am eternally grateful."

I couldn't help but notice the change of expression on Luc's face. Someone was asking him a question.

"John," Luc had a grin on his face, "someone who loves you would like to talk with you." I smiled. *"Hey Jaycee."* My words were directed to him.

*"Jacques, brother?"*

I couldn't help but notice Jaycee's voice was raspy. *"My dearest brother, babe, have you been crying?"*

"Um...Yeah, Jacques. I..."

*"Jaycee, I love you too. So damn much!"* As I felt my brother's emotions course through me, Luc pulled himself closer to me.

*"Sis and I want you to know just how deeply sorry we are for your loss, and we just want you to know that what happened to K.C. hurts us deeply. Trace will be punished... severely."*

*"Jaycee...Janine...Merci."*

*"You need not thank us, Jacques. You are our brother. What hurts you, hurts us. Jacques, my precious boy, you will never feel that pain again."*

*"Merci, Janine. I love you both so very much. I cherish you all."*

*"As do we, Jacques. As do we our precious, beloved vampire."*

*"Janine, no words can express what I am feeling."*

*"Jacques, we know. We know, brother."* Jaycee's voice was a hoarse whisper in my head.

*"Jaycee?"*

*"Yes, Luc?"*

Luc's hand ghosted over my ass. *"Before John and I rejoin you two, may I have a little more time,"* Luc winked at me, brushing his hand over my erect cock, *"with my baby boy?"*

Janine giggled.

*"Don't do anything I wouldn't do, little brother!"*

With that, Luc proceeded to show me just how much he loved me.

# ◈ CHAPTER THIRTY-SEVEN ◈

"Luc?" I could barely form his name. My motor functions were rebooting themselves.

"Yes, love?" His fingers played with my hair, his sweat-sheened, muscular body pressed close to mine.

"Thank you." I lightly caressed his face, our foreheads pressed against each other's. I didn't stand a chance. Luc, as promised, didn't even flinch. What had happened in the past, in my mortal life, was a distant memory. As he took me in his arms and made love to me, all I felt was my Sire, my love, my man! His feelings for me poured through my soul, intertwined with mine, leaving no doubt that Luc grieved with me over my mortal loss and had helped me to let go of the pain and guilt that plagued me. I also knew that nothing would separate us. I was Luc's and Luc was mine. Our connection, our souls, were linked for an eternity and nothing could, or would, ever separate us. I had wanted to explain further, but Luc now knew exactly why Trace's vendetta raged in him. Luc had, in his years of wisdom, put it into one very simple and conclusive statement.

"There are very few things in life that warrant taking a life. This John, is one of them. What Trace did, he will pay for." Luc's words were edged with steel. "We owe that to K.C. Justice will be served."

"Luc, babe. I just… ah… I just..." I felt myself choking up.

"Just what, John?" Luc stroked my brow, then he let his fingers gently caress my face.

"Luc, I just can't help but think that if I would have met you, been with you first...um...then, well..." Luc's eyes were studying mine.

"K.C. would be alive." Luc softly answered.

"Yeah, babe." I sighed. "Yeah."

"John," he was softly running his fingers through my hair, "that is so thoughtful and so damn loving of you. Hon, I know this sounds harsh, but," his eyes studied mine, "that is life. Unfair, yes...but, John, remember he lives on. Forever." Luc patted my chest. "In here, in your heart... Forever."

I dragged in a deep breath. Then another. What Luc did for me, taking away the angst, guilt and hurt, leaving me with only sweet memories of K.C., overwhelmed me.

"Babe?" I pulled Luc close to me. "I have to apologize." My eyes looked deep into his. His words had brought me peace, and more importantly, closure. I thought we were close, but what happened between us broke down any remaining barriers. We laid ourselves out to each other and exorcised any demon that could possibly rear its ugly head.

"For what, love?" Luc's fingers continued to caress my face.

"Luc? I feel somewhat foolish and ashamed at how I acted." My fingers softly ran across his defined pecs.

"Whatever for, John?"

"I was so afraid of how you would feel about me and my previous relationship that I...well...I was afraid of how you would react. I'm sorry love, I truly am. You, my boy, are," my breath hitched, "mine forever. What's in the past, is truly in the past. I have never felt as loved as I do now. To think that I will feel this way for an eternity with you," Luc tangled his legs with mine, "is all I need. Yes, Luc, you and my new family have given me everything a man could ever want. You, Luc," A tear formed and began to run down his face, "are the only one I will ever, ever need. As long as you are next to me, I have everything. I am yours for eternity, baby boy."

Luc began to cry. His body trembled with emotion. As he had done for me so many times, I pulled him into my arms and held him. As Luc wept, I focused carefully on the short time that Luc had reminded me that I had been here, marveling at how far we had come and at how hard it was to remember my arrival. Looking back, I recognized that from the moment I stepped off the plane and saw him,

I knew. I just fucking knew that Luc and I were meant to be together. To have him in my life as a mortal would have been a gift. Now, the idea that I would spend an eternity with him, was something that, even as a vampire, I could not comprehend. All the comfort, love, and protection this man gave me for this past week, damn it seemed like so much longer, culminated in this. This was my chance to repay this man that I had fallen so completely in love with. Letting him seek comfort and release from his angst and loneliness, and to know he will always be able to find refuge in my arms, along with my eternal devotion to him. God, I loved this boy so fucking much! As I held him, I could feel every emotion he was allowing himself to purge from his soul. Damn! I could only hold him tightly in my arms and let him know I would never let him go.

"I love you, John. I really do." Luc's voice hitched. "You are mine, always and forever." Repeating the vow that, from the first time I heard it, I knew was sacred.

"I know, babe. I know."

Slowly, I could feel Luc's face lifting from my chest. My eyes watched as his head tilted up and looked into mine. His eyes were red, this time from crying. His face was wet with tears. He gently pushed himself up so he was face to face with me.

"Hi." Luc's eyes looked softly into mine, his voice hoarse.

"Hi, yourself." I gently kissed the remaining tears from his face.

There was a soft knock on the door. Both Luc and I knew who it was.

I could sense what Luc wanted to ask, but before he could speak, I answered the question for him. "Jaycee, get yourself in here!" Luc and I watched as the door opened. With a look of concern on his face, there he stood. Jaycee. Our brother. My Sire's Sire. Try to explain this family tree!

"Luc, love, does a vampire need to be invited in by another vampire?" I was being totally serious, but apparently Luc thought otherwise.

"John, you goof!" He wiped a tear from his eye with the back of his hand, which I found totally endearing. "What do you think?" I noticed him trying his best to fight back a smile.

"Well, babe. I, um…" Luc started giggling, and from the other side of the room I heard Jaycee start to laugh as well.

"Well, this is just great! This isn't fair, babe. We didn't cover it in your 'Rule book', you little shit!" I playfully tickled him.

"Luc?" Jaycee started walking into the bedroom. "Jacques is right. I think we overlooked one."

"Oui, brother. I guess John's favorite author should have interviewed us first!"

I had all I could do not to start laughing. Luc and Jaycee were never going to let this go. Who knew vampires could be so much fun?!

"So, which of the two of you is Lestat?" I looked at Luc and did my best to give a serious looking evaluation, then Jaycee, who had started to make his way to my side of the bed. He was looking at me with this wicked smirk on his face, waiting for an answer. "Wait a minute! Don't answer that! I'd say, Luc. Jaycee, you're more the quiet, brooding type. You're the Louie of the family!"

Luc and Jaycee were both staring at me like I had suddenly gone completely mad. I knew that wouldn't last long, as both of them started to laugh.

"God, how did I exist before my boy?" Luc's eyes twinkled.

"Brood over this, Jacques!" Jaycee growled, ripping off his shirt.

"Oh my God!" I knew it was rude to stare, but, my Lord, Jaycee's muscles flexed. He was so damn cut, just like Luc. "God help me!"

"Hey, bro!" Luc giggled. "Careful, you'll make my boy go into shock!"

Before I knew it, Jaycee had divested himself of his clothes and was crawling under the covers. Both Luc and Jaycee started tickling me and generally teaching me a lesson. They were relentless. The more I begged for mercy, the more they inflicted, what they knew to be torture, on me. I had to do something fast! Even as a vampire, anybody who is ticklish knows this is pure hell. I had one trick up my sleeve that would bring me relief and drive them to the brink. I reached down and grabbed their stiff cocks in my hands and proceeded to swipe my thumbs over their swollen heads, which were leaking pre-cum. I fisted them, and with one slick stroke, both my mighty vampires caved in. Luc fisted the sheets and Jaycee's back arched off the bed, his heels digging into the mattress. A collective moan filled the room.

"My turn!" I stroked their hard, engorged cocks. What we shared next was as intense, emotional, and satisfying as what happened the last several times, with one exception. All the barriers and worries that had been part of our combined baggage were gone, checked at the gates. Yes, what we were going to have to come to grips with tonight was still there, but with nothing between the three of us, emotionally, that could distract us, a potential threat was gone. The connection that Luc, Jaycee, Janine, and I had, would allow us to overcome the obstacle that was threatening our family, our very existence.

"Hey, John?" Luc's hand rubbed my chest.

It was early evening. The sun had set and the full moon was high and shining brightly in the Parisian sky. The classic arched windows in our townhouse allowed a perfect view of the City of Lights including the Eiffel Tower. It allowed the soft, white light of the full moon to illuminate the bedroom in a soft glow that let me see the two men who meant everything to me. Content and at peace after our love making, even if it was temporary, having Luc's and Jaycee's bodies wrapped around mine was all I needed, but I knew very well what we have to face. At that moment, seeing the celestial portrait painted in the evening sky, my mind was on someone else who meant the world to me... My sister, my wolf, my Janine.

"Yeah, baby boy?" My eyes studied his.

"Hey, are you okay?" Luc pulled himself closer.

Even now, after what we had just shared, I was overwhelmed at the desire that still burned in me. Having Luc's and Jaycee's hard, muscular bodies pressed closely to mine only fueled the fire now set to ignite again.

I felt the soft brush of Jaycee's hand on my shoulder.

"If I may, brother? You've been so quiet. Did you want to be alone with Luc? I...I can, um... I can leave." His blue eyes told a whole different story.

"No way, Jaycee." I brushed his face with my fingertips. Luc smiled and Jaycee's body instantly relaxed. "If there was ever a time we needed to be together, it's now."

"Did we do something, John?"

"Why would you ask that, Luc?"

"It's just, um, you've been so quiet." Luc was so concerned, I was beginning to feel guilty, but I had to force back a smile at the tickling bout I went through. Worry lines appeared on both of their foreheads. I knew what I was doing was just a little bit naughty, but hey, they deserved a little payback!

"Oh God, Jacques." Jaycee's voice was shaky. "Please tell us so we can make it better."

"You can't make it better, Jaycee." I feigned, at least I tried to sound as if my world had come to an end. Holy shit! If you would have told me a month ago that I would be where I was, teasing two very powerful vampires and getting away with it, well, crazy didn't begin to describe it!

"Um, John? Whatever Jaycee and I did...I'm sure that..." Luc stuttered nervously.

I couldn't do this to them anymore. Placing my fingers on Luc's lips to stop any further concern, I looked at Luc, then Jaycee.

"You sweet, adorable boys. How could you possibly improve upon our lovemaking?" Giggling, I no sooner confessed when Luc and Jaycee showed me what we were partly known for... Fangs!

"You, mon cher, shall know our wrath!" Both Luc and Jaycee were on their knees leaning over me, their faces so close I could feel their warm breath. Luc was trying so hard to do his best Dracula voice and all I could do was giggle. Jaycee immediately lost it. I watched as Jaycee let himself fall next to me. Apparently laughs are contagious, because a second later Luc was on his side next to me, giggling so hard he was having a hard time catching his breath. I looked at Jaycee, then Luc. I was a goner. Damn! It felt so good to just laugh, however short-lived it might be.

Luc, propping himself up on his elbow, kissed me on the cheek. "Seriously, baby boy, where were you?" His cheeks were still flushed.

"Boys, I just, I'm having a hard time, knowing, um..." I had to take a deep breath as I was on the verge of losing it and I couldn't. I wanted to be strong for them.

"It's Janine, isn't it?" Luc ran his fingers across my face.

"Yeah, Luc. It's Janine." I took one of Luc's hands into mine. Holding it, I found myself nervously rubbing his fingers with my thumb. "I know she's with her pack. I know Sam and Christian have Elena and Trace detained. But something doesn't feel right. Fuck, boys, I don't know. I know we haven't had any problems with Alec, but shit! He's out there doing the same thing as Janine. Only he is just as much a psychopath as Trace is. I can't help but be concerned. Do we know if Alec has aligned with anyone to help him, if he were to want to seek revenge?" Fuck! *If* he were to want...He does! He made that perfectly clear.

"Jacques, Luc, if it makes you feel any better," Jaycee put his hand on my chest, "while you were with Luc earlier, Janine and I contacted Sam and Christian and our contacts in the vampire and wolf communities. No one has heard of anything untoward. Hell bro, no one has seen Alec since the other day when Adrian laid him out on the street."

"Merci, Jaycee." I faced him and softly kissed him. "I have to be honest with you. I don't like the sound of that. Please, don't take offense but, although I appreciate you and love you, babe, I am still damned scared. Please forgive me, but I won't feel relieved until I know that bastard is dead. I don't know what I'd do. I couldn't imagine my life without any of you."

"Jacques. God knows I love you too, so very much." Jaycee nuzzled my neck. "You aren't alone in your feelings."

"Luc? Jaycee?" My voice was apprehensive.

"Yes, love?" Luc answered. His head rested on my chest.

"Christ! How do I say this? Um...Trace. If we are to find complete peace and freedom from this psychopath. God!" My voice began to stutter, falter, at what Luc and I had come to terms with earlier.

"We are with you, John." Luc started kissing my hand that was still holding his. "Just like Alec, Trace must, and will pay. Keep in mind, it's not just you, Jaycee, and I that are looking after Janine tonight. We have Sam and Christian and the vampire and wolf community on our side. Remember, babe, there is still a kill order on Alec. I have not rescinded that. Like Jaycee said, you are not alone in your feelings. He will be dealt with swiftly. He has become a liability, a threat to our safety, and that of the mortal community of Paris as well." Luc kissed me lightly on my chest. "I sense Trace's punishment is weighing heavy on your mind."

Jaycee was lying next to me on his side, his head propped on one hand. "It's okay, bro. As Janine said, you have a beautiful soul. Though it is justified, we know, Jacques, the thought of killing Trace is troubling you deeply. You know you have our full support, love."

"Merci, Jaycee." By this time, Luc had also propped himself up, so both my boys were giving me their full attention. "Luc, I will take full responsibility for this. It needs to be done." I gently kissed Luc on the chest. "For the way K.C. died, and the unbearable loss I felt, Trace must pay. I owe that to K.C."

"Say no more, babe. Free your mind of the guilt. I can feel it coursing through you. Give it to me. Let it go." Luc's red eyes locked onto mine and I felt a warmth flow through my body, the anxiety I felt was dissipating.

"Luc, bro, allow me to share some of that with you as well." Jaycee kissed my cheek. His eyes had become deep red too. I felt a sudden peace sweep through me.

"Better, bro?" I felt Jaycee's fingertips lightly stroke my arm. I could only nod as I looked at the two men lying next to me.

"Good. That's all Jaycee and I will ever want for you. Peace, happiness, and our love. Trace shall be dealt with... Swiftly!" Luc brushed my face with his hand.

The guilt I felt was gone. *Elena, I begged you, I warned you. You just couldn't fucking listen. Trace is a dead man. Neither I, nor my Sire, my brother, or sister have done anything to warrant this obvious wish to destroy us. Trace got away with murder once and I will be damned if he thinks he's going to get away with it again! Why the fuck didn't you listen to me?*

I found comfort in the closeness of my lover and Jaycee. I once again turned my sights toward the window and the work of art that is Paris. Then, ever so slowly, I looked at the men who have come to mean everything to me.

"Luc, my love? Jaycee, babe?"

"Oui." They both answered in unison.

"Hold me, please. Hold me tight and never let me go." With no further words, I closed my eyes as I found myself in their loving embrace.

*"We need to go pay a visit to Elena and deal with Trace."* My hands took hold of Luc and Jaycee.

*"I wouldn't fucking do that if I were you, brother!"*

*"FUCK!"* I sat up so fast, if Luc and Jaycee hadn't been with me, I would have flown out of bed.

*"Jesus, baby boy! Hey! It's Luc! What is it?"* Luc and Jaycee instinctively sat up and wrapped their
arms around me.

*"Aww, isn't that just fucking sweet. Baby boy. You fucking make me sick, John."*

I literally felt ill. Every part of my body shook, and I was so taken aback by Elena's sudden onslaught, I couldn't even form the words to tell Luc and Jaycee.

*"If I were you, brother dearest, I'd stay the fuck away, because frankly, you are not going to like what has taken place."*

"John? John! Hon, it's Luc! Babe, wake up!"

What the hell? My eyes shot open, and much to my surprise, Luc and Jaycee were pressed tightly against me, their arms wrapped around me. "Jacques? Hey, bro, what the hell is going on? You must have been having a nightmare." Jaycee's concern was evident in the worried look on his face and his somewhat shaky voice.

"Baby boy. Do you remember anything?" Luc's voice shuddered, and his body trembled, as he lay next to me. Neither my Sire nor my brother wanted to let go.

"Fuck! It was so real. It was Elena. She was harassing me and warning me not to come to see her. She said I wouldn't like what I found. It was so fucking real!" I looked at Luc then Jaycee. I scuffed my face with my hands in frustration. "I was just dreaming? What the hell!"

"Yeah, babe. You scared the hell out of Jaycee and me."

My "I'm sss..." was cut off by Luc.

"No, lover. No apologies. We need to pay a visit to Elena and Trace. This has to stop. It's bad enough she was tormenting you when you were awake. Now you can't even rest. Damn her mind games!" Luc's eyes became deep red and his fangs began to descend.

"Easy, Luc!" Jaycee reached over and gently squeezed his arm. "This will end tonight."

"It's okay, Jaycee." I let my fingers run down his arm. "Luc, babe, I'm okay. I'm right here and your brother is too. Hey, love. I'm here." My fingers ran through his hair. Jaycee and I watched Luc relax. "That's it, lover. Just like you taught me." As hard as I tried not to, I felt what Luc was feeling and I felt the same way. I was pissed!

"This has to stop! No one fucks with my family. No one! Damn it! Where the hell has my sister been? She hasn't contacted me and now she does this!"

"She can't any more, babe." Luc softly answered me.

"Why not, Luc? It sure seemed real."

"You're a vampire, lover. Immortal. She is a mortal."

"What's that got to do with...?" Like I said several times already, I'm a little slow on the uptake. I'm undead. Preternatural. I knew, but it still caused a chill to run up my spine. "That was a nightmare."

"That's right, Jacques." I felt Jaycee's hand rub my shoulder, relaxing me. "She can no longer pierce the veil that separates our two worlds. Janine has seen to that. Similar to what you did, but the difference is, you were protecting us."

I shook my head. With Luc and Jaycee by my side, my mind revisited my nightmare. Again, I could feel my gums tingling, my fangs pushing out. It was my connection to Sam and Christian. I knew they were more than capable, but I still worried about them. My anger was consuming me and my body was responding. I didn't like what I felt, but this was serious. Life and death. My fists clenched the sheets. I felt muscles in my body contract, and before I knew it, I let out a growl, low and guttural.

"Elena, if any harm has come to Sam or Christian, I have no fucking problem killing you either. I fucking hate you, Elena. If you have to die...so be it! No one, not even my sister, threatens my family and gets away with it. You bitch!" Shit, hadn't meant to say that out loud.

"Luc, Jaycee. Oh my God." I looked at both of them, my eyes wide open. I could feel my whole body shake. "I am so sorry!"

"Mon amour." Luc's voice trembled at my onslaught. "Easy lover. I know you've been through so much, but we'll end it tonight. Together! Understand?" Luc pulled himself close to me.

I felt Jaycee's hand on my arm. "Luc is right, bro. I'm sure we can reason with Elena. She will need to accept this, and if she loves you, as you've told us, she will understand."

"It was a nightmare, John." Luc squeezed my arm.

"Nightmare or whatever," I looked at Luc, then Jaycee, "we need to go and pay Elena and Trace a visit." My voice was tinged with hatred. Not for Luc and Jaycee, but my reprehensible sister and that bastard Trace.

"Whatever you want, babe." Luc's hand cupped the back of my neck and pulled me into a kiss. "Jacques, you won't be alone." I turned my eyes to Jaycee's and brushed my lips against his.

Squeezing the young men's hands in mine, I gently said, "Je t'aime, boys."

"Je t'aime, Jacques," Jaycee replied.

I closed my eyes as I savored the feeling of Luc's head coming to rest against mine. "Everything we have, everything we are, everything we do, John, is for you."

I lifted my hand and caressed the face of the man I had fallen for, and died for. I'd do it again. I didn't even need to say anything. Luc knew.

I reached over and gently pulled Jaycee's head to mine. "This has gone on long enough; it ends tonight." There was such determination in my voice, I felt a shudder run simultaneously through their bodies.

# CHAPTER THIRTY-EIGHT

We had taken a shower and cleaned up. God knows I desperately needed Luc and Jaycee, but there was no time for that. We had an eternity. I won't deny that I was fucking terrified, but I had Luc and Jaycee by my side. Janine's life was in danger and I made a promise. I swore to Janine that nothing would happen to Luc. That promise, protecting my brother, sister, and the love I had for them, along with my newly discovered vampire powers, gave me an inner strength I never dreamed possible. I would give my life, if necessary, to protect the people who have become my everything. I am immortal. Preternatural. My compassion, caring, and love for my family make me who I am. Being a vampire defines me. Who knew that it would take dying to give me the strength to become the type of person I wanted to be, to be proud of who I am? To give me the strength to stand up for my beliefs and convictions, to not let people decide what I should be, how I should act and behave. It sounds cliché, but Luc, he completes me. He is the key to what has been missing in my life. He is my only and we won't be saying goodbye anytime soon. I will make my journey through eternity with him, inside my heart and standing right by my side. No, we wouldn't be saying goodbye, not that night, or any night. I would make sure of that!

"Holy shit!" I said with a grin, as I opened the armoire in our bedroom.

I had not yet gotten a look at the clothing selection Janine had put together for me. All I could do was stand there and stare. There was clothing from every top designer in the world. Shirts, sweaters, and tailor-made suits were all neatly organized. Huh? How did she get my size? Shoes for casual and dress. Ten tuxes. Ten? God love her! On the top shelf, still in its box, was a Stetson identical to Luc's. There was a note attached to it. I opened it, and in Janine's elegant handwriting it simply read, "For our other cowboy!" I found myself giggling to myself, remembering Luc's absolute humiliation the other day at the park. Bad, John. BAD! Material things had not really been a high priority for me before I met my immortal family, and even though I still feel the same way, well, hell! What would you do? God! I had so much love for Luc and Jaycee and my forever stunning wolf, my sister Janine. They had promised me the world. I don't know how long I stood there and just stared.

"What the hell do you wear to this fucking party?" Luc let out a small grunt of frustration as he entered the room.

I giggled. Luc did that to me. Just the sound of his voice centered me.

"Well, love," I replied. "I don't think a tux is appropriate."

"You know, love…" Luc padded up behind me, warm and fresh, his body glistening, still wet from his shower. God! He smelled good. Was there time? He pressed his lips onto my bare shoulders. The tat on his forearm rippled as his muscular arms wrapped around my waist. The heat of his hot, soft, and young flesh pressed against me. I leaned back, wanting to feel every inch of him. His head popped up over my shoulder, looking at me in the mirror hanging on the one closed door of the four-door armoire. Don't even ask. No reflection? Debunked, much to Luc's amusement.

"What you're wearing now is fine with me, babe, but where we're going, I don't think you arriving in a pair of briefs," Jesus, John! Luc's hand caressed my chest, "would go over well." God, I loved his need to touch me. I knew this wasn't an appropriate time, but every time he did, heat scudded through my veins. I watched his eyes roam over my body as he reached for a pair of my underwear.

My eyes followed as I watched him pull them up. "You know, babe," my eyes fixated on Luc, "not that I'm complaining, but aren't they just a bit too…" Luc didn't let me finish my question.

"I really couldn't care less, John!" He had hesitated, and with my briefs up to his knees, he looked up at me and grinned. "I need to feel close to you, babe." Luc made a point of teasing me as he finished slipping them up to his waist, snapping the waist band for effect. "Good?" he asked, looking at me for approval.

"Uh...Just...Fuck me, Luc! Yeah, babe. Good!" I turned and looked at my Sire. Running my hand across his face, I stood there and stared at this man who meant everything to me. My life, my love... my vampire. Once again, time stopped and the world belonged to us. It was just Luc and I. When I mentioned that to him, he explained that it was the connection, the bond that was between us. We were literally one. We could momentarily, together, stop time. I had to take a couple of deep breaths. No mortal love, not even the one I shared with K.C., compared to this. What I had with K.C. was good, in every mortal way. What I had with Luc, well, there was nothing to compare to, and there would never be a need. He was mine for fucking ever. God, I needed him.

"John?" Luc placed his hand on my chest over my heart. "Hey..."

"Jesus, Luc. I love you. I need you so damn much." My voice choked with emotion.

"John, baby, I know. God, I need you too. What we have to do is the hardest thing you have ever had to face." Luc leaned into me, wrapped his arms around me, and rested his face on my chest. "Just know that Jaycee and I are by your side. You will not face this alone."

"I know, babe," I leaned into his embrace, "but, I'm not exactly... God! Luc! What the hell kind of help am I going to be to you and Jaycee and Janine? I'm not exactly adept at being a vampire." I lifted Luc's chin so our eyes met. "What if I fuck something up? Luc, you and Jaycee have such confidence in me, but I'm not even attuned to what powers I have."

"John, love," Luc's hands gripped my arms, "just remember, Jaycee and I will be with you. In here," he tapped my forehead, "and here." Tapping my chest. "We will be with you every step of the way. I know this is hard to believe, but Sam and Christian will be there too. Every vampire and werewolf you have been introduced to can connect with you. You not only have your family, baby boy, but you have the community with you as well."

I couldn't even begin to comprehend what Luc had just told me. I wasn't even going to try. I trusted Luc; his word was his vow. His vow was his promise to me that I belonged to him. He reminded me of that fact in everything he said and did for me.

"Remember, mon cher, I am your Sire. It is you I protect. I shall do so no matter what I must do, even if I have to give my life." His hands gripped my arms a little tighter.

"Luc, babe. Don't you even dare think that! No! Just NO!" I said firmly. I pulled back, looking at him, but not breaking our embrace. "I can't. I won't. Not again! Please, baby, promise me...not again!"

"John, babe, I know you are struggling with this, but you must accept the fact that I am your Sire. John, just as you have pledged your life to me, I have pledged mine to you." Tears streaked down his face.

"I know, Luc, but, God, what if..." Damn! I could feel my voice start to choke up. I could feel the tears burning my face as they fell. They were blood red.

"Hey," Luc put his fingers to my lips, "don't even think that way, love. Remember what we talked about with Janine? Your self-confidence? Love, you have shown your strength in so many ways. You have to realize, mon cher, that we would not allow you to walk into a dangerous situation on your own. We'll have your back, just as you'll have ours!" Luc's eyes and expression showed me his total faith and belief in me.

"Baby boy, it's not me I'm worried about. I don't care what happens to me. It's...um...It's you, love, and my brother and sister. If anything happens to you because of me, Trace, or Elena, I would die." I took Luc into my arms, burying my face in his soft, shaggy hair. "I would die."

"That, my love, is not going to happen. What we have," Luc rubbed his hand over my heart, "cannot, and will not, be taken away from us. I will not let it. I swear, John. You see," Luc's embrace grew stronger, "if something happened to you, then I, too, would die, baby boy. Life without you..." Luc paused, then tilted his head ever so slightly, his blue eyes looking into mine. "What was it you said, babe? If I lost you, I would beg for death. It's the only way I can even imagine getting over you."

"Jesus, Luc. I fucking love you." More tears ran down my face as I held him in my arms. His words, his touch, somehow gave me the confidence that I needed.

"I, John, love you. No one but you. Now why don't we see what you should wear for this little family reunion." He placed a gentle kiss on my chest and began to flip through my shirts.

Despite what was going to take place, I looked at Luc, watched him, and smiled with reverence for the man I had lived for, died for, and lived for again. Looking up at my reflection in the mirror, Luc softly smiled. His eyes mirrored his love for me. God, with Luc by my side, I felt like I could do anything. I prayed to God that feeling was right.

# ❧ CHAPTER THIRTY-NINE ❧

It was after midnight by the time Luc, Jaycee, and I came to a decision on how we were going to handle this situation.

Janine was still with her pack. Before she left, Janine explained that the pack's hunt usually lasted until early in the morning. She vehemently expressed that she would be ready to rejoin us. Although Luc, Jaycee, and I expressed concern for our sister's safety, it was not open for discussion. Janine, being the matriarch of our family, as she gently reminded us, would not accept sitting on the sidelines as this whole ugly mess went down. As much as we hated the idea of Janine being put in harm's way, Luc and Jaycee gently reminded me that you do not debate, disagree, or argue with a wolf.

Luc, bless him, showed me a few more tricks I have up my cape. Yes, I giggled. Our first step was to go where Sam and Christian had detained Elena and Trace. I found myself having to hold back my anger at the mention of his name.

Elena? It was anyone's guess how she was going to feel when she saw me. I honestly don't know if she knows I am a vampire or not. Count that as one thing that would not go over well, but what the fuck would? I'm sure Trace has her so damn brainwashed that I don't stand a chance. I never did. Well sis, things have changed. I really couldn't care less what Elena thought anyway. She was now a part of my past; my mortal life. I was literally dead to her and I could only think of one way of convincing her… red eyes and fangs. Hell, it convinced me. While Luc and my brother handled Trace, I was going to try and talk some sense into Elena. God help me! But if either one of them, Trace or my sister, tries to harm Luc, Jaycee, or Janine, they will regret it… with their life. Period. There would be no bringing them back. Either Elena accepted this, or God help her!

Trace? Fuck him! He would finally pay. I had no problem with that. Given the chance, I would welcome the opportunity to end his miserable life.

"Babe?" Luc's gentle voice brought me back to reality. "Adrian has the limo downstairs. Are you okay, mon cher?"

I looked at Luc, memorizing every detail of my boy. Every hair on his head, that forever young and beautiful face, his blue eyes, lips, broad shoulders, and defined chest. My God! He took my breath away. Losing him was not a fucking option. I walked toward him and gently wrapped my arms around his waist, pulling him to me. There it was… that sweet, gentle whimper. The sound that exemplified the love that Luc had for me. My intelligent and powerful vampire. Knowing I was the only one that elicited that response from him gave me a rush and magnified my need to have him as close to me as physically possible. What we had defied explanation. Our minds were eternally linked and we knew each other's next move.

Luc's lips were now pressed against mine. His mouth opened, wanting me to devour him. I did. My tongue tangled with his. I tasted his warm, sweet mouth. The passion and love I felt from Luc filled my heart and soul. My body felt like it was on fire. Both of us clutched at each other's hair, our fingers tangled up in each other's soft, long locks, not wanting to release each other from our kiss, our fangs nicking each other's lips. Fuck, Luc's blood was so sweet. Desperately, Luc pulled his body to me. It felt like he wanted to climb into me. I grabbed his waist, pulling him tight against me. I felt his hard cock press and rub against my thigh. My muscles flexed to give him a firm, hard place to seek release. He reciprocated. Luc's breaths were short and choppy. He continued to grind against me. Luc was gone, I wasn't far behind.

"*Jesus, babe! Uuunnhh, I…love…you.*"

"*Luc, babe! Uuunnhh. You're… Oh my God! You're my life.*"

"*Come, baby. Come with me.*" I thrust my cock against his. "*I feel you, John."*

"Feel...uungh...you. Now. Babe. Now!"

We did. Wave after powerful wave of ecstasy swept through both of us. We felt each other's orgasm, and our own. I pulled Luc's head to my shoulder, and with my other arm, held him tightly against me. For long, languid minutes, we caressed and kissed each other. Silently. No words. It just wasn't necessary.

Luc and I became aware of Jaycee as he gently put one of his hands on each of our shoulders. Luc and I brought one hand over to Jaycee and gently tangled it in his thick, black hair. Our lips parted and we both looked at him. His fangs worrying his lower lips, his eyes gazing into ours. He pulled us to him, desperate for our touch and our love. "Please forgive me. Please...I...I..."

I didn't let him finish his thought. I kissed him. "Nothing to forgive." I kissed him again, clutching at one of his arms. "God, Jaycee, my forever brother. I love you," I whispered, trying to catch my breath.

"My Sire, my brother. I adore you. I cherish you. I love you." It was Luc's turn. His lips met Jaycee's. There was an urgency, a powerful moment between Luc and Jaycee that I had not witnessed before. This was not a farewell kiss. It was one of love in the purest form possible. As their fingers tangled in each other's hair, I could only respect and fall deeper in love with both of them. Then I found myself being pulled into their arms. Lips to lips, mouths to mouths, we surrendered to each other. I felt Jaycee's body shudder. The three of us, our bodies pressed together, touched, caressed and spoke words of love and courage. Luc and I proceeded to show Jaycee just how much he meant to us.

This was not goodbye. This was finishing something that started a long time ago. Our love for each other empowered us so we could move forward. Justice would be served tonight. This was the merging of the strength of three vampires. One newborn and two who were wise beyond their years. Beside them, and with the strength they fed me, I felt like I could do anything. Honest to God, they took away my fears. They gave me courage and strength like nothing I experienced as a mortal. Nothing, and no one, would divide or separate us. We belong to each other, always and forever.

Coming back to reality, one we were ready to face, Jaycee tousled our hair. "So brothers, let's take care of some business, shall we?"

"Sounds good, bro. John?" Luc and Jaycee looked at me with nothing but love, pride and total confidence.

I took a moment to collect myself. "Promise me one thing, boys?"

"Anything, my love." Jaycee brushed aside a lock of my hair that had fallen into my eye.

"When this is over, promise me that both of you will take me in your arms and make love to me. Please?"

"As if you needed to ask, babe." Luc's smile connected me to him on a deep emotional level. That one simple gesture was going to be the weapon in my arsenal that no one would see coming.

TO PARIS WITH BLOOD

# ✦ CHAPTER FORTY ✦

We had been in the limo about fifteen minutes. I sat between Luc and Jaycee, our hands linked together. I was looking out the window noticing the boulevard we were on. It looked familiar. I had been on it before, but I just couldn't place it. Paris was still in its glory. In the distance, the Eiffel Tower glowed gold. Besides an occasional couple coming home from a late night out, or someone out for a walk, the city slept. But Paris herself was alight, and the view was so breathtaking, I knew this was now my home forever. Yes, I knew we would travel, Luc had assured me of that, but Paris, she was my home.

"Hey there, bro." I acknowledged Jaycee as he started to lean into me. Putting a hand on his head, I gently pulled him to me, his head coming to rest on my shoulder. His thick, soft, black hair brushed against my face. An immediate warmth coursed through my veins. We were all a bit weary so we decided to wait and feed before we confronted Elena and Trace. We agreed that we needed to have all the physical and mental strength we could get. I gently placed a kiss on Jaycee's head. "Je t'aime, Jaycee." Ever so gently, he squeezed my hand in response. His warm breath softly caressed my neck.

"Rest, brother," I whispered, kissing his forehead again and letting my fingers run through his hair. I leaned over, burying my face in those thick, black strands. God! He smelled so good. "Better, brother?" I whispered in his ear.

"Oui. Merci, my dear brother." I watched his sculpted chest rise and fall as he dragged in a tired breath. Then he lifted his head, looked into my eyes, and whispered, "I will cherish and love you until the end of time."

My God in heaven. I remembered the things that went through my head about this man, my brother, less than a week ago. How could I have ever thought Jaycee possessive? Elena, almost convinced me Jaycee was plotting to kill Luc to have me for himself? God, that night at Janine's, I thought about his words. "From the first moment I saw you on the concourse, I knew you were the one for my brother." This strong vampire vowed to die for me if necessary. Oh God. Jaycee, my precious brother, I am so sorry.

I felt the sting of tears running down my face. I caressed his cheek, letting my fingers glide over his perfect skin. "Je t'aime, mon cher," my voice hitched, "only God himself knows how much." I felt him push his head closer to me, then, with a soft sigh, he released his hand from mine and I felt it gently trace its way across my stomach and clutch my side. The scent of his thick, black hair, the scent of Jaycee, just like Luc, would stay with me for an eternity. I felt a gentle smile forming on my face as the now familiar sting signaled my canines descending.

I was at peace being a vampire, and thanks to my family, I did feel more confident about my role in the vampire community. I had to wonder how the people back home, who had a problem with me being gay, would handle this. I'd laugh, but at the moment their narrow-minded opinions were not worth wasting any further thought or concern on. It really didn't matter as I would never see them again. So much of what I read was, and is, fiction. Pure fiction. Luc, the little shit, so enjoyed being able to debunk those myths. He still wanted to contact my vampire expert, as he kindly referred to her, and have a real interview. Knowing Luc the way I did, he probably had it at the top of his to-do list after this fucking nightmare was over. What I know is, there was no blood-lust when Luc turned me. How do you dispel centuries of misguided conceptions? Blood-sucking monsters? Yeah, right! What I wouldn't give to teach my very own version of 'Vampire 101'! Well, I still have my soul and I still love my Lord. The crucifix that I wore when I arrived in Paris still adorns my chest. When Luc first discovered it, I watched as he gently placed it in his hand. Then, as he looked into my eyes, he kissed it and offered a prayer to our Lord for giving me to him. My heart still beats. I'm still me. Just new and improved. I could only shake my head as my tongue ran across my fangs feeling their razor sharpness.

I was brought out of my thoughts by the feeling that someone I loved very much was wanting my attention. I turned my head toward my Sire and my eyes met with his. How long he had been watching me, I don't know. The serene look on his face momentarily took my breath away.

I took a deep breath. "Hi," I whispered.

"Hey, baby boy," Luc squeezed my hand, "what's going on in that intelligent head of yours?" He asked quietly, showing respect for Jaycee. "Are you okay?" His deep red eyes gazed into mine. His eyes had turned their vampire red and his fangs glistened in the evening light.

I leaned towards him, kissing him softly. My eyes lingered on his face for a moment. "I'm fine, babe." I couldn't resist. I raised my hand and ran my fingers through his long, thick strands. I was rewarded with that sweet, adorable whimper. "All because of you, my eternal young man."

Luc shook his head gently. "God, John, have I told you lately how much I love you? Do you know how much you mean to me?" His hand came up to gently brush my face. Then just as gently, he once again entwined his fingers with mine.

God, I don't deserve this. How could he love me, especially now? I put my head down and started to turn away from him, unable to face him with the guilt that was eating at me.

"John, love, I know what you're doing. Please. You are not fine." Luc immediately cupped my chin and pulled me back so I was once again looking at him. "What the hell is going on?" It was said out of concern, not anger, and worry lines creased Luc's forehead.

"Luc, babe..." I had to put my head down again, overwhelmed. "I...I don't understand. How can you love me? Babe," my voice was choking up, my eyes glassing over with tears, "look what I've done," I responded pensively. "Luc, oh God, Luc. All I've done so far is put you, Jaycee, and Janine in harm's way." I just couldn't face Luc. Once again, everything was conspiring against me. Elena. That bastard Trace. Fuck! Of all times to lose it. Why now? I needed to be strong, but the dam opened and the tears came. "Luc?" I was losing control. Unable to continue, I looked into his eyes, begging for his touch, something to let me know that everything was okay between us. He had read my mind and his answer was clear. His love for me was undeniable. With no hesitation, Luc ran his hand across Jaycee's arm, which was still firmly wrapped around my waist. Luc's hand clutched the other side of my waist and he put his head on my shoulder, pressing soft kisses to my cheek. I felt his fangs gently rub across my neck.

Jaycee, meanwhile, had fallen asleep. I was grateful for that. At least my brother did not have to see this. It was a small consolation.

"Oh God, baby boy," his lips softly brushed across my cheek, "when are you going to cut yourself some slack?"

"Luc, look what I've done. If I hadn't come..." I was fighting back the tears, but it was a losing battle.

"If you hadn't come, John, I would have spent an eternity trying to get over you." Before I could even respond, Luc tilted his head and kissed me. It wasn't a gentle kiss, but it wasn't rough either. It was passionate, gentle, strong, and soft. The kiss, I knew, mirrored all the feelings Luc had for me and it was the most intense experience I've had with him. Luc had just made love to me with nothing but a kiss. I could swear that Luc had just shared his soul with me.

"I did, babe." Luc answered. His eyes were deep red, his fangs, like mine, were fully extended. "John," Luc pressed his forehead to mine, "I watched you with Jaycee. Look at him now, babe. Here we are, the three of us, and Janine out there somewhere." His hand gestured towards the city. "Yes, we are going into a very dangerous situation here, but John, despite everything that is happening, what we have to face," Luc glanced over at Jaycee, still asleep on my shoulder, "don't you think I saw what you did for my brother, my Sire? My God, John, the love you showed him...the care." Luc leaned back, never breaking eye contact with me. "John, you are mine, but do you remember when Janine talked about you having someone for Jaycee? Do you remember when you said Jaycee deserved perfection?"

As Luc spoke to me, I felt one of his hands come to rest on my shoulder. The other, which had been on my waist, was now resting on my face. Carefully, without disturbing Jaycee, I leaned a little closer to Luc. My eyes looked into his. "Yeah, babe, I remember. Luc, like I said before, Jaycee deserves perfection. Nobody, at least nobody I know from my mortal life, deserves Jaycee. And, Luc, I don't know anyone in our world." I took one of Luc's hands and squeezed it gently.

Luc was listening to me, but I was having a hard time concentrating on what I was saying due, in part, to his smile. God! Could it be any bigger?

"John, my love. Believe it or not, you do know someone!"

"Huh?"

"The key word, John, is perfection." Luc squeezed my hand back.

As I was listening to Luc, and occasionally rubbing Jaycee's thigh with my free hand, I could feel what Luc was thinking. "Luc? No. Are you thinking? No. Really, Luc?"

"What am I thinking, lover?" Luc squeezed my hand again and his eyes briefly looked at Jaycee who was sound asleep, totally unaware of what was transpiring between his brothers.

"Baby boy." My breath hitched. "Me?" "Oui, mon cher."

"But..." If I looked how I felt, I probably looked like a deer caught up in the lights of an eighteen- wheeler.

"John, you and I shall share an eternity together. You are mine, forever."

"Luc, babe. You are mine! Fuck, Luc. Did I do something wrong?" I started to panic. Thoughts of Luc leaving me raced through my head. My heart started racing, my pulse thrumming. "Luc... I don't...Babe, you have to help me out. I don't understand. Don't you want me anymore?" My voice was full of panic, but quiet, with respect for Jaycee.

"Oh my God, John. Pardonnez-moi!" Luc, my confusion and assumptions now apparent, pulled himself as close as he could to me. "Oh God, John. I am so sorry. This is my fault. God, John. You're mine. I fucking love you. Of course I want you! You are mine! I'm doing a lousy job of explaining this. Just listen... OKAY?"

I was shaking so hard, my head was pounding. I tried to hold back the sobs. Luc's hand stroked the back of my head, rubbing the base of my neck.

"Easy, baby, easy. Let me try this again...okay?" Luc's eyes pleaded. "God, John. I'm so damn sorry. I fucked this up so bad." Luc pressed his forehead against mine.

I dragged in one deep breath, then another. "Please, Luc, 'cause I'm losing it here."

"Oh shit, John. Okay, love." He dragged in a deep breath. "Right, as you know our family tree is...um...unique."

"Very much so, babe." I felt a calmness overcome me and I knew it was Luc. I managed a half smile. "It's pretty basic if you think about it. Let's narrow it down, John."

"Sure, love." I gave Luc my full attention, wiping a stray tear from my face.

Luc was wearing that shit-eating grin of his, so I knew he was up to something. I had an idea, but I needed to hear it from Luc first.

"Okay, babe. Here's how it is."

I watched him, and though I would never admit it to him, his actions were adorable. His eyes looked up as he put a finger to his chin. *Yep, pretty basic stuff, babe,'* I thought. He looked down for a moment, and using my fingers, he started counting. My vampire genius at work! I had to turn away briefly. I didn't want him to see the smile that was trying to break free.

"Jaycee is my brother and Sire. I am Jaycee's brother. Janine is my sister. With me so far, babe?" "Yeah, makes perfect sense!" I couldn't help but giggle. "Luc, love?"

"Yes, John?"

"I sure am glad our brother is asleep. If he heard this, I think he would have us committed!" Luc giggled.

I could feel my initial panic gone, replaced now by the enjoyment I was getting out of my lover explaining where he was going with this.

"Oh, I don't think so, babe. Anyway, back to our little family tree! I am your Sire, John. You are my partner, lover, and brother. You and Jaycee are brothers. Janine is your sister!" He paused, his head nodding back and forth, running it through his head. "I think I've got that right!"

"And to think I was having a hard time understanding the difference between a first and second cousin." I started to giggle, but, yes, I felt bad. Luc was really into this, but he could have made it so much simpler. I took his hands and squeezed.

"Luc, love?" I tried my best to look respectful.

"So you understand?" He was looking at me expectantly.

For a moment I looked at him, smiled, and shook my head. "I adore you, Luc. As informative as this little genealogy lesson was, all you had to do was say" I leaned into him, my forehead pressed against his, "you, love, are ours, always and forever! Emphasis on *ours*, babe." I tousled his hair.

There it was, that little whimper. I smiled. Everything righted itself again. "In other words, baby boy," I brushed my lips across Luc's, "I am yours, you are mine, and Jaycee is ours." I smiled and leaned into Luc, kissing him with all the love I had. Breaking the kiss, I held Luc's face in my hands. "My heart is yours. I fell hard for you in the airport, the first time you touched me, and again when you kissed me. I fall in love all over again every time you look at me. I am looking forward to falling in love with you a thousand times a day for the next several millenia."

Luc literally fell into me, his head coming to rest on my chest. "Luc, I am yours, and you, babe, are mine. This guy," I turned to Jaycee, "is ours. Completely."

As if on cue, Jaycee, his hair rumpled, lifted his head from my shoulder and looked at us. "What did I miss?"

I leaned over and kissed Luc. "I love you, babe! Oh, and Luc?"

"Yes, John..." He looked at me with a *'what the fuck just happened'* expression on his face.

I chuckled and put a hand on his shoulder. "Luc, I have to say, this gives a whole new meaning to *ménage a trois*!"

"You, goof!" Luc jabbed me in the arm.

"As long as I'm still *your* goof, babe!" My fist lightly reciprocated.

Looking curiously at both Luc and I, Jaycee shrugged his shoulders and said "Really? Come on. What did I miss?"

Turning to Jaycee, I kissed him and replied, "Later, love, later." I winked at him. Jaycee looked at me, then Luc. I wouldn't have believed it if I hadn't seen it with my own eyes. Jaycee. Three-hundred-plus-year-old Jaycee. Powerful, immortal Jaycee. A vampire... with puppy dog eyes!

We had gone several miles at least. Like before, the road and buildings looked familiar, but I still couldn't place where we were.

"Luc, love?"

"Yes, John?" Luc was looking out the limo's window. I knew he had been in deep thought.

"This is the way to our club, isn't it?" I finally recognized several buildings.

As he turned back to me, I noticed the concerned look in his eyes. "Yes it is, babe."

"Is that where..." I started to ask Luc, but instead Jaycee's hand came up and gently turned my head to face him.

Jaycee leaned into me and brushed his lips against mine. Just like his brother, his deep red eyes reflected his concern. His eyes looked into mine. "Yes, brother. We have Elena and Trace at the club, in our suite."

The club would be closed. I briefly had this image of Elena and Trace tied to two old metal folding chairs in some dark, ominous warehouse, with a lightbulb swinging from a frayed cord hanging above them. Now, knowing where they were, I don't even think you could call it being *detained*. Knowing Sam and Christian, they probably offered them something to drink, at least Elena. Fuck Trace! If anything, I should contact them and offer Trace up as a late night snack.

"Merci, Jaycee." I let my head rest on the soft leather of the seat and rubbed my eyes. " Pardonnez-moi. Damn, you could have thrown Trace into the Seine for all I care!" I let out a huff of air, beginning to feel the effects of not feeding.

Jaycee, sensing my frustration, didn't have to say a word. Just feeling his fingers running across my wrist calmed me.

Luc, God bless him, had been watching the interaction between his brother and I. He looked at me, squeezed my hand, smiled, and simply said, "What did I tell you, babe?"

"Again, I ask...What did I miss?" Jaycee's frustration and growing impatience for an answer began to take the form of a two-year-old throwing a temper tantrum.

"Whatever are we going to do with him, John?" Luc squeezed my leg.

Though I appreciated Luc's and Jaycee's attempts to keep me, for lack of a better word, sane, the closer we got to our destination, the more anxious I felt.

"So, it will be the three of us, Sammy, Christian, E... E... Elena, and that bastard, Trace?" My voice trembled.

"No, mon cher. There will be others." Luc answered. A comforting smile formed on his face.

I was on edge, but I knew in my heart that Luc and Jaycee had this under control, more than I realized. For the first time since I'd been in the limo, the intercom buzzed. I had never really talked to Adrian, or even had the privacy glass separating the front seats from the rear, come down.

Luc answered. "Yes, Adrian?"

"Lord Luc, may I have a word?" Adrian asked.

Jaycee must have seen my expression. I felt him lightly squeeze my hand. "Yes, dear brother, he speaks!" A grin formed on his face.

"Of course, Adrian." Luc answered. "Oh, and Adrian, please put the divider down." With that, the glass separating the front and rear seats of the limo smoothly slid down. I glanced at Luc and Jaycee, then looked forward at Adrian. His eyes looked at me through the rear view mirror.

"Bonsoir, my Lord Jacques, mon cher."

It took me a few moments to realize that Adrian was addressing me. "Merci. Bonsoir, Adrian. Please, call me Jacques."

"As you wish, Jacques. May I have permission to address you?"

"Adrian, first of all, it is a pleasure to finally meet you! After all you've done for us, why on earth would you feel it necessary to ask my permission? You need never ask, Adrian."

I could tell from the look in Adrian's eyes he was taken aback by my question and subsequent response. After a few moments he seemed to be comfortable, but not before getting a reassuring nod from Luc and Jaycee.

"It is an honor to finally speak with you and welcome you into the family. I thank you for your kindness." I could sense the sincerity in his voice. "Jacques, what you did for my family in the limo showed great courage! A mortal, facing Alec…!"

"What did I tell you, Adrian?" Luc interjected.

"You are right, Lord Luc." I could see Adrian's eyes shift to look at Luc.

"Right about what, Adrian?" I asked.

"Jacques, you are the answer to the family's prayers. I am very happy for you and Lord Luc. If I may speak openly, Jacques, you two were made for each other. You and Luc are preternatural perfection."

Preternatural perfection? Holy shit. I could feel my face turning red, and as I turned my head to look at Luc, his face was beaming and, to my delight, as red as I feared mine was!

"Oh my goodness. Please forgive me for embarrassing both of you. Lord Luc…"

My Sire cut him off before he went further. "Adrian, our faithful servant, you have nothing to apologize for. Understood?" Luc looked at me and squeezed my hand.

"Yes, Lord Luc."

"Adrian, I'll second that!" Jaycee leaned forward and patted Adrian on his broad shoulder.

Adrian smiled at me through the rear-view mirror. His fangs glistened in the Parisian moonlight. "I want you to know that I have sworn an oath to my lords Luc and Jaycee, and Lady Janine, to protect all of you with my life if necessary. I will be with all of you tonight, every step of the way."

Adrian was a mystery. I really didn't know much about him and Luc and Jaycee had not offered up any information. Then again, I hadn't asked. What I knew of him did speak to his character. He was dedicated and loyal to Luc, Jaycee, and Janine. What really blew my mind was that he hardly knew me, but I could feel that same protective instinct towards me as well. Always present, ready to serve night or day. *Day*...interesting. Where did he get his attributes from? I hadn't thought about that. And he was about a century or so, (did I just say century or so?) younger than Luc, Jaycee, and Janine.

"Merci, Adrian. I want you to know that I sincerely appreciate what you are doing for us."

"I wouldn't have it any other way, Jacques." With that said, the privacy window once again closed. "Babe?" Luc leaned into me. "I know you have questions about Adrian. I promise, when this is over I will tell you his story and how he came to be with us."

"That story, Luc, I'm looking forward to!"

"He *is* rather good looking, brother. Isn't he?" Jaycee looked at me and smiled.

"So you think so, do you, Jaycee?" Luc looked at me and winked.

"Jaycee, my brother. Are you," I leaned closer to Jaycee, "are you blushing?" At that moment, as I gazed at him, the image of Jaycee as a powerful, immortal vampire was replaced with that of a young, innocent college boy whose sexual feelings were being discovered for the first time. My God, he was stunning. Luc apparently noticed it too.

"Oh, brother." Luc giggled. "Jaycee, you are so busted!"

"Okay, little brother. You got me. Sure, Adrian is a handsome young man, but there are only two men in my life," Jaycee leaned into me and cupped my chin with his hand, "that are mine. You, my baby brother," his eyes never left mine, "and Jacques, my precious, extraordinary boy." I went weak as he kissed me, his fingers threading through my hair. His forehead pressed gently against mine. At the same time, I felt Luc's lips press kisses down my neck. I tilted my head slightly to give him better access. The world, and all the worry and fear, disappeared. Reality took a back seat. Our love for each other was all that mattered.

Now who was blushing?

Then reality...life...came back. The limo approached the entrance to our club. It was pitch black.

*'Ahhh crap!'*

Something was wrong, terribly wrong. I didn't need to feel their concern coursing through me to know, their faces said it all.

I looked first to my Sire. Luc's face was taught, his fangs visible by the moon, which was casting an ethereal light into the limo. A low, guttural sound emanated from him. I didn't need the light to know that his eyes were deep red. Jaycee had been looking out the window, but as he turned to look at us, his face showed the same concern. I felt their rage course through me and I knew something bad had happened in the club. Our connections were so deep and complete, my body reacted. To sum it up, quite simply, there were three very pissed off vampires in the limo. Wait, make that four. One was in the front seat.

The window separating us from Adrian slid down, and Adrian turned, his one arm draped over the front seat, looking back at us. Yep, he was definitely pissed.

"My Lords?" Adrian's face was drawn tight with concern as he looked past me to Luc and Jaycee.

It only took a moment, but I knew what Adrian was thinking, what he was about to ask. Leaning forward, I grasped Adrian's arm with my hand. "No fucking way, Adrian! No. Fucking. Way! Please forgive me, Adrian. I mean you no disrespect, but I will not sit idly by as my Sire and Jaycee go in there."

"Lord Jacques, mon cher, it is for your own protection." His deep red eyes were full of concern.

"He's right, John." Luc was rubbing my back.

The feelings coursing through me were new to me. The old me probably would have cowered and jumped in the front seat with Adrian. The new me? Fuck that!

"Listen, Luc." My red eyes locked onto his. "I will not sit here and do nothing but watch, wait and wonder what the hell is going on in there. We discussed this, hon!"

"But, John." Luc's concern for me was palpable.

"But no, babe!" My hand reached up and grabbed him at the base of his neck, pulling him to my lips. It was no gentle kiss either. Our red eyes met each other's, our mouths connected, and our fangs nicked each other's lips. Our blood began to merge. I felt the urgency of the situation that was at hand. As a last resort, Luc flooded me with all the knowledge he could possibly give me before we faced whatever the fuck was going on. At the same time, I felt his total unequivocal love burn through my entire body.

"Fuck, John, I love you. I fucking love you so much." I knew, as my Sire, all he wanted to do was protect me, but he also knew that I had inherited his stubbornness. He knew I would never break my promise and I would stand beside him through good or bad. My hands reached up and grabbed two handfuls of that lush, thick, black hair. Breathlessly, I licked my lips, tasting his very essence.

"God in heaven, I love you, Luc." With that said, I found myself pulled into Jaycee's embrace.

"Jacques...brother?" I expected no less of Jaycee. His eyes begged me to listen. "Please!"

"Jaycee, my brother." I turned to look at him. His eyes were the same deep red.

"Damn it! I love you, Jacques." Then with the same determination, Jaycee pulled me to him.

As with Luc, I felt Jaycee empower me with everything he could teach me, and yes, I felt the love he had for me course through my body. We connected both mentally and physically. His kiss was as deep and powerful as Luc's. I would not let anything happen to either one of these men. As Jaycee gently pulled back from me, I looked at him. Between my Sire and my brother, I felt feelings and strength that I had not felt up until this very moment.

I cupped Jaycee's face into my hands. "I fucking love you too, Jaycee. More than you will ever know and, like Luc, the love I have for you is for an eternity."

I was a vampire. Any remaining mortal trace of me had been completely exorcised. Any doubts, insecurities, or lack of self-confidence were gone. They were replaced by a strength and feelings that were new to me, but at the same time they were feelings and knowledge given to me for the sake of my survival. More important to me was the survival of my lover, my brother, and Janine.

Without a word, Jaycee leaned over me and pulled his brother to him. With a tear streaming from his eye, he gently brushed his hand across Luc's face. With the same love I've seen so many times, he kissed Luc. My hands reached up and ran a hand through their hair. Several moments passed. Then, with the same tenderness, both Luc and Jaycee turned to me. Their fangs brushed my neck and they wrapped me in their embrace.

The silence that followed in the limo was palpable. What we had shared was something that no one but the three of us would ever understand.

I leaned forward, tapping Adrian on the shoulder. He once again turned to face me. "Yes, Jacques?"

"Adrian, would you do me a favor, s'il vous plait?"

"Lord Jacques, anything."

"We are going into the club. It's obvious something is terribly wrong."

I turned to look at Luc and Jaycee. "If it's alright with you, I would like Adrian to pull the limo around to the private entrance."

Luc and Jaycee took my hands. "It's your call, babe." Luc brushed his hand across my face.

"If that is what you want, Jacques." Jaycee's hand brushed my thigh.

I knew they were being as supportive as they could. I also knew they still wanted to protect me and the hesitancy to allow this was still weighing heavily on their minds.

"I, um, I just have a feeling that we are not going to get any resistance from my sister, but, um, damn!" My chin dropped to my chest.

"It's not Elena you're worried about, love. It's Trace, isn't it, babe?" Luc's hand came to rest on my thigh, gently squeezing it.

"Yeah, baby boy, it is. I want Adrian to be ready, just in case we need to get her out of there. That is, if I can get through to her." In my former life, Elena was my sister. If she, by some miracle, came to accept what Trace was responsible for, I owed that to her. It may have been adrenaline coursing through me, but I knew that this rebirth of self-confidence was given to me by the two men that mattered the most. Jesus, they, along with Janine, were the only thing that mattered to me.

"Lord Jacques?"

"Adrian, please. Call me Jacques, okay?" I gently smiled at him.

"Very well." Adrian's eyes gave away his discomfort with my request.

"Hey, Adrian." I leaned forward, putting my hand on his chin and drew his face up to make eye contact with me. "Listen to me. You have told me you are willing to die for Luc, Jaycee, Janine, and I. Adrian, please. Call me Jacques!" With that, my hand still on his chin, I pulled him to me and kissed him. Poor guy. I know I had totally thrown him off guard, but what better way to show him what he meant to me.

I turned to look at Luc and Jaycee. Both of them were sitting there smiling at me, their fangs framing their eternally young and perfect faces.

"Lord Luc?"

"Yes, Adrian."

Adrian turned to face us. "You have *got* to hang on to this man." Adrian looked at me and smiled.

"Oh trust me, Adrian. John is mine. He's not going anywhere!"

"John," Luc tousled my hair, "you never cease to amaze me. God, baby boy, I am so lucky!" My eyes met his. "Always."

Luc's eyes, just as red as mine, returned the look I was giving him, and not missing a beat, he answered, "Forever!"

Out of the corner of my eye, I saw Jaycee and Adrian shaking their heads, smiling, and loving every minute of it.

"Adrian?"

"Yes, Jacques."

"Before you take the limo to the private entrance, would you please get me and my brothers a drink. I think, looking at Luc and Jaycee, we will be needing it."

"As you wish, Jacques. Right away." Adrian closed the dividing window and I heard the front door open, then close. Jaycee, smiling at me, turned and opened the rear door for Adrian. Dutifully, he stood there waiting for permission to enter.

I leaned around Jaycee, stealing a kiss, and before Jaycee could even react, I looked out at Adrian and gave him permission to enter the vehicle and join us. Luc and Jaycee sat there, softly shaking their heads, looking at each other and smiling.

"What?" I looked at them both, utterly clueless.

"Nothing, brother." Jaycee giggled.

"Luc?"

"Nothing, babe." Luc had that shit-eating grin on his face again.

"Adrian, are you buying this? Because I'm not." Adrian just smiled at me as he attended to his duties.

I noticed he was preparing only three glasses.

"Uh, Adrian." I reached forward and placed a hand on his knee. "Where's yours?"

"Jacques. M'Lord?"

"Adrian, don't Lord me for Pete's sake." I let out a huff. "Pour yourself a glass too!" Luc and Jaycee giggled.

"But..." Adrian was obviously shocked.

"No buts, Adrian. Just do it! If it makes you feel better, that's an order!" I chuckled. Adrian looked at Luc and Jaycee like I had just lost my mind.

"Adrian," Luc pulled me close to him, "I suggest you do as my boy says." Jaycee leaned toward me, kissed me on the cheek, and tousled my hair.

"Luc, baby bro, you sure do know how to pick them." Jaycee laughed light-heartedly.

Luc gave me a look that made my cock take immediate notice. Taking one of my hands in his, Luc squeezed it, looked at me and said, "My vampire! Jaycee, yes, I sure as hell do!"

I pulled Luc to me and kissed him.

The sound of Luc's whimper filled the rear of the limo.

# ❈ CHAPTER FORTY-ONE ❈

As I had requested, Adrian pulled the limo around to the private entrance located at the rear of the club. Adrian would wait for us in the limo, ready to get us out of there once, hopefully, I was able to talk some sense into Elena. The plan itself looked good on paper.

Enter Murphy's Law. Usually plans on paper seem to go, what's that word Jaycee uses? Ah yes, poof! My brothers and I had exited the limo and were standing just outside the private entrance to the club. The entrance door and private elevator inside were secured by both voice and retina recognition. Good God! For a moment there, I felt like I was in some spy movie sans the guy with no identity, but an ultimatum!

I checked my watch and found that it was earlier than I thought. God, this night was going so damn slow. Janine and her pack would be wrapping up their hunt soon and despite our begging her to stay away, she would be with us. I learned my lesson, I guess we all did...you don't debate or question a wolf. Especially when that wolf is the matriarch of the family.

"Damn, Janine, just hunt all night, okay?" I wished like hell she could hear me. I took some consolation that at least she would be with her pack and safe. I just wanted this done and over with. Fuck! I picked up a rock and threw it, trying to work out some of my frustration. Apparently I had gained some strength. The rock I tossed finally connected with a window of an older building, two blocks away. A dog barked in the distance and two vampires jumped. "Excusez-moi, Luc and Jaycee." I kicked the pavement with the toe of my shoe, a little more gently, lest I crack the sidewalk.

"It's okay, babe." Luc walked over to me. "Nice arm." Luc gave it a light squeeze, trying his best to lighten my emotional load.

"Jacques," Jaycee came up beside me as well, "do you want to go up and see your sister?"

"Oui, Jaycee. It's time... Time to end this."

Jaycee and Luc, their protective side showing, started toward the entrance in front of me. I knew we were going to get through this ordeal, but after what Luc and I discussed in the limo on the way here, I couldn't let Jaycee wonder what the hell was going on. I really needed to do this for Jaycee. I kept putting him off in the limo. I can feel that he thinks something is wrong between us, but far from it! I just wanted it to be more damn special than this. At the same time, I needed Jaycee to know... I wanted him to know. After everything Jaycee did for his family, I wanted to give him some happiness. Just in case... God forbid! No, John, get that out of your fucking head right now.

Taking a deep breath, I reached out and snagged Luc's hand. "Luc, babe. Can I talk to you for just a moment?" I tried to come off casual, but I could see by Jaycee's eyes that he was thinking otherwise.

Luc walked over to me, his one eyebrow crooked, curious about this sudden request. "Luc, love?" I placed a hand on Luc's elbow and leaned in, speaking softly.

"John? What is it, love?"

"I know this is lousy timing, but I need to tell Jaycee."

"John," Luc ran his hand, palm side up, down the side of my face, "I think it's exactly the right time. Tell Jaycee." Luc glanced at him. "Tell him, baby." Luc tilted his head up and kissed me. "Je t'aime, mon cher... toujours."

"You're right, baby boy. Always and forever."

"May I be with you, John?"

"Oui, Luc. Absolutely. You, love, are part of this too."

I watched as Luc walked over to Jaycee and took his hand. After exchanging a few words, he leaned into Jaycee and kissed him. Then, still holding his hand, he led Jaycee over to me. Jaycee looked absolutely scared to death. As he approached me, my heart was beating a mile a minute. Not because of what I was about to tell him, but about how he would react.

Luc and Jaycee were standing in front of me. I smiled at Luc, then taking a deep breath, I looked at Jaycee. He looked like a little boy unsure of what he did wrong, thinking he was going to be punished.

"Brother, come here." I held out my arms. Hesitantly, Jaycee released his hold from Luc's hand and walked up to me, his head down. "Hey, bro. You have nothing to fear. Come here, babe." With my arms still outstretched, my hands gestured for him to come to me.

For several moments Jaycee hesitated, unsure, his head still down. I watched him as he slowly lifted his head, his now blue eyes questioning my motive. He walked to me and hesitantly let me embrace him.

"Hey, it's me, hon." My arms were now wrapped tightly around him. "It's okay. Hug me, dammit!" I immediately felt the tension in his body start to ease and his strong arms pulled me tightly to him. He sighed and I felt the relief pour through him as he pressed against me. "That's more like it!" I took one of my hands and pulled his head to me. I stroked his hair, taking a moment to inhale and savor the unique scent of Jaycee. Well, that and the cologne that I insisted he wear. 'London' for Jaycee, 'Touch' for Luc. We stood there for several moments locked in each other's embrace. I felt the steady beat of his heart as it pulsed against my chest, his head cradled on my shoulder.

Without letting go, Jaycee leaned back to look at me. "Jacques, have I made you angry? Disappointed?" Light creases formed on his forehead and his eyes began to tear up. "Oh God, I hurt you!"

"Hey, Jaycee." I placed a hand on his chest. "Why in God's name would you say, let alone think, that?"

"Um. It's...well...You've been so quiet since I woke up." He started to fidget and looked away. With oh so worried eyes, he looked back into mine. "Jacques, I'm sorry. I was tired and..."

I looked at Luc, who was standing next to Jaycee. Luc had to look away. I couldn't believe it. Well, yeah, come to think of it I could. The little shit was trying not to laugh.

"Jaycee. Is that what you think is wrong? The fact you fell asleep on my shoulder?"

"Oui, bro."

"Oh, babe! First of all, why, in all that is holy, would I be mad at you for that? Jaycee, I love the closeness we share. You should know that by now."

"What did I do wrong then, mon cher?" Jaycee's eyes now begged me for an answer.

I pressed my forehead to Jaycee's. "It's not what you did wrong. It's everything you do right!" I pulled Jaycee to me and kissed the very breath out of him. "Brother, I so wanted to do this differently, but Luc and I, ah, Luc and I wanted you to know of a decision we made that directly affects you."

"A decision?" Jaycee questioned, as he glanced at Luc.

"Yes, brother. We are hoping you approve." Luc ran his hand down Jaycee's arm.

Jaycee looked at Luc, then back at me. He reached over and snaked his fingers through Luc's hand, then mine. Jaycee's eyes came back to mine, his blue eyes begging me to tell him. "Tell me, Jacques. Please." His hand squeezed mine.

Tilting my head slightly, I took a moment to look into his eyes. My free hand came up to caress his face. Letting my hand follow his cheek, my fingers traced his lips. "You are so beautiful, brother."

I heard Luc's soft whimper. Glancing at him, his mouth moved without making a sound. I read his lips. "I love you, John."

I smiled and then returned my attention to Jaycee. I let my hand slip from Jaycee's grip. Reaching up, I cupped his face in my hands and pressed my lips to his. I didn't want to, but I pulled away, still holding his face in my hands. My thumbs caressed his mouth.

"Jaycee, my brave, courageous, and loving brother. You can stop wanting. You can stop wishing. You can stop being lonely." I looked away. I needed to collect my thoughts, not wanting to lose the momentum. Turning back to him, I gently let my hands fall. I took one of his hands and Luc took the other. "Jaycee, I wanted this to be special, but I didn't want to face what we are about to walk into..." My eyes glanced towards the entrance, "without you knowing."

"Knowing what, Jacques?" His eyes moved from mine, to Luc's, and back to mine. His face showed his confusion. I looked at my Sire. He gently nodded his approval.

"It's okay, baby boy." Luc approached me and, leaning into me, let his lips brush against mine. "It's more than okay… it's perfect! Go ahead. Tell him." My breath hitched as I watched Luc look at his Sire. "Tell our brother."

My hand came up to wipe a tear that fell from my face. I had to drag in a couple of breaths. Fuck, why couldn't this just be over with? *'Pull it together John!'* I mentally scolded myself. The three of us had become an impenetrable fortress. The walls were strong, built on our immortality, but the foundation was stronger yet because the foundation was built on love. The love of three men, three vampires, and one extraordinary wolf.

"Jaycee. Since the first time I saw you, I knew. I knew you were in love with me. I know that seems hard to believe. I was a mortal, but I felt it none the less. At first I thought you were possessive, even...forgive me...jealous. Bro, please forgive me. My sister even had me half- believing that you were plotting to kill your baby brother to have me. Damn, Jaycee! I wouldn't blame you if you were angry, but it crossed my mind. For that, I am truly sorry. I dismissed it immediately." My eyes begged him for forgiveness.

Jaycee dragged in a deep breath. "Jacques, there is absolutely nothing to forgive." Hearing Jaycee pardon me, so to speak, I too had to drag in a deep breath.

"I, in my mortal life, lost the only man I thought I would ever love. I never thought I would love again. That is, until I met you, Jaycee," I turned my head to look at Luc, "and my Luc. God, Jaycee, I don't know what I did to deserve this. Since then I've become a vampire and a brother and have the love of a man I never thought I would have again. I will *never* question that *ever*! To know I will be loved for an eternity is a fantasy come true." I once again wrapped my arms around Jaycee's waist. "Jaycee, you gracefully, respectfully stepped back, allowing me to fall in love with your brother. Despite the fact you are Luc's Sire, you gave him to me. Without you, mon cher, what I'm about to say would not be possible."

Luc put his hand on my shoulder. "Before you go on, may I say something?"

"Of course, Luc."

"Jaycee, my Sire, my brother. What John is about to tell you is something that both of us feel. Neither of us can ignore the fact."

"Ignore what fact, little brother?" I couldn't help but feel sorry for Jaycee. He had no idea where this was headed.

"Just listen to what John is about to tell you. Okay?"

"Of course, Luc." Jaycee looked at me. A soft smile began to form on his face. "Take your time, bro. We have forever." Which in turn caused Luc and me to relax and smile as well.

"Jaycee, babe. What is it that you have always told me? What is it that you told me the first time we met in the airport?"

For a moment Jaycee's expression went blank. Of course he knew, but the implication of what it meant, and the magnitude of how it would affect the three of us, suddenly caused a new and powerful realization to impact him.

Jaycee whimpered. "You, love, are ours...always and forever."

"Jaycee, my love." I pressed my forehead to his. "I am Luc's. I love Luc. He is what I live for, but I've gotten to know you over time, Jaycee, seeing your smile, hearing you laugh. Then, when I became a vampire, I felt your pain, your angst. Knowing how you really felt about me, well, I realized, Jaycee...Jaycee, I realized that I loved you too!"

"Are you telling me what I think you are, Jacques?" Jaycee's eyes were swimming in tears.

"I am Luc's. Luc is yours. And, my dear brother, you are ours. You, dear Jaycee, are loved completely and you will never be alone."

Luc leaned into his brother, kissing him on the cheek. "It's the three of us, big brother. You have us both."

I kissed Jaycee on the forehead. "If that's all right with you?" My hand ran through his hair.

The tears that were welling up in Jaycee's eyes began to fall. He wrapped his arms around me and kissed me. Then, his deep red eyes looking into mine, his voice barely a hoarse whisper, he said, "Yes."

Luc came to my side and leaned in to me. I held Jaycee tightly, knowing that the three of us shared a love so rare that nothing and no one would destroy it... but it was to come with a heavy price.

# ◆ CHAPTER FORTY-TWO ◆

The private elevator quietly made its way to the suite in the nightclub.

We were two floors away from our destination when Luc reached to the control panel and pressed stop. I didn't need to see the look on his or Jaycee's face to know something was wrong. I felt it too, and my blood ran cold.

"It's Christian and Sam, John." Luc gripped my hand hard.

"I know, babe. I'm feeling something too." I rubbed my thumb on his wrist, noticing his pulse was through the roof.

Jaycee, who had been standing to my right, was now facing both of us.

"What is it bro?" Luc asked. Jaycee's eyes were the deepest red I ever remembered seeing.

"It's Sam and Christian." Jaycee closed his eyes tightly, his head tilting slightly, desperately trying to get a fix on what was happening. Luc and I watched him, fixated. Suddenly his eyes opened wide, and dragging in several breaths like someone just punched him in the gut, the shock registered on his face.

"What is it, Jaycee?" I grabbed his arm.

"Oh God! It's Sammy! He's hurt bad!" A look of pure terror swept across Jaycee's face.

I hit the resume button on the elevator. "Fuck!" I pounded my fist on the elevator, leaving a dent in the steel door. "Enough is fucking enough already!" I was acutely aware of my new abilities. It felt like I had just been injected with a dose of adrenaline. Both my physical and mental acuities seemed to intensify one hundred fold.

"Babe!" Luc grabbed my hand with more strength than usual. He wasn't angry, he intimately felt every change in me. He was doing what he needed to do. Protect me. Protect me from myself.

"Luc! No! This ends now! Fuck Trace! Fuck Elena!" Our eyes locked on each other's. My jaw was clenched, my eyes stared deeply into his. Despite the urgency of the situation, I leaned into Luc and kissed him. It was no gentle kiss, but it wasn't meant to hurt. It was meant to show him the power of our love and he reciprocated in kind. When we finished, I reached up and threaded my hands through his hair. "I fucking love you, Luc! I caused this and I have to finish it."

Luc's eyes had shifted back to blue. "I know, baby boy," his voice hitched, "just please be careful. I can't...I won't lose you!" Then, in one blink his eyes were back to their deep red. "You have us, John. Do what you must. Jaycee and I are right here with you." His voice was edged with steel.

Every feeling Luc showed me, whether physical or emotional, showed and proved how much he loved me. This was no exception. His blue eyes. His undying, eternal love. His deep red eyes. The strong, confident, and wise vampire, who would stand by me through anything, giving his life if required. No fucking way. This boy was mine for an eternity.

Silently, Jaycee moved in front of me. "Je t'aime, mon cher." His kiss, the total opposite of what Luc and I just shared, was gentle and sweet. I returned his kiss with no hesitation.

"God, bro. My love for you will last for an eternity." Jaycee leaned into my touch as I ran my fingertips down the side of his face.

The elevator doors quietly opened. We were prepared for the worst. I was ready to rip my fangs into something...someone to be precise.

Jaycee grabbed my arm. "Easy, Jacques." His voice was gentle, but as I looked into his eyes… may God help anyone on the receiving end of his wrath.

Exiting the elevator, we cautiously walked down the hallway to the expansive living area. The scent of blood flooded our senses. Death, once again, had come to visit, but this time there would be no rebirth. Life was coming to an end.

Memories of what Luc and I shared played through my mind. The sweet taste of his blood red tear. The excruciating pain of my mortal body dying. Luc's fangs piercing my neck, him drinking my blood and forever taking me for his own. It was not meant to be tonight. Reapers had come to lay claim to what they thought would be theirs. Not if I could help it.

Luc had told me how Sam gently picked me up and carried me in his arms to the waiting limo. How he held me in his arms on the way to Luc's apartment and then carried me to Luc's bed. Sam and Christian stood guard outside our bedroom protecting Luc and I through my transformation.

Sam was there for me when I needed him, now it was my turn to return the favor. In one split second, the three of us saw the scenario we feared the worst, the one we dreaded. As much as we tried to prepare for it, it still made me sick and full of rage. Then my red eyes locked onto her. There was the woman who betrayed me through her jealousy, the woman who brought a fucking shit storm down on our family. That bitch, Elena!

She was huddled on the sofa, her face emotionless, but her eyes betrayed her. They reflected something far more sinister. The ornate antique table that had been in front of the sofa was obliterated, smashed into bits and pieces. The suite was in ruins. The flat screen monitors, the audio system, and the communications center. It literally looked like a bomb had been set off, but it hadn't. It was Sam and Christian. They had fought back, had fought for their lives. My senses were on overload. I felt my fists clench. I stood there, feeling a rage I never felt before, and one question kept repeating over and over in my head. Where the fuck was that bastard Trace? I knew Luc and Jaycee were seeing the same thing. I felt their anger, like mine, course through me. Then, as fast as these thoughts entered my mind, they were pushed aside when I felt pain shoot through my chest. It wasn't mine. It was...Oh God! It was Sam's. Directly in front of Elena, on the floor, Christian was on his knees. He cradled Sam in his arms. Blood pooled around them.

"Oh my dear God. Christian? Sammy?" Luc stammered, visibly shaken. Before I knew it, I was next to Luc. I wrapped my arm around him and he leaned into my embrace. This was the first time I felt such despair in Luc. His heart was aching. As my Sire, his sorrow was my sorrow; his pain was my pain. This was not acceptable. The promise I made to Janine and Jaycee came back to me and this, so help me God, would be the last time Luc or my family endured pain of this magnitude.

Christian, in tears, looked up at us. "Please help." His eyes reflected desperation and fear. His voice was shaking, on the verge of a total breakdown. My heart ached, but I wasn't the only one. I felt Luc's and Jaycee's emotional pain as well.

As the three of us rushed to Christian's side, I could see Elena pushing back into the sofa, her hands gripping the cushions, her knuckles pure white. Her eyes were fixated on me. "Elena!" I spat. Leaning into her as close as I could get, I looked at her with nothing but contempt. "I will fucking deal with you soon, but so help me God, if you fucking move, I *will* kill you!" I knew Elena wouldn't move. Even though we had lost contact with each other, I knew my sister, and right now it was taking every bit of her strength to come to grips with what she was seeing. Her brother. A very fucking pissed off brother, with fangs. She was literally scared to death. *'That's a first!'*

"You're a...You...John..." Elena cowered.

I pressed her shoulders into the sofa. She winced as I applied what I knew to be almost enough pressure to break her shoulders. "Not such a smartass now, are you, Elena?" Tilting my head slightly, I could feel the corner of my mouth form into a smirk. I bared my fangs and growled. "Keen observation skills, sis. Yes. Yes I am! I am a vampire! Now, do me a favor. For the first time in your life, just sit there and shut the fuck up!"

"John, it wasn't..." I refused to give her the final word. No longer would I tolerate her *I'm always right* attitude.

"It wasn't what, Elena? It wasn't your fault? What part of *leave me alone* didn't you understand? Elena, I don't have time for you now." I bared my fangs at her, enraged. "So help me God, Elena. If you move, you're as good as dead. I will personally rip your throat out! You had better pray Sam doesn't die!" I released my hold on her shoulders, but continued to lean in as close as I could to her. "You are dead to me, Elena. Damn you, damn you straight to hell!"

I turned my attention back to Luc and Jaycee. Dropping to my knees between Luc and Jaycee, I immediately reached and pulled them close to me. What I saw made me weak. Sam had been attacked so viciously, so savagely, my mind couldn't even comprehend the injuries that were inflicted on him. A large, claw-like gash cut through his face. His shirt was shredded. Another claw-like slash had ripped his chest open. His life source, his blood, was flowing from him. There were other cuts, not as deep, not mortal, that covered his body as well. I took in a sniff of the air. I knew exactly who else was injured. I recognized his sweet, young smell.

"Jesus! Christian!" I quickly moved to his side.

"Jacques, it's nothing." I put my hand on his shoulder and he immediately winced and let out a moan. "Nothing? Bullshit, Christian! Let me see!" Gently leaning him forward, I noticed blood seeping through the tattered shirt on his back, below his right shoulder. I began to unbutton his shirt.

"Jacques, please. I'll be okay. We need to help Sammy." Tears fell down his face. "I can't lose him!" He was literally shaking in my arms.

"You won't, Christian. I swear to you!" I cupped his face in my hands and softly repeated, "You won't! I'll be damned if I lose you!" I brushed my hand, palm side up, over his much too pale face. Christian relaxed long enough for me to remove his shirt. The same gash, identical to Sam's, was causing considerable bleeding and, although he wouldn't admit it, Christian had to be in considerable pain. Although the blood loss was not as rapid as Sam's, I could tell Christian was not fairing too well. Pure adrenaline, fear, and concern for Sam were the only things that were keeping this boy going. He needed attention too. Fuck!

Luc and Jaycee had taught me that minor injuries were not a problem for vampires. We had a natural ability for our body's defense system to expedite the healing process. A mortal wound however, involving sudden, massive losses of blood, were too much for a vampire's system to neutralize and heal. The blood we carried in our system was our life source. The loss of blood was too much for our bodies to defend. What could heal Sam and Christian was pooling on the carpet underneath us. They were both dying before my eyes.

"Babe!" Luc looked up at me. "We're losing Sam." A tear ran down his face.

"NO!" Christian sobbed. He pulled Sam to him, aggravating his wound and causing the blood loss to quicken. He gasped for air as his ashen face betrayed his attempt at concealing his suffering.

"Hang in there my brave and loyal bodyguard." Running my hand through his hair, I gently kissed the top of his head. Then leaning down, I pressed a kiss to his wound. "Stay with us, Christian. Hey, look at me!" I gently cupped his chin in my hand and tilted his head. Our eyes met each other's. "Sammy needs you...and I need both of you!"

Hold it together, John. Just fucking hold it together. No one was going to die on my account tonight, or ever.

"Brother! Oh God!" I grabbed Jaycee's arm. "What can we do?"

Jaycee looked up at me. Blood red tears were running from his eyes. "Nothing, brother... nothing." His voice filled with anguish.

*Nothing* was not a fucking option.

I reached over to Christian. "This is all my fucking fault. I am so sorry, Christian."

Christian reached for me, his bloody hand grabbing mine. His red eyes were pleading with me. "No, Jacques! Oh God, no, it's not...but, Jacques...I love him. I can't lose him. Take my life if necessary, Jacques. Don't let Sammy die!" My God, the love he had for Sam. He didn't even know his own life was in jeopardy, and if he did, he didn't care. He was willing to die for his love. I knew the feeling.

"Christian, love, that won't be necessary." I looked down at my hand covered in Sam and Christian's blood. "Hey, Christian?" My hand brushed his cheek, my thumb pausing to wipe a tear from his face. "How long have you and Sam been together?"

I glanced at Luc and Jaycee, tears of red ran uncontrollably down their faces. "I promise you both, no one is dying tonight!"

"Um, one hundred years now, Jacques." I watched as he looked down at his lover, his hand caressing Sam's face. "Why, Jacques?"

"Christian," I put my hand to his chin, "you've only just gotten started."

"What if this were Luc or Jaycee?" I had my answer. I knew exactly what I was going to do.

"John, babe. This wound, this attack, it has all the signs. The injuries," Luc sniffed the air, "the scent."

I leant forward and kissed Luc on his cheek. "I know. A wolf, baby boy. A fucking werewolf named Alec!" I grabbed Luc's arms. "Baby boy, do you trust me?"

Luc's whimper was enough, but pressing his forehead to mine, stroking my cheek, he answered me in what was barely a hoarse whisper, "With my immortal life, John."

"Jacques?" Jaycee leaned into me. "What are you thinking?" My precious bro's lips quivered as he choked out his question.

"Jaycee," I brushed a lock of hair off of his forehead and looked into his eyes, "I need yours and Luc's help. Can you do that for me?"

"Of course. Anything, Jacques."

I paused and looked at them. "Have I told you lately how much I fucking love you?"

Just as Sam and Christian had pledged their life to protect me, I would do what was necessary to save them. I would do anything. No one was dying here, but someone would pay dearly for their part in this nightmare. Reaching up, I grabbed Elena by the leg and pulled her onto the floor. Her struggles were in vain. She was no match for my strength. I would get the answers from her later; I would get the cure from her now.

"John, love." Luc's eyes pleaded with me. "Don't."

"Luc, babe. If she had listened, if she had only listened and stayed away, none of this would be happening." I looked down at my sister, her eyes glazed over in pure terror. "Luc, no, as much as I want to, I'm not ending her life. But, babe, she has something these boys desperately need. She'll help us whether she wants to or not."

My eyes glared at her. "Elena, I warned you!"

"Oh no, you monster!" Elena screamed, struggling. "I will not be a part of this."

"You *made* yourself a part of this the moment you ignored my request to stay away and got on that fucking plane! You have no one to blame but yourself!" I stopped and looked at Sam and Christian. "You know what, Elena, I'm tired of wasting my breath on you." My sister screamed as I grabbed her arm and my fangs ripped it open.

"Luc, Jaycee, let me get to Sammy." Luc and Jaycee, still on their knees, moved to the side as I dragged my sister over to him. Holding Elena firmly in my grasp, I brought her arm over Sam's chest.

"Christian, hold your man. It's going to be okay." Please, God, let me be right.

Luc and Jaycee reached down and opened his wounds to allow as much of Elena's blood to enter his system as possible. I had ripped open a large artery in Elena's arm. I watched as blood poured from her into Sam's mortal wound. My sense of hearing told me how much longer I could allow this before Elena died. I could hear her pulse and heartbeat. Quite honestly, I didn't give a damn if she died, but I would not start my life as a vampire, with a murder rap hanging over my head. At least not with regards to Elena. Trace? That was a whole different story. What I wouldn't give to suck the life out of him.

"John?" Luc gently squeezed my arm. "I think that's good." As he looked at me, I saw a glimmer of hope in his eyes.

"Christian, my precious boy, let Luc and Jaycee tend to Sammy. I need you to come to me. That's an order, young man!" He flinched, but then relaxed when he saw my smile. I reached my free hand toward him, waiting for him to take it.

Elena's heartbeat and pulse were weaker, but I knew she was in no danger… yet. I forced her to sit next to me. Due to blood loss, she was too weak to fight back. She had not uttered one single word. This was music to my ears.

I watched, and my heart skipped a beat, as Luc and Jaycee picked Sam up and carried him to the sofa. With Sam safely cradled in their arms, Luc gently ran his fingers through Sam's thick, auburn hair. Jaycee softly ran his hand across his leg. A sense of pride filled my heart as I watched my Sire and my brother. Their care and concern for the people they loved was overwhelming to me. As Sammy lay there, I watched his breathing. It was still difficult for him, but definitely less painful. Carefully, Luc and Jaycee removed what was left of Sam's torn shirt. Both of them pulled their shirttails free and proceeded to clean Sam up as best they could. Taking a deep breath, I watched Sam's mortal wound begin to heal. That's a good sign, isn't it?

Jaycee, a soft smile forming on his face, looked at me and just shook his head. I bowed my head and closed my eyes, overwhelmed at the reverence and love my brother was showing me.

"*I need you, John.*" Luc's plea echoed through my mind.

"*Not as much as I need you, baby boy.*"

"*Je t'aime, babe.*" Tears streaked down Luc's face. "*Pour toujours, mon amour.*"

"*Oui, Jacques. Luc and you together...forever. This is as it should be.*" Jaycee affirmed my thought, and looking at his brother, he brushed his lips across Luc's hand.

Would our love conquer and help us to get rid of this nightmare? Looking at Luc and Jaycee, I knew it could. Anything was possible with them by my side.

Christian was so damn weak. It broke my heart as he took my hand

and made his way to me. His eyes never left mine. "Here, Christian." I gestured for him to sit between my legs, his back facing me. "Hey," I whispered in his ear, "look at your man! Have faith Christian. Just relax. Let's concentrate on making *you* better, so you two can get back to holding each other, loving, and making love to each other." Christian leaned into my embrace, his hand still wrapped in mine.

"Merci, Jacques."

"No need, Christian. No need at all." I kissed him lightly on his cheek.

I had held Elena's arm with one of my hands directly on the gash I inflicted on her, stopping the blood loss. "Ready for another donation, Elena?" I sneered.

"Christian, this will take but a few minutes." My face pressed against his.

"Jacques?" He turned his head to face me. "How can I ever repay you for saving Sam and I?"

"Hey, let's just concentrate on you and Sam right now. Okay?" I gently put my hands on his shoulders. "Christian, lean forward. Easy. That's my boy." He did as instructed, though slowly, as he was extremely weak and to the point of passing out. With my free arm, I held him securely.

Not saying a word to her, I pulled Elena's arm over Christian's wound and released my grip. Her blood began to cover and heal Christian's wound.

I couldn't help but notice the curious look on Elena's face. "You mean that actually works?" Her laugh, though weak, was wicked. "What a fucking shame!" she huffed. Her comment earned my elbow in her face. I knocked her unconscious.

I sat there on the floor. Dragging in a few breaths, I suddenly realized that we had staved off a tragedy. For the first time, the full events of the evening sunk in. Taking in another breath, I shuddered. For the most part things were in control. Sammy. Christian. The reaper would not take them tonight. My eyes found their way to Luc and Jaycee. I could see they were exhausted, but they were still attending to Sam. Fear not, brothers. We will have our sister back, this I promise to you...on my very life. I looked back down at the boy in my arms and sat there in quiet contemplation.

"John?"

My heart skipped a beat, knowing full well who was summoning me. Luc. I lifted my head to see him and my brother looking at me. Gentle, loving smiles greeted me. I smiled back. Their hair was rumpled, their clothes askew. My God, they were so fucking beautiful, and they were mine.

"Hey, baby boy." I choked back a sob, my eyes focused on Luc.

"John, my God! Do you have any idea what you just did? You saved Sam and Christian's life!" His voice was shaking. "Are you okay?" The concern in Luc's voice shook me to my core. I was on an emotional precipice. I knew that the slightest display of affection, just the sound of my Sire's voice, could push me over the edge.

"Yeah, Luc. Just a little tired and um, hungry. Don't worry though, babe. Sam and Christian are more important right now."

"Bullshit, Jacques. I won't have my brother in any discomfort." The rush of concern I felt flowing through me from Jaycee, pushed me just a little closer to the edge. "Hang tight, Jacques. I'll take care of you."

"Merci, Jaycee. Love you."

Jaycee, like his brother, never ceased to amaze me. He raised his hand to his lips and blew me a kiss. All I could do was look at him, softly shaking my head. I reached up making a grasping motion with my hand. "Got it, bro." I winked at him, and despite it all, I felt a small smile trying to break free. Break me free from the pure hell we were in. I couldn't help but notice my boy watching our interaction. He winked. Any mortal boyfriend would have thrown a punch, but, then again, we were anything but mortal.

*"Hey, Luc! I love you, baby!"*

*"Love you too, my knight in shining armor!"*

*"Your wish,"* I grinned, *"is my command, Sire!"*

Just for a moment, our connection made me forget. I forgot the pain and suffering, what Sam and Christian bravely endured, missing Janine. I wanted to laugh, needed to laugh, but this was not the time or the place. Luc understood, but gave me a thoughtful nod. He knew just what it meant to me, and of course, that whimper. *"God, I need you, Luc."*

*"Soon, John."* Luc's voice whispered in my head.

A promise. A pledge. God, I adored him and wanted him so damn desperately. Silence filled the room and then, well, leave it to my brother...

"Ah, excusez-moi my liege. Why don't you and your Sire get a castle?"

Jaycee, my precious, funny, and hotter than hell brother! Laughter filled the room, briefly. Then it struck me. Yeah, we had talked earlier, but I knew. Never again would anything separate the three of us. No thought would be kept from each other. The three of us would spend eternity together, bonded by a force to be reckoned with. Centered and kept in control by Janine. Janine. God in Heaven! Keep her safe.

I felt Christian's hand squeeze mine. Looking down, I watched as Christian gingerly adjusted himself in my lap so he could see me. I pulled him close to me, my hand caressing his defined, muscular chest.

"Christian. Hi!" I squeezed his hand back. "How's my bodyguard?"

"Jacques? SAM!" With all that had happened, and in his mentally and physically weakened state, Christian had momentarily lost track of where he was and what had happened. He was startled, and in his panicked state, he tried to break free of my embrace. "I need to help Sam!"

"Christian. It's okay! Everything is fine!" Gently restraining him, so as not to aggravate his near mortal wound, I gently ran my fingers through his hair. "Easy, Christian. We're here now. Remember? He couldn't be in better hands!" Putting my hand to his chin, I guided his face up to where he could see Sam.

"Sammy!" Christian once again struggled, desperately wanting to get to his man. "Please, Jacques. I need... I want to be by Sammy!"

"God, Christian. I know you do. You will, my brave, handsome boy." I rubbed his arm and kissed his cheek. "You, young man, scared the life out of us." I could hear Luc and Jaycee giggle. Even Christian managed a grin. "You are going to stay right where you are and rest! I believe you are still my bodyguard? So if I were you, I'd listen to me."

"Sam is going to be just fine, Christian! Thanks to that incredibly hot vampire who is holding you in his arms!" Jaycee reassured him, grinning from ear to ear.

"Yeah, and don't get too used to that!" Luc chuckled.

Christian relaxed back into my embrace. "You know, Luc." Christian looked up at me. "He *is* hot!" I could feel the tension in him dissipate, and I saw his lips curve into an angelic smile. "Sammy and I," Christian reached up to touch my face, "Jacques, we owe you so much."

"No, you don't. You would have done the same for us, but you and Sam must do one thing for me." My hand lightly caressed what were now minor scars, but moments ago had been mortal wounds, bleeding to death. My God, that works fast! I looked at Elena, still passed out on the floor. *'Well, finally. You did something for someone other than yourself.'* I thought.

"Jacques? Hey." I felt Christian's fingers gently run up and down my face, bringing me back to reality.

"Christian, babe. I'm sorry. You and Sammy need to do one thing for me."

"Anything, Jacques. Anything!" His voice was still weak.

"Promise me that you will never look for another job." I smiled.

Christian, still in my embrace, leaned forward, cautiously testing his shoulder. "The pain. It's gone!" Christian sighed, then he turned and looked at me, smiling. "Jacques, would you consider being ours?" The look on his face, and his adorable smile, lifted a weight off my shoulders. Sammy, though still in bad shape, was healing at a rapid rate, and gave us a few moments of hope. Hope that we would be able to end this nightmare, once and for all.

I tousled Christian's hair. In return, Christian turned and kissed me. It was so gentle and full of love, I felt my heart flutter. "Rest for a while. Just rest, Christian." I pulled him close to me, his head coming to rest on my chest. In an act of devotion, he placed his hand on my chest...over my heart. I felt his body relax into mine and watched as his eyes closed. "Rest well, Christian." I gently kissed his forehead. "Just sleep. It'll be better when you wake up."

"Promise, Jacques?" His eyes, half closed, looked at me, needing that extra assurance. "I promise, beautiful boy."

Christian was asleep in my arms. My senses were on high alert. I had to remind myself how deep we slept, the sleep of the undead. I just needed to see. I sighed as Christian finally took a breath. At rest, in deep sleep, a normal respiratory rate for mortals is about twelve breaths per minute; for vampires, it is one.

I brought Elena's arm to my mouth and began to lick the gash on her arm, healing it. I don't know exactly how it works, but vampires can actually heal injuries on mortals. Something in our genetic makeup, and the fact we are immortal. I really didn't understand. Only human blood could repair such horrific injuries to us, as evidenced on Sam and Christian. I looked at Elena with contempt. I bet you never thought you'd end up saving what you set out to destroy. *'The irony is on you, Elena.'* I thought. My relationship with her was over, but we still needed her. My sister Janine was out there. So help me God, Elena would help us. I was careful not to transfer any of Sam's or Christian's blood into her wound. The last thing we needed was an *eternal* Elena. I let her lay on the floor where she had passed out, partly due to the blood loss, and partly due to my elbow. You'll live, Elena, but after we are done with you, you may wish to God you were dead.

"Babe?" Luc's voice, was a soothing balm to my frayed nerves. "Look!" His eyes were locked on Sam.

Christian jumped out of my lap. "Whoa! Christian! That was a mistake!" I was up and caught him. Dizzy, he fainted and fell back into me. Scooping him up into my arms, I carried him over to Sam. One hundred and eighty-five pounds of solid muscle, yet it felt like I was carrying a puppy in my arms. A puppy. I grinned.

I remembered what Luc had told me about vampires living forever at the age of physical maturity, and realized that Christian had matured quite young. For all that he was born more than a hundred years ago, he was forever just barely eighteen. My mind flicked through the faces that I had met a few nights past. It seemed that nearly all of the family that I had met who could claim more than a hundred years of life were quite young in appearance, especially those of less aristocratic demeanor, quite probably due to the evolutionary need for adult males among the working class. My bodyguard was just a pup. *Oh, for the love of all things holy! Despite all the madness, here I was thinking about age and puppies.'*

I heard Luc giggle.

I looked up at him. I was a little, for lack of a better word, irked. But the moment I saw him, he took my breath away and heat scudded through my veins. He just sat there and waggled his eyebrows at me.

"What am I going to do with you, Luc?" I could only shake my head and grin. "God, I need a drink."

"I can give you something better!" Damn that sexy voice of his.

"Behave yourself!" I scolded him. I could hear Jaycee was enjoying every minute of it. Leave it to Jaycee to find this funny.

"Oh, God, you two! You're killing me here!" He was desperately trying to control his laughter. "I can't...Shit! My side hurts!"

"Good!" I chuckled.

*'Holy shit, that means that not only is Christian a puppy, but Jaycee, Sam, and my little shit, Luc, likely aren't far past puppyhood! Oh God, I'm surrounded by puppies. Well, at least Luc is paper trained.'* I thought, laughing to myself.

"*Hey, smart ass!*" Luc was looking at me with that adorable grin.

"*I heard that!*" Jaycee was looking back and forth at us. "*You sure you two aren't married already?*" Luc whimpered.

Feeling Christian move, I looked down at him. Cradled in my lap, his head was resting against my chest. He was still sleeping. Reality was sinking in. My God, the thought of these two men gone... I quickly shook the image out of my head. Still sitting on the floor, I held him in my arms, my hand pressed to his chest, feeling the slow beat of his strong, young heart. Looking at his shoulder, where previously a death blow had been struck, there was nothing but perfect, bronze skin. No scars or reminders left of the brutal attack that almost took his life. I dragged in a breath, letting out a sigh of relief.

The brush of Christian's hand over my face, brought me out of my ponderings. "Jacques, my hero!" I blushed, realizing Christian had been watching me look at him. With a wink, he smiled at me.

"Hey there, Christian." I tousled his hair.

I felt his hand cover mine, which was still softly resting on his chest. "Jacques." A tear ran down his cheek. "You caught me. You didn't let me fall."

I was back at the edge of that emotional precipice.

His eyes were focused on mine. The expression on his face was so full of love and adoration for me that I felt myself blush. "Jacques, I hope I'm not out of line. I am your bodyguard, and my one and only duty is to protect you. I would die for you, Jacques."

"Christian, my God! Young man, you almost did! What brought this on?" My hand gently ran across his chest.

"It's just, well, the way you saved Sam. And now, here... us. You saved me too. You mean everything to me, Jacques. My God, you are so beautiful, Jacques. I mean..." He started to blush.

As my hand stopped, coming to rest over his heart, I looked into his blue eyes. What is it with all these gorgeous men and their incredible, blue eyes? Must be a vampire prerequisite.

"Christian. It's okay! What's going on in that head of yours? What are you thinking?"

"I wish I had a brother. I wish you were my brother." His eyes misted over. One more emotional nudge.

"Um, I'd want him to be you because..." Christian's voice hitched, "I really love you, Jacques. I knew it from the first night I saw you." Looking down, he entwined his fingers with mine. Then, as he lifted his head and looked into my eyes, he choked back a sob and said "I really do love you, Jacques."

And over I went.

"I love you too, Christian." Tears were spilling down my face. "Christian," I dragged in a deep breath and held Christian's face between my hands, "it looks like I have a baby brother!" Christian, returning the favor, caught me. I held him as tight as I could. I don't know if it was the violent attack and near loss, the anger over an ultimate betrayal, or the emptiness over Janine's absence, but at that moment, for the sake of our sanity, our emotions allowed us to purge the horror we had seen and replace it with love.

The five of us, with Sam on Luc's and Jaycee's laps, gathered as close together as possible, and joined hands. It was then we heard Sam let out a huff of air, his hand slowly moving to his chest. His eyelids fluttered. Luc gently brushed a lock of hair from Sam's eyes. Then, for a few moments, his eyes opened. Just enough moments to reassure his man that he would be back in his arms soon. Enough moments for Christian to hear, "There's my boy." Long enough for Christian to lean forward and place his head next to Sam in time to hear the words he needed to hear from Sam. "Love you, Christian."

I looked down at Christian. He didn't need to ask. I knew what he wanted. "Luc? Jaycee? My baby brother needs his man."

I gently helped Christian stand up, I didn't want him to take another tumble. He leaned into me, but his eyes were seeing only one thing. Sam.

Getting up, Luc and Jaycee laid Sam back down on the sofa, propping a pillow under his head. Christian looked at us, and smiling, crawled onto the sofa and promptly proceeded to wrap himself around Sam. We watched as Sam, as weak as he was, found the strength to wrap his arms around Christian. Bringing his one hand up, he pulled Christian's head softly into the crook of his shoulder, burying his face into Christian's hair. There was no need for words. None at all.

I was immediately surrounded, and those two sets of strong arms wrapping around me told me, without words, how much I was cherished, adored, respected, and most of all, loved. What followed was a dream, one that I did not want to wake up from. Warmth spread through my body from head to toe as Luc, facing me, kissed me, slow and gentle. He whimpered. My heart skipped. His hands seeking, touching, and wanting every part of me. Jaycee, standing behind me, took his hands and ran them through my hair while kissing the base of my neck. His hands, like Luc's, touched me and sent warmth through me from my head to my toes. Luc's whimper and Jaycee's soft love-filled moans. They were consuming me, possessing me, and, God help me, loving me. Then I heard those words. Words I had not heard for what seemed an eternity.

"You, love, are ours." The promise that infused me to my very soul.

"Always and forever." Jaycee whispered, completing the vow that bound the three of us together. "If only Janine were here. God, boys, I miss her so much."

"We will see her again. Babe, we will get her back." Luc trailed his fingers down my face. For a few brief moments the three of us just stood there. No words were needed. I felt Jaycee move away. "I'll be right back, Jacques."

With Luc still in my embrace, his head resting on my shoulder, I took a few moments to look at Christian and Sam. Neither of them were going anywhere anytime soon, but that was just fine! Seeing them together, healthy, alive, and being able to share their love for each other, that's all I wanted for all of us.

As I turned my attention back to Luc, Jaycee returned with four glasses and a bottle of Luc's 'Special Reserve'. Don't even bother trying to figure out what 'Special Reserve' means. I will tell you this, it's not what you're thinking. It's *not* human blood! Luc tried to explain it to me. I'll understand...maybe in one hundred years or so!

"Just what the doctor ordered." I sighed.

Jaycee handed me two glasses. "Why don't you give one of those to your little brother?"

"I just, with everything that's happening, it just felt like the right thing to do, you know?" I looked into Luc's eyes for approval.

"John, my love. What you did for him," Luc's arm gestured towards the two men on the sofa, "for Sam. No explanation is needed. I would expect nothing less from you babe."

"Just promise us one thing." Jaycee put his hand on my shoulder. "Don't ever, ever change."

"That is one promise I know I can keep, Jaycee. Your brother, the man I love, made sure of that." That whimper.

"Luc, hon. Jaycee, babe. Would you excuse me for just one moment?"

I walked over to Christian. I thought for sure I would find him sleeping, but he wasn't. I looked at him. His arms were carefully wrapped around Sam. Their bodies were pressed together and Christian's leg was swung up and over Sam's hip. I watched as Christian lightly pressed kisses on Sam's face and chest. My God, what a heartwarming sight. Thank you, God. Thank you for keeping them together. I suddenly felt myself blush as I realized I had been watching a very private moment between lovers, but Christian needed to be fed. I leaned over and gently ran my fingers across Christian's bare, broad shoulder.

"Christian. Excusez-moi?"

"Hey, big brother." He turned his head, his eyes meeting mine. With a soft smile, he winked at me.

"Here, baby bro, drink this." I handed the glass to him. "It will help take the edge off for now."

As he turned his body toward me, I couldn't help but notice Sam's chest. What I saw made my heart skip and my pulse race. "Luc? Jaycee? Can you come over here please!" My voice was filled with excitement.

"What's wrong, Jacques?" Christian had propped himself up next to Sam to accept the drink I offered. "Nothing's wrong, baby bro!" I pointed to Sam. "Look at Christian!"

Luc and Jaycee had come over, both of them were looking much better. As a matter of fact, we all were, including Sam. Where his chest had been slashed open leaving a mortal wound, there was only perfect, bronze skin. It was completely healed! My eyes shifted from Sam and looked up to find Luc and Jaycee looking at me.

"My God, babe!" Luc whispered breathlessly.

"Holy shit, Jacques!" Jaycee's face couldn't hide his amazement. Signs of relief, and their love for me, shone on both of their faces.

Before I knew it, Christian was up and embracing me. Christian's emotional dam broke. He wept. I did the only thing I could, I wrapped my arms around him and pulled him tightly against me. I held him and let him purge himself of all the pain and worrying he had endured this evening. Stroking his hair, I whispered words of comfort and support, words of love.

"Jacques?" Tears were streaming down Christian's face as he pulled back just enough to look at me. "I know I've said this before but, thank you. I love you so much!"

I wiped a tear from his face.

"Christian, like I said, you would have done the same for me... for us. It's going to be okay! I pulled Christian back into my arms. Do me a favor, please."

"Anything, Jacques. Anything!"

"Don't ever let him go!"

"Je vous promets!"

"Christian, I know you do. I know you promise. Christian, I'm so proud of you!"

"Jacques, what did I do? How could you be proud of me? I...I let all of you down."

"Why would you say that, let alone think that, precious boy?"

"I let Alec get Trace."

"Actually, Christian, Alec can have him. Despite what I think of Elena, she is unscathed. You did exactly what I would have done." My eyes looked up at Luc. "You protected the most important  person in your life."

A tear fell down Luc's cheek.

Christian wrapped one of his hands in mine and pressed back into me. With his head resting on my shoulder, I gently kissed him on the cheek, then nuzzled my face in his hair.

"Merci, Jacques." He squeezed my hand.

"Never, Christian, never would I allow such a love to be destroyed by anyone." I looked up to see Luc and Jaycee looking at me.

"Jaycee?" Luc was addressing his brother, but his blue eyes were locked onto mine.

"Yes, Luc?" Jaycee's eyes, as blue as Luc's, never wavered from mine.

"You, me, and John...always?"

"For fucking ever, baby bro!"

# ❈ CHAPTER FORTY-THREE ❈

About an hour had passed. Elena, thankfully, was still passed out. I didn't want to deal with her, but at the same time I wanted to shake her awake and ask her exactly what the hell went down. I wanted some fucking answers. My anger for her burned inside me, but right now the discussion Jaycee, Luc, and I were having was far more important. We still had Alec and Trace to deal with. Christian and Sam sat across from us at the dining room table which, amazingly, had gone unscathed. The four crystal glasses from the other evening were still sitting where we left them. The only exception was that now five fresh ones were filled. All of us were exhausted, but before continuing this battle, we must deal with first things first. The need to feed was overpowering. What we drank before had taken the edge off, but with what we were facing, we needed our full strength.

I felt a serene smile spread across my face as I looked at Sam, this strong, handsome vampire was once again fully intact. No scars, not even a scratch, remained. He was sipping on a glass of Luc's 'Special Reserve'. Luc noticed his restraint, obviously not used to the attention.

"Sam. Hey! You're still weak. Drink up. Trust me, I have plenty more where that came from!"

"Sammy. Luc is right. We almost lost you and Christian. You look great, but how are you feeling on the inside?" I asked.

Sam took another drink, then set the glass down on the table and reached a hand across the table to me. I accepted his offering and he wrapped my hand in his. His thumb gently rubbed my wrist.

"I really appreciate your concern, Jacques. I feel fine. Just a little tired. I don't remember much though."

"I thank God you don't, Sam." I squeezed his hand.

Christian leaned into him, resting his head on Sam's shoulder. Sam kissed him on top of his head.

"Christian? Is it okay if we ask you some questions? I know they may seem redundant, but maybe something slipped your mind." Luc leaned inward, his voice soft and compassionate. He took in a soft breath. "You had more important things on your mind."

"Of course, Lord Luc."

"First of all, no more of that, Christian. It's Luc, Jaycee, and John, or should I say, big brother?" Luc turned to me and winked. Jaycee tousled his brother's hair. "That goes for you too, Sammy!"

I watched Christian and Sam's reaction. They both blushed. Christian started to say something about proper respect, but he didn't get very far. I didn't let him.

"Hey, baby bro. Listen to Luc, okay?" I winked at him. "Trust me, you do not argue with my Sire!"

"Wait! Baby bro?" Sam looked at Christian, then me, a puzzled look on his face. "Sounds like I missed something!"

"Sammy." Jaycee interjected. "Jacques there," his hand gestured to me, "has adopted Christian!"

At the word adopted, Sam pushed his chair away from the table and walked around, heading, and looking, directly at me. Without flinching, he pulled my chair back, signaling me to stand.

I glanced at Luc, who just shrugged his shoulders. *"Gee, thanks, Luc!"*

*"You're welcome!"*

*"You are so gonna get it!"*

*"I can't wait!"* Luc winked.

A vision of Luc making love to me flashed through my mind. I immediately felt my cock take interest. It had been so fucking long.

Jaycee, the little shit, decided to target me rather than Luc. I wanted to crawl under the table. Now I know what Luc had to endure.

"Sam, I can explain!" I stood up. "Really!"

When did he get so tall? Sam didn't say a word. He just stood there looking at me.

"Sam, it all happened..." Before I could get another word out, Sam silenced me by placing two of his fingers on my lips. A smile began to form on Sam's face, dimples in his cheeks appeared, and little lines formed on the sides of his eyes, which sparkled like diamonds. My memory flashed back to the first time I met Sam at the club. No...John...No, that is absolutely impossible. It can't be.

What came next surprised everyone. Without a word, Sam put his hands on my waist and pulled me into his arms. God, for such a big man he could be so gentle. Before I knew it, he took one of his hands and tangled it in my hair, pulling my face to his. Our lips met, and he kissed me. It was soft and gentle. The love I felt from him overpowered me. It was not meant to be sexual. It was to say thank you, I love you.

Keeping me in his embrace, he leaned back and looked at me. "Jacques, with all my heart, with all that I am, for the love of my man, I thank you. Christian and I will never be able to repay what you have done. Christian told me of your bravery, and the love and compassion you showed." He paused and gently kissed my forehead. "I had brothers, Jacques, but that is another story. My young man," his eyes briefly glanced at Christian, "was an only child. For a man as honorable and brave as you to accept him as your little brother, speaks not only of your character, but your feelings for us as well. Christian and I love you with all our hearts!"

My knees went weak. Sam, his hand on my elbow, guided me to my seat. "I guess that clears up the 'Lord' thing!" Jaycee chuckled.

I was still trying to figure out what the fuck just happened when Luc decided it was a good time to lean over and kiss me. It was meant to be, oh God...sexual.

I didn't want it to end, but I needed air, and I didn't want to do something to Luc that wouldn't be appropriate in present company. I looked into my lover's eyes and saw a promise of things to come. My attention to Luc was gently interrupted by the feeling of a hand softly taking mine, fingers becoming entwined with mine. Once again, with my newly-acquired powers, I knew by touch alone who needed me.

"Excusez-moi, Jacques." Christian was standing next to Sam.

"Hey, little bro. Everything okay?" I looked up into Christian's eyes.

"More than ever." A single red tear ran down Christian's cheek.

"Then, Christian, why the tear?" I stood up and gently took my thumb and wiped the tear away.

"Um...I...Jacques..." Christian was becoming flustered. "Is it real, or was I just dreaming?" He raised his hand to wipe away another tear.

"Christian," I squeezed his hand, "is what real?"

"I really have, um...I really have a brother?"

I smiled and softly laughed, shaking my head. "My precious, Christian," I let my fingers softly run down the side of his face, "yes, you really do!" I tousled his hair and brought my hand down to cup his chin. "I love you, little bro!" I had started to lean into Christian, when, much to my surprise, Christian eagerly brought his lips to mine and kissed me. With no hesitation, he showed me that eternal youth is absolutely beautiful and I was the lucky one to be shown how true that is.

"I love you too, bro! This is so cool!"

"You, babe, have your hands full!" Luc giggled.

And then it hit me. *'An eternally eighteen year old brother.'*

*"Yeah, and an eighteen year old lover!"* I shot back at Luc. Luc blushed.

*"Thought you could sneak that one past me, did you?"*

Luc whimpered.

Then it dawned on me. Hit me smack upside the head! I should have known by the grin on Jaycee's face that he was listening. All I could do was look at him. *'Aahh! Double crap!'* Regardless, I couldn't help but smile, and as I did, something else hit me.

Christian and Sam had returned to their places at the table and I sat down again. "Luc?" I turned to him and took his hand. "Babe, after what just happened with Christian, can I run something by you and Jaycee?"

"Babe, you don't have to ask!"

I turned my attention to Sam. "Sam, you just shared a little something about yourself with me. I want you to know you can tell me everything, when you're ready."

"Of course, Jacques. I appreciate your understanding, and I will."

I turned back to Luc. "Everyone should have family, Luc. Jaycee, you with me on this?"

"Of course, bro. What are you thinking?"

"What I'm thinking is, Sam and Christian have been with you for, oh hell, a long time. Right?"

"Yes, babe. A long time. They have watched over us and saved us so many times, I have lost count. Luc looked at them lovingly.

"May I ask a favor then, love?" I was excited by the prospect and hoped Luc and Jaycee would feel the same way, but I guess I didn't have to wonder.

"Yes! Absolutely!" Luc knew what I was getting at and gave me the answer before I asked the question. Luc turned to look at Jaycee. His smile and a nod were all I needed.

"What's going on, Jacques?" Christian's eyebrows drew together.

"We'll need to stock more of that special reserve Luc has!" I could tell by Christian's expression, he was trying his best to figure out what was going on, but he shrugged his shoulders and looked at me, confused.

"Sammy. Christian." Jaycee stood up with his glass. "I'd like to propose a toast!"

Following his lead, we all stood up, raising our glasses. Poor Sam and Christian were still puzzled, as they stood and looked at each other, but still respectfully raised their glasses to meet ours.

"To Sam and Christian! Welcome to the family!" With that said, we toasted, drank, and took the next few minutes to enjoy the momentary happiness that filled the room.

"It's a damn shame that it took something this wrong, to bring about something so right. Ironic, isn't it?" I shook my head.

Taking our seats, I glanced at Jaycee. He was happy, but as he looked at his watch, I knew it was time we pressed forward. Janine was still missing. Our family was not complete.

"Pardonnez-moi, but time is slipping away. Christian, what can you tell us about what happened here?" Jaycee asked. "I hate to push it, but Janine was supposed to meet us and she is, um...She's," Jaycee's voice hitched, "missing." I reached for, and took one of Jaycee's hands into mine.

"I understand, Jaycee. God! Jaycee, I am so sorry. Everything was under control. With all due respect, Jacques, your sister... Well, she isn't a very polite person."

I huffed out a breath. "Don't take it personally, Christian."

"We, Sammy and I," he turned to look at his man, "we were watching Elena and Trace. What a complete asshole!"

"You're too kind, Christian." I gave him a grin.

"Anyway, out of nowhere, Alec busted through the door to the suite." Christian added.

"Fuck!" Luc became agitated, slamming his fist on the table. "I forgot to take him out of the security bypass program."

I grabbed his arm. "Luc, no! You will not blame this on yourself. Listen to me, all of you. This is not anyone's fault."

"It all happened so fast. I'm sorry, so sorry." Christian began to tear up and Sam immediately put an arm around him.

"Hey, bro. It's okay." I reached over and touched his hand. "What did I just say? You are not to blame yourself for this. Understood?"

"It's just when he attacked Sam, all I could think about was..."

"Your boy." Jaycee answered for him. I couldn't help but notice Jaycee glancing at his brother, then me.

"Yeah, and that's when Alec took Trace."

"Christian, did Trace put up a fight when Alec approached him?"

Christian thought a moment, then with a slight tilt to his head, he shook his head back and forth. "No, Jacques. Come to think of it, no. As a matter of fact, Jacques, neither did Elena. It was like... shit! It was like both of them were waiting for him. God! Jacques, Luc, Jaycee...I let you down." Sam wrapped his arm around Christian and pulled him close. Suddenly a rush of forgotten events filled Christian's head. He looked down at the table. I could tell things were coming back to him; he was remembering what had taken place. Slowly he looked up at me, his face once again ashen white.

"Christian, what is it?"

"Trace, Jacques! Trace!"

"What, Christian? What about Trace?"

"He turned, shifted. He was already a wolf!" He started to shake and Sam took his hand. "Jacques, oh my God! He was already a wolf! Elena did nothing. She sat there, cold, calculating. She just laughed this evil laugh."

I felt the fury and anger in me build, but for Christian's sake, I took a deep breath, reining my emotions in. "Easy, Christian. Hey, it's okay! Go on. Trust me, Christian, I know that laugh. What happened then?"

"Oh, God! Then he went after Sam! Jacques, I'm so sorry. I...All I could think of was saving Sam. I tried to get him off Sam, but...Oh, God! Jacques! Trace attacked me! Jacques, please forgive me." Christian's eyes pleaded with mine. He was physically shaking.

"Christian, babe. It's okay. You did good, Christian, you did really good! Just take a few moments."

"Come here, hon." Sam pulled him back into his embrace. "Jacques is right."

I slowly stood up. Luc put his hand on my arm. I felt his concern. I looked down at him and leaned over, kissing his forehead. Then I turned and set my sights on Elena. I had the sudden urge to drain every drop of blood from her body. All this time, Elena and her concern for me, it was all a trap. Part of a plan that I did not see coming until now. Well, Elena, payback is a bitch. I hope you're fucking ready! No one fucks with my family. No one!

I turned back and stood behind Luc. I let my hands run down his arms, to his waist. I closed my eyes. Just touching him, feeling him, it centered me. Opening my eyes, I placed my hands on his shoulders. God! They were so tight. I rubbed them gently, and Luc leaned back into my massage. "Luc, it was a fucking set up! They wanted this. It was just a distraction. They knew we would be preoccupied with Sammy and Christian. They wanted..." My voice caught.

"Janine." Luc and Jaycee answered in unison, in what was barely a whisper.

"Oh, God! Jacques, Luc, Jaycee. What have we done?"

"Christian. No! Don't make me go big brother on you! I would have done the same thing." Luc looked at me and reached up, taking one of my hands that was working on his shoulders. He entwined his fingers with mine. "We will, so help me God, get our sister back. I promise." Luc stood up and threw himself into my arms. "I promise, baby boy." I whispered into his ear as I let him lose himself in my embrace.

It was then I heard Elena regain consciousness. I brushed my lips across Luc's. "Give me a few moments with her, babe."

He nodded. Jaycee stood up and took his place beside his brother.

I actually felt a little calmer, though this nightmare was by no means over. One fire at a time, I guess. But this fire was out of control, and the person responsible for fanning the flames, was in this room. I was not about to let her burn down what I had built. If anyone was burning, it would be Elena, burning in hell. As I turned and looked at her, I felt my hands clench together. I felt nothing but contempt for this woman that I no longer knew, or wanted to know.

I felt Luc's hand on my arm and turned back to him.

"John, are you sure?" He looked up at me. Fine worry lines appeared in the corners of his eyes. Fear showed in his beloved eyes.

I would not allow him, or anyone in this family, to go through any more pain on my account. Either Elena cooperated, or she would die. There was no in-between, no gray areas, no bargaining, no compromise, and no fucking forgiveness.

"Yeah, baby boy, I'm sure. I love you for your concern, but please do not be afraid." I cupped his face in my hands. "I have to do this." My voice was confident and determined.

"Of course I understand, but that doesn't mean I have to like it." He pulled me to him and kissed me. "I love you...always."

"Forever, Luc." I turned and walked toward Elena. I could feel Luc inside me, calming me.

I growled as I approached her, just for effect. "Elena, you should be on your knees thanking my lover, because right now, if it wasn't for him, I would rip your heart out."

As I got closer, she stood up. Looking down at her arm, she looked back up at me with pure hatred in her eyes. She lunged toward me. I guess she forgot about my red eyes and fangs, and what that meant. I grabbed her around the shirt collar and lifted her, feet kicking air, dangling off the floor.

"You monster! Let me down!" she screamed. "How the fuck could you do this to me?"

"You've got a lot of nerve asking that, Elena." I glared at her and twisted her shirt collar, momentarily cutting her breath off. Like tossing a rag doll, I threw her through the air and she hit the floor. "Sorry, I was aiming for the couch, bitch!"

Elena picked herself up off the ground and flung herself at me. She had always been quicker than me, but now the joke was on her. I let her beat on me with her fists for a moment, but she recoiled instantly as I growled and bared my fangs, grabbing her wrists.

"Enough! Those days are gone, Elena. I don't have time for this fucking shit. I told you to stay away. I told you I would kill you, and that asshole Trace, if any harm came to the people that I love. You really are a selfish bitch, aren't you, Elena? The *only* person that ever mattered in your life was, and is, you! Now..." I pushed her back down on the sofa, "you will listen, and listen good! Because if you don't," I snarled, "what I did to your arm earlier will seem like a paper cut!"

"I dare you!" Elena glared at me.

"Really?" I smirked. "I dare you? Really?" I felt my body tense, hands open wide, ready to throttle the life out of her.

Before I knew it, Luc and Jaycee were by my side, their hands holding mine. I smiled as I glanced at them, squeezing their hands. "You wonder why I love them? God, you really are too much, Elena."

"So, Elena." Jaycee growled. "We meet in person." I watched him giving her the once over. His eyes were deep red, and his fangs...

"Huh, nice touch, love." I chuckled.

"Trace will kill all of you! You fucking monsters!" Elena's voice sounded threatening, yet it lacked heat.

"Really?" Luc snarled.

*'God! He was so hot when he vamped out.'*

*"Vamped out? Really?"* Jaycee looked at me and grinned.

The levity, as brief as it was, was needed. Luc and Jaycee were always one step ahead of me when it came to my thoughts and emotions.

"He already got one of you!" Elena glared at me. I knew she meant Janine. It hit me like a punch in my gut. My knees went weak. I would have fallen if it weren't for Luc and Jaycee catching me. I had not been fully aware of how powerful I was, but before I knew it, I broke free of Luc and Jaycee's hold. Leaning over her, I wrapped my hands around Elena's throat. "What the fuck did you do?"

"She should really learn to keep that boyfriend of hers on a fucking leash." Elena stared into my eyes, as cold as ice.

Jaycee snarled.

The smile on Elena's face gave me chills. "Jacques?"

"Yeah, bro?"

"May I have a little chat with her?"

"Jaycee. The bitch is all yours." Stepping back, I felt Jaycee's hand brush mine.

I watched as Jaycee leaned forward, bracing himself against the back of the sofa. His face was mere inches from Elena's. In the meantime, I leaned into Luc as he gently took my hand and entwined his fingers with mine.

*"My baby boy?"* I felt Luc's hand come to rest on the small of my back.

As he put his head on my shoulder, he whimpered. *"Yes, John.*

*Until the end of our days."*

Without my vampire sight and hearing, I would have missed it. Missed the sound of Elena's sharp intake of air, the flicker of pure terror in her eyes. If Jaycee or Luc could not break her, she would break herself. The realization of Trace's abandonment was sinking in. I should feel sorry for her. Should.

"Elena? How much do you know about werewolves?" His red eyes pierced hers.

"They can fucking kill you!" Her voice was defiant, but was that fear I saw on her face?

"Yeah, they can, they can *try*." Jaycee's emphasis on the word try, and the smirk on his face as he said it, made Elena squirm. "What else?" Jaycee leaned closer to her.

Luc and I watched Jaycee. His power of self-control, and his calm demeanor, seemed to make Elena squirm that much more.

*"Remind me not to get my brother pissed off!"*

Luc squeezed my hand. *"You're kidding, right babe? You are his hero!"*

*"Babe, God knows how much I appreciate that sentiment, but..."*

*"John, babe. You're my hero! For what you've done for us. For your love, bravery, and compassion. Jaycee and I owe you everything. Like I told you before, babe, you owe us nothing."*

I turned to Luc. I knew. I knew he was looking at me. *"Luc, love. Can I hear it one more time?"*

Luc smiled. *"You, love, are mine...ours...always and forever."*

I cherished the moment Luc and I were once again alone together, wishing we could forget the world. Then the shrill, irritating voice of Elena snapped Luc and I back to reality.

"Frankly, you freak, that's all I need to know." Elena snarled.

Unimpeded by her ranting, Jaycee continued. "How did Trace react to Alec's overtures?"

Jaycee's line of questioning made sense, perfect sense. Yes, we had made an educated guess, and that is what we were going on. We just wanted her to admit the fact that this was all an orchestrated, premeditated plan devised, in part, by Elena. She picked the perfect scapegoats but that, I'm sure, Elena knew would be easy. Alec is an idiot. Fuck! Trace is an idiot. So, dangle the right prize, which happened to be my sister Janine, in front of Alec, and promise a very jealous Trace payback, well, there you go. Elena always was a manipulative, self-serving bitch, and she was proving it again. But this? Friending vampires and werewolves? What the hell did she think this was? Facebook? Oh, John has friends in France. I'll just weasel my way in.

"What...What do you mean by Alec's 'overtures'?" I could tell Elena was trying to read him. "He...He allowed it?"

"He didn't struggle, did he Elena? You would think a man like Trace, a man of such strength and free-will, would be in charge of his life! Shit! From what I've heard, by all accounts, why would Trace want to be a wolf? Wasn't he here to help rescue Jacques? Hell, I would have thought he would go down screaming and kicking!" Jaycee looked at us with a decidedly cocky smile on his face. Leave it to my brother. He was enjoying every minute of this.

Luc and I nodded and smiled at him.

*"I think Jaycee missed his calling, babe."*

Luc turned and looked at me. His one eyebrow arched in question. *"How so?"*

*"Oh, I don't know? Prosecutor? Detective? Yeah, detective! CSI Paris! He could walk around at night, investigating and interrogating. He could wear sunglasses at night and get away with it!"*

*"You, goof!"* His fist lightly slugged my arm. *"I know what you're doing, mon cher. Merci! Love you, babe."*

*"Love you more!"*

"Jacques. Luc." His smile grew even bigger. "Alec has finally found his mate."

"What do you mean, mate?" It actually sounded like Elena had no clue. For a moment, I couldn't believe that Elena had not factored that in, but then again... Oh! This was too fucking good. Elena didn't factor in that Trace was gay.

"Well, Elena, you see," Jaycee stood up next to me, "wolves mate for life."

"In other words, Elena, your little plan has, shall we say, backfired in your face. You see, Elena, the pull, the desire, the yearning between werewolves, if they are true mates, is so powerful that nothing, and no one," he made it a point to lean a little closer to her, "can stop it. It is, indisputably, the strongest physical and emotional connection a werewolf has with another female, or in this case, male!" I didn't need to see the look on my brother's face to know he was enjoying himself. "There is only one person...*one* that wolf will ever claim for their own. Trace letting Alec turn him without any struggle means his allegiance, his love and devotion, belongs to Alec, now and for eternity. Trace will obey anything and everything Alec asks him to do! By now you're nothing but a little, albeit annoying, problem."

Luc stepped forward, bending down towards Elena. "If I were you, Elena, I'd be very concerned about myself. Very!" He straightened up again, taking my hand.

"Oh, really? God! I thought vampires were supposed to be intelligent. That is fucking bullshit! Trace is strong and independent. No one tells him what to do! What the hell are you talking about, mate? Trace...He's...He's straight." Typical Elena. Stubborn to the end, but Jaycee and Luc were breaking her down.

Luc nudged me. "She has absolutely no idea what her so-called boyfriend has been up to, has she babe?"

I almost felt sorry for her. No. I guess I didn't. I leaned over next to Jaycee and looked directly in her eyes. "Elena. You're dead to me. My feelings for you died the day I became immortal. So really, I couldn't care less what you think, but shit! This is too much!" I found myself letting out a wicked little laugh. "Elena," I leaned into her, "he likes boys, a lot!"

She spit in my face. "Liar!"

I grabbed her around her neck. It took all my willpower, but I put just enough pressure on her throat to cause her to choke. My hands wanted to do more. At this point in the game it was all about standing my ground and using the self-confidence that Luc, Jaycee... a knot formed in my throat... and Janine had given me. After years of her constant sarcasm, abuse, and smartass remarks, my transformation had finally helped me find the strength to stand up for myself and those I loved. Right now I was fighting for Janine. If necessary, I would drain the life out of Elena for an answer. Who's the monster? Until Janine was standing next to us, unscathed, her hands touching and caressing us, until the smell of lilacs permeated the air in her presence, I guess the jury is still out.

Standing back up, I took a moment to look at her. "I wonder, Elena, how your blood tastes?" I bared my fangs. "One more time, Elena. Try me! Anyway, where was I? Oh right...Trace likes boys."

"Fuck you, John. I know you've had a hard-on for him since the day you saw him, but he picked me! He fucking picked me! Trace, gay? I think not!"

"Oh, I think so." I paced a few steps back and forth in front of Elena, rubbing my hands together. "Remember my little road trip to Miami with Trace in the rig. It was a warm, beautiful night in Georgia." I leaned forward, face to face with Elena. "Trace treated me to a great supper. We grabbed a shower at a truck stop, and then Trace found this great place to park the truck for the night. Elena, it really does pain me to tell you this, but I fucked him so hard, he cried...for more! Funny, I figured him for a top!" I stood up and found myself, once again, between Luc and Jaycee. Elena went ashen white, but apparently she had one more card to play… the desperation card.

"Funny thing of it is," Elena sneered, "you didn't even bother to factor in the wolves downstairs."

"What the fuck is that supposed to mean, Elena?" I had come to hate her voice.

"Well, where are the fucking wolves that were downstairs?"

"Again, what are you saying, Elena?" I felt my hands begin to squeeze her throat.

"Easy, baby." Luc put his hands on mine, taking hold of them.

"Let's just say Janine has her fucking paws full right about now."

"You bitch!" I once again found my hands wrapped around Elena's throat. I wanted to rip it open.

Instead, something came over me. It overpowered me. I knew what I had to do.

"No, John." Luc had been listening to me.

I turned to Luc and Jaycee. "Babe, I know you don't want this, but I promised Janine I would protect you. Now, with what is happening, what we've been through, Luc," I grabbed his arms, "I need to do this. You and Jaycee," my breath hitched, "fuck! I love you both so damn much." I dragged in a breath. "This is my fault. I need to end this. Besides, if I stay here, I will kill her. I want, I need you both to stay here with Sam and Christian and watch Elena. If she so much as moves," I turned to look at her, "do me a favor and end her."

As I turned back to face Luc and Jaycee, Sam and Christian had come over and were standing in back of them.

"Bro?" Christian walked over to me. "Leave that to Sam and me. While you and your Sire and brother were dealing with Elena, we had a heart to heart talk and well, we would still like to be your bodyguards. If that is acceptable?"

I looked at Luc and Jaycee.

"That's your call, babe."

"Jaycee?"

"I agree with my baby bro."

I paused, looking at all four of these men, and took a moment to address their request.

"Christian and Sam. First of all, I appreciate everything you've done for me, for Luc and Jaycee and...for Janine. I couldn't expect more. Your dedication and loyalty to us went beyond the call of duty. Which brings me to my second thought. We are now family! Being a bodyguard to me... No. I will not require your services any longer."

"But, Jacques." Sam's eyes pleaded with mine.

"Sammy, I love you, but let me finish. Here's the thing. We are family. What do families do? They love, protect, and guard each other every single day of their lives. Just as we," I acknowledged Luc and Jaycee, "look out for each other, we will be looking out and caring for you every day now too! Just as you will be, for us."

It took a moment for what I said to sink in, but when it did, Sam and Christian immediately embraced me. Luc and Jaycee joined us.

I knew it was coming... It came.

"You fucking sick bastards. Trace and Alec are going to rip you apart."

I was having a hard time visualizing my past life, my mortal life. The years that Elena and I spent together growing up, there was nothing. Those memories are gone. Yes, in a way it was sad, but if I could still remember those times, when Elena was my sister, I could not dislike this woman. I would care about her wellbeing. Our defenses would have a weak spot. Did I have regrets? No! I wouldn't change a damn thing. I wanted love and I found that, and more. The deceit and violence that occurred here tonight were all the doing of someone I didn't know anymore. What I did know is, if anyone were dying tonight, it would not be one of us.

"Sammy? Christian?"

"Yes, Jacques?" Christian stepped over to me, eager to please. *'Yep, a puppy!'* I thought, lovingly. "What we were talking about, before. I was totally serious. If she tries anything," I turned and glared at Elena, "end her life."

"They wouldn't dare!" Elena shrunk back into the coach.

"Oh, they would, Elena. You brought this on yourself. As far as

I'm concerned," I leaned over her, inches from her face, and bared my fangs, "you are dead to me."

Luc was trying, but I knew he was struggling with my decision. I looked at him and pulled him to me. I let my lips brush across his, tasting his mouth, his very essence.

"Luc, I promise you. It will be okay." My fingers gently ran through his hair.

"It better be." Luc pulled me tighter to him. I could tell it was taking every ounce of his protective instincts to allow this. I felt his warm breath against my neck as he buried his face against me. "Just please, babe…Please, mon cher… Come back to me."

"I will, baby boy. I will."

"Don't be so sure of that, Luc." Elena's sarcastic response was silenced by Jaycee's fist connecting with her jaw.

I laughed as I watched Elena cringe and hold her jaw as two very pissed off vampires sat on either side of her.

"Oh, I'll be seeing you again, Elena. You can count on that!"

Luc and Jaycee embraced me once again. Then they each pulled up a chair and had a seat. Make that *four* very pissed off vampires.

# ✦ CHAPTER FORTY-FOUR ✦

As I opened the door from the private entrance, my mind was still reeling. I realized I had a long way to go before I was anywhere close to controlling my vampire instincts like Luc and Jaycee did. Hell, they had more than three hundred years advantage on me! God bless them though. If it weren't for them, I would have ripped Elena's throat out. My mind flashed to Christian's anguish, Sam's pain, and how Christian held Sam in his arms. I knew first-hand how Christian felt, but all that mattered was that Sam and Christian had survived. I found great solace in that. What if that had been Luc? I knew my mortal memories were disappearing, fading into nothing more than a tattered picture, but I felt a knot form in my gut as the pain and grief I felt when I buried K.C. flashed through my mind. Losing Luc?

"No fucking way!" I shouted to no one...I thought.

"Jacques, are you okay?" Worry lines creased Adrian's forehead.

"Ah, yeah. Merci, Adrian." I dragged in a couple of breaths, involuntarily shuddering.

Adrian picked up on it immediately. "You're shaking. I'm sorry, but if it helps, your fears and frustration are completely warranted." His concern was appreciated. "If I may?" Adrian, now standing closely beside me, put his hand on my elbow and escorted me to the limo.

I noticed his eyes scanning the grounds surrounding the club.

Adrian being ever vigilant. When this was over, his faithfulness would not go unnoticed. Like Sam and Christian, his loyalty and his selfless, abiding love for our family would be rewarded. Never, not even in my mortal life, have I ever met anyone as devoted or reverent.

I don't know why, but I thought about the century age difference. Luc, love, you have some explaining to do. I felt a small smile forming on my face as I realized I would have an eternity to get to know all the answers. Sammy, Christian, and Adrian. Yeah, babe, a lot of explaining.

"I am so sorry for what happened, Jacques. Besides the obvious, how are you holding up, sir?" His hand gently squeezed my elbow. I grinned and softly shook my head. He still hadn't grasped that I had banned any type of formal prefixes when addressing me.

"Pretty good, all things considered, Adrian." I leaned into him. "I'll be okay once we finish this completely." We were now standing next to the limo. I noticed Adrian's hand was still on my elbow and I could feel his sincere concern for me. "Ah hell, Adrian! That is a lie." I put my head down. "Adrian, I don't know what came over me in there. When I was mortal, I wouldn't hurt anyone."

"Jacques, you must stop punishing yourself." Adrian placed his hand on my shoulder. "You are a vampire and you are struggling with new emotions you never had to contend with as a mortal. Yes, we live for an eternity, but it comes with a price. It's not foolproof. As you found out tonight, it is fraught with danger. Jacques, you will adapt." I felt him softly squeeze my shoulder and for just a moment, a rare moment, Adrian smiled at me. "The love you have for Lords Luc and Jaycee, and Lady Janine, is more powerful than you know. Eternal love, Jacques, is something only a very few are fortunate enough to achieve. Jacques, you are young! You have done an exemplary job of handling your transformation. Do not be so hard on yourself! Besides," Adrian looked into my eyes, once again squeezing my shoulder, "you have Luc. You are a very lucky man! After all, he waited three hundred and fifty-seven years for you!" Adrian, much to my surprise, let out a small laugh.

I still had a hard time processing that. I stood there shaking my head, feeling my heart pound. "Hell, Adrian, don't I know it." I paused, noticing Adrian bow his head in reverence. "Adrian, you knew what was going on, didn't you?"

"Yes, Jacques." Adrian's head was still lowered, his hands fell to his side. "I should have been there."

I tilted his head up to look at me, brushing a lock of his long, blonde hair from his forehead. "No, Adrian, don't put that on yourself. You did exactly as you were told. If anyone should be apologizing, it is me for putting you through such an ordeal. Adrian, may I share something with you? I hope that is not too forward or makes you uncomfortable?"

"Sir… oh pardonnez-moi… Jacques, of course."

I couldn't help myself. Everything that happened tonight: Sammy, Christian, not knowing where Janine is, missing Luc and Jaycee. Fuck! Why couldn't I be stronger? This was not the time for self- pity. Some vampire I am.

"Adrian? I...I...um...shit!"

Adrian was one step ahead of me. He softly ran his fingers down my cheek, then cupping my chin in one of his strong hands, he looked at me, nodding his head.

"Merci beaucoup. I care about you too, Jacques." His strong arms surrounded me and pulled me close to him. I felt one of his hands gently guide my head to his broad shoulder. For a few moments, Adrian held me and no words were spoken.

"Thank you, Adrian." I whispered in his ear.

"Jacques, thanks are not necessary. I think we both needed that."

He gently let go of me and opened the rear door. I had one foot in the limo when I turned, hesitantly, to look at Adrian. "May I sit up front with you, s'il vous plaît?"

"Oui. Of course." He shut the rear door.

I started to walk around the vehicle, but before I took more than one step, Adrian was once again by my side. My arm was now securely wrapped in Adrian's. For some reason, the dynamics of our relationship were changing… noticeably. This was not a bad thing, just different, and not even my vampire intuition could pick up on it. I looked at Adrian. His eyes vigilantly perused our surroundings. Almost like, God I can't believe I'm thinking this, he was expecting something to happen. '*John, paranoid now.*'

"Merci. Merci beaucoup, faithful Adrian." I thanked him as he opened the front passenger door for me. I leaned into him and hugged him. Taking several deep breaths, I got into the limo. Adrian closed the door and proceeded to walk around to the driver's door. He got in and started the engine.

"Where may I take you, Jacques?"

"Janine's townhouse please, Adrian. Elena told us otherwise, but I need to start somewhere. God, Adrian. I don't know how to tell the truth from the lies with Elena. She's always been so damn good at telling me what I want to hear."

"I am very sorry, Jacques. I just wish I could do more."

"Adrian, you are. Please keep doing what you are doing."

"You need only ask, Jacques. Janine's townhouse, then?"

"Oui, Adrian."

"Very well."

The limo proceeded to leave the club. A slight feeling of panic formed in my gut… Not for myself, but for those I left behind. I closed my eyes and pictured Luc. His thick, shaggy hair. His eyes. His face. The arms that so eagerly embraced me. His beautiful body pressed against mine when we made love, and that endearment. His sweet whimper. An urgency swept over me. I know we had just left, but when I was away from him, all I wanted was to be next to him. I pushed every other thought away that was racing through my head. I concentrated on one thing only… My baby boy.

*"Luc, babe. Please tell me you can hear me Luc?"*

Silence.

I realized that Luc had other things on his mind. His sister, listening to Elena's rantings and threats. Concentrating, I pushed myself to empty my mind of everything that emotionally stood between us. I let my mind replay the last time we made love. The touch of our eternally young bodies, Luc's lips pressing against mine. The feel of him inside me. Our bodies moving as one with each other. Smooth, muscular heat to smooth, muscular heat.

*"Luc, baby? Please?"*

His whimper. Like a drowning man, I dragged in one deep breath, then another. Thank you, God!

*"Luc, my baby boy."*

*"Oh God, John, my love."*

*"You're with me. Thank you, Lord!"*

*"I'm with you, John. I'll always be with you."*

*"Always and forever, Luc."*

*"I love you, mon cher. God, I love you! I fucking miss you!"* Luc's voice hitched.

*"Be safe, hon. I love you too."* I felt the corner of my mouth

quiver, hearing Jaycee's voice. I felt a tear sting my eye, then run down my face. As I remembered Luc's words to me, and the connection to my family, strength replaced fear and confidence replaced doubt.

*"I will never forget what you did for my Sam. Je t'aime, Jacques!"* Christian. My little brother. I could picture him. His blonde, shaggy hair. Hey! Just like mine. Those vivid, blue eyes. Like mine. Why do I feel a pattern developing here? I could picture his eternally young smile beaming at me.

*"I love you too, Christian. Don't ever forget that. Promise?"*

*"I promise, Jacques."*

*"You make us so damn proud, Jacques. It is a privilege to have you in our lives. How do I thank you for saving my life?"* It sounded so good to hear Sam, his voice strong, vital, and healthy.

*"Sammy, no words are necessary. I just ask one thing."*

*"Anything, Jacques. Anything."*

*"Sam...Christian...Promise me you will watch over and protect my boy and my brother."*

*"With our lives, Jacques."* Christian answered.

*"Please, all of you...my dear family. For the love of all things holy, if Elena tries anything, I mean anything...end her. Promise me?"*

*"Oui, my love. Oui."* I knew it was tearing Luc apart to actually think of killing her, but no fucking more will I have her and Alec threatening us.

"Adrian." I turned to him. "It's time to get our sister back."

"I am one hundred percent in agreement with you, sir...um...Jacques."

As always, the more urgent the matter, the longer the drive seems. We were approaching Luc and Janine's residences on the Rue de Montmorency.

"Adrian. S'il vous plait. Pull over here." I pointed to a lit corner. Adrian pulled the limo up to the corner, but did not stop the engine. I was about to get out when Adrian took hold of my arm and began to speak.

"Jacques, it looks like the Rousseau family is having their weekly meeting. The Rousseau family, Jacques, goes back to the sixteenth century. Luc will introduce you to them at their next meeting. They are allies and protectors of the mortals as well."

My God! The house was huge, three stories, French provincial architecture.

The limos in the circular drive were roughly the same year as ours, give or take one or two years. All appeared as if they were just driven off the showroom floor. All the shades were open and candles lit each room in the house. I noticed there was a soft glow coming from what may have been a parlor. My curiosity was piqued! I would look forward to the meeting with the Rousseaus.

"Adrian, thank you for the information." I began to open the door.

"Jacques, we are not quite there. Let me take you to Janine's residence."

"Adrian, I appreciate your concern, but if Alec and Trace have Janine there, I would rather have some element of surprise."

"Jacques, if you don't mind me asking, it had to be Alec that turned Trace. After all, it would be surprising, if not unthinkable, that someone from the wolf community would turn him."

"Adrian, *nothing* would surprise me. Seriously though, Adrian. We believe he did. He needs allies and who better to align himself with than Trace? Adrian," I reached over and placed a hand on his, "when this is over, I promise I will tell you why."

"Jacques, there is no need. It is none of my business. It is obvious though, that Trace carries a great hatred for you and those you love."

"That obvious, huh?" I leaned back and wearily rubbed my eyes.

"Jacques?" Adrian had pulled the limo completely to the curb and it appeared we were three to four city blocks away from Luc's townhouse. Funny, as a human I would have taken Adrian up on his offer and had him drop me off closer. As a vampire, this was nothing more than a walk out to the mailbox. As the limo stopped, I again went to open the door. Immediately, I felt Adrian's firm, yet gentle grip on my arm.

"Adrian? Everything okay?" There was concern in his deep red eyes.

"Jacques, please be careful. Someone desperately wants you back."

"I will, Adrian. I desperately need to be back with him." I quietly sighed. "God be with you."

"Merci, Adrian, and with you as well."

Once again surprising me, Adrian leaned toward me and placed a gentle kiss on my cheek. "Jacques, I have no doubt I will be seeing you again. I will head back to the club and see if there is anything I can do."

"I would appreciate that. Thank you." I squeezed the hand that was still holding my arm. *"You need only call if you need me."* Huh, he too had the ability...

*"And here I thought..."* I chuckled, *"you had a private listing."* We both softly laughed, although our levity was charged with worry, and yes, fear.

I exited the limo, took one last glance at Adrian, and watched him pull away. I summoned everything I had in me. Everything that I knew was made possible by the two men that I desperately missed and loved.

The early morning air was damp and the sky turned an ominous grey as a fog settled over the city. I instinctively put my hands in the pockets of my suit coat. I smiled, remembering Luc and I debating what I should wear. It seemed a totally moot point now but Luc, being Luc, insisted I wear my black suit.

I found myself remembering the two of us standing in front of my armoire. *'After much deliberation, and Luc finally putting his foot down, I did as he insisted and chose one of my black designer suits. I found myself powerless. No is not an option, especially when your lover is standing there, wrapped in only a towel, his perfect, muscular body still warm and wet from the shower. I'd never say no to him. What Luc wanted, I would give him.'* "John, babe." Luc was putting the finishing touches on my tie. *"You are a vampire. You are strong and powerful. You, love, don't need to bare your fangs to prove that."* He turned me so I was facing the mirror. *"Damn! Just damn! You look good enough to sink my fangs into!"* I looked at him. His X-rated stare was going to give me wet dreams for weeks. *"Fuck, baby boy. When we get out of this, have at it!"*

I felt something metallic in one of my pockets. It was a flask. I paused and pulled it out. Shit! It was stunning! It was classic in design. I tipped the flask over to see the bottom. Of course! Where else would it have come from? Why didn't that surprise me? As I turned it on its side, my finger brushed against what felt like engraving. Sure enough! And what I saw almost brought me to tears. It read 'John, always and forever mine. Love, Luc.' I stood there smiling like a goof. "Ah, what the hell!" I unscrewed the cap and, saluting my family, I took a drink. Luc's private reserve. Just when I thought nothing could surprise me, Luc did it again. Almost immediately, I felt the warm rush of potent blood rejuvenate me. I headed out into the unknown, knowing whatever I faced, my family would be with me.

I was about four city blocks away from Luc's townhouse. About eight from Janine's. It was then I heard him. I hadn't used my cell phone since I arrived. I thought of reaching for it. *'What was emergency here? 999?'* I thought. Well, John, that's just dumb. Imagine *that* call. "Ah, yes. I'm a vampire and I am being followed by someone or something. I am so fucked."

Just goes to show, what looks good on paper..."Fuck me! Damn it! Why the hell didn't I stay with Luc?" Basically I was yelling at myself. I began to make a run for Luc's apartment. For some reason, I could sense he stopped his pursuit. He just bloody stopped in his tracks. With every nerve I had left, I turned around to face him. I took a deep breath. "Oh my God! You?" Why the fuck was I even surprised?

"Aller!" He said. It was one word, one simple word.

"Go, Alec? You son of a bitch! Go?" Something was happening to me. He just stood there and looked at me. What was it Luc told me? Werewolves can control a vampire's mind, make them do things they don't want to do. God help me. Alec was a walking sexual fantasy. His thick, black hair and steel blue eyes penetrated me and held me, pulling me to him. What the fuck! No, this wasn't happening. John, pull yourself together. He's ruining our lives. He already tried to kill Sam and Christian, but, my God, his perfect smile, those fucking feral eyes, burned into mine. All of a sudden I wanted him. God, I hated him, but I didn't give a shit at that moment. I was losing control. No!

"Go!" Alec commanded me. "Go before I do to you what I have been craving to do!"

"So fucking do it already! Just fucking do it!" I had just lost my mind. I was exhausted, worn... He was beating me down. John, don't look into those fucking eyes!

"Don't tempt me, Jacques! You belong to someone else."

"Yeah. Luc. You son of a bitch!" I hissed.

Then a new voice barked out a command. "Turn around, Jacques! Turn. Around." Damn! The pull he had. No, I would not allow this bastard to get to me. Remember, John. Remember what Luc and Jaycee taught you. Remember your sister. I steeled my nerves. It will not end this way! You need to, you must, get Janine back. I knew who it would be, but I had to, for my own satisfaction. So I did, and as I turned, Alec smiled, not at me, but at who was in front of me.

"Bonjour, John. I have been waiting for you... a long fucking time."

Yep, I was right. Pure white fangs, and oh shit...those eyes...wolf eyes!

"Hello, Trace." My eyes, I knew, burned red and my fangs emerged. When did the son of a bitch learn French? Dickhead.

# ✦ CHAPTER FORTY-FIVE ✦

I stood there, frozen in place, unlike several Parisians who passed by very quickly. A shiver went up my spine as I briefly acknowledged them.

What the hell was going on? That same look of fear and pity for me was etched across their faces. As they passed, I could have sworn I heard one of them say "May God be with you." For some reason, I was drawn to that one person. As it turned out, with good reason. Literally, in the blink of an eye, the young man who said it flashed his deep red eyes at me. A vampire among mortals. Holy shit! Just as Luc had promised, I was not alone, but I could not let on. I quickly shrugged it off, knowing that I still had several obstacles to get through. One of them was not getting myself killed.

Like some horror flick, sans directors or extras, the scene had been set, and the cast was in place. The streets surrounding us were now completely empty, save myself, Alec, and Trace. Unlike the movies, there would be only one scene and one take. Fuck it! Action!

"Trace, you bastard, I really have no time for this. I really don't have time for you. Yeah, you're a real man, Trace. What? You need Alec?" I briefly turned around and looked at him. "For what? A bodyguard..." I paused, tilting my head slightly, "or a good fuck?" I felt the smirk on my face; I looked at him with nothing but contempt. My God! This used to be someone who mattered in my mortal life.

Now I was looking at a complete stranger and I could see who he really was... A cold-blooded killer!

Trace growled. "I'm going to rip your fucking heart out, John!"

"Impressive, asshole! Before you wolf-out on me, may I have a word with your homophobic dipshit of a boyfriend?" That's it, John. Throw gas on the fire. I watched as Trace's fists clenched and unclenched. "Oh, I promise, buddy, you'll have the chance to explain to Alec why this is so easy for you. You *have* told Alec that you've killed before, haven't you? You remember, sweet, precious, innocent, and beautiful K.C. You did tell him, didn't you?" I snarled. "Besides, wasn't he your best friend, you bastard? Killing me should be easy. If only you would have come to terms with the fact you were gay... that you loved him. I wouldn't have stood in your way. Instead, you took your insecurities out on K.C. You are nothing but a fucking four-pawed coward!"

Trace's wolf eyes turned solid green. I know it didn't matter, what was done was done, but it sure the fuck felt good to finally tell him exactly what I thought and felt about him.

"Just hold that temper, Trace." That temper. The one thing that hadn't changed. "Let me have a few words with your new friend, or should I say mate?" This time Alec growled. Hmmm, I think I hit a nerve. I knew I was pushing it, but in the last several days things had begun to fall into place. Pieces to this puzzle began to put themselves together.

Crap, I was probably going to be ripped to shreds, so why not have some fun with these two fuck-ups?

"Trace, s'il vous plait, excusez-moi. I need a few minutes with Alec." Then, as if Trace were no longer there, I turned and stepped toward Alec.

"Who the fuck do you think you are, Jacques?" I had quickly learned to avoid looking directly into Alec's and Trace's eyes.

"Ah, the last time I checked, a vampire, you douche bag. I really don't feel like wasting my time with you, Alec, but you fucking crossed the line. First with my sister, Janine, then trying to butcher Sam and Christian. Did you actually think you were going to get away with this?"

"Trying? What the hell do you mean trying?" He was surprised by my revelation. "They're dead!"

I sensed he wanted to push for confirmation. Self-doubt? Well, what do you know? I actually hit him with the proverbial curve-ball. So I confirmed what he wanted to know. Hell, not only would it give me the satisfaction of knocking him down a few pegs, but it would also gave me an edge. The complete power Alec thought he had on me no longer applied. "No, actually, they are very much alive, thanks to Elena! Oh, by the way, they are severely pissed off!"

"No... How? You d-d-didn't!" Alec stuttered.

"Didn't what, Alec? Let Sam and Christian drain the life from her? Kill her? No, unlike you and Trace, I have morals...to a point. She is very much alive and hating every minute of it."

"What do you mean, hating?"

"God, you are such an idiot! Like I said, Alec, you may have the looks, I'll give you that, but...why, in the name of all that is holy, am I even trying to explain this to you? It's like talking to a second grader." I smirked. "Alec, do you actually think she willingly helped to save their lives? I have to say, she put up a good fight. It was...how should I say this...pathetic, but satisfying, to see her take the punishment for something you and her supposed boyfriend were responsible for. After all, it's not like she's an innocent bystander in this. She is a part of this so-called plan, but I have a feeling it will be short-lived if you and Trace succeed."

"You bastard, Jacques!" He roughed his face with his hands in obvious frustration. "You think you're so fucking smart."

"Now, now, Alec." I chided him like a child. "She got off easy. I'd keep one thing in mind though. Luc, Jaycee, Sam, and Christian are keeping her company. After what the three of you did to our family, well... When I left the boys were terribly hungry." Maybe I was becoming somewhat over-confident, but damn, I couldn't shake the feeling that Luc and Jaycee were standing right next to me. Our connection was strong and I was coming to the realization that it was a force to be reckoned with.

I felt Trace move toward me.

"Back off, Trace! Now!" Huh! He actually backed off.

What happened next seemed to end before it even started. I had a feeling of protection, like a veil enveloping me, a shield. It was new, yet so damn familiar. One thing was sure, it wasn't Luc or Jaycee. Their presence was still separate. For a moment, I swore I even smelled their scent. I quickly pulled myself together.

"Anyway, Alec. Where was I? Ah, that's right...Trace. You turned him, didn't you?"

"Yes, I did." Alec answered smugly.

"Interesting, Alec. Did Trace ask you to, or did you have to force yourself on him? Attack him? I understand wolves mate for life, right? Please, feel free to correct me."

"Yeah, what about it, Jacques? Janine's my mate."

"I would have to disagree. Especially after what I saw in the limo the other day. Janine despises you. She kicked you to the curb, dipshit. Not exactly my perception of love. Anyway, so you turned Trace." It was meant to be a statement.

"Yeah, I did. What damn business is it of yours anyway?"

"No reason, Alec. Hell, I know my time is running out. I'm just curious. Besides, if it's not that big of a deal, what's the harm? So, again, Alec. Why?"

"Why?" He snickered. "To finally rid myself of you and your, what's your name for him, baby boy. Trace is going to help me get Janine back, then turn Elena, to have her for himself."

"But, Alec...Where is the logic in this master plan of yours? Janine is done with you. Your true mate is standing right there." I pointed to Trace. "I don't see where Janine and Elena fit into this?"

"What a bunch of bullshit, Jacques! I really don't need to listen to any more of your idiotic attempts at rationalizing this, or for that matter, trying to save your ass. I can destroy you anytime I want." He took a step toward me.

A threat? Sure, but Alec was reaching now. Had I actually put a seed of doubt in that thick head? I pressed on.

"Point taken, Alec. I must say, the power you have over me right now, is somewhat impressive." I said sarcastically. I knew that the strength and courage I was feeling was due to Luc and Jaycee. The cockiness, admittedly stupid, was my own doing. "Well, before you both commence with my demise, let me tell you a little story."

I closed my eyes, connecting with Trace. I felt so much of his mortal side still struggling with his immortal side. I knew from experience, if I hit the right nerve... Well, hell! It was worth a shot.

"Jacques? What the fuck are you doing?" Another step. He was closing in on me. I also noticed that Alec's canines had lengthened and his eyes were now fully grey, his wolf eyes. Janine had explained to me that while in that stage, their vision was limited, especially at night since wolves could only see in black and white. I wasn't sure this was going to help, but I'd take any help I could get. I especially liked knowing I had the advantage when it came to seeing in the dark.

"*I love you, Luc.*"

"*Always, lover. We are closer than you think.*"

"*I know, baby boy. Just a thought away!*"

"*If you only knew!*" His words came to me slow and deliberate. Luc was sending me a message.

"What the fuck am I doing, Alec? For your benefit, to get this little story accurate just for you, I had to reach back to the time I was mortal. Forgive me for my fucking rudeness, asshole." Alec snarled.

"*That's my boy!* Luc's voice was filled with his confidence in me.

"*God, Luc. I need you.*"

"*I need you more, babe.*"

Damn! My love for Luc surged through every part of my body. I wouldn't fail. I couldn't. I had come too far to let our love be destroyed. Losing the man I loved? I would not go through that again.

"You see, Alec, before coming to Paris, Trace and my sister..." I paused, rolling my eyes, "dated. At the time, I knew that Trace," I pointed in back of me, "wanted me, but Elena had her claws dug so deep into him, he became her very own little puppy. That's right, puppy." I laughed, a definite sarcastic edge to it. I paused and put a finger to my chin. "That is fucking ironic, isn't it? A puppy... A puppy who grew up into a big, bad wolf. Get it, dipshit?" I shook my head. Jesus, they could rip me to shreds. "Anyway, I admit it, I had feelings for Trace, but he was obviously taken. I would never have done anything to hurt Elena. Later, I fell in love with someone else. His name was K.C. More irony...wouldn't you agree, Alec?" Still keeping my eyes from connecting with Alec, I took several more steps towards him. "Trace couldn't handle it. You see, Alec, Trace is gay. He was in love with me, but couldn't come to grips with how he was feeling. Instead of just fucking dealing with it, he murdered my lover because he couldn't have me."

I turned slightly toward Trace and growled, baring my fangs. I wanted to rip Trace's throat out. "You fucking son of a bitch, Trace!"

"You bastard, John!" Trace growled.

"Shut up, Trace! Just shut the fuck up! Oh, I know you want to kill me. Hell, you already have, a long time ago in our other life. Remember? You'll fucking have your chance, but for now, just do me one last favor and back off and shut your fucking muzzle!"

*"Funny, the angrier I get, the less control they have over me, and the more control I have over them."*
*"You learn quickly, John."*
*"Are you spying on me, babe?"*
*"Yes."* Luc whimpered.
*"Baby boy, don't ever stop. Ever!"*

"Have you looked at him, Alec? Look at him! He has it so bad for you that, well, you really should have done a little more research on his past before you sunk your fangs into him. Shit! I'm a vampire, and I can feel his need for you! God, Alec, are you really that stupid, that inept?"

I turned toward Trace and pointed. "Alec! Look. At. Him!" Alec flinched with every word. Trace's head was down, his chin on his chest. "What is wrong with you, Alec? He is your mate and he's still in love with me. Alec, take a moment and think. Why the hell would he come to Paris with Elena? Where is she? She was left on her own in our club, our suite. Trace had no problem leaving the supposed love of his life among not only us, but a community. A community you used to be a part of. He had no problem leaving a mortal among vampires and werewolves. Get a clue, man!" I glanced at Trace. He looked, for all the world, like a broken, rejected, and whipped dog. "Alec, they've been together thirteen years. They've been engaged so many times, I lost count. God! Alec! Think! What other fucking explanation could there be? Trace murdered K.C.! Why? Me! Now he's here. Why?" I was so frustrated all I could do was look up at the sky and scream. "ME!" Why the fuck was I trying to help him? "You know what, Alec?" I turned back toward him. "You deserve him!"

"You are fucking insane, Jacques! He loves Elena."

"Really, Alec? Who are you trying to convince? Me or you? Elena told me she can't even stand to have him touch her!"

"That's a fucking lie, John! You know it!" Trace screamed.

"Oh really?" I half-turned to Trace. "Think, dumbass. When's the last time you...Fuck! Never mind! Trace, you are such an idiot."

Turning back to Alec, I kept the momentum going. I needed to turn them on each other. Call me screwed, but it was the best plan I had at the moment. "Has anything I said to you registered in that canine brain of yours?" I stood there, clenching my fists, not so much at the anger I felt for him, but for his ignorance. "I guess not. I knew from the moment I met you, you had nothing going for you besides your fucking pretty boy looks.  Let me try this one more time.  He killed my mortal boyfriend!  He killed him in fucking cold blood!  Alec, history is going to repeat itself.  He needs to finish this, but there's one thing missing, Alec.  Think!"

It was as if someone had flipped a switch in Alec's fucked up head.  "Luc."

"Jesus, Alec.  You're finally figuring that out?  Once again, someone is standing between Trace and his obsessive desire for me.  Why the hell do you think I'm here?  Do you actually think I'd put my lover in danger?  I'd die first.  Besides, there's a catch that neither of you see.  Alec, for God's sake.  Trace is your mate!"

I dragged in several breaths.  I was exhausted, but God, the strength in me.  I thought for a  moment.  It was like Luc and Jaycee were standing right next to me.  My nerves were shot, but there was a calmness in me.  I actually felt the love and strength of Luc and Jaycee giving me the courage to continue.  I felt that familiar heat scudding through my veins.  It was as if, I swear to God, it felt like they were right next to me, Luc to my left, Jaycee to my right.  God!  What's up with that new feeling?  It was like a shield surrounding me.  *John, snap out of it.*

"Trace, step up.  Admit it!  Don't you and your asshole mate have the advantage here, anyway?  I loved K.C.  You were so damn jealous, you took away my only mortal love.  He was your best friend, Trace.  Now, my God, Trace, you want to take away the man I have chosen to spend eternity with.  How am I doing so far, Trace?" I said, without turning to look at him.

"Fuck you, John."

"Sorry, Trace.  That'll never happen again."

That comment earned me a growl.  I couldn't help it, I started to giggle.  God help me!  I was losing it.  I knew I was pushing and taunting.  I should have been dead by now, but I was holding on.  I gave thanks to my boy Luc, my brother Jaycee, and whatever or whomever was shielding me from Alec's and Trace's wolf powers.  Maybe I could stop this, but my words...the truth...did not seem to be getting through to either of them.  A little bit of me was falling apart.  God!  All I wanted right now, was Luc's strong arms around me, and to surrender myself to him.  God, I needed to feel him in me, making love to me.  *'Come on, John.  Shake it off.  Hold on!'*  So that's exactly what I did... I held on. I held on to the strength of knowing how deeply loved I was, and to the desire, want, and need, to return Janine to our family so we would be complete again. So help me God, as long as my heart was beating, I would not give up. Enough was enough! I turned and looked directly at Alec.

"I have to admit, I never thought I'd say this about you, Jacques. You are one tough, smart vampire. Either that, or just plain suicidal." He chuckled. "For what it's worth, Luc and Jaycee trained you well!"

"Gee, I don't know whether to be flattered or insulted." I said with absolute sarcasm. "Alec, just humor me here, would you? Did he struggle when you turned him? Did he beg for his life? Did he tell you that he loved Elena?"

"No. So?" Was that my imagination, or had I just piqued Alec's interest? I forged ahead. "Was Elena in the room when you did it, Alec?"

"Yeah. So what? I still don't get your point."

"What about, Trace?" Silence. For just a moment, I thought I was getting through to him. I should have known better.

"Alec! What about Trace?" God, I wanted to end this. How clueless were they?

"He gave no resistance." I noticed Alec's eyes shift to Trace. He dragged in a deep breath. "He seemed to enjoy it." His smile was pure evil.

"Alec, why is it that a vampire is explaining what you did? Elena knew what was happening! Why wasn't she throwing a fit? Why do you think Trace was enjoying it?" It was like talking to a fucking brick wall... A wall I wanted to beat my head against. "Even though it's none of your business, Alec, do you think I struggled when Luc took me and made me a vampire?"

"I know what I did, asshole. He asked me to turn him so he could be powerful enough to destroy you. They both knew you were a vampire and that was the only way to kill you, your Sire, and your brother." Alec's wolf eyes returned their gaze to me.

"God, Alec. You have been given way too much credit! You actually bought that line of shit? You're a fucking disgrace to your species." I met his gaze, baring my fangs. I must have a death wish. Funny, I watched him as his eyelids closed halfway and his face became taught. He was trying to pull me into his spell. His feral eyes, reflecting the light of the moon, stared into mine. I met his stare, laughing.

I felt nothing. No pull, no control.

"What the hell!" Alec stomped his foot on the pavement.

"Alec, what are you? Two!" God, was I pushing it! "Whatever kind of control you think you have on me, is obviously not working. I suggest you save your strength. Alec, again...Look at Trace. Look into his eyes."

"Why should I do what you ask?"

"Humor me, asshole!"

God, I just wanted this to be done and over with. I just wanted Luc, and I wanted Janine back with us. He looked at Trace. I watched him. I didn't need to see Trace, Alec's eyes betrayed what he saw.

What he saw was...Shit! This was just too good! He saw his mate.

"Alec." Trace whimpered. "I did it for us. Yes, I did it so I could rid myself of John and Luc at first, but the moment I saw you, I was drawn to you. Then you turned me...Alec, please! Fuck! I want you so much! I love you! I'm yours!"

"Didn't see that one coming, did you, you son of a bitch?" I growled, baring my fangs at him.

Alec stumbled backward as if he had been hit with a battering ram. "No! This cannot be happening. I am not a fag! But..."

"But, what, Alec? What?" I smiled. "Feeling something you don't want. If it makes you feel any better, he sure the hell is good in bed."

I couldn't see Trace, but I could feel his emotions. I had hit a nerve. Trace just needed to be pushed, and I knew him well enough to know I had given him the shove he needed.

I turned to look at Trace. What I saw was not the mortal Trace I had known, loved, and come to hate. I turned back to Alec. He glared at me and I knew my time was just about over.

"You, Alec, are a first class fuck up!" All the contempt and hatred I had for him was surfacing, churning in my gut like a poisonous stew. "Look what you've done. You turned Janine. I'll give you that one since it was with good intentions. Janine sacrificed herself to destroy a vampire that was going to, literally, destroy her family. I find that somewhat noble on your part."

"What the fuck are you talking about, John? I turned her because she was meant to be my mate!"

"Alec, did no one give you a clue about what it is to be a werewolf? Maybe I should lend you some of my books and movies." I couldn't help but giggle.

"Jacques, if you don't fucking shut up, I'm going to end you!"

"Come on, Alec. If you wanted to end me, you had so many chances already. Don't worry, I'll let you try. Just let me give you a few more facts. I know you really don't care, but Trace does. After all, if Trace wanted me dead, knowing the way he feels about me..." I purposely turned and looked at him, "he would have killed me by now. Alec, can't you see what's going on? He still fucking loves me, and now he loves you too." I turned back to Alec.

*'Fuck, I am so going to die.'*

*"No, you're not, baby boy. No, you are not."*

*"Promise, babe?"*

*"Would I let you down?"*

*"God, I love you!"*

"Anyway." I turned back to Alec. "Janine never had those feelings for you."

"Yes, she did!" Alec snarled.

"Like the feelings Trace has for you? Like the feelings you have for him?" I pointed at Trace. "It was Trace that came to you, sought you out. How am I doing?"

Alec began to answer.

"Shut up, Alec. Shut up and listen!"

"What about Elena? Was she with Trace? WAS SHE?" My voice reverberated through the streets.

"Yes, but Elena..." Alec was starting to lose it. I watched as he began putting the pieces together in his mind, revisiting the time Trace and Elena confronted him.

"But what, Alec? Did she put up a fight when you turned Trace? Did she scream? Beg for his life? It was Trace, all Trace, wasn't it Alec? Alec, I know I'm pushing my limits with you, but think back. Think back to when you turned Trace. How did Elena react?"

"She...Fuck! She just sat there and smiled."

"Alec. I hate to tell you this, but you were double, triple...Ah! What the hell does it matter? They used you for their own fucking separate agendas."

"No one uses me, Jacques!" Alec's words, as harsh as they were, lacked heat. The truth was overwhelming him.

"Alec. One more thing, before I kill you both." *'Fuck! Did that just come out of my mouth?'* "Who attacked Sam and Christian?"

I noticed Alec's hands shifting to paws. He growled, his voice becoming lower. "Alec...Who?"

"I thought I killed Sam. I left Christian to Trace."

"You know, as werewolves, you both suck!" Suck? Oh my God in heaven. Did I just say that? I started to laugh.

I'm actually fucking surprised I was able to keep them at bay as long as I did. I'm really surprised I was able to even get halfway through this conversation. Honestly, it was like Luc and Jaycee were standing right next to me. They were, sort of. The proof? That adorable, beautiful smile, that one simple gesture. The one single weapon in my arsenal that Alec and Trace did not see coming. My baby boy, and my precious brother Jaycee, standing directly behind Alec, dressed in matching black suits. Luc, only you, my precious boy… A formal massacre.

# ❧ CHAPTER FORTY-SIX ❧

Within seconds, Alec had fully shifted. Given his stature as a man, I knew he would be big, fucking big. His fur was jet black and his feral, grey eyes burned into mine. His face was drawn taught as he snarled and growled at me. Strong, deadly jaws showed his full set of teeth, including his two large canines. Now fully extended, they could tear the flesh from someone as precisely as a surgeon's scalpel. His paws were big, with long, razor sharp claws.

For a split second, my mind visualized them slashing into Sam's body. My God, the pain he must have endured. How he survived, was nothing short of a miracle. Alec let out a howl that should have woken the whole neighborhood. For that matter, it should have woken the dead. He was hunched over and poised to pounce on me.

Then, I heard another growl. I turned. It was Trace. He was impressive too. Trace, being a little shorter than Alec, was a bit smaller in wolf form, but still fucking big. God! Christian, my little bro... The thought of Trace trying to take away yet another person I loved, only fueled my hatred and rage towards him. My heart ached at the thought of what Sam and Christian had faced, what they endured for us. What was pushing me past reasoning, was that they suffered, they almost died, just doing what they were asked...What I asked. I knew in my heart they would do it again, if required. The contempt and anger I felt for these two bastards was consuming me. I wanted them dead. I picked up a sudden shift in Trace's eyes. He glanced at Alec, but then, once again, stared into mine. Curiously, it was not with the intensity he showed towards Alec. There was a hesitancy, but I knew if Alec didn't get me, Trace would. Trace's allegiance to Alec was complete. He was Alec's mate, whether Alec wanted it or not.

I can't really explain why I did what I did next. I looked at Trace, and for just a brief moment, I remembered. I remembered my mortal life with my sister and Trace. Moments before everything went south, I remembered my beloved K.C. lying in his casket. Trace had relegated him to the past tense. All because he couldn't admit the cold, hard truth that both he and I knew. He had loved me and was still *in love* with me. The evil look in Alec's eyes wasn't in Trace's. The intensity wasn't there either, but he was Alec's mate now. He belonged to him for an eternity. Now, here he was coming to grips with what his depraved jealousy had cost him. It all could have been preempted if he would have had the guts to admit he was in love with me.

The pathetic irony of it was, once again, he would not, ever, have me. He would be forever in love with someone who would never want him or love him. He would never feel the love I had and have. Let the punishment fit the crime! Did I feel sorry for Trace? No. Did I pity Trace? No. I couldn't. Alec and Trace would not rest until each and every one of us were dead. There was one more reason why I knew Trace would never be loved the way he wanted to be loved... Standing directly behind him were Sam and Christian.

Trace had no chance to react. He didn't sense it. He had no idea what was coming his way, that hell was about to be unleashed. Unlike myself and Luc, Alec never took the time to teach or help Trace through the transition. Vampires may not be able to match the brutal strength that werewolves have, but we do have powers that can give us an edge: our speed and our night vision. Maybe if he had known, he would have had a chance, but he didn't. What happened next was a blur. It was a blur to Trace, but my vampire eyes saw it all.

Trace bared his fangs at me, and with one last growl, he hunched over and leapt at me. Death on four paws. In the blink of an eye, Sam and Christian were on him. Sam had him in his arms, pulling him into a choke hold. Trace's rear paws were flailing and kicking at thin air, in a desperate attempt to escape the hold he was in. I watched as Sam's hands got a choke hold on Trace. Then, with all the strength he had,

Sam lifted Trace over his head and threw him to the cement walkway. Hard! Trace howled and I heard the sick snap of bones. Landing on his back, he was momentarily stunned. Within seconds, Sam was straddling Trace, his strong hands wrapped around Trace's throat like a vice. Pulling his head back, Sam growled, opened his jaws, and buried his fangs into Trace's neck. Trace yelped. Then Trace's long, sharp claws tore into Sam's arms. I saw Sam flinch, but Sam's concentration and resolve did not waiver. Blood poured from the mortal wound Sam inflicted on him, his howl was becoming a whimper. I was watching Trace die and I felt nothing. For all practical purposes, he was already dead to me.

It was then I heard a vicious snarl behind me that gave me the chills. It was Alec. He had been prepared to pounce before the attack on his mate. I knew Luc and Jaycee were there, but my God, Alec was so big. What were their chances? Fuck! As much as I loved them for what they were doing, I didn't want them in any danger. As for my chances, I suddenly got the answer. Searing pain shot through my shoulder. Alec had gotten to me and dragged me to the ground. His jaws were opened wide. He was foaming at the mouth, ready to tear my throat out. With all the strength I had, I wrapped my hands tightly around his powerful mouth. My strong hands were like a vise as I clamped down. He was so close I could feel his breath. He was struggling hard, trying to break the grip I had on him. Another sharp pain ripped through me as he swiped one of his front paws across my chest. I flinched, but knew that I had to maintain my hold. Those teeth could tear me to shreds. The pain I was feeling was intense, and I was feeling somewhat disoriented, most likely from the loss of blood. I looked into his wolf eyes. I have never seen such hatred or evil! I was looking death in the eye.

Luc and Jaycee were on the ground next to me. Their eyes deep red and their fangs bared. I felt them using every ounce of preternatural strength they had to keep Alec's mouth away from me. More importantly, I felt them give me inner strength and their love. Despite the hell we were going through, an inner peace swept through me. It was then I looked at Luc and Jaycee.

*"If I have to die like this, just remember how much I loved you. Promise me you will not grieve for me. Tell Janine how much I loved her. You both have given me more than I ever would have dreamed possible. Please, get the hell out of here! I couldn't bear it if you were*

*hurt. Please!"*

*"No, John. We are not going anywhere! Don't you fucking give up! I will not lose you! Not this way! I know it hurts, but hang on. Please!"*

I looked at my boy, knowing he was feeling my pain. His eyes were filled with such determination. I knew he wasn't going to abandon me, no matter how hard I begged him.

*"Luc, I love you so damn much!"*

With pure determination, I was able to turn my head slightly, just enough to look into Jaycee's eyes. *"Jaycee, my brother...Promise me... Promise you will take care of your baby brother."*

*"Jacques, so help me God, it is not going to end this way. This is not fucking acceptable."* Tears were rolling down Jaycee's face.

*"I love you too, Jaycee."*

*"Always and forever, my beautiful brother."*

Alec lashed out with one of his paws, but it was his turn to hurt. Jaycee somehow managed to catch that paw in his hand, and he proceeded to break it. Alec tried to howl, but with my grip on his mouth acting like a muzzle, it came out a muffled whimper.

"Take that, you bastard." Jaycee snarled.

*"I need you both to be strong for me. You need to get out of here, now!"*

*"No fucking way, John! I won't live without you. We won't live without you! We will die first, babe."*

*"Luc?"* My voice, thick with emotion, came to a halt.

Time stopped. It literally stopped. It was a howl, but at the same time, my God, it sounded like...There was only one thing that would stop Alec dead in his tracks... His mate. Whether he accepted it or wanted it, regardless of how much he denied it, Trace was his, and I knew his basic primal instincts were screaming at him to protect his mate. Trace's pain was his. He was feeling that now, intimately. What happened next would possibly save our lives. Our eyes, even Alec's, looked over at the struggle between Sam, Christian, and Trace. Christian, on his knees, was bent over Trace's head and had forced Trace's mouth open. In once single motion, Christian snapped his jaws apart, and Sam beheaded Trace. He was shifting back as the final death strike was executed by Sam. The punishment Trace was dealt, was quick compared to what he did to K.C.

*'So be it.'* I thought. *'Justice had been served and my precious*

*K.C. could finally rest in peace.'*

I knew it wouldn't faze Alec. I looked back at him, and I swear, the son of a bitch was smiling. Trace was dead. As much as I tried, I didn't feel anything.

"Well, fuckhead, you got what you wanted. That's all you're going to get." I glared into Alec's eyes.

*"You are so right, my precious, immortal vampire, my beautiful brother."*

Those words, words spoken to me after my transformation. That voice, soft and loving. That scent, filling the early morning air. God in heaven... Lilacs. Please Lord! Please!

"Janine?" My voice was barely a hoarse whisper.

*"Jacques, I need you to be strong. I need you to be brave, mon cher. My brothers cannot hear this. I need you to do something for me."*

*"Anything, Janine. Anything to save them. Just tell me!"*

*"I love you, Jacques. Push Luc and Jaycee away... NOW!"*

I summoned all the strength I had, and as Luc wrapped his arms around Alec's middle, temporarily giving me room to move, I rolled to my side and pushed Luc away. Still not in full control of my strength, I inadvertently sent Luc through the air. Instantly Sam was there to catch him. I briefly watched Luc trying to struggle out of Sam's arms. The shock on his face gave way to fear.

"Sam! Let me go! John, babe. Why?" I heard the desperation in his voice. "Sam, dammit, please!" Luc tried to break free of Sam's hold, but he was not going anywhere. I guess Sam was not going to relinquish his duties just yet.

I made sure the grip I had on Alec's mouth was still firm. I needed to keep it shut. I knew if I lost control of that, Alec would rip me to shreds.

*"Jaycee, babe. You're next!"* His brow furrowed. Questioning my cryptic comment, he hesitated, and looked at me. As he taught me, his hesitation was my opportunity. *"That's my brother! I love you!"* With all the power I had left in me, I pulled my legs back and kicked Jaycee as hard as I could. *"I'm sorry, Jaycee. God, I am so sorry!"*

The force sent Jaycee reeling back with enough force to lose his grip on Alec. I guess my little brother hadn't resigned yet either. As with Luc, Christian firmly wrapped his arms around Jaycee. Damn! I was impressed. Despite his size, he was small in comparison to Jaycee,

Christian knew what he had to do.

*"I love you bro. I promise you. Jaycee isn't going anywhere."*

*"That's my boy!"*

Alec, momentarily caught off guard, hesitated in his assault on me.

I could hear Luc and Jaycee struggling, swearing, and begging to be released, but that was not going to happen.

*"Jacques, my love, move your cute ass!"* Janine did not have to tell me twice.

*"I love you, sis."*

As happened with Trace, the next few seconds were a blur. I moved so damn fast, I surprised myself. As I let go of Alec completely, I dug my heels into the ground, like a runner waiting for the gun to fire. I launched myself forward, towards Luc. He caught me in his arms. We all looked up as we heard a growl echoing through the streets, a growl we all knew very well.

"Janine?" Luc struggled to say her name, still trying to catch his breath.

"Yes, Luc. Our sister!" Sam released his hold on Luc. Instantly, I grabbed him and pulled him to me, hungry for the feeling of my lover's body pressed against mine.

There we were, Luc and I, Jaycee, Sam and Christian, all looking at a very pissed off werewolf. We had managed to separate ourselves from Alec, but, by the looks of it, he would have one of us in a matter of seconds.

The howl we heard, our sister's, was now much closer, surrounded by members of the *community*.

Alec was hunched over, ready to pounce. I knew that the death of Trace didn't emotionally impact him, but he was now completely out of control. Whether he wanted to admit it or not, he had just watched his mate die. I knew he hated it, he couldn't help it. There was no use denying the chemistry that drove the most primal of emotions and needs of wolves for centuries. He had just watched his mate die at the hands of the people he had come to despise the most. He studied us, his eyes glaring. His every move was calculated and deliberate. Looking, deciding. He wanted us all dead. We were staring down the face of a cold-blooded killer with four paws. Fuck! Who am I kidding? Those are claws!

Five vampires against one werewolf. What were the odds? Regardless, he would not get near the men in my life. I would die first.

"Come on, asshole." I yelled. "It's me you want! It's always been me! Well, here I am." I just wanted his attention turned away from the others. If I could keep him focused on me, Janine would have a target. A killing machine that was aimed at me. I had to keep him distracted. It was worth a shot. Apparently, his only thought, his only mission, was to kill me. What the fuck? He was completely oblivious to Janine and the circle of vampires and werewolves that surrounded him.

*"Jacques, do not move."*

*"Janine, I need to do this."*

*"You, my precious brother, have done enough."*

We watched, but it was over before it started. Alec, muscles taught, leapt directly at me. It was working, but I didn't factor in one thing, my Sire's complete devotion to me. Before I could react, Luc stepped in front of me.

"John, no! I will not let you die! I can't!" I felt him push his body back into me. "I fucking love you too much." The determination in his voice broke my heart.

"Dammit, Luc...NO! I won't have you die for me! I love you too. Luc. That's why I have to do this." Despite his strength, I pushed him aside. My love for him was, and would forever be, more powerful than any preternatural power I may have inherited.

Alec was now in mid-air. Despite it all, he actually looked elegant. My God, the strength, the grace! It seemed like Alec was in flight. His eyes were beautiful. *'Wait a minute!'* Fuck, he was playing with me, trying to take control of me again. *'His eyes.'* I thought. *'His fucking eyes. Look away, John! Look away.'* I turned and focused on Luc and I could feel myself gaining control again.

Luc grabbed my arm, desperately trying to get in front of me. "Sam!" I yelled. With no hesitation, Sam grabbed Luc and pulled him back. Christian did the same with Jaycee. They upheld their honor to us, with unflinching loyalty. Preternatural shields, their only mission, to protect Luc and Jaycee.

*"Christian, baby brother, you and Sam protect my boys! Please!"*

*"With our lives, Jacques. I... I really...."*

*"I know you do. I love you too, Christian."*

I stood there, before the men I loved. The pledge I made to Janine had now come full circle. My promise to her, my pledge to protect Luc. Hell, yes! With my life. Now, not out of obligation, but because of my love for the whole family, I would die for all of them. If Alec wanted them, he would have to go through me. No fucking way in hell, would I allow him to harm any of them. I braced myself as Alec, in flight, neared his target... Me! I raised my arms and gestured to Alec with my hands, avoiding his eyes. "That's right, you bastard. Come on...I'm right here!"

"John, baby... NO!" Luc screamed.

"It's alright, Luc! Everything is going to be okay!" Thanks to my powers, I could feel the heat of Alec's breath as he closed in on me. I stood firm, waiting for the impact. He wanted one thing... Me. Fine. So be it.

*"My brave brother, my brave vampire. Fear not! Stand strong! Your love and faithfulness to us will be your shield, our shield. Be still, Jacques! Do not move! Do. Not. Move!"* Janine's voice strengthened me to my very soul.

*"Janine!"* I gasped, overwhelmed at her control of me. That protective shield I felt overcome me earlier... It was Janine!

What I saw next, defied explanation. Out of nowhere, there was our Janine. Petite, absolutely breath- taking, jet black hair flowing in the early morning air. She was an angel sent to deliver us from evil. An angel with fangs. Out of the corner of my eye, I saw her. Her eyes locked onto her target, and she lunged forward. Her target was Alec.

We stood there, the five of us, in stunned silence. Two wolves on a mid-air collision course. *"Luc...Jaycee..."*

*"Me too."* Luc knew.

*"Always and forever."* So did Jaycee.

Alec couldn't have been more than three feet away from me, at least, that's how it felt. Fuck it! If I had to die, I wanted to look the bastard in the eye. I raised my head, staring directly at him. *"Alec, you bastard...Burn in hell!"* I wanted the last words he heard, to be mine. I wanted him to know, in his last moments on earth, how much I hated him! His mouth was open wide for the kill. He was so intent and determined, so focused on me, his protective senses must have been shut down. It worked! He didn't sense or see anything but me. It happened quickly. Janine's attack on Alec was precise and deadly. In one swift motion she collided with Alec, both of them crashing to the ground with a sick thud. It was a quick struggle, as Janine and Alec wrestled for domination. Alec had lost control and it worked to my sister's advantage. Within seconds, she had Alec on his back. As she struck Alec across his forehead with her paw, her claws, sharp as razors, tore into his eyes, blinding him. With no hesitation, she sunk her teeth into Alec's throat and with lethal accuracy, she ripped his throat open. She was shaking, tearing, and then finally, with a growl and one swift tug, Alec was dead. It happened so quickly that, ironically, Alec, after all his smart-ass sarcasm, threats, and rantings, died in silence. There was not even a whimper.

My eyes perused the buildings, streets and sidewalks. As far as I could discern, no one had witnessed the hell that had visited their neighborhood. Once again, peace and quiet were restored to the streets of Paris. I stood there, my knees and my whole body shaking. Janine, still in wolf form, trotted toward me.

Exhausted, I dropped to my knees and wrapped my arms around her neck, burying my face in her thick mane. Her hair was every bit as soft in wolf form, and there was still the scent of lilacs. It was as if every bit of strength, both physically and emotionally, took a hike. I felt myself collapse onto her. Luc immediately fell to his knees behind me and wrapped his arms around my waist, pulling me into him. With all the strength I had, I reached out to Janine. That's all it took. The relief I felt overwhelmed me and I started to cry. Janine gently licked my face. *"Oh my God, Janine. Oh my God. Are you okay?"* I gently scratched her between her ears.

*"Yes, Jacques. I am so proud of you, brother. You were so brave."*

*"I would do anything for my family...Anything, Janine."*

Jaycee had knelt down next to his brother. I felt him kiss the top of my head. *"Je t'aime, brother."*

"John, my love for you is eternal, my beautiful, brave vampire." Luc pressed a kiss to my face.

I gently let go of Janine and she turned her attention to Jaycee. I watched her lovingly, gently, put one of her paws on his arm. Then she proceeded to lick his face. His laughter was tempered with tears and quiet sobs of relief. Jaycee pulled her to him and pressed his forehead against hers.

As I turned to look at my boy, I found him looking at his hand. Taking his finger and tasting it, he quickly pulled me into him.

"Luc, sweetheart. Are you hurt?" I saw the blood on his hand.

"John, love. No. I'm okay. It's your blood, babe. You're bleeding. Let me see." Luc pulled away in order to look at my shoulder. I watched as he studied the wound Alec had inflicted on me in the struggle. I remembered it had stung, actually it hurt, but I gave it no further thought.

"Jaycee?" Luc tried to remain calm, but he was shaking.

"What's wrong, little brother?" Jaycee quickly came to his side.

Janine joined us. Sitting as close to me as possible, I felt her pressing against me, protecting me. I scratched her lightly between her ears. She licked my face. I looked at her and, I swear, she smiled.

"It's John, brother! Alec, the bastard, he hurt him!"

"That son of a-..." Jaycee suddenly went quiet as his hand gently checked me for other injuries. "Luc?" I watched as Jaycee brought his hand from my chest up to his mouth and tasted the blood on his hand.

"CHRISTIAN!" Jaycee frantically yelled.

Janine was sitting directly in front of me, licking the blood that was coming from the gash in my chest.

I don't know if it was the adrenaline, or if I was in shock, but until the wounds that Alec inflicted on me earlier were brought to my attention, I really hadn't felt anything. Now, in the aftermath, I felt the same sickening feeling come over me that I had right before I passed out in our suite at the club. This time, two things were different. Last time, I was on my way to becoming immortal, a vampire. This time, I was on my way to dying. Last time, my last memory was of Sam picking me up. This time, it was my little brother. Before I knew it, Christian, responding to Jaycee's call, ran to me and swept me up in his arms.

Looking down at me, I felt Christian's hot tears hit my face. "Don't you fucking die? Please, Jacques. I need you brother. I love you so damn much!"

Then, as before, everything went black.

# ❦ CHAPTER FORTY-SEVEN ❦

It was about an hour before the sun would rise over the streets of the city I loved. The city where I found love in so many different ways. The most precious being Luc, my beautiful baby boy. Janine and I were sitting in one of the parks we visited when I first arrived. Janine was doing her best to comfort me, but an eternity without him… How the fuck was I supposed to deal with that?

"Why, Janine? Why did I come? This is all my fault." I squeezed her hand as she pulled my head to her shoulder. Deep red tears stung my eyes as they fell down my cheek. They hadn't quit falling since the funeral.

"You know, you're right, Jacques." Janine suddenly pulled away from me, pushing my head off of her shoulder.

"Janine? What?" I looked at her, confused. Janine was looking back at me with pure hatred in her eyes.

"What? You actually have the nerve to question me! Didn't you hear me the first time? Why the hell did you come anyway?"

I started to pull away from her, as her eyes shifted, her wolf eyes. "I don't understand, Janine." My heart was racing.

"Thanks to you, Jacques, Luc and Jaycee are dead! Do you fucking hear me? Dead!"

"No, Janine. No, you...You… You killed Alec, and Trace is dead."

"Wake up! What the hell kind of dream are you having?" She

snarled at me. "You killed them. You killed my brothers!"

"No! This can't be happening!" I felt myself losing control, tears coursing from my eyes. "Luc and Jaycee are not dead!"

*"Wake up, John!"*

"Luc and Jaycee are alive!"

*"John! Wake up!"*

Janine grabbed me by the shoulders and started to shake me. *"Wake up, Jacques!"*

"Please tell me this is a joke, Janine. They are *not* dead!"

"They are, and you," Janine glared at me, "are responsible! Live with that!"

"No! God! No! Luc! Jaycee!" I yelled.

I found myself lurching up in bed, waking at the same time I sat up, feeling the scalding tears in my eyes.

Strong, warm arms wrapped around me, pulling me close, settling my head against a solid shoulder. "John, I'm here," A soft voice, I knew so well, whispered into my ear. "I'm here."

The voice, the heat, the familiar scent and touch, filled my senses. I had to. I pushed away just enough to see him. To see my Luc. I saw those worried, and oh-so-beloved blue eyes, gazing into mine.

"Luc?" I touched my palm to his cheek. "I had the most terrible nightmare. I thought...I thought I'd lost you and Jaycee."

"We're here, babe, thanks to you." Luc's voice was quiet, filled with emotion.

"We're here? You mean, Jaycee, my brother, he's okay?"

A warm, gentle touch of a strong hand brushed my face. I turned, and there, much to my relief, was Jaycee. His mesmerizing blue eyes never left mine as he leaned over and gently kissed me. "Hi, beautiful."

Relief washed over me as my eyes gazed upon a very much alive Jaycee. Luc gently ran his fingers across my shoulder, wanting my attention.

"God, John. You were so brave. You protected all of us. You set yourself up as a target. We were so damn worried about you. You took a couple of strong hits from Alec, then passed out from blood loss. You've been out so long, babe."

"How long?"

"Twenty-eight hours." I noticed moisture glistening in Luc's and

Jaycee's eyes. "Damn it, John! I don't know what we would have done if you hadn't opened your eyes ever again."

"I just...I just knew that I had a promise to keep. I promised to protect you and Jaycee." I looked at them both. "I couldn't imagine a world without either of you."

Luc and Jaycee each burrowed one of their hands into my hair and pressed their foreheads against mine. "We love you so much, John!"

"I love you too. God! I love both of you so much!"

Then, pulling themselves as close to me as they could, Luc and Jaycee took turns. First Luc, then Jaycee, brushed their lips against mine. Then the kisses... They both kissed me long and slow and sweet. I tasted the salt from their tears, or maybe it was my own. We clung together, letting the pain and relief flow from us, until, at last, we were purged.

"Where are we, Luc?"

"In our bed, babe."

I looked at him, this man that I was so in love with. "Is it really over? This isn't another dream?"

"No, Jacques." Jaycee brushed a finger across my lips. "This... You, us, right now, our love for you... It's all very real!"

I felt myself sink into the bed, exhausted, but relieved. "It was so damn real."

"The dream, John?"

"Luc, it was no dream... It was a nightmare."

"How so, bro?" Jaycee pressed his body closer to me.

"It was Janine and I. She was blaming me for getting you both killed." In that moment between the three of us, dead silence filled the room.

"John, love. There is something you need to know." Luc was worrying his lower lip.

"Little brother, I don't know. Maybe we should give Jacques a little time to rest first." Jaycee looked at me, his eyes full of concern. "He's been through so much."

"Hey." I reached for a hand from each of them. "I just slept for twenty-eight hours. I think I'll be okay."

"I know, babe, but this news is a little disconcerting."

"Luc, after all we've just been through..." I squeezed his hand. "I appreciate you wanting to protect me, but I think I can deal with it. Okay?" I smiled, reassuring Luc.

"You're right, John. You've more than proven that you can take it and kick ass!" Luc smiled and let out a small, sweet chuckle.

Jaycee giggled. "I swear, Jacques, you are trying to Americanize Luc."

"Your point being?" I couldn't help but grin at Jaycee. "After all, when your brother changed me, he did acquire some of my DNA, did he not?" I brushed my lips across Jaycee's.

"Ah, Jaycee. My boy has you on that one!"

"What have you created, Luc?" Jaycee tousled my hair.

Luc turned his attention from his brother to me. He placed his warm, strong hand on my heart. "You are my eternal love. My reason for living...Forever."

I pulled Luc to me and kissed him. "Luc, I thank you so damn much for choosing me." After a few moments, I turned and looked at Jaycee. "My dear brother, I thank you for giving him to me." I saw the need in my brother's eyes and, with no hesitation, I pulled him to me and kissed him.

We laid there, our bodies pressed together, in quiet solidarity. "Luc, Jaycee, tell me, please." I looked at Luc, then Jaycee. "Tell me why I would have such a terrible dream. Please!"

Luc and Jaycee rested their hands on my chest. I watched as my Sire gathered his inner strength to tell me; I knew he was struggling. "Luc, baby boy, whatever it is, I promise it will be okay."

"We have information coming in from the vampire and wolf communities. That night at the club, John, when we found Sam and Christian. Elena told you that no one else was at the club. Do you remember that?"

"I will never forget, Luc. I guess at the time there were more urgent things to attend to. I thought maybe she was just playing with us, but that's okay. Go ahead."

"She was right. Sam and Christian were so worried about Janine, they sent all the others out to search for Janine."

"My God, Luc! That was so fucking dangerous, as we found out! We almost lost them!"

"I know, Jacques, but go easy on them, okay? They thought they could handle the situation. They had no idea that Alec had turned Trace until later. As far as they knew, they were dealing with two mortals and one wolf."

"You're right, Jaycee. It's just, hell, none of us saw this coming.

Besides, I could never hold that against Sam and Christian. They almost paid the ultimate price."

"Well, we know what happened next." Luc had placed his head on my chest. "Thanks to their sacrifice, the others found Janine and rescued her. God only knows what would have happened if it hadn't played out like it did."

"Luc, Jaycee? I know this is off topic, but where were you when I was out for all this time?"

"With you, babe." Luc kissed my chest.

"So, neither of you slept yet?"

"You're all that matters bro." Jaycee wrapped his arm around my waist.

"Come here, Jaycee." I pulled his head to my chest.

"Have I told you lately how much I love you both?"

"Always..." Jaycee sighed.

"Forever..." Luc whimpered.

"You both need to sleep." I let my fingers run through their hair. "I'll watch over you."

"God, bro. That sounds so good!"

"John, there's just one more thing we need to tell you."

"Of course, Luc. What is it, babe?" I let my fingers run through his hair. "No one can find Elena and Adrian."

For just a moment, I pictured Adrian coming back here, and finishing Elena off. That wouldn't have been a problem, it would have been a fucking relief. No, what I feared was worse, far more sinister.

*"Adrian and Elena are together."*

*"Our thoughts exactly, babe."*

"Are we safe?"

"Yeah, babe. Vampires are outside of our townhouse. We've shared our suspicions. Janine has temporarily taken Jaycee's room."

"Sam and Christian?"

"They're here too, bro." Jaycee smiled. "By the way, your nightmare? That's all it was. Just a nightmare. Janine is in her room, Sammy and Christian have kept her updated. Needless to say, she was beside herself worrying about you, Jacques. She even came to our room to check on you herself."

I felt a tear run down my face.

"Just forget it, Jacques. Your mind was absolutely overwhelmed with what took place. You saved all of us, my hero!" Jaycee wrapped an arm around my waist and kissed me. Luc pressed his body against mine, as our legs tangled together.

"That...um...and this, makes me feel so much better!" I smiled.

"We can tell!" Luc said. His hands roamed my body. "Here's what we are going to do." Luc shot me one of his 'take me now' looks.

I looked at Jaycee, who in turn, winked at me. "Most definitely, yes!" Luc and Jaycee immediately started to let their hands wander. "But first...Sleep!" I smiled to myself as I remembered Luc telling me the same thing when he turned me.

Luc and Jaycee looked at each other, their heads still resting on my chest, and gave up. Letting exhaustion and relief consume them, they fell into the sleep of the undead. No matter how long it took, I would be there when they woke up.

# ❧ EPILOGUE ☙

A light snow was beginning to fall as I turned my car into the long approach to our country home. It was still close to Paris, but far enough away to afford our family their privacy. *Our family.* I smiled thinking about it. We had grown in size. With Sam and Christian part of the family, the townhouses in the city were just a bit too small. To be honest, as I walked those streets, I couldn't shake the image of what happened there earlier this year. With the support and dedication of the wolf and vampire community, what happened that night was erased. No evidence was ever found, but the memories remained.

Halfway up the drive to the estate, I looked in the rearview mirror, smiling at the gifts that packed the back seat. There was one gift, though, that sat in the console by my side. Luc and Jaycee made me swear to behave and be sensible. Did I ever listen to them? They reminded me that this was the first Christmas of many, many more, but this one was special... Eternally special.

As I approached the main entrance, there he was. My baby boy, my Sire, my Luc. God! The longer I was with him, the hotter he got. He was fucking beautiful. He just stood there, leaning against one of the Barocchio columns that adorned the expanse of the front of our home. As I pulled into the circular drive and put the car into park, I took a deep breath. I had to. What I saw took my breath away. He was dressed in black khakis, a crisp, white dress shirt, and a black pullover sweater. Looking at that long, thick mop of shaggy, black hair cascading over his collar, all I could think was… Mine!

*"Always and forever, babe! I missed you. Get your cute ass over here!"*

*"Yes, my Sire!"*

I jumped out with the small black box in hand. I hit the lock button and ran around the car, straight into my lover's outstretched arms. Instantly, I felt Luc's strong arms wrapping around me, pulling me into his embrace. I tilted my head and let him run his fangs up and down my neck, one of my favorite new kinks. My hands traveled down his back and I grabbed his sweet little ass. I pulled him up. He wrapped his arms around my neck and his strong thighs and legs, encircled my waist. Our lips met, our mouths opened, and we kissed, playfully rough. Luc's sweet whimper caused heat to scorch through my veins as we ground our hips together. Our erect, stiff cocks rubbed against each other.

*"Fuck, Luc… Just fuck!"*

*"I couldn't…unhh…have said it…unhh…better!"*

Luc and I were oblivious to the front door opening.

"Pardonnez-moi, brothers."   Jaycee lightly tapped me on my shoulder.

I opened my eyes and looked at Luc. I couldn't help but giggle. Luc was looking at me, but, by the look in his eyes, he was someplace else. Turning my head, maintaining my hold on Luc, I looked at Jaycee.

"Oh, my dear brother, this better be good." I grinned.

"Um…I just…Oh boy." Jaycee was blushing.

"Luc, babe?" I let him down easy. "Can you stand?"

"Huh?"

I brushed my fingers across Jaycee's lips, then kissed him. "What is it, precious brother?"

"We've been waiting for you, Jacques! Your little brother wants to decorate the tree!"

This was Christian's first Christmas with his new family, his first having a brother. He was still talking about our adventure going out onto the property to find the perfect tree. I had a talk with Luc, Jaycee, Janine, and Sam, explaining how much Christmas meant to me. I found out we all shared the same feelings. Out of respect for Christian, him being Sam's partner, I wanted to make sure it was okay to spoil my little brother rotten. Needless to say, I got his blessing. I shook my head, remembering the look on his face yesterday when I took him to the stables and presented him with a young Clydesdale. He looked at me in disbelief. He looked at the horse in disbelief. As he petted the horse's handsome, striking face, I heard quiet sobs and saw his body start to tremble. I placed a hand on his shoulder and Christian jumped into my arms. I held him tight. God, I loved that kid!

"Well then, Jaycee, we mustn't let him wait!" I turned to Luc. "Hey, babe."

"You do know, John, we are going to finish what you started!"

"Oh, brother! And I mean that literally!" I waggled my eyebrows at him and he let out a soft laugh. "Come on, we mustn't leave Christian waiting!" I took Luc's and Jaycee's hands into mine and softly shook my head as I watched them take their place... Luc to my left, Jaycee to my right.

"What about the gifts?" Luc looked back.

"Would you help me get them later, babe?"

"We both will. Knowing the both of you, you won't make it back into the house." Jaycee nudged me on my shoulder with his free hand.

"Hey, Jaycee. Could you give us just a few more minutes?" He looked at Luc and me with a twinkle in his eyes.

"I assure you, precious brother, we will behave. I just need a moment with Luc." Jaycee leaned toward me and gently kissed me. "Take your time."

"Tell my baby brother I will be there shortly!" Knowing Christian, he would probably throw himself into my arms.

"I promise...And you better! He's got a bad case of missing you!" Jaycee made his way back in and closed the doors. Damn! He was dressed identical to Luc. To hell with the gifts! I'll just have Janine put a bow on my two men!

"Is everything okay, baby boy?" Small worry lines creased Luc's forehead.

"Couldn't be better." I pulled him to me, letting him rest his head on my chest. "Hey, I have something for you, and I couldn't wait until this evening." I handed Luc the small black box.

"What did you do, John?"

"You'll see." I placed my hand on top of his. "Open it."

I watched as my boy slowly opened the box. Luc's breath hitched and his eyes brimmed with tears as he studied what was in it. "May I?"

"Yes...Yes, please." Luc's hands were shaking.

I carefully removed the necklace, and as Luc lowered his head, I placed it around his neck. I lifted the crucifix, the same one that I wore, and placed it in my hand. Kissing it, I looked up, and thanked God for the beautiful, amazing man who I, literally, gave my life to.

"John...What can I say?" He fell into me, wrapping his arms around me. I stroked his shaggy hair and kissed the top of his head. His soft, sweet whimper was all I really needed.

"How about, 'always', Luc?"

"Even better, 'forever', John!"

We walked into the entryway of the estate and made our way down the hall to the great room where a fire had been lit. There, looking at us, was the most perfect gift I could ever receive. Janine, Sam, and Christian were waiting for me. Luc and Jaycee were by my side. I just stood there. I felt a tear run down my face. I knew it! Christian came running up to me, hugged me, and gave me the sweetest kiss I ever tasted.

"Je t'aime, Jacques! I'm so glad you're home!"

"My precious boy, God knows, I love you too!" I tousled his hair and softly kissed him. Janine approached us. I noticed she had an envelope in her hand.

Gracefully she walked up to me and gave me a soft, gentle kiss on my cheek. "Jacques. How was your trip to Paris?"

"Magnifique, ma chere...Merci!"

"This came for you in the mail today, love." Janine handed me the envelope.

"Who's it from?" Luc asked, leaning into me.

There was no return address on the envelope, but it did have an air mail stamp on it. Sam walked over, joining us, with drinks in hand.

I leaned into him, and brushed my lips over his. "Thanks, Sammy!"

"You're welcome!"

"Who's it from?" Christian's eyes looked into mine, curiosity showing on his handsome face.

"Let's find out!" I flipped the card over and, lifting the seal, opened the envelope. It was a Christmas card. I felt my heart stop.

I felt Luc and Jaycee squeeze my hand.

On the front of the card was a picture of a Cardinal, sitting on a snowy covered branch. On the top, the card read 'To my brother, at Christmas'.

I felt sick. Luc, feeling my hand shake, took the card from me and opened it. Inside the card it read: Though miles separate us,

We will be close, Always and Forever.

Love, Elena and Adrian

*'Aahh crap!'*

# ❧ FINNIS ☙

# ᕙ About the Author ᕗ

Jeffrey Niewinski was born and raised in Wisconsin, where he still calls his home.

Jeffrey has two son's: one residing in Littleton , Colorado and the other in St. Paul, Minnesota, along with two granddaughters.

After a varied and interesting career path, which included being a veteran radio announcer in the 80's at WIFC-FM, in Wausau, Wisconsin, he decided on an early retirement.

Thanks to his friends in France and a very interesting picture sent to him, an idea and story sparked his imagination.

With the encouragement from Family and Friends, To Paris, with Blood was born.

~ Because a publisher should stand behind their authors~

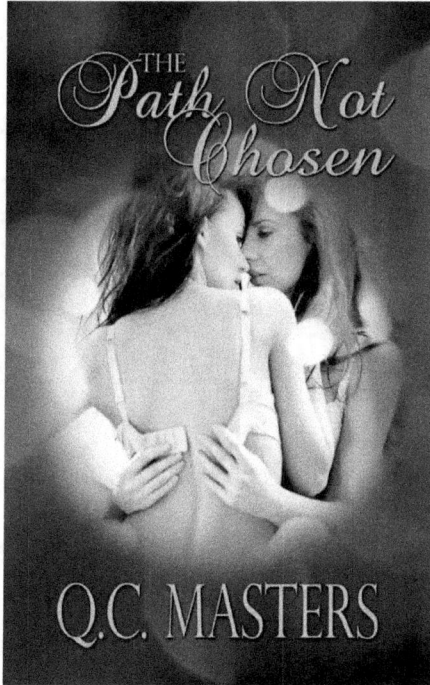

# THE Path Not Chosen

## Q.C. MASTERS

What do you do when you meet someone who changes everything you know about love and passion?

Paige Harlow is a good girl. She's always known where she was going in life: top grades, an ivy league school, a medical degree, regular church attendance, and a happy marriage to a man. So falling in love with her gorgeous roommate and best friend Alyssa Torres is no small crisis. Alyssa is chasing demons of her own, a medical condition that makes her an outcast and a family dysfunctional to the point of disintegration make her a questionable choice for any stable relationship. But Paige's heart is no longer her own. She must now battle the prejudices of her family, friends, and church and come to peace with her new sexuality before she can hope to win the affections of the woman of her dreams. But will love be enough?

www.shadoepublishing.com

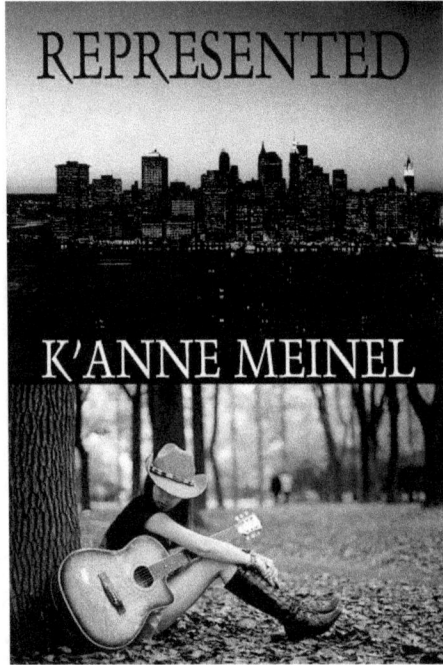

Coming out is hard. Coming out in the public eye is even harder. People think they own a piece of you, your work, and your life, they feel they have the right to judge you. You lose not only friends but fans and ultimately, possibly, your career...or your life.

Cassie Summers is a Southern Rock Star; she came out so that she could feel true to herself. Her family including her band and those important to her support her but there are others that feel she betrayed them, they have revenge on their minds...

Karin Myers is a Rock Star in her own right; she is one of those new super promoters: Manager, go-to gal, agent, public relations expert, and hand-holder all in one. Her name is synonymous with getting someone recognized, promoted, and making money. She only handles particular clients though; she's choosy...for some very specific reasons.

Meeting Cassie at a party there is a definite attraction. She does not however wish to represent her despite her excellent reputation. She fights it tooth and nail until she is contractually required to do so. In nearly costs them more than either of them anticipated....their lives.

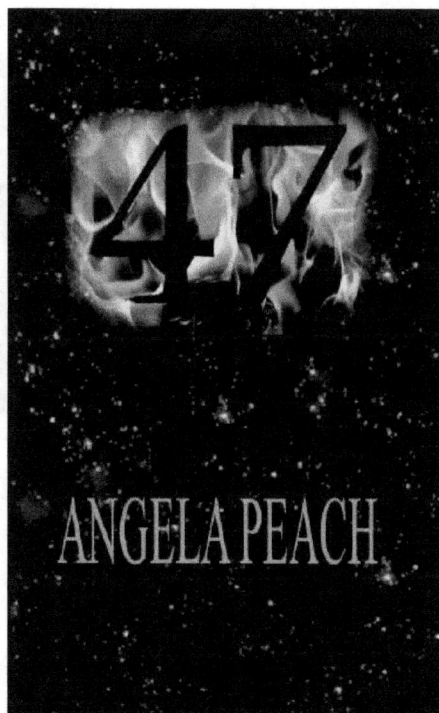

*As I watch the wormhole start to close, I make one last desperate plea ... "Please? Please don't make me do this?" I whisper.*

*"You're almost out of time, Lily. Please, just let go?"*

*I look down at the control panel. I know what I have to do.*

*Lilith Madison is captain of the Phoenix, a spaceship filled with an elite crew and travelling through the Delta Gamma Quadrant. Their mission is mankind's last hope for survival.*

*But there is a killer on board. One who kills without leaving a trace and seems intent on making sure their mission fails. With the ship falling apart and her crew being ruthlessly picked off one by one, Lilith must choose who to trust while tracking down the killer before it's too late.*

"A suspenseful...exciting...thrilling whodunit adventure in space...discover the shocking truth about what's really happening on the Phoenix" (Clarion)

***www.shadoepublishing.com***

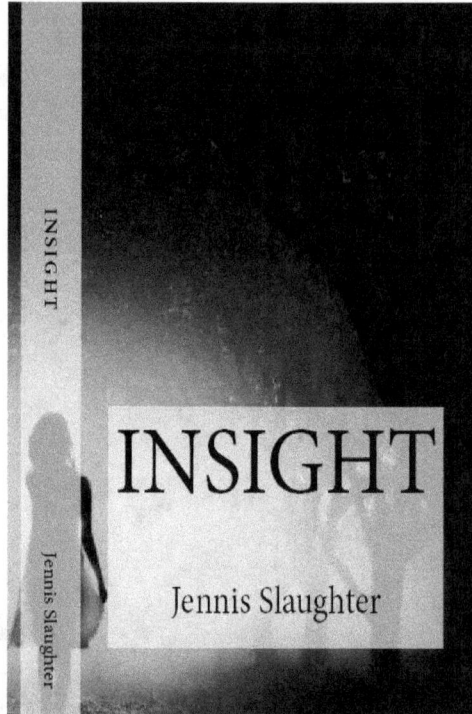

When Delaney Delacroix is called to locate a missing girl, she never plans on getting caught up with a human trafficking investigation or with the local witch. Meeting with Raelin Montrose changes her life in so many ways that Delaney isn't sure that this isn't destiny.

Raelin Montrose is a practicing Wiccan, and when the ley lines that run under her home tell her that someone is coming, she can't imagine that she was going to solve a mystery and find the love of her life at the same time.

*www.shadoepublishing.com*

~ Because a publisher should stand behind their authors~

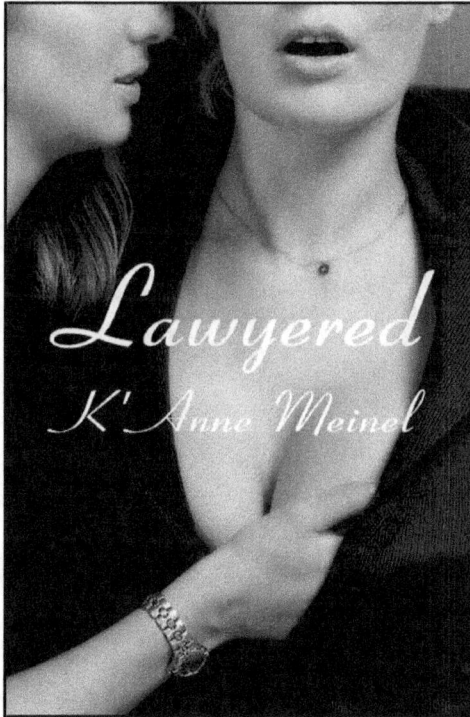

*Lawyered*
*K'Anne Meinel*

Discovering that you don't have everything you thought you wanted is a surprise. Getting a promotion, finding new friends, learning you are attracted to women....

Nia Toyomoto has worked hard all her life to prove she was the best; she graduated early from high school, college, and got the dream job in Manhattan. Becoming a partner at the tender age of thirty she thought she had it all until the law firm made demands about her personal appearance and a few other things that made her change her life for the promotion. Then she realizes having everything isn't all that it is cracked up to be without someone to share it with...

A successful lawyer in the big city, choices have to made, sacrifices and surprises await this beautiful and talented woman....does she make the right ones though?

**www.shadoepublishing.com**

~ *Because a publisher should stand behind their authors~*

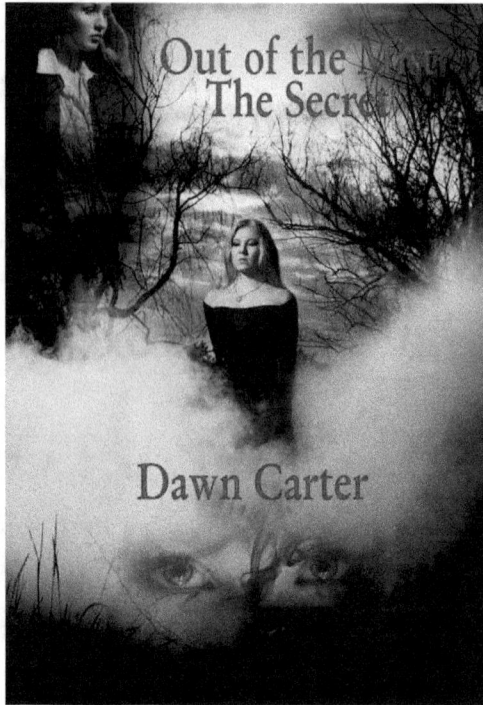

*What happens when two women, from different worlds collide?*

*Jordan Watkins, self-assured, successful attorney, who trusts no one, dates often but believes it is not in her genes to have a successful relationship. All that changes when she meets and falls for Angela Gratace, who is still discovering her identity.*

*Angela did not mind being alone, it came with the territory she had learned in her youth. Keeping to herself was the best option. But, that was before Jordan Watkins walked into her office, and into her heart, turning everything Angela believed in upside down.*

*Thrown into a whirlwind of emotions, Angela is now faced with the dilemma of having to admit she is not only attracted to the young successful attorney, but also women. Struggling with her identity, Angela questions if she is gay, straight or bi-sexual, or just going crazy. Will she risk everything she believes in, or face her demons, and choose happiness, or die protecting the secrets, lies and betrayal, of a past she tried hard to forget.*

***www.shadoepublishing.com***

~ *Because a publisher should stand behind their authors~*

# RIDING THE RAINBOW

## GENTA SEBASTIAN

*A Children's Novel for ages 8-11*

Horse crazy Lily, eleven years old with two out-loud-and-proud mothers, is plump and clumsy. Her mothers say she's too young to ride horses, she can't seem to get anything right in class, and bullies torment her on the playground. Alone and lonely, how will she ever survive the mean girls of Hardyvale Elementary's fifth-grade?

Across the room Clara sits still as a statue, never volunteering or raising her hand. To avoid the bullying that is Lily's daily life she answers only in a whisper with her head down, desperate to keep her family's secret that she has two fathers.

Then one day Clara makes a brave move that changes the girls' lives forever. She passes a note to Lily asking to meet secretly at lunch time. As they share cupcakes she explains about her in-the-closet dads. Both girls are relieved to finally have a friend, especially one who understands about living in a rainbow family.

Life gets better. As their friendship deepens and their families grow close, their circle of friends expand. The girls even volunteer together at the local animal shelter. Everything is great, until old lies and blackmail catch up with them. Can Lily and her mothers rescue Clara's family from disaster? Or will Lily lose her first and best friend?

*www.shadoepublishing.com*

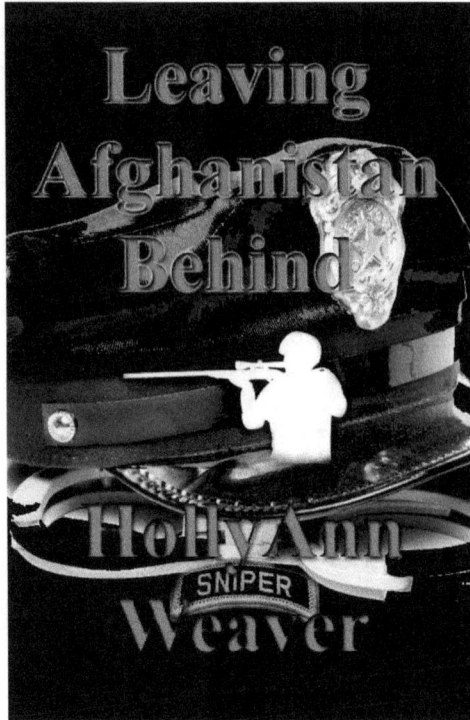

Amelia Gittens had the credit of being the first and only woman thus far in the United States military of being a sniper in combat, made possible by being in the Military Police unit of the crack 10th Mountain Infantry Division. After retirement she joins the City of New York Police Department, and suddenly finds herself involved in a suspect shooting incident which soon encroaches upon her entire life. In order to protect her therapist who has been targeted as a revenge killing, Amelia takes on the responsibility as if she was still in the Army, treating it as a tactical maneuver.

www.shadoepublishing.com

~ *Because a publisher should stand behind their authors~*

When U.S. Marine Dakota McKnight returned home from her third tour in *Operation Iraqi Freedom*, she carried more baggage than the gear and dress blues she had deployed with. A vicious rocket-propelled grenade attack on her base left her best friend dead and Dakota physically and emotionally wounded. The marine who once carried herself with purpose and confidence, has returned broken and haunted by the horrors of war. When she returns to the civilian world, life is not easy, but with the help of her therapist, Janie, she is barely managing to hold her life together...then she meets Beth.

Beth Kendrick is an American history college professor. She is as straight-laced as they come, until Dakota enters her life, that is. Will her children understand what she is going through? Will she take a chance on the broken marine or decide to wait for the perfect someone to come along?

Time is on your side, they say, unless there is a dark, sinister evil at work. Is their love strong enough to hold these two people together? Will the love of a good woman help Dakota find the path to recovery? Or is she doomed to a life of inner turmoil and destruction that knows no end?

**www.shadoepublishing.com**

*If you have enjoyed this book and the others listed here Shadoe Publishing is always looking for first, second, or third time authors.  Please check out our website @*
*www.shadoepublishing.com*
*For information or to contact us @*
*shadoepublishing@gmail.com.*

*We may be able to help you make your dreams of becoming a published author come true.*

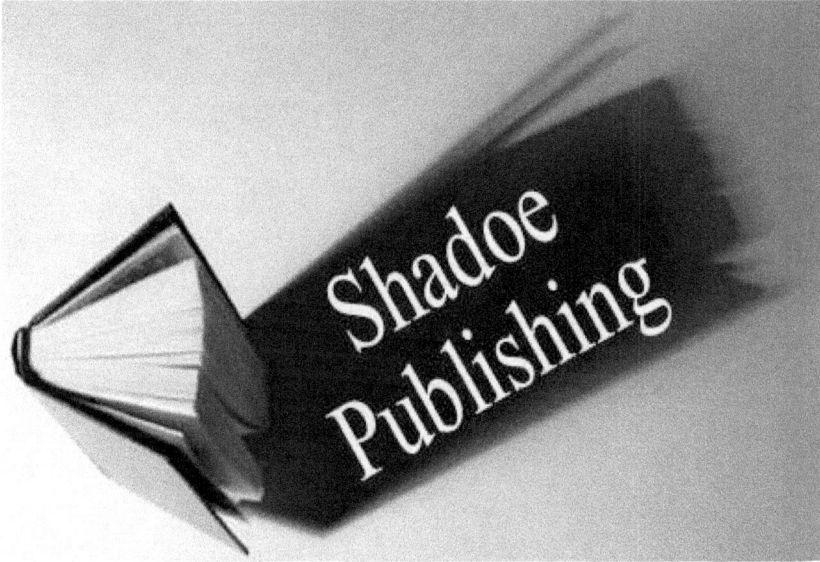

www.ingramcontent.com/pod-product-compliance
Lightning Source LLC
LaVergne TN
LVHW051449080426
835509LV00017B/1714